Transition

Transition

by

Charles M. Sell

MOODY PRESS
CHICAGO

to Ginger, my wife

All Scripture quotations in this book, except those otherwise noted, are from the *New American Standard Bible,* © 1960, 1962, 1963, 1968, 1971, 1972, 1973, 1975, and 1977 by The Lockman Foundation, and are used by permission.

Library of Congress Cataloging in Publication Data

Sell, Charles M., 1933–
  Transition.

  Bibliography: p.
  Includes index.
    1. Life cycle, Human.   2. Adulthood—Psychological
aspects.   3. Developmental psychology.   I. Title.
HQ799.95.S4   1985   155.6   85-4822
ISBN: 0-8024-0406-5

1 2 3 4 5 6 7 Printing/BC/Year 87 86 85

Printed in the United States of America

Contents

PART 3
OLDER ADULTHOOD

Preface

I have just completed a lifetime journey in nine months. My intensive study has taken me down the fast lanes of young adults and along the rigorous trails of the elderly. Though I have been studying adult development for years, I have looked at adults more intensely while writing this book. I am as excited as a tourist just back from the Holy Land. There was something awesome about my trip. My respect and compassion for people has grown with every step through the complex terrain known as the adult life span.

I have been strapped to a hang glider with young adults, sensing the surging excitement they thrive on. I have gone down jungle trails with young missionaries and have come to better fathom the inner force that drives them to teach the poor how to tend gardens and how to know Christ. I have felt the passion and the anxiety of newlyweds and have picked up a new awareness of a mother's mixture of feeling as she gazes down on her newborn. I have felt the confusion, disorientation, hurt, and anger that viciously agitates the divorced and attacks the parents of a dying child.

I have fought depression with the forty-year-old factory worker as he monotonously feeds pieces of metal into a thunderous stamping machine for eight hours a day. I have felt excitement, too—the euphoria of the middle-aged man or woman who has seen a dream come true or who has dared to dream again.

I have sloshed through the grief of the young widow and the old widower. I have been in the lonely rooms of the single and the disappointed homes of the married. I have sat in the so-called empty nests of the mid-lifer, some of them sad, and others jubilent with love.

Strolling slowly and quietly with the elderly who drink deeply of life has been most refreshing. Yet I have been touched by the anger—of the frustrated, strong, capable older worker who has been stashed away on some shelf by retirement. I have been most saddened and bewildered beside the aged person slouched in a nursing home's wheelchair, having outlived every living close friend and relative.

Come with me on this journey; the next time you meet an adult in transition, you will have something to say. Better yet, you will know when it is best not to speak. You will know what to do for them and with them. You will shed fear, too: no longer will you be so terrified of grief, sickness, depression, and death. You will sense that a Christian cannot only *go* through life's transitions, but *grow* through them.

Also, you will learn a great deal about yourself. Like a medical volume, this book will help you understand some of the hurts of life. It may help you more easily diagnose your mental, spiritual, and psychological self. When you are hurting, you may be able to know whether you are having just a bit of psychological indigestion or whether you have a more serious problem. The extensive index will enable you to find specific information about yourself or someone you are trying to help.

Transition is a summary of the current research about adults and how they develop. More than a book describing life's crises, it portrays the potential of life's transitions. It not only analyzes the problems, it seeks answers.

It offers guidelines to help you through your own passages. It gives suggestions on how to help others, whether you are a trained counselor or not. I have also tried to explain to those of us in the church how we can build churches that stimulate adults toward maturity and minister to adults in trouble. We must resist the tendency to view all adults alike. Too often we teach and speak to them as if we can simply mold them into the shape of our words. But our words are heard by adults in various stages of change. Adults cannot be shaped as if they came out of a can of Play Dough. We must strive to make our message, our counsel, and our programs relate to where they are in life's journey.

Transitions is the first book to speak to Christians and the church about the entire adult span. It was made possible by a sabbatical granted to me by Trinity Evangelical Divinity School, where I teach. My wife Ginger contributed enormously as researcher and typist. We have drawn from scores of sources, seeking to put technical knowledge and complex issues into readable terms. Because it covers so much of the adult landscape, *Transition* will sometimes be more superficial than I would like it to be. In some places I wanted to deal with more sides of the issues. At times, I wanted to share more biblical insights. But there just was not space. *Transition* is a start toward delivering to those who care about adults some information they need to counsel, teach, and love. I hope it will be a helpful start for you.

CHARLES M. SELL

Introduction

ARE STAGES JUST FOR KIDS?

My mother had a favorite saying. When any of us acted like a buffoon or suddenly turned sullen, she would console herself with "It's only a stage." That idea carries many harried mothers through a lot of hard moments. It gives hope, bestows patience and, most likely, keeps them sane. A mother reassures herself, her husband, and anyone else who will listen that the children will get over or through it. Kids outgrow their moods and hatred of the opposite sex. It is predestined, say the experts; it is normal for kids to be abnormal sometimes. Kids come from the delivery room preprogrammed. Like geraniums in the backyard, children, too, will come to full bloom. After all, did not the apostle Paul admit that when he became a man he put away childish things (1 Cor. 13:11)? It is just a matter of time.

Could it be that adults are also preprogrammed for stages? Until recently, the adult landscape was seen as a long stretch of featureless years with childhood at one end and senility at the other.[1] So-called stages stopped when adulthood arrived. Mom could not comfort herself with, "*I'm* going through a stage!"

Many experts now say she can. A stage may explain some of the confusion, hurt, or depression adults feel. Adulthood is a cavernous territory replete with tunnels, valleys, and passageways. You and I could be stumbling through one of them right now.

Sheldon was stumbling through such terrain when I talked to him awhile ago.[2] He had been in an emotional cellar for weeks, his wife told us. She could not understand him. Could we? "When I read in the newspaper some acquaintance has died, I wish it had been me," he lamented. In his mid-fifties, Sheldon was in the gloom

1. Daniel J. Levinson, *Seasons of a Man's Life*, p. x.
2. The name and some details have been changed, but the situation is true.

of one of life's difficult transitions. Many transitions are unwelcome. They disturb present circumstances and cause discomfort.

If life could be treated like a video player, a button could be pushed to keep a favorite scene on the screen. Perhaps that explains why photography is a popular pastime. A photograph defies the clock. It stores a cherished moment on a piece of paper to somehow keep it alive. Perhaps our cry is not "Stop, world, I want to get off," but "Stop, I like it fine right here." But life goes on—from one thing to the next, one crisis to another. Life may better be described by prepositions than by nouns. Life seems to be en route: to, from, into, out of, through. Fixed points are few, transitions many.

No marvel one of the recent best-selling books is titled *Passages*.[3] In robust style, Gail Sheehy wrote the script modern adults are acting out in mid-life. Reading it, they cried out in astonishment, "That's us." In its pages the lost had found themselves. Not that they discovered a way out of the woods; rather, Sheehy showed them that wandering there is OK. Life is made up of passages. The glory does not lie in arriving; it lies in getting there.

The notion of transition is typical of a society smitten by the concept of change. *Static* is out; *dynamic,* in. Everything is evolving. Like snowflakes, words like *continuity, becoming, transition, passage,* and *crisis* fill contemporary air.

Nonetheless, even the experts disagree over whether or not adult stages, like those in childhood, actually exist. In order to determine the validity of stage theories, it is necessary to see what developmentalists mean when they talk of transition.

TRANSITIONS AND THE COMMON COLD

Like the common cold, adult transitions are easier to recognize than to explain. Paranormal transitions are easier to spot than normal transitions because they often appear to be more traumatic: divorce, death of a spouse, or the loss of a job, for example. Paranormal transitions include some positive things, too, like entering a better job, moving to another city, or adjusting to winning a sweepstakes. Though those can all look good, they include their share of stress.

Even if most of the traumatic life crises are escaped, it is still necessary to plod life's normal passages. Being more subtle, these are more difficult to recognize. They are called normal because they are typical to life, although not all adults will experience them. Some normal transitions, such as getting married, having a child, and losing a spouse, deal only with married people; by remaining single, some adults will miss those. Also, some adults will not go through all of life's transitions because they will not live long enough to retire or become seriously ill, both normal transitions for the elderly.

The so-called mid-life crisis is the most famous normal passage. Raising teens, adapting to the empty nest, and caring for aging parents are some of the major adjustments for middle adults. Young adulthood has some obvious transitions, too: choosing a vocation, marrying, and becoming parents, for example. Besides those,

3. Gail Sheehy, *Passages.*

there is the less obvious crisis in the early thirties. Older adults face life's most difficult normal passages: retiring, facing a major illness, losing a spouse in death, and coping with physical disabilities.

Transitions are mysterious, like an underground passageway I once saw in a tour through a castle. The castle's rooms were gigantic, the woodwork extravagant, and the huge beams in the inner part of the towers projected massive strength. But what captivated me the most was that underground tunnel. A half-mile long, the escape route led from the castle to the stables. It was strikingly different from the rest of the castle. The vast ballroom offered its visitors the feeling of dignity. A sense of comfort overtook us in the luxurious bedroom suites. Serenity filled the garden room. But the secret tunnel was mysterious and unnerving. It held no comfortable chairs because it was not a place to rest. No artwork adorned its moist, dark stone walls. It was not a place to browse. The tunnel was not made for stopping. It was for those en route with a sense of urgency. It turned your mind to either the past or the future: either you would concentrate on the extravagant castle you were leaving behind or on the stables ahead.

Life's transitions are like that, going *from* somewhere *to* somewhere. The present circumstances may seem like a void. It would be pleasant to turn around and go back to the security left behind. But because that is impossible, it is necessary to keep groping for what is ahead; then there will surely be a resting place. Uncertainty cries out "How long?" And anxiety questions, "Will I ever get through this?" Drawn to the past by warm memories and yearnings, the future simultaneously beckons with a mixture of hope and fear. Sometimes depression opens its dark pit. Above, the grass is green, the sun shining on gleeful men, women, and children. But those in transition feel distant from them, pressured by the urgency to get on, to get through and out.

Listen to a bereaved widow and you will sense this image of a tunnel. Talk with a man who has just lost his job and you will catch the anxiety. Share some moments with an elderly person who has just left his old neighborhood and you will feel the awesome mystery of another transition. After all, the most revered Psalm speaks of walking through a valley and the emotion of fear that can be found there.

THE ANATOMY OF A TRANSITION

MARKER EVENT

A transition often begins with some marker event. A birthday, for example, can become an entrance into a normal transition. The thirtieth, fortieth, or sixty-fifth are the most notorious. The onset of a serious illness can also signal the beginning of a transition. Hooked up to machines in a hospital, a middle-aged man may become aware that he is entering some new phase of life. Bad news (your wife has died; you are being laid off; your husband has filed for divorce) can be the beginning of a paranormal crisis. Sheldon, our earlier example, most likely entered his transition when he received news that his son had left his wife. That caused a short-circuit in his system, because his beliefs about marriage contradicted what he was hearing.

INTERNAL AND EXTERNAL FACTORS

Psychologists do not agree on whether internal or external causes begin normal transitions. Does some sort of inward change come first, coloring the person's interaction with life's circumstances? Or do outward events alter a person on the inside? A woman at mid-life will serve as an example. If she gets panicky about her past choices, especially anxious about her appearance, and sometimes downright depressed, is it because some inner forces are at work? Or is she out of sorts simply because of what is happening to her: her energy level is lower than before, her children will soon be gone, and the wrinkles keep showing up. She cannot climb out of the pits by telling herself, "Life begins at forty."

Some psychologists believe that many *internal* things generate movement to another stage. Erik Erikson is the most prominent developmentalist to think so. He compares human development after birth to the embryo's growth before birth.[4] Each tiny change within the womb is dictated by the substance of the embryo itself. The process is similar to a developing photograph. The print slowly appears because it contains within it all that it is to be. Many who study development see it as an unfolding of what was fundamentally *given* from the start.[5]

Those holding that view believe that good changes take place in adults as they proceed through stages, which take adults from simpler to higher levels.[6] The adult at mid-life is different in a very distinct way from the adult in his twenties. He has not only increased in years and experience; he has elements within that could not have been present earlier.

Progress through the stages is according to a fixed pattern. One stage follows another, and no stages can be skipped. Certain tasks of one stage must be completed before the person can advance to the next. Compare it to what happens in the embryo: the heart must develop to a certain place or the embryo's growth will be jeopardized. Lack of development at one point hinders future growth.

Some psychologists differ with that view. Not using the word *stages,* they talk of *phases.*[7] Focusing on *external* circumstances, they study how adults cope with changes related to aging. Adulthood has its seasons to deal with: the springtime of youth, the harvest of mid-life, and winter of advancing age.

Not enough research has been done to determine which viewpoint is correct.[8] The most attractive view is that the external and internal are interactive. Each acts on the other, and each is explained by reference to the other.

Take, for example, Sheldon. In his fifties, there were a number of circumstances working on him. His son's marriage was breaking up and a daughter had serious marital discord. His aging, handicapped mother-in-law needed constant watching and assistance. At work, there was talk of early retirement. Even though he was in good

4. Erik Erikson, *Identity and Life Cycle,* p. 53.
5. Gabriel Moran, *Religious Education Development,* p. 18.
6. Psychologists holding this view include Erikson, Kohlberg, Fowler, and Perry.
7. Psychologists holding this view include Levinson, Sheehy, Neugarten, Lowenthal, and Weathersby.
8. Douglas C. Kimmel, *Adulthood and Aging,* p. 85.

health, he still had plenty of physical signs he was slowing down. Couple that with what was happening inside. He was thinking about how the bulk of life was gone. All the decisions, efforts, and plans he made in the past were bearing their fruit in the present. His children's marital problems joined with his internal discord. He was asking, "How and where did I fail, if I did fail?" He was about to finish his vocational race, and the anticipated advancements had never come. No hope of promotion helped him get out of bed. His children's problems made him re-evaluate his yesterdays. All the while, his aging mother-in-law reminded him of the old age toward which he was headed.

Sheldon needs to pour energy into both internal and external adjustments. He needs to budget his time so that he can help his mother-in-law, do what he can for his married children, keep plodding at work, and get enough rest. A lot of personal fuel will be burned up by the mental work he has to do. He will be scrutinizing his past while modifying his image of himself. It will take time and effort for him to accept himself as a person near the close of his life's vocation. In addition, he must see himself as the kind of father who could have two divorced children. Cherished ideals and dreams will crumble under the footsteps of reality.

EMOTIONAL REACTIONS

Sheldon's transition will be generating all sorts of emotions. Guilt and disappointment will grip him. He will grieve for his losses: his vocational hopes, his self-image, his stamina. Sometimes, coping with those emotions can use up enormous amounts of energy.

A transition can be a tempest of mental quakes and emotional tremors. People struggle to keep their balance. Trying to master emotions, exhaustion may overtake them. Stress may give birth to physical pain and even illness.

Symptoms like the following should drive a person to seek help:

- ongoing fatigue that does not seem to have any physiological cause
- a feeling of weight on the shoulders, or the sense that you are about to cry and don't know why
- a new physical ailment (backache, headache, digestive problem, etc.), or one that has been judged by a physician as not "serious"
- the need for drugs, liquor, or medication (even aspirin) in order to help make it through the day
- sexual disinterest or dysfunction
- a change in behavior, such as quarreling if the person has not previously been argumentative or silence in someone who is normally contentious
- change in appetite
- a change in sleeping habits[9]

9. Laura J. Singer, *Stages: The Crises That Shape Your Marriage*, pp. 253–54.

TRANSITION AS CRISIS

What has been discussed so far seems to say transition is spelled c-r-i-s-i-s. That may or may not be true, depending on how transition is portrayed and crisis is defined.

Psychologists who view transitions as internally triggered maintain that each transition is a crisis. Erikson views a transition as a turning point, similar to a medical crisis in which the ill person will either get better or worse. Erikson is talking about a psychological fork in the road.[10]

At certain points in adult life, an inner disequilibrium disrupts the expected flow of events. The adult is knocked off balance in such a way that he must deal with it. Ahead lies potential disaster. For example the young adult arrives at an intersection where the choices are between intimacy and loneliness. At that juncture, the person must acquire the skills required for marriage and other close relationships. If the art of intimacy is not learned, the outcome is painful isolation. Precariously poised on a fence, the adult in transition will fall on one side or the other. The outcome will affect future psychological growth.

Not all psychologists look at transitions that way. Some define a crisis as a time of emotional trauma and stress. They have found that some transitions are a crisis for some people but not for others. Daniel J. Levinson notes that 62 percent of the men in his study experienced "a moderate or severe crisis" during the period he called "the Age Thirty Transition," and 80 percent of the men in "the Age Forty Transition" had "tumultuous struggles within the self."[11] Not all studies confirm those findings, but all studies of mid-life show it is traumatic for some people.

Studies show that any transition can become a stormy period. Adults and counselors need to be aware when those times can happen so that they can take those factors into account when a person is suffering emotionally or spiritually.

UNEXPECTED CHANGE

One prominent developmentalist, Bernice Neugarten, has found that most transitions are not stressful; it is only when transitions are unexpected that they cause trauma.[12] A crisis occurs whenever the event is "off time," when a transition is either too early or too late. For example, because people generally expect marriage to last a lifetime, a divorce creates an unexpected change. When illness causes early retirement, the transition is "off schedule." Those happenings are normal in one sense: marriage is expected to end eventually and retirement to occur. Those events create a crisis if they unexpectedly take place early in life. The crisis is not the event, Neugarten claims, but the timing.

---

10. Erik Erikson, *Children and Society,* pp. 65–68; 263–73,
11. Levinson, p. 87.
12. Bernice L. Neugarten et al., *Personality in Middle and Late Life: Empirical Studies,* pp. 290–91.

FEAR OF IMPENDING CHANGE

Fear can cause a crisis. An approaching phase of life may be seen as threatening and damaging. Many people tremble at the thought of turning thirty, seeing the last child go to college, or retiring.

Sometimes the crisis is not over fear of where one is going, but sadness over what one is leaving. Some persons are overwhelmed with a sense of loss when facing a transition period.

UNEXPECTED DEMANDS

Some people experience a crisis simply because demands upon them are surprisingly difficult or different from what they imagined. Taking care of aging parents may be tougher on individuals and marriage relationships than previously envisioned; the severe emotional distress comes as a shock. And many adults are not prepared for the sense of loneliness and worthlessness that retirement can bring.

CUMULATIVE EROSION OF ENERGY

Massive amounts of energy are sometimes poured into coping. When the demand exceeds the supply, it can wreak mental and emotional havoc. Imagine for example the drain on a mid-lifer who cares for a set of aging parents and labors with a rebelling teenager while coping with menopause.

UNRESOLVED EARLIER ISSUES

If one carries unsettled earlier issues into a transition there will most likely be trouble. Marriage can be tough for a young adult who has not made a proper distance between himself and his parents during the teenage years. Or a person who has not established a fairly stable view of his identity during young adulthood may have a particularly severe mid-life transition.

SEVERAL TRANSITIONS AT THE SAME TIME

Some research shows there is more stress when several transition events occur simultaneously. For example, E. Palmore and others report that retirement, widowhood, or severe physical illness have few negative effects on a person's life adaptation. But when two of those events occur at once, they tend to impact that person severely.[13]

CAUGHT UNAWARE

Life's passages may be more foreboding to the person who is not aware he is in one. He has no good answer for the nagging voice that says "What is happening to me?" A

13. E. Palmore, et al., "Stress Adaptation in Later Life," *Journal of Gerontology* 34 (1979):841–51.

Christian, especially, may feel guilty about his doubt or confusion. He wonders where the joy and peace have gone and blames himself for being unable to snap out of it.

Such a person, going through a normal phase of life, thinks he is abnormal. That in itself can multiply the anxiety and anguish. But "no temptation has overtaken you but such as is common to man" (1 Cor. 10:13). Trials are not unique to any one person. Paul did not say that to excuse us from the need to face temptation. Rather, he wanted to convey that no trial is so unique that it cannot be handled. God will be faithful to all who trust Him during trials.

To get through a transition, it helps to know the terrain. If we know what is happening, we can know what to do about it. But knowing is still only a portion of the answer. Our negotiating passages may be affected by what we think about them. Are they positive or negative? Are they to be resisted or welcomed? Are adults in transition getting older or better? Those questions comprise another major issue in developmental studies.

DEVELOPMENT OR DEMISE

Some developmentalists are ecstatically optimistic about the potential of adult transitions. Viewing growth as internally regulated, they see man headed for some higher form of existence. Transitions are not unwelcome intruders. People should reach out to them and seize the chance to mature. Declining? No, aging is ripening.

Compare what happens to adults with what happens to youngsters. At puberty, around age twelve, a revolution takes place in a human being. Physical changes transform the person socially and emotionally. Some research shows that intellectual changes take place. The newly emerged teenager has a new capacity to think. That does not mean the teen has more knowledge and experience. It means he has a new inner structure, or tool, to think with. It is something a child does not have and cannot have until that level is reached. That is why schools begin to teach algebra at that time: the teen has the mental equipment to handle it. Nobody suggests that is bad, saying, "Poor kid, she's aging." Rather, she's maturing. People celebrate, believing the new thinking apparatus and the childbearing capabilities are just great.

Some experts think the celebrating should be extended to the adult years. People have the potential for new structures and capacities until the end of life.

Psychologists who think that are called structuralists. They maintain that when someone successfully goes through a transition he emerges at the other end as a new creature. And each newness is better than the one before. They say that stages are hierarchical; like Jacob's ladder, every rung goes higher, higher.

Aging has not always been viewed that way. Yes, things got better up to a certain point, but after that it was downhill. Puberty was like springtime, menopause like fall, and old age, cruel winter.

Some psychologists not only make mid-life one of life's great turning points, they maintain old age has the greatest potential of all. Only beyond the midpoint can a person obtain true *wisdom.*

That which is developing within is a unique self. Every mid-life crisis, according to C. J. Jung, is a spiritual crisis. Jung proclaimed a need to die to the self of the first half of life and liberate the new man within.[14] Structuralists invite people to look inside themselves for the light to get through life's tunnels.

THE RELIGIOUS DEVELOPMENTALIST VIEW

Religious persons with that perspective see development as the work of God. God moves in the evolutionary process in the world and mankind toward His highest handiwork. Janice Brewi and Anne Brennan explain in their hopeful book about mid-life, "We sense that creation is ongoing in time and history and that we have the freedom to enter in our ongoing creation in the choices and decisions we make."[15] They employ the image of the new birth to support their view biblically. Man is born again and again as he becomes what God intends him to be as a result of each transition.[16] Though change is a crisis, it is not something to be feared. Each crisis can be embraced with confidence in the process and hope for what lies beyond.

Some maintain that crises, tensions, and conflict can be turned into the most promising aspects of life. "Discontentment has the power to open us to the Mystery. All that is creation in man stems from a seed of endless discontent. New insight begins when satisfaction comes to an end, when all that has been seen, said and done looks like distortion."[17] Those who successfully negotiate the upheavals along the adult pathway will find increasing maturity if they reach beyond the tensions they feel.

Some claim that looking inside oneself for direction is the same as looking to God. The further down one goes into oneself the closer one gets to deity. They picture the self as a well. The further a man plunges into its depths, the more complete is the separation from his own culture and even his own self-interest. The more a man moves into his privacy and individuality, the more he becomes connected to the wholeness and richness of the universe. At the deepest levels he feels he is going beyond himself. As he moves through the well of the self into the dimension beyond it, he comes to the underground stream where he experiences the unity of being. After that long inward journey, renewal and transformation begin.[18]

---

14. Carl J. Jung, *Modern Man in Search of a Soul,* trans. W. S. Dell and Garry F. Baynes (New York: Harcourt, Brace and World, 1933), p. 109, cited by Janis Brewi and Anne Brennan, *Mid-Life: Psychological and Spiritual Perspectives,* p. 31.
15. Brewi and Brennan, p. 47.
16. Ibid.
17. Abraham J. Heschel, *Who Is Man?* p. 31; Brewi and Brennan, p. 16.
18. Brewi and Brennan, pp. 21-22.

With that outlook, all of life becomes sacred. Man is seen as part of the evolving universe, and God is the ultimate point upon which all reality converges.[19] If all is evolving toward God, then change is good and the most sinful act would be the refusal to change.

That viewpoint is appealing because it transforms the common pessimistic view of aging. But evangelicals will have trouble with its theological moorings.

THE THEOLOGICAL PLATFORM

The religious view's basic points are that (1) human nature has within it the capacity to develop to lofty dimensions; and (2) the architect of that evolution is God. God, they say, is closely connected with the natural world, and His salvation and creative work is within those processes. In theological terms, they stress the *immanence* of God as contrasted with the concept of *transcendence,* a term used to portray God as separate and above creation.

The second point will be examined first. Evangelicals also believe that God is immanent. "In Him we live and move and exist" (Acts 17:28), affirmed the apostle Paul. But God's immanency is not the source of salvation. Redemption comes from outside mankind. The new birth and the new creation are achieved by the Holy Spirit, not the human spirit. Scriptures are careful to distinguish between the new man and the old. Growth in salvation comes from the transcendent God who is separate from, over, and above His creation. The Bible clearly distinguishes God's working within the world (His immanence), from His supernatural working (His transcendence).

Religious developmentalists have to depart from that viewpoint in order to closely connect the natural man and deity. The theologian Paul Tillich is often referred to in their literature and helped to form their thinking.

Tillich explains that there are three viewpoints on the relationship of God to the world. He dismisses the first two and then embraces the third. In the *primitive* view, God, the highest being, is alongside and above all other existing beings. "In this position he has brought the universe into being at a certain moment, governs it according to a plan, directs it toward an end, interferes with its ordinary processes in order to overcome resistance and to fulfill his purpose." Eventually God will bring His work to a conclusion through a final catastrophe. In *naturalism* "God is the name for the power and meaning of reality. He is not identified with the totality of things . . . but he is a symbol of the unity, harmony and power of being; He is the dynamic and creative center of reality."[20] The term *God* is here interchangeable with *universe.* Tillich rejects that because it fails to account for the religious experience of the "holy."

Tillich contends for a third viewpoint, which he claims is not really new. It is similar to the naturalistic viewpoint but with a radical difference. Like it, this view includes the immanency of God in all things. God is not alongside things nor even above them, he asserts, but "He is nearer to them than they are to themselves." God is

---

19. Pierre Tielhard de Chardin, *The Divine Milieu,* p. 44, as cited by Moran, p. 73.
20. Paul Tillich, *Systematic Theology,* 2:6.

also transcendent, but not in the way the primitive view defines it. God is not spatially separate from the world. There is no superworld of divine objects. Rather, transcendence means that within itself, the finite world points beyond itself. It is self-transcendent.[21]

That view of God is central to the theology of many developmentalists. In some respects God and human nature are one. The potential for development and growth is there; that potential is God. To put it in biblical words, developmentalists would say that people are moving toward the kingdom of God, toward the new creation. Transitions are the wombs in which men are ever born again and again.

That type of reasoning is possible whenever God is pictured as the potential within creation toward which creation itself moves. Yet that view of God is distinct from the Christian orthodox position based on Scripture. To depict God in that way, one must reject the Bible as revealed truth and replace it with religious experience.

Tillich has clearly done that by saying that all knowledge of Him is found in experience. God, he says, does not reveal Himself in words and therefore, cannot be known objectively. All talk falls short of any rational understanding of who He really is. When he describes God, Tillich does not describe the God of Augustine, Luther, Calvin, and other orthodox theologians.

For one thing, Tillich refuses to say that God is personal. Secondly, Tillich does not clearly distinguish God from the created world. Though he does use the term *transcendence,* critics claim his concept of God is not really different from that of naturalism or pantheism.[22] He has not been able to define God's transcendence in a way that truly makes God distinct from the world. That is because for Tillich God is the mysterious ground of all being who is beyond human comprehension. When he does portray Him, Tillich's God seems to be one with the universe, and is identified with man's "becoming." How neatly the concepts of naturalism, evolution, human development, and a liberal idea of salvation are woven together!

Evangelicals refuse to adopt such a philosophical view of biblical truth. Certainly, God cannot be comprehended perfectly or entirely. But Scripture has taught something true about Him. He is a personal God who has spoken about Himself. When the Bible speaks about Him, He is not merely some impersonal force within the universe. To picture God and His connection with the world in that way is to make biblical words mere symbols, devoid of literal meaning. One must wrench Jesus' words about the new birth from their biblical context to equate them with what happens in the mid-life crisis, as if God's salvation is worked out in natural growth instead of supernatural intervention.

Along with their concept of God, religious developmentalists are unbiblical in their perspective of human nature. The Bible does not indicate that human nature is as reliable as they suggest. To recommend that man look inside himself for guidance in his adult journey is to put a trust in the human heart that Scripture warns against. Human nature contains within itself deceitful, destructive elements. "For out of the

---

21. Tillich, pp. 6–9.
22. See Donald M. Luke, "Paul Tillich," in *The New International Dictionary of the Christian Church,* ed. J. D. Douglas (Grand Rapids: Zandervan, 1978), p. 975.

heart come evil thoughts, murders, adulteries, fornications, thefts, false witness, slanders" (Matt. 15:19). The pattern for Christian maturity is not found within, but in Jesus, the author and finisher of our faith.

AN EVANGELICAL VIEW

Although their theology cannot be accepted, some of the optimism of those researchers and writers can be embraced. Evangelicals can see some of the potential in adult development. If psychologists find more solid evidence that qualitative changes do take place in adult transitions, there would be no reason to reject that on theological grounds.

First, biblical theology does affirm that God is immanent. God works in both nature and man, apart from the direct work of His spirit in salvation. He sends rain on the just and the unjust. Although God's being within all men is not enough to bring salvation, He does work within their natural development. Some Christians identify that activity of God in nature and man as common grace.

Second, although believing human nature is sinful, evangelicals do not claim it is all bad. The doctrine of total depravity concludes that sin has affected all parts of man, but it does not judge man to be totally bad. Depravity renders man unable to do anything to bring about his own salvation. That is what Paul meant when he said, "For I know that nothing good dwells in me, that is, in my flesh" (Rom. 7:18). But that man cannot justify himself does not mean that he cannot do anything that is morally, socially, or intellectually right. Even fallen man is made in the image of God (James 3:9). For those reasons, child development is viewed positively. It is good when a baby learns to talk and to think logically. Children are nurtured in order to develop their human faculties. To believe there may be qualitative changes in adults does not contradict what evangelicals believe. It represents a new view of the adult, but not an entirely new view of man.

My perspective of human nature reflects both the potential and perversity inherent in it. Human nature does not contain within itself the direction for Christian maturity, which results only from applying God's truth to life. Jesus set the standard: "Sanctify them in the truth; Thy word is truth" (John 17:17).

Perhaps there is some potential in the natural process of growing older. A positive attitude toward old age is one of the bright concepts religious developmentalists have given to us. But the Bible points to the labor and sorrow of life's later years (Ps. 90:10). Some developmentalists say old age can be a land of promise, overflowing with the milk of human wisdom and the honey of spiritual sensitivity.[23] The Bible speaks of that, but not too loudly. Old age can produce wisdom (Job 12:12), but that wisdom is skimpy compared to the wisdom revealed by God. When God makes a revelation, He takes away the discernment of the elderly (Job 12:24-25). Greater wisdom, not gleaned from human experience, is revealed. Heschel, an expert on aging, cites a Hebrew proverb as a clue to the Jewish idea of wisdom in old age: "A

---

23. For example, Abraham Heschel, "Religion and Aging in Contemporary Theology," p. 139.

wise old man—the older he gets, the wiser he becomes, a vulgar old man—the older he gets, the less wise he becomes."[24] Wisdom is something someone takes into old age with him in order to grow old successfully.

It is certainly possible that there are new avenues for growth as one ages. Perhaps one ought to enter old age as one enters the senior year of a university, in exciting anticipation of consummation, as Heschel suggests: "The years of old age may enable us to attain the high values we failed to sense, the insights we have missed, the wisdom we ignored," he says. "They are indeed formative years, rich in possibilities to unlearn the follies of a lifetime, to see through inbred self-deceptions, to deepen understanding and compassion, to widen the horizon of honesty, to refine the sense of fairness."[25] Perhaps old age can bring a greater detachment from this life and a stronger tie to spiritual values. One can accept that God causes growth in all human beings as they age, but redemptive growth will require something beyond the immanent working of God. That is achieved by His supernatural ministry within those who believe. By God's grace, transitions can be pathways to higher ground.

ISLAND TO ISLAND

An adult transition is like traveling from one island to another. We leave solid ground in order to move on. Usually we are vulnerable while traveling between islands. Paul Tournier describes the reaction to that in-between time as the "anxiety of the middle way."[26] Life has moments when we are like a trapeze artist swinging high above the crowd. He stuns the audience by letting go of one bar to seize another. Between the bars, he is precariously afloat in midair. The audience gasps as he dangles on nothing but his fading momentum. His life depends on his ability to grab hold of the bar swinging toward him. Between the letting go and the grabbing on, there is no turning back. This *middle* is a sort of no place.

Creating a feeling of being out of sorts and out of place, transitions are really life's most crucial places, leading to either renewal or ruin.

The idea of being in a transition is nothing new to the Christian view of life. The Bible sees all of life as a pilgrimage. God is the only certain solid ground. One of the earliest biblical examples, Abraham, knew about transitions. "By faith Abraham, when he was called, obeyed by going out to a place . . . and he went out, not knowing where he was going" (Heb. 11:8). He experienced the sadness and anxiety of letting go. His security came from resting in the promises of God. He endured because he walked by faith and not by sight.

Transitions will be less mysterious, less threatening, after you have read this book. Getting through life's passages will still require, above all, a firm faith in God. "God is faithful, who will not allow you to be tempted beyond what you are able, but with the temptation will provide the way of escape also, that you may be able to endure it"

---

24. Abraham J. Heschel, "The Older Person and the Family in the Perspective of Jewish Tradition," in *Aging and the Human Spirit,* ed. Carol LeFevre and Perry LeFevre, p. 40.
25. Ibid., p. 39.
26. Paul Tournier, *A Place for You,* pp. 164-69.

(1 Cor. 10:13). When you can't turn back and you don't know where you are going, trust Him. Cast all your anxiety upon Him, especially the *anxiety of the middle*. *Getting through won't always be easy, but it will always be possible.*

PART 1

YOUNG ADULTHOOD

1

Coming on Strong:
The Widening Perspective

Somewhere, sometime, it happens. It may be sudden, as it was for John W. A northern stranger sharing the hot summer sun with the people of the south, he stood in front of a house. Fresh from completing his first year of college, one thing occupied his mind: the selling of books. But the little girl's piercing yell blasted from his mind his salesman's fantasies. He never forgot her words; he lived them over and over again, and they became part of a story he told repeatedly. "There's a man in the front yard," she yelled. "A man." John actually looked around to see who the girl was talking about when the realization hit him, knocking him off his psychological balance. Mentally he tumbled, picked himself up, and was never quite the same again. In the eyes of others, he had become a man. Now, he knew, he must become a man in his own eyes.

Other young adults enter adulthood less suddenly. Some "marker event" may signal their arrival: marriage, enlistment in the service, voting. But that point in time, if there is one, is only part of a process that normally takes place between the ages of eighteen and twenty-four and may go on longer.

THE ATLAS AGE

By the time the young adult starts getting cues from others that his life's elevator has stopped at another floor, he has been receiving signals from his body, which has changed significantly from what it was in adolescence. Now it is a wonderful blend of balance, stability, and strength. At the top of their form from a physical standpoint, young adults are coordinated, graceful, and decidely more comfortable with themselves than teenagers.[1] Most are rid of the nuisances of adolescence: pimples, unpredictable sweating spells, clumsiness, and uncontrollable blushing.

1. Gene Bocknek, *The Young Adult*, p. 105.

Those have given way to more mature physical and emotional responses.

The body's condition may be largely responsible for what is happening in the young adult's inner world. Unconsciously, the physical strength and stability will be turning out streams of living confidence. Consciously, it will produce a satisfying sense of self-acceptance.[2] The endocrine glands have steadied their flow and have balanced up the various hormonal secretions. Psychologically, a corresponding sense of "getting it together" and "getting on" takes place.

That adds up to excitement, particularly when coupled with newly acquired freedoms. The young adult is ready to sail away into adult life, without all the limitations, self-doubt, and confusion of adolescence. Not that anxiety and fear are absent, but young adults have a confidence unmatched by any other stage of life.

That robust energy accounts for the first typical feature of young adult passage: activism. Like the enchanting yellow brick road of Oz, the path ahead is alluring, provocative, positive. But, it can also become like Pilgrim's pathway with its sloughs of despond. It is clearly documented that the young adult's activistic nature can drag him into disillusionment and depression.

GETTING INTO THE ACT

Radical idealism, activism, altruism are the words most used to characterize the young adult. With those traits, they make their mark on history. Hitler mobilized unemployed young adults as storm troopers, firing their enthusiasm with his dynamic speeches. The Peace Corp is made up mostly of young adults, and so was the Hungarian peace movement. Young adults are associated with compassion and sacrificial serving as well as change and revolt.

Their obvious social visibility shows up in religious movements. Take an imaginary snapshot of the contemporary evangelical movement and one might well ask, What could be accomplished without them? They are there, front and center, everywhere. They join with charismatic Bill Bright, leader of Campus Crusade, who invites them to "come, help change the world." They sit at desks in seminaries and Bible colleges, pondering their mission to the world. Many end up working long hours in grass huts translating the Scripture into all-but-forgotten dialects, offering help and hope to inner-city poor, or showing farmers in Central America how to get more crops from their small plots of ground.

History proves that societies, dictators, and church leaders have impulsively sought to control, contain, harness, and even manipulate and exploit the young adults of the world. Their social, political, and religious importance and impact would itself be a fascinating study. But the objective here is to understand the developmental traits that lie behind those contributions.

2. Ibid., p. 106.

A WIDENING PERSPECTIVE

Physical might is behind the activism, as has already been suggested. Their bodies are ready; so are their wills. They sense their own capacities, and so are ready for life's challenging tasks.

Social factors are also at work. The "I am capable" attitude is stimulated by their being welcomed into society at large. Permitted to go off to college or their own apartment, to marry, to vote, to buy alcoholic beverages, they are now finally "on their own."

Inner forces combine with new social roles. They seem to face the world in a way that is distinct from their adolescent days. It is not that they were unexposed to world conditions during their teenage years—as teenagers, they read *Time* and *Newsweek*, viewed television newscasts, and attended classes that directed their attention to social conditions and political affairs. The difference is that their perception has changed. They see and focus in on things in a different way, and thereby find new meanings.

Unlike young adults, teenagers look at the surrounding world in terms of themselves and their impact on others. The technical term for that perspective is narcissism. Not to be confused with selfishness, it refers to the way in which youths see most everything in relation to the self. Teens are in the process of forming a personal identity. Therefore, the world is a house of mirrors one walks through to find out what one looks like and who one really is. (That may explain in part why actual mirrors are so integral to teen life.)

But young adults undergo a major change. Identity is pretty much intact. Less occupied with self, they turn their attention outward. National and international events are now cast in a new light. The lens of their perception is decidedly wide angle—in fact, it gains a sort of infrared capacity to see things in new ways. It is not that the new vision is unrelated to the self. Rather, formerly the world was used to answer the question, Who am I? Now, the world is seen with the new question, What is happening to me and to everyone else? Things that were there all along are now seemingly discovered. The military draft, nuclear warheads, and underprivileged people are now linked to their own welfare, future, responsibility, and relationship with God.

That new perspective allures a young adult to a journey that may be as dangerous as a jungle path or as depressing as a trail through a rain forest. But he has discovered a new pathway and is anxious to see where it will lead.

RADICAL IDEALISM

Something must be done about the world, says the young adult. It must be evaluated and criticized. That may sound like what happens during the teenage years, but it is clearly not the same. The adolescent is idealistic and critical, sometimes viciously so. But inwardly, the adolescent is not able to handle his critical ability. Being too impulsive and emotional, the teenager does not think things through carefully, and so he does not *act*. Inner urgings and feelings overwhelm his control center so much that they spill over into his behavior, and the adolescent can only *react*.

Being more controlled and physically and emotionally balanced, the young adult can reflect and plan. And in doing so, he tends to distinguish himself from the age groups below as well as above. If I may make a careless generalization: the adolescent *reacts,* the middle or older adult *reflects,* and the young adult *reflects and acts*. All may view the same film, depicting an undernourished child. The adolescent may feel for the hungry-looking child and reflect upon who he is in relationship to the little boy or girl. The middle and older adult may want to reflect upon and discuss political and socio-economic conditions that have brought such a thing about. But the young adult wants to do something about it. He is driven.

A reservoir of confidence feeds his activism. Young adults have a basic trust in themselves and their own capacities. "Even after the most painful confrontations and greatest disappointments, they are typically able to pick themselves up, pull themselves together and prepare to try once again."[3] Their tough, vigorous approach to life puts them on a football field, pushes them off high cliffs while clinging to a hang glider, or permits them to bravely attack an enemy at war.

Sometimes they take dangerous risks, not because they want to be hurt or die, but because they believe in their ability to survive, to win. An acquaintance of Robert Kennedy, Jr., offered this explanation as to why Kennedy allowed himself to become involved with heroin. He pointed to the reckless Harvard days. "They were always testing the limits of what they could get away with. When you combine natural adolescent impulses with the sense of omnipotence they felt, it's a pretty combustible situation."[4] That same sense of omnipotence led young East Berlin men to throw stones at Soviet tanks during the 1963 uprising.[5]

Two other features of the young adult lie behind his radical idealism and his tendency to act. First of all, William Perry maintains that radical idealism is a necessary part of the development process, particularly the formation of values.[6] The young adult is in the process of making commitments to ideals and beliefs. Perhaps the process of choosing such values needs to include acting upon them. Inwardly, he is saying, "I cannot hold a value I do not act out." In other words, implementing values plays a role in formulating them. If a young adult were to embrace a set of beliefs without acting on those beliefs they would have little driving force in his life.

Perry also suggests that the young adult's attempt to put his beliefs to work is an unconscious attempt to test them. Values cannot be mere ideas, unrelated to life and behavior. Not worked out, they may not only be unimportant but also wrong.[7]

---

3. Bocknek, p. 111.
4. Melinda Beck, "A Kennedy's Bout with Heroin," *Newsweek,* 26 September 1983, p. 40.
5. Bocknek, p. 114.
6. William G. Perry, Jr., *Forms of Intellectual and Ethical Development in the College Years,* p. 124. See also Bocknek, p. 116.
7. Ibid.

Older adults are faced with the urgency of continually encouraging young adults to pursue Christian values. Older adults must permit them some risks, support them, and join with them. Granted, their activism sometimes pits the younger against the older. The older ones are troubled and disturbed by the reminder of what is left undone. Young adults become impatient when the older adults do not join them. Nonetheless, that friction affirms and reforms values for all adults. They need each other: older adults can temper the young adult drive when it is misguided; younger adults can goad the older by their energetic example and hard questioning.

The second feature leading to activism is the young adult's potential for innovation.[8] Young adulthood is a time of nonconformity. Older adults sometimes misunderstand that and so lump young adults with adolescents—who are decidedly conformists. During the hippie movement, most adults interpreted the odd dress and life-style as mere conformity to a group, though nonconformity to society at large. But, in reality, it was and is the adolescents and older adults who are conventional, while young adults are the open ones. Because of their newly secured identity, they are free to differ from others. Unlike teens, they are more individualistic, willing to wear hats they like and listen to music they prefer whether anyone else does or not. They want to try new things, to experiment, to anticipate that things can be different. Perhaps because they are entering a new period, they think they can also make a new world—or at least a new church, school, or community. And they are superbly enthusiastic. They clash with older adults over problems and challenges that those adults have by now learned to live with. The older generation does not want to bother or be bothered; they fling at the young adult the four words that inflame and frustrate them the most: "We've tried that before." To older adults, it is a sensible reason because they probably did try it. To younger adults, it is no reason, because they have not tried it. They think they have the power, the brains, and the will to succeed. What is a sensible reason to middle and older adults is a rationalization to them. Once they have tried and failed, it will become a reason for them, too.

As someone immersed in the vibrant young adult world at a seminary, I have had the privilege of sharing in the exuberant feeling for new possibilities. Each new group of students comes like actors out on a stage. The cast is new, but the play is always the same. The newly elected student council promises to do something about the chronic problems of seminary life. The script is typical: our relationships are shallow, the assignments are too demanding, the faculty members are not always available. Year after year, I have sat hunched over Styrofoam cups, listening to students in the lunch room or lounge discuss what needs to be changed and how. The student council acts, sends complaints and suggestions to the faculty and administration, plans more socials, tries out creative ideas. Some are effective and improve conditions. Many deeply imbedded problems remain, for it would take major innovations to solve them. The faculty, who are really in charge, are slow to make such changes. Still, each new wave of students floods the same ground with its idealism and energies, unaware that previous waves have washed the same shoreline in the same way, leaving it much the same as before.

8. Bocknek, pp. 116-118.

The seminary scene is a smaller version of what is played out on the larger stages of institutional and national life. Young adults' pressure for reform is usually tempered by other forces.

IS THE ALTRUISM GENUINE?

Whether we look at that tempering of young adult activism as good or bad depends on how we look at their activism. Some developmentalists have very positive opinions of it. Gene Bocknek asserts, "As a repository for idealism, they may have no peer among adults."[9]

But others question whether young adult vision is all that unselfish. Some offer developmental explanations that are not so favorable. Some Freudians, for example, maintain that it is a manifestation of adolescent rebellion. They see it as an extension of what Freud termed the Oedipus complex, wherein the son has an unconscious battle with his father for his mother's love, which leads him to rebel against the father. That reaction is projected to the world scene. On this view, antiwar demonstrations and college takeovers were attempts to seize power in order to resolve inner conflicts.

Those who want to see little altruism in young adult rebellion say that young adults call for change whenever they see their welfare threatened. In the sixties, for example, students were aware of how the Vietnam War and the military draft touched their own lives. The fact that the colleges have quieted down now that the personal threat has been removed is pointed to as proof for the argument.

But some studies indicate that young adult social revolts have been based on lofty values as well. Student leaders of several decades ago, for example, were not rebelling against their parents' viewpoints but were merely carrying out in activistic ways the values of social justice their parents held. Developmentalists do not have enough hard data to determine the precise nature of what appears to be young adult altruism. But it seems that the social and psychological evidence leans strongly in favor of a unique altruism blossoming in young adulthood. The mental and moral development described by Piaget and Kohlberg (which will demand our attention later) also leans in that direction.

Some maintain that that is due to the evolutionary process of human development: concern for humanity as a whole flourishes during young adulthood, leading to social progress.

Evangelicals can offer a theological explanation. Although a developing person is sinful, that person also bears the image of God. Given that the young adult has acquired a new ability to view the world, he may also have a new consciousness of rightness. "They show the work of the Law written in their hearts, their conscience bearing witness, and their thoughts alternately accusing or else defending them" (Rom. 2:15). Moral consciousness about social matters comes with new awareness of social issues. That it is difficult to conclusively judge the purity of that concern is quite understandable, for they are, like all of us, sinful. Thus their activism is a mixture of altruism and rebellion.

9. Ibid., p. 206.

The young adult described in this chapter may not match our experience. Many young adults we know may have little get-up-and-go—and even if they do, where they are going does not seem worth getting to. Such personal observations do not discredit the previous description of the young adult for three reasons. First, the difference between capacity and behavior must be distinguished. Sometimes, circumstances will repress tendencies in human development. In a very poor country, for example, young adults may not have the physical energy or opportunity for innovation. Second, individuals' differences will shape their development, and not all who have the potential to be innovative will be assertive. Third, not all young adults function at that level of psychological development. Some may still be on an adolescent level despite their age.[10]

It is feasible to describe as normal certain psychological characteristics of this stage: a sense of power, a capacity for a world perspective, an activistic stance, potential for innovation, a reservoir of confidence and outrageous idealism. That is the "stuff" of young adulthood. We are now pressed to reckon with what young adults do with those traits and how to respond to them.

10. Ibid., p. 118.

2

Clashing with Society: The Idealistic Pattern

Looking at the world through their newly acquired wide-angle lens offers young adults excitement and challenge, but little comfort. The political and social landscape is not picturesque. It conjures up the same sort of feelings that come from gazing at murals of battle scenes with soldiers in brightly colored uniforms smeared with blood, or paintings of Judgment Day with naked bodies scrambling over one another, faces twisted in anguish and torment.

The young adult's reaction is logical enough: he wants to do something about it. American adults of all ages who visit impoverished countries have a similar reaction. People walk littered streets amid public buildings with smeared windows and dirty floors, thinking, *Why don't they do something about this?*

The world the young adult sees clashes sharply with his acquired values. His family life has imparted respect for safety, fairness, prosperity, and love. He sees injustice, poverty, danger, hatred, oppression, and manipulation. As a child and youth, he knew those things were there, but before young adulthood he was like someone sitting in a large room, reading by a small cone of lamplight. He was conscious of the rest of the room, but only dimly. In young adulthood it is as if the lights of the room are suddenly turned on. Were it not for the sense of power the young adult feels, that vision of the world might do him in—which it apparently does to some, who escape through drugs or even suicide.

AN INTERSECTION CALLED "CLASH"

Most young adults are in for some inner conflict between self-interest and world concern. Parents, society, and his own inner voice are saying, "Get on with personal achievement. Get a job and a family"—symbols of success and adult status. But another voice, the spokesman for radical idealism, is saying, "Do something for the world you live in. Having a family is not as important as having a fling at fixing what you see to be wrong." The need to settle down clashes with the desire to go into all the world. Marriage competes with missionary work, and building a career sometimes interferes with serving others.

Those who deal with young adults on a regular basis see the struggle daily. A student once came into my office, for example, hoping that I could help him better define his life goals. Should he become a media consultant for missionaries working in the countries of Southeast Asia? The position was offered to him. Through pioneering ·in the use of films, projectors, and other educational media, he could contribute to scores of countries and millions of people. His masters degree in media and another in Christian education uniquely fit him to the challenge. But the job would demand a lot of him. He and his wife would be on the move constantly, in and out of one country after another, a life hardly compatible with raising a family. And the need for such a media consultant was far from clear; churches and missionaries in those nations might not be ready for expensive forms of media. His expertise might better be utilized in the States. His painful struggle was typical of the tension young adults feel.

That tension comprises one of the major crises of the young adult's passage. His mental and emotional balance will be at stake. The crisis may be resolved by ignoring the world's needs and concentrating only on the personal. The young person then moves toward a career without connecting it with significant service to the world. Denying his potential for innovation, altruism, and risk taking, the young adult becomes the established adult who has rationalized away a part of himself. The inward tension is gone, but it may leave a gnawing sense of uneasiness in its place.

The ideal would be a vocation that satisfies personal need for success while at the same time contributing to the world. A young adult might enter a business career in an attempt to implement his ideals there. Of course, those who go into helping professions or professional Christian ministry are also trying to balance the need for success with their contribution to society. But the inner idealistic voices are not easily quieted even in vocations that appear to be directly altruistic. Missionaries, ministers, counselors, and others who are involved with society's needs continue to have conflict. Their careers, like any others, can easily become means for satisfying ambition rather than for serving others.

Some solve the tension by using the financial rewards of a career for a contribution to the world's needs. A young man enters a sales career or a woman who likes to design houses becomes an architect in order to make money to give to missions and social work. That use of vocation is biblically approved. Paul said, "Let him who steals steal no longer; but rather let him labor, performing with his own hands what is good, in order that he may have something to share with him who has need" (Eph. 4:28).

Those who choose to follow the ideals of young adulthood will most likely fight some emotional battles. "The young adult stage is exciting and satisfying, an entry into the major life period, yet it is also characterized by disillusionment."[1] That disillusionment results from the painful conflict between idealistic desire to change the world and routine self-interest.

The idealism, of course, may not always be global, that is, oriented toward making some major social, spiritual, or political contribution. Idealism may be directed toward a small sphere, such as one's local church or school. It will also be directed toward personal matters like marriage. In our culture, a woman's idealism may be directed toward the context of marriage and family. (That is not to say a woman should not aspire to have a wider impact.)

But it is no doubt true that for young adult women marriage is the major arena for idealism and possible disillusionment. One study in a middle-class community discovered that newlywed women reported more depression than any age group except older women, whose depression stemmed from feeling life to be meaningless.[2] Temporary circumstances may be the most likely cause of those depressive tendencies. The young adult women studied were in a transition period that included the loss of their former social life and roles.

But such depression may also be related to conflict with ideals. Those who come to marriage with more global concerns may have difficulty seeing their role of wife and mother as a significant response to the altruistic voices within. I often observe that in young wives who give up a campus evangelistic ministry for motherhood. They find it hard to exchange the social contacts and rewards of ministry on a college campus for the daily routine of caring for one or two toddlers. Our culture does not help, because there is no longer a solid link between rocking a cradle and ruling the world. Although part of the answer to the meaninglessness felt by women is their participation in broader arenas, surely part of the answer also lies in stressing the enormous contribution a conscientious mother and father make to the world situation.

A woman's disillusionment may not be connected, however, to such altruistic concerns. It may result from her high ideals of marriage. Marriage may turn out to be not all that it was cracked up to be.

Whatever the cause of disillusionment and whenever it comes, it will be eased or compounded by what the young adult's expectations. Western society (and young adults within it) considers this stage to be, without exception, the most desirable period of life. Teenagers badly want to get there, older adults look back on it nostalgically. The young adult enters what is to be the prime period only to discover inner conflict. Much seems to be wrong; so much has to be done. "Small wonder," says one expert, "that this is a time when people often seek psychological help."[3]

The tension between world concerns and personal needs will not be completely resolved in this period. It will be a continual battle—and it may be worse later for those who fail to deal with it during the young adult years. If, for example, a person

1. Gene Bocknek, *The Young Adult,* p. 194. See also L. Rappaport, *Personality Development,* and P. Symonds, *From Adolescent to Adult.*
2. Marjorie Fiske Lowenthal, Majda Thurnker, David Chiriboga, et al., *Four Stages of Life,* p. 105.
3. Bocknek, p. 194.

silences his concern for world needs by plunging into work and pleasure, middle age may bring that concern to the surface once again, creating a crisis. The question, "What will I do with my life?" will change to, "What have I done with my life?"

MINISTERING TO YOUNG ADULTS

The young adult's conflicts are so profound that the solutions cannot be simple. The Christian finds Scripture calling for a radical approach to life: "whoever wishes to save his life shall lose it, but whoever loses his life for My sake, he is the one who will save it." (Luke 9:24) But other Scriptures temper, or at least qualify, that statement. Paul did not advise rich persons to become poor, but to not be conceited, to not trust in their riches, and to be generous and ready to share. (1 Tim. 6:17-19) When writing to housewives, he did not demand they give themselves to missionary or social work. Rather, they were to work out the implications of their faith within their context: "to love their husbands, to love their children, to be sensible, pure, workers at home, kind." (Titus 2:4-5). In other words, the Scriptures do not counsel young adults to submit recklessly to their radical idealism. Sensible concern for personal needs need not always be at odds with the will of God. Each individual will have to prove what is the good and perfect will of God for himself. A number of principles might help.

ENCOURAGING IDEALISM

First, the priceless idealism of young adulthood should be encouraged. It may be very costly for society and the church if it fails to encourage the mining and refining of that valuable commodity. Ignoring idealism may repress the creative activity of God and quench His Spirit. The bleak result for the young adult who denies it is a narcissistic preoccupation with self and the possibility of later regret.

The young adult should be encouraged to resolve inner conflicts for himself. It may be easy for older adults to tip the balance one way or the other, subtly or even overtly. Middle adults are fully aware of the demands personal needs place upon them. Knowing the vast amount of energy it takes to raise children and make a living, they may push the young adult to abandon broader hopes and aspirations. Older adults may force their life-style and values upon young adults and undermine their idealism. I can recall the shock I felt when my own twenty-seven-year-old son, caught up with helping inner city people, told us that he had only two shirts: the one he was wearing and the other that he wore at his wedding. But for him and his wife what they had was enough. He was resolving the tension between filling personal needs and performing a ministry in his own way. Though his way was different from ours, my wife and I knew acceptance and support were the only proper responses. Too many young adults are discouraged by older adults who carelessly press their life-style upon them.

OFFERING REALISTIC THINKING

On the other hand, the balance can be dangerously tipped in the other direction. We can encourage bold risky action that may needlessly lead to personal discouragement, harm, or death. Young adult idealism can breed ventures doomed to failure from the start. Risk and danger can be proper, but they should not result from unwise, or careless planning. A second response to young adult activism, then, should be realistic thinking.

Middle and older adults can help. Although middle and older adult thinking often amounts to rationalizing the status quo, it can also represent a link to the world as it is. Young adults need to reckon with that "wisdom" just as older adults need to be open to young adult visions. Solitary idealism can be as damaging as realism alone can be sterile.

Mature caution is not always apparent in contemporary fundamentalist and evangelical circles. The story is told of the man who, overwhelmed by the spiritual lostness of an African tribe, believed God had called him to go to them. He went alone, without knowledge of the people's ways or their language. He simply took a plane to the country, disembarked, and literally walked off into the jungle. In a few weeks, he was found—dead.

Few cases are that extreme, but they can still be disastrous. A Western evangelistic organization sent a couple to another English-speaking country to win people there. After having had overwhelming success in the United States, the couple had enormous expectations. Unheeded cultural differences, however, beat upon their enthusiastic efforts. The resulting disillusionment spilled over into their self-images and their marriage. They returned, divorced, and left professional Christian ministry. That organization's policy now dictates that such pioneering ventures will always be handled by more than one couple; more attention is also being paid to cultural orientation.

Leaders who send eager young adults into unrealistic ventures in the name of an omnipotent God are being unfair. God has not granted man omnipotence. Man operates within the limited range of his gifts and calling.

TEACHING FAITH

A third response to activism has to do with faith. Young adults need to be directed to faith in the Lord, even though they characteristically trust in themselves. In a preliminary study of the faith of certain evangelicals, James Cobble uncovered a tendency for young adults to misplace their trust. Though his sample was admittedly small, Cobble found that a strong dependence upon God for accomplishments is not widely manifested until middle adulthood.[4] That does not suggest that middle adult faith is always a good model to follow. Middle adult trust in God may sometimes be a virtue; sometimes it may be a cop-out. It is easy to point to examples like David who

---

4. James Cobble, *Faith and Crisis in the Stages of Life,* unpublished manuscript, 1983.

refused to take matters into his own hands as he could have when in a dark cave, with a spear in his hand, he considered executing the sleeping evil King Saul. Yet, there are many biblical examples of persons of faith who did act. One must be careful neither to substitute faith for action nor to use faith as an excuse for lack of action. Although there are times that call for trust without recourse to improving the circumstances, that should not be the general rule. Long ago Karl Marx called such religion an opiate to keep oppressed people content with their needless suffering. The Christian choice is not faith *or* action; it is faith *and* action. The young adult is inclined to forget the faith, while older adults may leave out the action.

Young adult growth in faith will also require learning that trust in God is not a mere supplement to achievement. True faith says, "I can endure all things through Him" (Phil. 4:13). Faith, the young adult will learn, must account for failure and suffering as well as success. It is not easy to teach young adults about failure. Perhaps only experience can do that. A student once told me how life tutored him:

> My faith was shattered when our campus leader died from a sudden heart attack. I couldn't pray, read my Bible. I could hardly believe anything he had previously taught us. But, a lot of thinking over many months brought me to see a deeper dimension to faith. My faith in Christ had to incorporate the fact that a dedicated Christian friend like my leader could die young.

Faith does not always reshape the world, but it does make acceptance of conditions as they are easier. Disillusionment, depression, and struggle are part of the baggage that go along with the journey on planet earth.

PROVIDING VOCATIONAL GUIDANCE

The fourth response of the church to young adult activism is a very practical one. It should be evident by now that choosing a job is loaded with spiritual, moral, and emotional issues. Martin Luther is largely responsible for calling a job a "vocation," that is, a calling. He broke down the distinction between secular and sacred vocations. All are sacred. One of the major tasks of young adulthood is choosing a vocation that takes into account world concern, individual gifts and abilities, and personal needs. That makes for a very complex choosing process. (I will deal specifically with the two major tasks of young adult passage, vocation and marriage choice, in chapters 3 and 5.)

MINISTERING WITH YOUNG ADULTS

So far, the discussion has centered on ministry *to* young adult activists. But what contribution will they make to the church? How will their ideas and energies be incorporated?

The church's reaction to young adults, like society's, is ambivalent. Their idealism is needed but, at the same time, they are threatening. Because the church tends to be a conservative social institution, it may see more threat than promise in young adult idealism. After all, the young adults of the sixties and the seventies contributed such things as increased drug use, new varieties of music, and a weakening of sexual restraints.[5] Young adults tend to focus on society's faults, limitations, and failures. Often feeling left out, they attack and criticize, perhaps because they have indeed been excluded from responsible positions.

In keeping with the Christian view of man, both the negative and the positive in young adult dissension should be recognized. Present political leaders now confess to the rightness of the Vietnam protests, and even the sexual revolution brought about by the young adult subculture has fostered new acceptance and understanding of sexuality. Issues they raise today about churches should be carefully studied. If nothing else, young adults will cause heightened awareness in those who listen.

Too often, young adults have found the church saying, "our way or stay away." Contact with alienated young adults in a project called "Religious Experiment Seminar" showed that many felt this way: "The Christian church has not allowed me the opportunity of full participation in its life. When young adults have been invited to serve on boards and committees, it has seemed like a token involvement. I and others feel that our suggestions are not taken very seriously, and sometimes not even heard."[6]

Church leaders recognize that young adults are the ones to call upon to get a job done. They will be even more effective if they are given cause to feel that they are working *with* the church and not merely *for* it.

Scripture gives no reason that age should exclude young adults from the church's ministry, social work, or even decision-making positions. True, Paul warned against putting a neophyte into such a spot. But a neophyte is a new convert, not necessarily a young adult. Paul chose the young Timothy for a major leadership role. Though Paul knew that Timothy's youthfulness might hinder his work with some people, Paul never indicated that he thought Timothy's age was a limitation (1 Tim. 4:12). The apostle John may have spoken highly of young adults, though it is not completely clear that he was referring to chronological age when he wrote, "I have written to you, young men, because you are strong, and the word of God abides in you, and you have overcome the evil one" (1 John 2:14).

A final suggestion relates to reaching young adults. Through the years, the church has had a difficult time keeping them within its ranks. Church statistics consistently have shown young people dropping out in their late teens and returning after they are thirty. A recent Gallup poll shows that this is not as true as it once was. Although part of the recent gain may be due to conservative social trends, it could also be related to changes in the church. Without sacrificing beliefs, churches have made significant innovations to accommodate themselves to young adults. Some have virtually established two kinds of churches. By holding two worship services on Sunday morning, one more contemporary than the other, they have appealed to all generations. Sometimes whole churches have taken on a young adult character. Church renewal has

5. Bocknek, pp. 196–202.
6. Larry A. LeFeber, *Building a Young Adult Ministry*, p. 20.

brought increased emphasis on relationships. Contemporary issues are discussed, and social concern is expressed in concrete service to others. Few evangelical churches dominated by middle adults are quick to change, but some have, and the resulting influx of young adults is evident.

Another phenomenon is the rise of young adult churches. One of the fastest-growing and now among the largest evangelical churches in the Chicago area was started and is maintained by young adults. Conservative in doctrine, with a pastor in his early twenties, a rock band, contemporary slide presentations, and upbeat sermons, the church has touched the lives of thousands of people. It is one of scores of young adult churches throughout the country.

Anthropologist Margaret Meade points out that older generations need the younger. In traditional societies, the reverse was more obvious. The younger needed the older to teach them the ways of successful living. Now, rapid cultural change sometimes renders middle and older adults outdated in their approach to life. That is most obvious in the technological fields where young adults hold the strategic jobs because the recency of their education gives them an edge. It is obviously not true in other areas of society that are not so fast moving. Meade's insight is, nonetheless, timely. She maintains that information must not flow from older to younger, nor from younger to older, but both ways.

I once saw a sign appealing for credit applications in our local Sear's store. "Young adults: Sears trusts you." Perhaps the church should consider adopting that same attitude.

3

Avenue to Adulthood:
The Tasks of Transition
and the Choice of a Vocation

His dream was to be a veterinarian, but he was a construction worker. Like two hot electric wires, the dream and reality short-circuited within him, spitting crackling sparks of doubt and discharging a current of anxiety through his twenty-one-year-old soul. After a meeting at which I was the speaker, he came to me to ask for prayer. Guilt kept him from dropping the construction job that he disliked: he could not bring himself to dampen his father's joy over his son joining him as a partner. Financial shortage kept him from entering college to pursue his dream. Remaining in construction would be simple, but not satisfying. Dropping his job to train to be a vet would be risky, but it was his passion. God's will was what he wanted. But God's will was what he did not know.

Why would anyone so young feel so desperate about the future? Because that young man was feeling all the pressure of entering the adult world. He sensed that time was running out. What he did not know was that he really had plenty of time. In the modern world, entering the adult world can be a long process, consuming a person's twenties and even a few years of the thirties.

THE TWENTIES' TASKS

According to Daniel Levinson, the *entering* period hands the young adult two essential tasks.[1] The first is *exploration,* to generate options and keep them open. The second is *creating a stable structure.* Family and society are saying "make

---

1. Daniel J. Levinson, *Seasons of a Man's Life,* p. 79.

something of your life," economic pressures demand settling down, and companion needs push toward marriage.

Those two tasks compete with each other. The exploration has to do with dreams; creation of a stable life structure deals with reality. Immediate pressures and opportunities may not lead in the dreams' direction.

STABILIZERS AND ADVENTURERS

It is not difficult to see that some adults choose one task over the other. Some settle down at the cost of betraying their dream, and others "hang loose" to keep their options open, moving from one job, place, or school to another.

According to Levinson, forsaking one or the other of the tasks has serious consequences, though each has its rewards. The *stabilizer*, who settles down quickly into marriage, family, and vocation, perhaps buckling under immediate pressures, will have some sense of security and, perhaps, maturity. Vocation, marriage, and a family all add to the status and satisfaction of being an adult. But if his dream is abandoned in the process (or never had time to formulate), he may have to deal with the results later. Levinson claims that those who succeed in an occupation that holds no interest for them will have to deal with the consequences of betraying their dream. Key choices have been made too soon.[2] Later, that person may say to himself: "Did I commit myself prematurely? Were my horizons too narrow? Do I want to maintain this life forever?"

The *explorer* will also face hazards. Granted, the adventure will probably be exciting, given the young adult's inner strength and creative spirit. But the explorer's life may be so loose, so transient that it does not provide internal security. In addition, he may lack support from parents and others who criticize, complain, and call him irresponsible.[3]

Most of the men in Levinson's study fell between those two extremes. In other words, they did both, attempting to include one in the other. He says, "The distinctive character of this developmental period lies in the coexistence of its two tasks: to explore, to expand the horizons and put off making firmer commitments until the options are clearer; and to create an adult life structure to have roots, stability and continuity."[4]

TENTATIVENESS

If finding oneself and making choices are more complex in our option-ridden society, then tentativeness on the part of young adults may be a proper response. The young adult should not pressure himself to decide too soon. Other adults should patiently support the young adult in his exploration.

Those who work with young adults repeatedly observe that tentativeness, even in

2. Ibid., p. 80.
3. Ibid.
4. Ibid.

regard to serving Christ. A young pastor will speak of his two years in the pastorate as "a great learning experience." The attitude seems to be "what I am now doing, I am not really doing; I am just getting experience for what I will *really* do someday." Not that young adults do not perform worthy and sacrificial service for the Lord and others, but they do tend to look at many of their young adult years as being on a pathway to somewhere.

The church has responded in a number of ways. Short-term missionary experience is one example of a provision for exploration without demanding a lifetime commitment. Churches are also quite open to those who change their occupations in the late twenties and early thirties. Seminaries and Bible colleges are filled with those who have left careers and jobs to train for ministry. It seems, too, that there is growing approval of those who decide to leave full time ministry. It is becoming evident that even those professions may not be lifetime ones, and people are permitted to leave without shame or fear of criticism.

Levinson extends the provisional quality of young adults' decisions to all choices: "Even when he makes relatively binding initial choices regarding marriage and occupation, they will have a provisional quality: if they don't work out, change is still possible."[5]

However, making the marriage contract so conditional becomes a problem because Scripture teaches the permanent nature of that commitment. The church must respond by helping young adults understand how to carefully select mates and to build solid marriages.

If Levinson is correct, the choices of the twenties will be put to the test in what he believes to be "the Age Thirty Transition."

THE THIRTIES' TRANSITION

The period of entering adulthood has pretty well come to an end by age thirty. Yet surprisingly, Levinson has found that people of this age are not all that "put together." "For most men, the life structure of the late twenties is unstable, incomplete and fragmented."[6]

Though temporary stability has been achieved, the young adult is still exploring. Beginning at about age eighteen, Levinson notes, he has a sense of urgency over what he will do with his life. That launches him into a transition phase that will end somewhere between ages thirty-one and thirty-four, at which time a settling down period begins.

Only 18 percent of the men Levinson studied had a fairly smooth thirties transition. He therefore, concludes that it is a very difficult period of life. "The difficulty may be so great that at times he feels he cannot go on."[7] Counselors and ministers should be alert to possible job and marital dissatisfaction. Persons during this period will need

5. Ibid., p. 79.
6. Ibid., p. 83.
7. Ibid., p. 86.

to work on the flaws of the life they have built, and they will need to create the basis for a more satisfactory structure.[8]

The Christian point of view stresses the importance of commitment. But that may be difficult. We live in an age of "commitment cripples," says popular speaker John Powell. It is necessary to teach the rightness of making some commitments tentative. Persons can be encouraged to change jobs, for example, in an attempt to pursue what they believe to be their dream within the will of God. Changes can be encouraged within present commitments. Sometimes modifications here and there can bring great fulfillment and make drastic, risky new choices unnecessary. Older adults can offer the love, care, and support that will help to see the young adult through the transition phase into established adulthood.

ADULTHOOD AT LAST

Until now the young adult journey has looked just like that: a journey. There have been few stopping places along the way. For the most part, the twenties are flexible and dynamic years, and the young adult train does not seem to arrive at a substantial stop until the thirties. *Settling down* is the name one researcher gives to this period.[9] Another calls it *established adulthood.*[10] "The individual now makes deeper commitments, invests more of himself in his work, family, and valued interests; and within the framework of this life structure, makes and pursues more long-range plans and goals."[11]

Bocknek describes several features of this period.

There is a deepened understanding of the workday reality. The blending of ideals and realism makes the established adult competent and productive. "If the young adult dares to plan great things, it is the established adult who can be depended on to get everyday things done."[12]

Experience results in greater effectiveness. Even if past experiences have not been successful or happy, the established adult has a better sense of what can be done, because he has done it. The young adult focuses on "readiness," but the established adult can reflect on achievement.[13]

Circumstances require handling basic ongoing concerns. Bocknek's comparison is very well said: "Given free rein, the young adult would change the world. Given the same opportunities, the established adult would keep it functioning."[14] The established adult has to bear much of the burden for society's continuance: care of the young, of aging parents, and of community needs. Young adults may think the preoccupation with keeping things going is a surrender of ideals, a selfishness.

8. Ibid.
9. Ibid., p. 85.
10. Gene Bockneck, *The Young Adult*, p. 176.
11. Levinson, p. 23. Levinson studied men only. The same might not be true for women, particularly because unsettling symptoms of menopause can be beginning for them.
12. Bocknek, p. 177.
13. Ibid., p. 179.
14. Ibid., p. 180.

But established adults are in the center of their world, no longer looking at it from the edge occupied by early young adults. They must handle immediate concerns while seeking to have a broader influence through the channels open to them: giving to missions, church ministry, personal evangelism, involvement in ongoing political processes, support of and membership in para-church and community organizations.

Before the young adult arrives at the thirties plateau, a lot of developmental challenges will have to be faced. Vocation, intimacy, marriage or singleness, morality, and faith all represent crucial young adult choices. The first of those areas to be looked at will be vocational matters.

THE VOCATIONAL VOYAGE

THE IMPORTANCE OF THE VOCATIONAL CHOICE

Not long ago I met a young man in his early twenties who had left seminary before finishing. We stood in a music shop where he was now a salesman. Feeling a need to explain, he told me of his journey from seminary to sales. Seminary and some church experience confirmed to him that he lacked gifts for ministry. Afterwards, while working at several different jobs that kept food on the table, someone mentioned to him that he might connect his interest and background in music to a vocation in a music store. He was certain God was leading, because the manager of the first store he approached hired him. As he talked, I picked up clues of anxiety. His job search had strained his relationships with his wife and her parents. He had gone through a difficult, complex passage, and self-esteem was in short supply. In our society, choosing a vocation is not the same as simply finding a job.

The importance of career has been inflated to enormous proportions. Personal and social identity are bound up with one's occupation. After asking your name, a stranger is most likely to ask next: "What do you do?" In this mobile, depersonalized society, one's occupation is the basis of more prestige and identity than one's name. In a small town in the past, the name Johnson might have given a person a sense of esteem and recognition; but today, unless one's name is Kennedy or Rockefeller, it gives little sense of identity. A job does.

Self satisfaction also comes from vocation. A paycheck is no longer sufficient for most people. The idea that a job should be fulfilling pervades our society.[15] Somehow a vocation must be linked with giving expression to the creative, unique person one is becoming.

God is also involved. A job is a *vocation,* which means *calling.* Viewing all jobs as callings makes it important that a person do not only what he likes, but what God wants. No wonder young adults pressure us to tell them how to know the will of God.

15. W. H. Miernyk, "The Changing Life Cycles of Work," N. Datan and L. H. Ginsberg, eds., *Life-Span Developmental Psychology: Normative Life Crises,* as cited in David F. Hultsch and Francine Deutsch, *Adult Development and Aging,* p. 276.

GOD'S WILLING AND OUR DECIDING

Finding God's will in any matter involves considering a number of factors.

God's Word. The young adult should consider the mission of the Christian and how he should contribute to it—for example, coupling a medical career with mission work, or simply being a doctor as an act of Christian love and opportunity to witness. He must also take into account ethical and moral principles, which point to jobs that are consistent with Christian truth and values.

Circumstances. The young adult should seek to understand his own life history, the realities of life now, and possibilities for the foreseeable future. For example, he may come to see that a strong desire to be a pastor is the result of years of parental pressure, or that a lack of finances for college training may signal God's will for the moment.

Personal gifts, talents, and desires. The idea that Christians can do all things through Christ is a misunderstanding of Philippians 4:13. A thorough assessment of personal attributes can help point the way to God's will.

The Holy Spirit. Biblically, it is clear that God does work personally in the inner self. People look within for conviction or a sense of certainty. However, a personal "feeling" must be only part of the total picture. A strong feeling that one must move in a certain direction may not be the voice of God, but a voice that comes from personal impulse or influences of others. That does not mean that those voices, even though not directly from the Holy Spirit, are necessarily wrong. Perhaps there are situations where one must do what one intuitively feels is the right thing to do.

Combining all of the above to make a rational (and somewhat intuitional) judgment is a sound way of making decisions. One other feature that traditionally has been included is peace. Using Colossians 3:15, "Let the peace of Christ rule in your hearts," some have suggested a right decision will always be followed by peace. However, that verse actually refers to acting in a way that results in interpersonal harmony with others. Obvious, some tough decisions may leave an uncomfortable feeling after they are made, while some wrong decisions may be followed by psychological peace merely because the unsettling period of decision is over. Tuning into the inner being when the decision is a moral one and when conscience may be warning of a wrong decision may be one aid to decision-making, but conscience is not always reliable (1 Tim. 4:2; Titus 1:15). Internal calm cannot always be expected when we make the right decision.

BACKGROUND AND VOCATION

The first two decades of life play an enormous role in shaping someone's job outlook. The childhood imagination at work in playing fireman, teacher, or nurse shapes expectations. Sometimes one of those will "stick" and become the stuff of one's dream of the future.[16] Idols chosen during childhood may also play a part: space pilot, singer, or pastor. One young man told how he had decided to go into the ministry largely because of a childhood decision. Watching the Christian education director of his church, he decided that that was what he wanted to be. A teenager may give up some childhood notions and choose work as part of a desire to be like someone (parents, friend, idol) or to be different from them (especially parents).

Forces are at work that a person may not be conscious of. Much depends upon geographical area, ethnic background, and economic situation. In high school, for example, a youth may easily be channeled into the "vocational" rather than the "college" track because teachers or counselors perceive him in a certain way. No doubt racial and sexual discrimination is present on that level.[17] That is why it is important that teens receive guidance in making their decisions. Their self-identity is not yet formed; they may be persuaded by temporary views of themselves, or guided by prejudiced or uninformed adults. Concerned people who know a youth's personality, potential, and dreams will be needed in the early teens. Consider the crucial role a junior high Sunday school teacher and youth pastor have in guiding teens into God's will.

Teens should be introduced to people who model various careers. They should be given broad and in-depth exposure to those in professional ministry, such as pastors, teachers, and missionaries as well as laypeople who integrate their jobs with Christian convictions. Books and films can bring them into touch with such people; large numbers of missionaries are where they are because of reading missionary biographies.

EXPERIENCE AND VOCATION

An individual may choose a job on the basis of a particular experience. A man may choose to be a fireman because his grandmother's house was destroyed by fire.[18] A field trip, short-term service, part-time job or volunteer work can shape a person vocationally. A teenage girl who works after school in a nursing home may say to herself: "I want a job where I can serve elderly people." Sometimes experience will come much later in life. For example, a young man may become a doctor because of parental expectations and pre-adult influences. Later, however, he may choose to go into psychiatry, building on his medical degree, because of contact with emotionally disturbed patients. Sometimes, therefore, a satisfying vocation can be found that builds on previous training rather than requiring a radical break with one's past. Many go into full-time Christian service that way. Businessmen become business managers in missionary organizations; doctors, counselors and other professional people practice their vocation in missionary situations. Parents and the church can help a great deal by enriching the experience of children and youth in ways

---

16. Theodore Lidz, *The Person, His and Her Development Throughout the Life Cycle,* pp. 392–409, as cited by Naomi Golan, *Passing Through Transitions,* p. 54.
17. Douglas C. Kimmel, *Adulthood and Aging,* p. 276.
18. Ibid., p. 277.

that will increase the chances for them to test themselves and discover more vocational options.

INTERESTS AND VOCATION

Explaining how a Christian can discover his spiritual gift or gifts, some say you should ask yourself: "What do I like to do?" There seems to be no clear biblical chapter and verse for that. But there may be a point here if "what you like to do" means "what you are inclined to do." An expert in vocational counseling, Richard Bolles, maintains there is a strong connection between one's interests and one's abilities. "Your interests, wishes and happiness determine what you actually do well more than your intelligence, aptitude, or skills do."[19]

PERSONALITY AND VOCATION

Occupational choice often reflects a "fit" in some sense between the person and the job.[20] No one knows for sure how to match a person's personality with a job. Personalities and temperaments are too complex to fit into neat categories. One study matching personality and vocation was done by John Holland, who refers to Douglas T. Hall's matching of six personality types with jobs as follows:

1. *Realistic*—Involves aggressive behavior, physical activities requiring strength and coordination (examples: forestry, agriculture)
2. *Investigative*—Involves cognitive (thinking, organizing, understanding) rather than affective (feeling, acting, or interpersonal and emotional) activities (examples: biology, mathematics, oceanography)
3. *Social*—Involves interpersonal rather than intellectual or physical activities (examples: clinical psychology, foreign service, social work)
4. *Conventional*—Involves structural, rule-regulated activities and subordination of personal needs to an organization or person of power and status (examples: accounting, finance)
5. *Enterprising*—Involves verbal activities to influence others, to attain power and status (examples: management, law, public relations)
6. *Artistic*—Involves self-expression, artistic creation, expression of emotions, and individualistic activities (examples: art, music, education)[21]

Choosing and adjusting to a vocation includes more than learning the specific skills of a job. A person will have to blend his personality with that of his boss and co-workers, as well as master the technical aspects of a particular job.

19. Richard Nelson Bolles, *What Color Is Your Parachute? A Practical Manual for Job-Hunters and Career Changers,* p. 85.
20. Kimmel, p. 279.
21. Ibid.

Few people will find a job that fits them in every way. Entering a job and staying there will require a great deal of adjustment, including the tolerance of certain dissatisfactions and personal inadequacies. For example, a minister may love to study and preach sermons, and even though he may not relate well to people, he may still succeed. Knowing when to compromise one's ideals for reality or when to use them to challenge reality is the tricky dynamic of all growth.

VOCATIONAL DEVELOPMENT

I have noted that Levinson distinguishes the vocational outlook of a person in his twenties from that of a person in his thirties. The twenties are the *novice* stage, during which time the young adult is tests and learns in order to move toward the adult stage of the thirties. In his head, a man (and more and more women who are career-oriented) creates a ladder. His ambition forms the concept of a future with definite rungs. Those rungs may lead to "the dream" or in another direction. He sees the ladder with both internal and external aspects. Internally, the meaning of the ladder is shaped by a man's concern with fame, creative achievement, power, human welfare, parental injunctions, and rejections from the past. Externally, the ladder's rungs may include status in the organizational hierarchy and reputation in the community or occupation. "The occupation usually provides a rough timetable for reaching various levels of advancement."[23] If he falls behind, he may become quite anxious, worried that the whole undertaking may be in jeopardy. That may cause problems in the early thirties or later at midlife.

Vocational life does not easily fall into place along any certain or even rational pattern. The young adult may go from job to job, entering one training program and then another until he settles in somewhere. The actual process may include being in the right place at the right time. Even after settling down, the person will usually have to get more training or may even change to another vocation.

The vocational passages will be different for the blue-collar and the white-collar worker. The blue-collar worker is in a tightly structured environment. He starts at the bottom with low pay and simple tasks. Climbing the ladder means moving to a better job classification and gaining some seniority. By his mid-thirties, he may have achieved the skilled worker status and feel fairly secure. Most likely that will be where he stays until retirement.[24]

For many blue-collar workers it is not that simple. They shift from job to job in the early years, looking for satisfaction as well as higher wages.[25]

---

22. Barbara M. Newman and Philip R. Newman, *Development Through Life: A Psychosocial Approach*, pp. 264–67.
23. Levinson, p. 142.
24. Emmanuel Kay, "The World of Work: Its Promises, Conflicts, and Reality," pp. 63–69; Naomi Golan, *Passing Through Transitions*, p. 60.
25. See Lillian Rubin, *Worlds of Pain: Life in the Working Class Family*, pp. 155–84.

Church leaders who have themselves been on the white-collar route may have some difficulty empathizing with the blue-collar worker's life. Not only should counselors seek to be in touch with their struggles, but as Christians we can support social and political action that will provide opportunities for them.

Starting out at a later age and after some college training, the young white-collar worker has high expectations. He senses his own worth and has some idea of what he wants to accomplish. Initially, he may know disappointment. But he is not as dependent upon his company or institution for advancement as is the blue-collar worker. He has "portable" skills and knowledge and can thus move from place to place, seeking advancement and fulfillment. The first years in the white-collar job market are quite exhilarating.[26] By the mid-thirties, he may be well on his way up the ladder and be recognized as a person with potential.

WOMEN AND VOCATION

Women are increasingly adopting careers and taking a place in the work force. Women who choose to marry and have children have a vocational trail quite distinct from men. More than ten years ago, researchers determined three main patterns among working women:

- *Conventional:* the woman drops her career when she marries or has children and concentrates on being a housewife with no intention of returning to work
- *Interrupted:* the woman may drop work for a period when her children are small but intends to resume it eventually
- *Continuous:* the woman interrupts her work only minimally or not at all if she has children.[27]

Recently, more women are choosing the third alternative, delaying having children until the early or mid-thirties.[28]

The issue of working women has become a problem for some evangelical and fundamentalist Christians. Certain crucial factors should be part of any discussion of that controversial issue. First, it is clear that not all women who work want to. The majority of working women are single, divorced, or married to a man whose income is not sufficient for the family's needs. Working is no option for them. Second, we should probably do more to raise the status of the role of wife and mother than to try to demean the role of a career. Much of the problem lies in the fact that vocation has been elevated as a source of satisfaction and prestige far above what it should be—for both men and women. Our society badly needs to recapture the sense of dignity (and even vocation) that goes with motherhood.

But, on the other hand, we should try to better understand the struggles and

26. Kay, pp. 63–69.
27. Rhona Rapoport and Robert N. Rapoport, "Further Considerations on the Dual Career Family," *Human Relations* 24 (1971):519–33, as cited in Golan, p. 63.
28. Golan, p. 63.

frustrations of a woman who wants to follow some career goals. After all, our society invests a great deal of its resources into providing equal training for men and women. We should recognize the frustrations of a woman who spends her college years preparing for a vocation, only to be asked to give it up a few years after graduation. Many women seek careers, especially after the children are grown, because they do not find the role of a modern housewife fulfilling.[29] Several studies have found that full-time housewives with school-age children have low self-esteem and an unusually high rate of psychological symptoms of emotional distress.[30] Although we should encourage Christian women to be more involved in community and church service during those years, they should not be denied the freedom to decide what best fits their needs and desires within God's will.

A woman must add her husband's and children's needs to her own in deciding whether or not to work outside the home. The evangelical view of the wife's role places her obligation to them above career goals. However, there are no studies proving a woman cannot be employed and still fulfill her homemaker role.

It might be well to recognize the problems a woman has whatever path she takes. If she takes the conventional path, she may face boredom and social isolation later on. That will not go away by simply telling her home is her place. She may also struggle with bitterness or disappointment because she gave up what seemed to be a promising and exciting career for what has turned out to be a less than exciting marriage.

If a woman follows the interrupted path, her problem will be related to re-entering the work force after being out for many years. She may be overcome with feelings of inadequacy and insecurity when she sees how changes have rendered obsolete her previous training and experience. Community groups, universities, and junior colleges are now providing re-entry classes for women who need information and support.

Today, vocation is important for men and increasingly important for women. The church is challenged to communicate a theology of work that deals with today's situation.

29. Myrna Weissman, et al, "The Educated Housewife: Mild Depression and the Search for Work," *American Journal of Orthopsychiatry* 43 (July 1973):565-73, as cited in Golan, p. 64.
30. Kimmel, p. 165.

4

The Tunnel of Love: The Intimacy Need

In the old amusement park ride called "The Tunnel of Love," a boy and girl sit close together in a little boat as it winds its way through a corridor of darkness. People gather at the exit where the couple abruptly breaks into the light again. They laughingly watch for a crimson blush or coy expression that betrays the couple has taken some advantage of the privacy.

The tunnel of love is an apt symbol of the adult passage into intimacy. The young adult enters into one-to-one intimacies that are unlike any previous relationships. Passion fires the quest to know and be known in new and exciting dimensions.

INTIMACY'S INTRICACIES

Developmentalist Erik Erikson stresses the importance of intimacy in adult development. Learning to be intimate, in his scheme, is the major young adult task. Tying personal development to the physical and sexual, Erikson places the sexual self at the core. The young adult must learn the art of sexually relating in marriage, but Erikson leaves no doubt that he is not just talking about the physical. Intimacy includes the ability to be committed to close and lasting relationships and the willingness to sacrifice and compromise as those relationships require. That capacity is necessary for friendships and partnerships as well as for marriage.[1]

REQUIREMENTS FOR INTIMACY

Christian theology affirms the adult's need for intimacy. "It is not good for the man to be alone," God declared (Gen. 2:18). *McCall's* magazine asked twenty thousand

---

1. Erik Erikson, *Childhood and Society*, p. 263.

women the question, "What is most important to you now?" Sixty-one percent replied, "A feeling of being close to someone." Surveyor Daniel Yankelovich says that *Playboy* magazine was surprised to discover that most men feel the same. The ideal lover chosen by the majority of men asked was described as "someone I could be totally open and honest with."[2]

Scripture urges couples to become one flesh. But to do this, they need to distinguish between intimacy and sexuality. Young couples are often deluded into the thinking that they achieve intimacy by being skillful at romance and sex. Intimacy demands sharing one's inner self—allowing another to explore the deepest caverns of one's being. The exploration includes:

- *The physical:* the touch of each other's bodies, the color of her eyes, the sound of his voice
- *The emotional:* making each other laugh, standing near while the other cries, enduring the other's angry outburst, being bored or depressed together
- *The intellectual:* discussing a book you have both read, sharing your concept of God, arguing about political views, discussing new ideas
- *The social:* liking the same people, having a long talk with another couple, meeting with a small group, going to a party
- *The spiritual:* sharing your highest longings, committing yourselves to certain values, worshiping at church, praying about personal matters in the other's presence

Intimacy requires development of *both* communication and companionship. It is not just talking together, but also doing together. The talking and the doing enhance one another. A couple can enjoy deep intimacy during a quiet walk by a lake, even if no words are exchanged. Intimacy, therefore, includes developing areas of life such as:

- *Recreation:* playing a game and sharing the joy of winning and the disappointment of losing, leisurely enjoyment of the same hobby
- *Creation:* redecorating the bedroom, refinishing a chair, building something together
- *Serving:* teaching a Sunday School class, working on a fund drive, ministering in the inner city, working to get a political candidate into office[3]

THE ABSENCE OF INTIMACY: ISOLATION

Learning the art of intimacy in young adulthood is as necessary as learning language in early childhood. Failure can be serious, for the only alternative to intimacy

---

2. "Sex Survey of Women," *Chicago Tribune,* 17 December 1979, Sec. 1, p. 14; Daniel Yankelovich, "New Rules in American Life: Searching for Self Fulfillment in a World Turned Upside Down," *Psychology Today,* April 1981, p. 85; M. Lasswell and N. Lobsing, "Sexual Intimacy: The Most Common Questions," *McCalls,* September 1979, pp. 65–66.
3. Charles M. Sell, *Achieving the Impossible: Intimate Marriage,* pp. 38–39.

is isolation. Loneliness can be a tragic human condition. Persons who cannot be intimate often commit savage acts against themselves or others. Erikson claims certain severe psychological problems are related to isolation.[4] A man, for example, may beat his wife simply because he is unable to permit her to invade his private self. He is so threatened by closeness he wants to destroy the one who tries to get near him.

Isolation can be severely painful. Without intimacy, a person feels unattached. Life is lived in a shell. Unable to permit anyone into the inner self, he stands like someone dressed as a medieval knight at a masquerade ball. When others around shed their masks, enjoying warm human companionship, he stands in a corner like an antique decoration that people soon come to ignore. He goes through life that way, unwilling to disclose himself, always telling himself that it is safer that way. In the meantime, he wastes away inside his metallic costume, afraid and alone.

It is well established that loneliness plays a major role in suicides. Although it is not fully documented that isolation can lead to murder, it is true that a number of individuals who have killed prominent Americans have turned out to be "loners": Lee Harvey Oswald, Sirhan Sirhan, and James Earl Ray, to name three examples.[5]

IDENTITY AS A PRECONDITION TO INTIMACY

SEXUAL IDENTITY

Erikson maintains that a person's sense of identity is tied to achieving intimacy. If a person feels reasonably good about who he is, intimacy can follow. The relationship between identity and intimacy is most easily seen in the sexual realm. Intimacy means both giving and receiving. In order for a woman to give and receive sexually, she needs to have a certain assurance of her identity as a female. Sexual intercourse challenges the personal identity. Honeymooning may be difficult for the person who is not sure who he is. Signs of dissatisfaction or disinterest can devastate an uncertain man. But if he is sure about his manhood, and believes that his maleness is not defined only by sexual performance, he can handle whatever happens. He will understand that sexual adjustment takes time. In other words, the more secure the identity, the less there will be fear of failure and rejection—and the greater the comfort with intimacy.

Sexual identity is crucial not only for the married. Knowing and accepting one's sexual self is vital to success in all interpersonal relating. Young adults sometimes have trouble being close because they have rejected their own sexuality. That happens because they have not distinguished genital sexuality from affective sexuality. Genital sexuality, of course, refers to overt forms of sex behavior. Affective sexuality has to do with the physical aspects of compassion, warmth, and gentleness in any human contact. Touch does not have to be genitally sexual to be pleasurable and satisfying. A father may find pleasure in running his hand through his nine-year-old daughter's silky hair

4. Erikson, p. 266.
5. John Altrocchi, *Abnormal Behavior*, p. 252.

or friends may find pleasure in embracing one another at the sharing of good news.[6]

For some young adults, sex is something to be controlled in order to build one's Christian character. In working with college students, we have found that many Christian young adults conceive of sex genitally and therefore fail to see the relevance of their sexuality. . . . As a result they attempt to deny a very significant part of their personality. [This leads to] repression and an unhappy compartmentalization of oneself. The end product is seeing yourself as your own worst problem and a tendency to reject your very self as too sinful to be forgiven."[7] Clark Barshinger has seen people grow through counseling and teaching. When they learn to accept their sexual feelings and fantasies, they are released to engage in more open intimacy with others on a non-genital basis. His conclusion expresses a powerful insight: "We have come to believe that it is our fear of our own sexuality that gives so much trouble in intimate relationships with others, regarding the question of purity. If the sexual part of me does not have to be rejected flatly, then I am free to meet you on a more mature, wholistic basis."[8]

PERSONAL IDENTITY

Erikson asserts that true intimacy cannot come before young adulthood, because a person is not sure of his identity until then. Teenagers have close relationships of a sort, but they are not capable of true intimacy. True intimacy requires accepting a person as he is. Adolescents seem to be incapable of that kind of acceptance. They are not able to allow another to get close while at the same time giving him the freedom to be himself. That is because adolescents are in the process of forming an image of themselves; they are narcissistic in that their main concern is with the formation of the self-concept. Because of that, their relationships typically involve self-adoration and absorption. In other words, a youth builds a relationship with someone because he sees that person as an extension of some characteristic of his own. A boy hangs out with the jocks because he thinks of himself as one. That confirms his identity, which is still in the formative stage. The other person is an object or instrument for enhancing his own view of himself.

Being certain about one's identity is necessary for achieving closeness to anyone. Uncertain about oneself, a person may feel he has nothing to offer. If he is not secure he may fear others will reject him, make fun of him, or do something that makes him feel uncomfortable about who he is. Such a person can even be anxious about losing himself; about being suffocated by another so that his personal existence does not seem to count.

MATURE INTIMACY

After the identity is more intact, it is possible for a person to form a mature, close relationship. A jock will see no threat in having an actor as a close friend, for example.

6. Clark Eugene Barshinger, "Living the Single Life: On Singleness, Intimacy and Maturity," p. 16.
7. Ibid.
8. Ibid.

Here is the difference between mature love and immature adolescent love: Youth's love is highly emotional and self-centered. Such love is caused by three factors: (1) The loved object loves the youth ("Wow, this cheerleader really sees me as something special; I love her for that"). (2) The loved object satisfies the youth's need for prestige and status ("Think of how I look walking down the hallway with her"). (3) The loved object represents some aspect of the youth's own idealized ego ("She really goes with my image of super-jock").[9]

When a young adult cannot love in a mature way it is gruesome. Some people in their early twenties have already divorced twice. People around them say they are self-centered and incapable of loving. They themselves say they have not yet "found themselves." They want freedom. That sort of problem may explain why three out of four teenage marriages fail. Self-absorbing reactions prevent mature acceptance, which is the essence of true love.[10]

An insecure Christian, unsure of his faith, may have trouble relating to those of other faiths. Getting close to an unbeliever carries too much threat. Friendship evangelism will be very hard for such a person. Prejudice may be bred by an insecure Christian identity. He comes to feel it is unsafe to really get to know the "outsider" for who he truly is. The outsider must remain what the insiders think he is, because the insider's identity is tied to that. That comes from basing one's identity on the wrong thing. If a person believes he is born again because he belongs to a certain group, then his spiritual identity is on very shaky ground. Such a person cannot be open to people of other groups for fear of discovering that some of them might also be born again—and that would destroy his image of himself. His prejudices must protect him.

The same insecurity may foster hostility. Witnessing can then become a competitive act; one must argue lest he lose his own faith. A whole group of people can behave that way. In their uncertainty they build walls of separation to protect themselves from close contact with the "enemy." From time to time they venture from their secure fortress to persuade others to join them, and their identity is affirmed every time someone is won over to "their" side. An insecure faith feeds on the souls that are "won." Identity is secured by numbers, and people become statistics. There is little true intimacy among such groups because they are held together by their supposed identity. They must be careful to always say the *right* thing, not necessarily the *honest* thing.

Groups and individuals can avoid such a shaky identity by establishing their faith on solid ground. Bible doctrine, church history, and studies of reasons for faith will help the Christian know who he is and why. The better the individual is grounded, the more genuine he can become in human relationships.

---

9. Gene Bocknek, *The Young Adult*, p. 138.
10. Ibid., p. 148.

NEGOTIATING THE TUNNEL OF LOVE

The trip through the tunnel of love is more exciting than it is simple. Andrew Greeley observes that "intimacy is always difficult, and when it stops being difficult, it stops being intimate."[11] Though difficult, love is an art that must be mastered.

The intimate person can include another person within the limits of his ego boundaries without demanding that the person change. His friendship is not conditioned on the other's complying with his wishes, beliefs, tastes, or patterns of life. It takes a bit of security to stand the strain of expanding one's boundaries; the Christian has the virtues of forgiveness, forbearance and love to help him stretch himself.

Another feature of intimacy is its lack of possessiveness. Intimate friendships are not based on selfish exploitation. Therefore, such friendships may not last forever. I recall my own painful growth in this area. During my teens, I looked at a friendship with another boy in permanent terms. After moving away, we wrote letters to each other with the closing, "lastingly yours." Eventually, we went our separate ways, and I felt we had betrayed each other. But now I know that true partnership is not possessive. An insecure person may view any close relationship as a means of solving the loneliness problem forever,[12] but realistically, not all relationships have a lifetime promise. Those who insist on such a commitment may lose out. Modern persons are equipped with wheels and wings. Today's relationships must have more depth in less time and without the assurance that the friendship will be lasting. We need to offer as much as we can of ourselves to those who fly in and out of our lives.

Another thing we must learn is that not all good relationships have great depth. The young adult comes to realize there are degrees of intimacy. Some friendships are built around playing on the company's softball team—nothing more. No attempt is made to increase the level of intimacy. Being a partner requires the ability to tolerate varying degrees of closeness. However, social scientists do warn that superficial relationships are limited in their effect. A person must learn to express true feelings. Doing so serves to strengthen rather than jeopardize his relationships.

THE NEED FOR SELF-DISCLOSURE

Self-disclosure is one of the basic routes to being intimate. Being a Christian helps here. Honesty should flow from a Christian as pure water from a mountain spring. It is important to understand what true self-disclosure is. It is not a sort of psychological nakedness, or a compulsion to tell everything. Being willing to share oneself with a lover or a friend is good, but the actual revealing must not be carried too far, too fast. Some thoughts may be better kept to oneself.

Self-disclosure should also not be confused with impulsiveness. Persons who go straight from the lung to the tongue do not usually have many friends. Proper timing is crucial. One study has shown that some people are lonely because they lack the

11. Andrew Greeley, *Love and Play*, p. 64.
12. Bocknek, pp. 138–41.

ability to know when sharing intimate things is appropriate. They distance themselves from others by disclosing things at the wrong moment.

THE NEED FOR UNDERSTANDING

Self-disclosure is but one side of intimacy. To the art of giving one must add the art of receiving. Though giving (self-disclosure) and receiving (understanding) are parts of the same process (communication), they are as different as the tongue is from the ear. Talking is trusting; listening is being trustworthy; talking requires honesty and a desire to be cared for; listening requires empathy and a will to care. A good talker can build his pride and keep his prejudices; a listener grows humble and gives up his stereotypes.

Of the two, good listening is the most difficult to master and thus the rarer. Most of us play the fool described in Proverbs:

> A fool does not delight in understanding,
> But only in revealing his own mind.
> (Proverbs 18:2)

Paul Tournier agrees: "Each one speaks primarily in order to set forth his own ideas. . . . Exceedingly few exchanges of viewpoints manifest a real desire to understand the other person."[13] It takes two good listeners to make one intimate relationship. Research that compared twelve troubled marriages with twelve non-troubled marriages confirmed that. Couples in a troubled union more often misunderstood one another and more often felt misunderstood. What astonished the researchers was the fact that the couples could not correctly identify the specific issues on which misunderstanding existed. In other words, it was not many misunderstandings that plagued their marriages; it was *the* misunderstanding. Most troubled couples are not as incompatible as they are incommunicado.[14]

Fortunately communication training is as plentiful as communication problems. Colleges and churches can provide courses and point to books. John Powell's, *Why Am I Afraid to Tell You Who I Am?* and David Johnson's *Reaching Out* are two outstanding selections among scores of others.

The problems of intimacy are too complex to be solved by reading a book or taking a course, though those can help. Intimacy demands feeling free and fostering freedom to be oneself. It is the "stuff" of life that should be part of a marriage and family. People who grow up in families without it will have the most difficulty with intimacy. For them, and for all of us, the best context for learning intimacy should be the church. It is to be a place of acceptance, where love covers a multitude of sins. It is to be a community of honesty, where every man speaks truth to his brother and sister.

13. Paul Tournier, *To Understand Each Other,* p. 4.
14. R. D. Laing, H. Phillipson, and A. R. Lee, *Interpersonal Perception: A Theory and Method of Research,* p. 86, as cited by Sherod Miller, Elam E. Nunnally and Daniel B. Wackman, *Alive and Aware,* p. 149.

It should be a place of warmth and harmony, for the fruit of the spirit is love, joy, and peace.

Not all marriages, families, or churches will at all times nurture impulses toward intimacy. Living with that situation is also part of the young adult task. The ideal human experience is not always intimate. Maturity, according to Erikson, demands that people learn to live with some isolation, just as a baseball team lives with some numbers in the loss column. What is important is that there are enough wins to offset the losses. It is necessary to live within such an intimacy-isolation tension in marriages, friendships, churches, and selves. The way to do that, according to Erikson, is through love.[15]

HANDLING CONFLICT AND COMPETITION.

Intimacy does not exclude conflict and competition. Being close permits expressing our assertive energy. Life demands initiative, and individuals cope constructively with problems by formulating ideas and taking action. If a person asserts himself for the welfare and productivity of the group to which he belongs, that is healthy. Self-assertiveness is not always selfishness. If we accept this, then we must face what will logically follow: competition and conflict.

Some research confirms the suspicion that Christians tend to avoid conflict. Crisis manager Speed Leas recently did a study of churches in conflict. In an article entitled, "Why Pastors Are Fired," he states flatly that churches do not know how to handle conflict when it comes, primarily because they do not accept it. They tend to ignore conflict like an unwelcome guest. Eighty-three percent of the churches he approached refused to talk about why their pastors were dismissed. He concludes that Christians tend to sweep their differences under the rug.[16]

I will now give five suggestions for handling conflict.

(1) To be successfully dealt with conflict must be accepted. If we allow people to 'ᴀe productively assertive, then their ideas and plans will naturally compete with one another. The only way to avoid conflict is to demand that people stifle their energy and creativity—a high price to pay for peace. Jesus was a man of conflict *because* He asserted Himself, as did Paul, Peter, and others of Christ's followers.

The issue is not whether we will be competitive. The issue is whether we will compete for the proper ends and in the proper manner.[17] Developmentally, young adulthood is the period for discovering how to compete and conflict in a mature way. The key element in the young adult's ability to do that is the management of the aggressive feelings that are generated in human interaction. Hostility and aggressiveness are not necessary to assertiveness. The mature adult learns not to allow strong feelings of anger and hatred to motivate or control his actions and reactions. Even in a touch football game, a person may block his opponent violently out of some deep

15. This analysis is from Gabriel Moran, *Religious Education Development*, pp. 32-33.
16. K. L. Woodward and E. Salholz, "Why Pastors Are Fired," *Newsweek*, 23 March 1981, p. 80.
17. The principles given here are from Bocknek, pp. 143-45.

emotional hostility. "It has become increasingly apparent from interviews with professional athletes that many find competitive sport to be a socially acceptable method for venting raw desires to inflict pain and punishment on others."[18]

Young adulthood is the time to learn how, in the words of the apostle Paul, to "be angry and . . . not sin" (Eph. 4:26). To learn how to do this, a person must study his own emotions, constantly analyzing the feelings behind his actions.

(2) A good competitor must be tolerant of failure. We may be prone to think that failure is not a part of God's plan for us. We may see it as a signal that God has not led us. We may even retreat and give up. But to succeed, we must cope with failure. It may cause us to back up and reconsider our direction, but failure need not cause us to quit. Setbacks teach us about ourselves and our lives. They can be occasions for moving forward in ways that would be otherwise impossible.

(3) Handling competition requires knowing when to be competitive. An immature person may view most human encounters as occasions for conflict. The mature know that there are countless situations in life where losing and winning are irrelevant. "People who make everyday social contact into a game of who is smarter or wittier debase and dehumanize those relationships."[19]

(4) Successful competition requires distancing oneself from accomplishment. Achievement must not be elevated to a higher level than it deserves, even though today's culture makes so much of it. A person's worth is too easily judged by his successes. As a result, some endure their days with little self-esteem. John Quincy Adams is an example of one who coupled amazing success with a lack of self-worth. He held more important offices than anyone else in the history of the United States. He served with distinction as President, Senator, Congressman, minister to major European powers, and participated in various capacities in the American Revolution, the War of 1812, and events leading to the Civil War. Yet, at age seventy with much of that behind him, he wrote, "My whole life has been a succession of disappointments. I can scarcely recollect a single instance of success in anything that I ever undertook."[20] Such is the fate of those who base self-regard on attaining unrealistic ideals or surpassing the feats of others. "When they measure themselves by themselves, and compare themselves with themselves, they are without understanding" (2 Cor. 10:12).

(5) Managing competition requires an understanding of what it means to strive. Struggle is conducive to psychological growth and well-being. It is healthy to strive to become what one can become. Self-actualization is like the unfolding of a flower or the growth of a seed. Self-fulfillment must not, however, come at the expense of others or the will of God. When self-actualization is the only standard, other values and persons are often cast aside. Self-fulfillment is then reduced to selfishness.

Striving must be controlled by worthy goals. Self-expression is not enough. If a person pursues unworthy goals, he will feel unworthy. He may feel trivial even when others bestow praise and reward. A highly successful football player, for instance, may

18. Ibid.
19. Ibid.
20. John F. Kennedy, *Profiles in Courage,* p. 35, as cited by Donald Felker, *Building Positive Self-Concepts,* p. 1.

feel demeaned if he feels the sport is overrated. He may even become cynical about society and those within it whose values, to his way of thinking, are distorted. "The schism created by the difference between personal goals and publicly acclaimed ones inevitably leads to alienation and self-estrangement, with resultant damage to one's own ego integrity."[21]

Morality must not be sacrificed for personal achievement. Life's games must be played fairly. Unethical and unbiblical striving will wreak havoc with inner integrity.

If, while reading this chapter, you have been struck by the complexity of interpersonal relationships, I have done my job. The young adult learns a sophisticated system of relating to people. It takes time and requires patient effort to become an artisan of intimacy.

21. Bocknek, p. 145.

5

Down Lover's Lane: From Courtship to Parenthood

Judge us moderns by the music on our radios and one conclusion would be clear: mating matters. Lyrics and music in endless variations celebrate falling in love. Surely, we judge no human path to be more exciting than the bridal path!

Our society does not, however, clearly define for us the passage to marriage. In popular terms, it is more likely something a person falls into instead of travels towards. Our language lacks a good modern designation for this period. *Courtship* sounds old-fashioned, yet there is no word to replace it. That may be a symptom of the fact that the process is not well defined or even often thought about. In Western culture's past, attention was called to courtship by the many rules and customs that regulated it. Today, the patterns of dating and mating are so divergent and vague that it is impossible to talk of a normal route. Confused persons rely on Abby Van Buren and Ann Landers to sort out the right and wrong way of selecting a mate and entering a marriage.

COURTSHIP

The haphazard way we go about choosing a life partner may underlie the problems we have living with the ones we choose. If a person's selector is bad, his adjustor better be quite good. One counselor put it bluntly: "The problem with American marriage is American courtship."

Scripture gives some guidelines for courtship, but does not offer precise patterns. In both Old and New Testament times, parents chose mates for their children. That, by the way, is still the practice in most of the world. But to impose that on Christians living in the West would be unwise for many reasons. It is better to integrate the following biblical tenets with modern life.

1. A person should seek a husband or wife—the process is not to be left to chance (Gen. 2:24; 1 Cor. 7:2).
2. A Christian should seek God's will, deciding whom to marry based on sound reasons as well as circumstances and feelings (1 Cor. 7:24).
3. The Christian should marry only another Christian (1 Cor. 7:39; 2 Cor. 6:14).
4. A sound reason to get married is to have sexual satisfaction (1 Cor. 7:1-7).
5. Romantic love is possible before marriage (as in the case of Jacob, Gen. 29:20), but it is not always present before marriage (as in the case of Isaac, Gen. 24:67).
6. Love can and should be developed after marriage. True love is something under a person's control; it is not merely something that controls us (Eph. 5:25; Titus 2:4).
7. Persons should get their parents' advice and consent before marriage, though they are not always subject to parents when they are adults (Gen. 24:67; Eph. 5:28; Titus 2:4).

The above instructions should be mixed with our understanding of the modern courtship process in order to guide people successfully through it. Though the process is not well defined, certain patterns do emerge when closely observed. Four stages, each one narrower than the previous, are as follows[1]:

FRIENDSHIP

DATING

ENGAGEMENT

MARRIAGE

Friendships with the opposite sex help young adolescent achieve a number of things: knowledge about the opposite sex; some comfort in being with them; increased awareness of the various personality types. Young people may not be conscious of what they are learning, and are probably unaware of the connection between being a friend and selecting a mate. We can call that to their attention.

During the dating stage, the adolescent's achievements should be similar to those in the friendship period. In addition, dating gives additional chances to learn what kind of person he or she ought to marry. Casual and steady dating is usually for fun and recreation. "Going steady" serves the youth by giving a sense of security: it provides someone to take to socials and be attached to.[2] But even if a youth is not conscious of the process of selecting a mate, the dating stage provides a chance to try out his personality in a relationship and discover more about the opposite sex. Theoretically, it is best for young people to date many people to accomplish that. When the final

---

1. I first learned of the four stages from a lecture by Howard Hendricks, Dallas Theological Seminary, in a course titled The Christian Home, 1957.
2. David F. Hultsch and Francine Deutsch, *Adult Development and Aging*, p. 261.

choice is made, a breadth of dating experience may make the person more certain he or she has found the right one.

Dating is a passage with considerable risks. People can exploit one another. A woman can be hurt when a man wants to move toward a sexual relationship before deciding on marriage. Once sex is involved, breaking up becomes more traumatic and difficult. Breaking up is another dating risk. Being jilted can create a crisis, particularly when the person's ego identity is not fully developed.

Parents and friends play a strategic role in the young person's dating life. First meetings of couples are most often arranged by friends.[3] Parents and church leaders who want to introduce young adults to potential mates should take note of that and provide good social opportunities. Young adults can also be helped to sort out the criteria for choosing a good mate. Young adults are trying to determine the relative importance of romantic love, compatibility, friendship, and other factors. They need to be encouraged not to marry because of mere romantic involvement.

Relatives and friends can become mirrors for young couples. Couples watch for affirming statements or signs from others that indicate to them that they are compatible. If they are grossly mismatched, they can be helped by a close friend who is frank with them about it.

Unfortunately, many will eventually marry for insufficient or wrong reasons. They may lose most of their good judgment during courtship and marry because society expects them to or because parents have pressured them. Sometimes an unconscious desire to improve themselves, or even missing their father or mother, will make them yearn to say "I do."[4] Some of those reasons shove teenagers into early marriages. As the divorce rate for them shows, such marriages are extremely unstable and should be prevented if possible.

Some pastors try to head off unlikely matches by maintaining a close friendship with the church's youth. Such a pastor encourages the youth to talk to him about any relationship that is getting serious.

ENGAGEMENT

Engagement, the formal promise to wed, is usually preceded by informal pledges. In the college setting, that may be a "pinning," with fraternity pins acting as preliminaries to engagement rings. Formal engagement, however, still serves a major purpose. The announcement to others causes the couple to be seen differently. People now begin to treat them as a unit more than they did previously. When the bond is institutionalized in that way, the couple's relationship may actually change.[5] They begin to view each other as part of a more permanent unit. Communication, conflict,

---

3. Robert C. Ryder, John S. Kafka, and David H. Olson, "Separating and Joining Influences in Courtship and Early Marriage," *American Journal of Orthopsychiatry* 41, no. 3 (April 1971):450–65, cited in Naomi Golan, *Passing Through Transitions*, p. 68.

4. William J. Lederer and Don D. Jackson, *The Mirages of Marriage*, pp. 42–46.

5. Mark L. Knapp, *Social Intercourse*, p. 22, as cited by Kathleen M. Galvin and Bernard J. Brommel, *Family Communication: Cohesion and Change*, p. 207.

and all of the other aspects of a more formal relationship may become more crucial for them. They either try to work harder at relating or their fear of losing what they have may make them less able to face their differences. They may begin to assume aspects of marital roles; a man who believes strongly in wifely obedience, for example, may begin to boss his fiancée, possibly causing trouble between them.

Others will be affected. Parents, particularly mothers, may feel abandoned by their engaged child.[6] Engagement may provide the beginning of the struggle of grown children and parents to separate.

Engagement also pressures the couple to look closely at their decision to marry. Misgivings may come when things do not "feel" right. Because as many as 50 percent of engagements are eventually broken, it is important that a couple be open to changing their minds.[7] Engagement is not the final commitment.

Premarital counseling during this period will help a couple to become sure of their decision and prepare for their marriage. To be effective, premarital counseling must involve the couple in spirited interaction concerning how they are communicating and relating. Studies indicate that simple little talks from the pastor are inadequate and pretty much a waste of time. Four to six two-hour creative sessions are usually needed to produce any significant results.

Most pastors now require premarital counseling and are giving it high priority in their schedules. Tests, books, questionnaires, and study materials are now plentiful. Norman Wright's *Premarital Counseling* provides much of the needed content and resources. Many churches are training lay persons to do such counseling, not only to save the pastor's time, but because a lay couple can sometimes relate better to the couple before and after the wedding.

WEDDING

The wedding is an important marker event. Spiritually, it crystallizes and celebrates the couple's commitment in God's sight. Socially, it solidifies their pledges in the sight of others. The wedding ceremony shows that marriage is more than a couple's commitment to each other. Society has a stake in what happens to marriages since the stability of the family affects the welfare of society and its individuals. The scriptural statement that "A man shall leave his father and his mother" (Gen. 2:24) implies that the leaving be a publicly recognized act. Couples who live together without a wedding and a marriage contract are not fulfilling the biblical requirements.

Today, more than one million persons of the opposite sex are living together as unmarried people. The U.S. Bureau of the Census included a category for them on their census forms for the first time in 1980: "POSSLQ, People of the Opposite Sex Sharing Living Quarters."[8] Though the number of such couples has been rising

---

6. Pauline Bart, "Depression in Middle Age Women," *Women in a Sexist Society,* ed. V. Gornick and B. Moran, pp. 163–86 as cited by Galvin and Brommel, p. 207.
7. Norman Wright, *Premarital Counseling,* p. 38.
8. Dennis B. Gurnsey, *A New Design for Family Ministry,* p. 116.

(doubling in eight years), they form only 4 percent of couples living together.[9] It is not known whether all POSSLQ's are sexually involved (for example, an elderly man and a live-in housekeeper, or a college student rooming in the home of an aged woman). However, because most are under thirty-five and nearly the same age, it appears true that some young people view living together as an extension of the courtship process, if not a complete alternative to marriage. Evangelical churches will continue to face that challenge to their own ethical views. Evangelicals can contribute by continuing to urge people to make public marriage commitments as well as by holding the wedding ceremony in high regard.

HONEYMOONING

Is any event in life as mysterious as a honeymoon? Strange stories circulate, making it seem that Murphy's law applies. Today's couples know of marriage failure and are worried about a bad start. Some are not prepared for the possible surprises. One woman tells that she was not able to enjoy making love because she knew her mother would know what they were doing. Most couples seem prepared for the fact that the honeymoon can be stressful, although it is no serious problem for the vast majority of couples. Good humor, prayer, and understanding enable them to handle any problems that may arise. Not all couples choose a honeymoon period, although experts recommend they have such a break to relate without the day-to-day pressures at home.

HANDLING THE CULTURE SHOCK

The relationship has a new character the couple needs to adjust to. Even couples who have lived together report: "It's different now that we are married."[10] Sharing the same bed, using the same bathroom, undressing freely in front of each other are specific acts that are part of a broader adjustment. In a sense, each must adjust in a new way to a person from another sub-culture. She may love learning about the "world of men" but sometimes find his ways upsetting. He has the same experience with her. A successful marriage requires building a bridge between the "cultures." Each must see that certain peculiarities come simply from the fact that each is a different gender, having grown up in somewhat distinct environments.

PLAYING THE PART

Role-taking also confuses the relationship. Persons change after marriage because of the matter of roles. When Richard Burton strolled out on the stage as King Lear, he

---

9. Spencer Davidson, "Proliferating POSSLQ," *Psychology Today.* November 1983, p. 84.
10. Rhona Rapoport and Robert Rapoport, "New Light on the Honeymoon," *Human Relations* 17 (1964):33–56.

was in some sense no longer Richard Burton, and was judged by how well he transformed himself into the part. Being a husband or wife is similar. A couple walks from the marriage ceremony onto a stage.

A person will actually change because of the new role he has taken. That can be good, but it can also be troublesome, depending on the script. For example, a man may think that dating and long romantic evenings are for boyfriends and girlfriends but not for husbands and wives—who have plenty of time together just running the household and watching television. He may suddenly stop taking his lover out on dates now that they are married. He is the same person, but he has changed roles.

Whether changes are good or bad depends on whether couples agree on each other's script. They judge each other based on their role expectations. It is not that they have not been appraising each other all along, but, after marriage, the standards change. Now each is to see how the other measures up to the new part. To use the above example, if the husband soon stops all the romance, the wife will be disappointed if she thinks husbands should be as romantic as boyfriends.

All that role-playing is threatening, though things like it have been experienced before. With a new job, for example, there is pressure to measure up and succeed; boss and employee communicate to find out what is expected. Similar, though more complicated, dynamics are at work in marriage. Even though they may have agreed on husband-wife roles before marriage, it will take time to communicate and work out the details. The adjustment takes time because it requires change, either in behavior or expectations, and change is rarely easy.

SEXUAL ADJUSTMENT

The beginning of sexual harmony will, of course, be a prominent part of the honeymoon period. But, sexual harmony may take months or years to develop. The first days of the honeymoon may be unfavorable to sexual adjustment because the wedding, as well as events leading to it, is usually a stressful time. Anxieties couples bring to the marriage bed can also interfere. Reading and hearing about frigidity and impotence stirs their fears.

Marriage manuals describe problems that can arise and give frank, insightful advice on being good sex partners. The couple's total relationship must be brought to the sexual uniting. Communication, patience, understanding, and all the other dynamics of their personal oneness will make the physical part satisfactory. If there are difficulties, those skills will enable them to solve the problems before they unduly strain the marriage.

It is most important for couples not to permit the "downward spiral" to set in. If honeymoon sexual encounters are not as fulfilling as expected, a couple should resist permitting disappointment to interfere unduly with their relationship. Otherwise a temporary situation can be turned into a long-lasting one. Both may become depressed and feel responsible, even guilty. Or one may blame the other, if not in actual words then by his or her mannerisms. If the initial disappointment is taken too seriously, it will create this spiraling effect: the couple brings the negative feelings to the next encounter, and without the confidence, trust, and comfort necessary for a satisfying sex relationship, they may experience the same problem. A couple needs to be patient. They should get all the knowledge they can from books and counselors if their sexual adjustment is not satisfactory.

THE FIRST YEARS OF MARRIAGE

Families and individuals are too different to predict with any accuracy the conflicts a couple will have. However, researchers have charted stages of marriage and family development in helpful ways.[11] The following description will not fit everyone, but it will help to identify some of the possible transition periods.

FIRST DAZE

Marriages are made, though it is commonly thought that they just happen. In her candid article "The Death of a Marriage," Barbara Spense admits that she and her husband were plugged into that idea. "Right before we were divorced, my husband said to me, 'Marriage should not have to be work. You fall in love, get married, and that's it.' He was partly right. You get married and that's it, but now I know that that is when the work begins."[12]

Some of the tasks couples work at are learning to live with each other's habits, trying to be both a full-time employee and a marriage partner, deciding at which family's house to celebrate holidays, telling one another when they are angry, and dealing with in-laws.[13] That list shows that just being in love will not make a marriage work.

During the early years, the couple will continue to work on the tasks begun during the honeymoon: adjusting to each other's peculiar ways, getting used to role-playing, and learning the art of intimacy. After the honeymoon, they make their adjustments in the midst of the pressures and demands of relatives, work, and friends. That can complicate as well as help. Suppose, for example, an in-law insists the new husband is not playing his role properly. That now figures in the bride's judgment of the groom's measuring up. On the positive side, friends might tell them how well they are doing, giving them welcome affirmation that all is well.

---

11. Laura J. Singer has described stages based upon her counseling experiences in *Stages: The Crises That Shape Your Marriage*. Ellen Galinsky draws on her experience and research to chart stages of parenthood in *Between Generations*. Kathleen M. Galvin and Bernard J. Brommel formulate stages based on various researchers in *Family Communication: Cohesion and Change*.
12. Barbara Spense, "The Death of a Marriage," *His*, February 1980, pp. 1-5.
13. Galvin and Brommel, p. 209.

PATTERNING

This early stage is a patterning period. Like new pieces of furniture, the couple will be placing in their home patterns of relating that might be with them for a lifetime. The way a couple handles conflict, for example, is set in concrete by the end of the second year, according to some experts.[14] That alone should press the couple to put time and energy into constructing good patterns. They will want to be careful not to allow initial problems to bud, blossom, and grow into bitter fruit. For that reason, many pastors are coming to realize that post-marital counseling sessions make sense. By meeting with a couple three to six months after the wedding, counselors can help to identify problems at the bud stage. I know of one pastor who with his wife conducts small group sessions for couples who have been married six months. They call it the "twenty-thousand-mile-check-up." After a year, couples go through the "fifty-thousand-mile-check-up."

Relational skills newlyweds work on include self-disclosing, handling conflict, affirming, listening, and sharing feelings.[15] Practical issues relate to handling finances, church relationships, homebuilding, career and educational planning, and social life.[16] All of those should be the subject of premarital counseling and should be incorporated into marriage seminars and post-marital counseling sessions.

Handling conflict should be singled out as one of the most crucial skills a couple needs. Whenever one person becomes an obstacle to the other in the close confines of marriage, communication becomes difficult. It is easy to talk when there are nice things to say; the real test of communication comes when you care enough to talk about the very worst. If a couple has a problem between them they cannot discuss, it will create a proverbial "sleeping dog." Neither can mention the problem lest it arouse something they cannot handle. If another such problem arises, the distance between them increases.

Research has shown that newly married couples often develop a "wait and see" attitude. They neither *talk* about nor *do* anything to solve a problem between them. Wives more often than husbands openly talk about differences. Men speak openly about financial problems but not about desires for more frequent sex. Wives complain six times more frequently than husbands about the amount of time spent at home.[17]

If couples do not learn to share under the stress of conflict, misunderstanding can eat away at their relationship like acid. A study of problem couples proved that to be the case. *Misunderstanding* was ruining their marriages, not *misunderstandings*.

---

14. Ibid., p. 210.
15. See Charles M. Sell, *Achieving the Impossible: Intimate Marriage,* for specific guidelines for these skills. Also see Galvin and Brommel for more research in this area.
16. Galvin and Brommel, p. 207.
17. Beverly R. Cutler and William G. Dyer, "Initial Adjustment Processes in Young Married Couples," *Love, Marriage, Family: A Developmental Approach,* ed. M. E. Lasswell and T. E. Lasswell, pp. 290–96 as cited by Galvin and Brommel, p. 210.

When questioned, they could not recall specific problems. What they did sense was a general misunderstanding.[18]

OPTICAL ODDITIES

Perspectives will change with the marriage experience. For example, earlier if one partner had become depressed, the other would simply have said, "Well, that's O.K. There are many reasons to get depressed." However, after some years of marriage, the other person may percieve the depression differently, for example, "I must not be a good wife, or I would have made him happy by now."[19] Despite the potential for problems, research has indicated that the first years are usually happy ones and differences are not taken so seriously that they erupt into crises.[20]

Special mention should be made about the newlywed's interactions with the in-laws. Studies have shown that couples will probably have regular contact with them throughout life.[21] Relatives will affect the new pair in specific ways, but the broader problem is that there are three distinct small group systems interacting with each other: the couple, the husband's parents, and the wife's parents. Different values and patterns of interaction offer plenty of opportunities to clash. If one partner does not get along with an in-law, tension will be created. He or she will be caught in a conflict of loyalties. Couples will need a long range view, recognizing that how they relate to in-laws in the early years will be important to the future relationship. They feel they have little need for the extended family at present, but they will need each other as time passes.

CHILDREN

The next major marriage transition period occurs when the two become three or more. How and when individual couples go through this stage will vary a great deal. Some will decide to not have a baby until they have been married for many years, while others will have one the first year without deciding.

THE DECISION TO HAVE A CHILD

In modern times, couples not only decide when to have the first baby, but whether or not to have one at all. In the past, having a baby was not a major decision because married couples were expected to. After all, the psalmist sang of children as

---

18. R. D. Laing, H. Phillipson, and A. R. Lee, *Interpersonal Perception: A Theory and Method of Research* (New York: Springer, 1966), cited by Sherod Miller, Elam E. Nunnally, and Daniel B. Wackman, *Alive and Aware*, p. 148.
19. Monica McGoldrick and Elizabeth A. Carter, eds., *The Family Life Cycle: A Framework for Family Therapy*, p. 16.
20. Galvin and Brommel, p. 210.
21. Lillian Troll, Sheila Miller and Robert Atchley, *Families in Later Life*, p. 7.

a gift of the LORD. . . .
Like arrows in the hand of a warrior,
So are the children of one's youth.
How blessed is the man whose quiver is full of them.
(Psalm 127:3-5)

In the past, many arrows made a full quiver; now, just the thought of one makes couples quiver. Family planning does not deny the psalmist's contention that children are a blessing of the Lord. That scriptural truth, however, must be applied in a world wherein issues like overpopulation pressure couples to have fewer children. Some decide to have a childless marriage. Theologians seem to offer no objections to their doing so, believing that if it is permissible to use birth control techniques to limit the number of children to one, it is permissible to limit it to none.[22]
Couples need to prayerfully consider their motives for having children. Having a child for the wrong reason may be as negative as not having one for the wrong reason. There are four categories of motives:

- *Egotistic.* Wanting a child who will look like me, who will carry on my admirable traits, who will be successful, or who will carry on my name; feeling the pride of creation; wanting to stay young in heart; desiring fulfillment
- *Compensatory.* Making up for an unhappy family background; compensating for lack of satisfaction in a job; desiring to feel more secure about masculinity/femininity (can be especially dangerous)
- *Conforming.* Being like most people; pleasing parents; forestalling social criticism (not as dangerous as compensatory motives, but still a poor foundation for becoming parents because the desire is not to have a child but to please someone else)
- *Affectionate.* Wanting a real opportunity to make someone happy, or to teach someone about all the beautiful things of life; desiring the satisfaction of giving to someone else and helping someone grow and develop (good reasons for wanting to parent a child)[23]

Although it is desirable to have the affectionate reasons, many also decide to have a baby because of the experience it provides. The psalmist sang:

Behold, children are a gift of the LORD;
The fruit of the womb is a reward.
(Psalm 127:3)

22. For further information, see Charles M. Sell, *Achieving the Impossible: Intimate Marriage*, pp. 199-202.
23. William Granzig and Ellen Peck, *The Parent Test*, p. 19, as cited by H. Norman Wright and Marvin N. Inmon, *Preparing for Parenthood*, p. 1.

Most of the reward is in the experience itself. Giving birth provides an opportunity to participate in God's creative work. "A woman giving birth to a child has pain because her time has come; but when her baby is born she forgets the anguish because of her joy that a child is born into the world" (John 16:21, NIV).

"Deciding to have a child is still about the most impactful decision a woman makes,"[24] although the decision will not always be a logically calculated one. Perhaps Mark and Anne Hanchett are correct when they suggest that most Christian couples conceive simply because they are doing "what seems natural in God's plan for His creation."[25]

Delaying pregnancy for a few years after marriage is a good practice. The complications of pregnancy and the presence of the baby are demanding. It is better that a couple work well as two before increasing the number.

THE PREGNANCY

Ease of adjustment in the initial weeks of a pregnancy will probably depend on whether or not it was anticipated. If a baby was wanted and pregnancy hoped for, conception can be a "blessed event." If not, it can be a shock. Pondering the threatening changes and responsibilities, a man or woman might think: *We are not having a baby. We are having a disruption!* The woman may feel that her life plans as well as her body have been violated. Trying to help his wife come to grips with those negative feelings, the husband may feel challenged and become disturbed since he was responsible for having impregnated her. He becomes ambivalent; his fears and anxieties are aroused. That raises the abortion issue. Doctors may ask: "Is this pregnancy convenient?" and then suggest aborting it if it is not. Such a casual view of conception and abortion is grossly distinct from the Christian viewpoint. Christians know that having a child is ultimately the Creator's work, not theirs. Although it is a joint venture, once begun in conception the process is in His hands. Nonetheless, some Christian theologians advocate abortion under certain circumstances, as when the pregnancy threatens the woman's life.

Pregnancy begets joys and challenges for the couple. For the wife, it can be discomforting, especially at first: swollen ankles, sore breasts, nausea, vomiting, fatigue, heartburn, bleeding, and bloatedness are some of the usual physical difficulties. Although women often talk about those matters, they do not often discuss the sensation of pregnancy. The following description by a pregnant woman is as rare as it is beautiful.

> Your notion of bodily integrity is violated in a much more dramatic fashion than the advent of your first menses or the first act of intercourse.... You are bound to feel at times that your body has been possessed and that you have lost control of your own person. You can view it as a violent siege, an opportunity for physical transcendence, a chance to

---

24. Robert Gould, *Transformations. Growth and Change in Adult Life,* p. 97.
25. Mark Hanchett and Anne Hanchett, "On Having a Family," *The Stony Brook School Bulletin* (February 1980), p. 1.

see if your body functions properly, or a slight inconvenience—well worth the price—but pleasure and pain will always go hand in hand, and ambivalence is the only correct, the only possible emotional posture.[26]

Emotional issues of pregnancy may cause some temporary changes in the couple's relationship. Because she uses so much emotional energy concentrating on her womb's occupant, a wife may have little left to support her husband. He might feel neglected or unloved and, at times, feel that his wife resents him.

One study found that wives do not become more emotional in dealing with conflict during this nine month transition. It did find, however, that husbands avoided conflict, especially during the last stages of the pregnancy.[27]

The prospective mother's feelings might be mixed: her fears mingle with the joy of giving birth. Will she be a good mother? Will the baby be OK? Can she handle the change?

The couple will also grapple with practical questions. Besides arranging finances and getting baby things ready, they will face some choices: gynecologist, birth situation (home or hospital), and whether or not to use the natural birth method.

For the most part, the pregnancy period is a happy time, filled with warm closeness, especially if the couple shares their fears as well as their joys with each other.

LIFE WITH BABY

As soon as the baby takes his first breath, the mother and father take on new roles. The fact that giving birth to a baby has considerable impact upon them can be seen in their first reaction, which is often a sort of denial—"I'm a parent; I can't believe it!"

Anxiety over ability to perform the mother or father role is typical. The thought, "I'm not ready to be a father," raced through the mind of one of my friends as he sped through traffic to the hospital with his wife who was ready to deliver.

The parents' views of one another will change. Now each will have two roles to perform. It is most natural that the husband worries that his wife's role of mother will interfere with her functioning as a wife. She, on the other hand, may be concerned about his being a good father. In the past, mothers may not have expected fathers to do much for the child because it was traditional for mothers to care for them. Experts contend our society is still too "mother-centered," and challenge men to be more involved in childcare. From the beginning the infant needs to have positive contact with the father in order to have a solid self-concept and identity.[28]

Couples with young children undergo other changes in the marital relationship. It becomes more difficult to have romantic and sexual encounters. Caring for the

26. Angela Barron McBride, *The Growth and Development of Mothers*, pp. 30–31.
27. H. L. Raush et al, *Communication Conflict and Marriage*, p. 204.
28. John Nash, "The Father in Contemporary Culture" in *Love, Marriage, Family: A Developmental Approach*, ed. M. E. Lasswell and T. E. Lasswell, pp. 353–62, as cited by Galvin and Brommel, p. 213.

children until evening makes it tough to find quality time together when each is not too tired. Going out on "dates" is more expensive—requiring paying a babysitter—and not as convenient—if children are sick, for example. During this stage of marriage, couples need to realize that the marital relationship may not be the same as before, while recognizing that the situation is temporary. The degree of difficulty in maintaining marital intimacy fluctuates through the life cycle. A difficult period should not be a basis for judging the whole marriage. Couples should thrive on closeness when circumstances make it easy, and strive for it when circumstances make it hard. All the while, they must accept the fluctuations and think of the marriage in terms of the whole life span, and not just a particular part. It should also not be forgotten that children can add a new richness to the couple's intimacy.[29]

Having the first child affects the relationship the couple has with in-laws. If the child comes early in the marriage, its arrival will probably give the new family a more distinct identity of its own. Recognizing that they are now their own family in-laws will probably not insist they "come home" for holidays and other occasions. The child's birth will also complicate the relationship with the couple's parents, because a grandparent-grandchild relationship has been created.

SCHOOL STEPS

The next major transition for a family is when the child goes off to school. This raises issues related to separation, authority, and interpretation.

Separation. During pre-school days, a child becomes increasingly independent of and separate from parents by visiting friends, staying overnight with grandparents, playing across the street, and so on. Going off to school is a powerful marker event of greater independence and separation. It is ominous, signalling to the parent that future separation is inevitable. Putting the child on the bus for the first time can be emotionally unsettling, testing the parents' ability to "let go."

Authority. Authority becomes an issue in a number of ways. Because the child's world has grown wider, parental authority is carried out in new ways. Communication of the family's rules, values, and standards becomes more difficult. As the child comes under other influences, old beliefs and ways may be challenged.

Interpretation. Interpretation is also dominant at this time. Ellen Galinsky maintains that parents will be pressed to interpret themselves as parents. Their patterns of parenting will be undergoing constant evaluation and change as their child's behavior away from home makes them question what they have been doing.[30]

THE CHURCH'S INFLUENCE ON FAMILY STAGES

The church's ministry of discipling finds a natural base in the home and family, where children and adults alike should be nurtured, grow, and mature. Being Christ-

29. Howard Clinebell and Charlotte Clinebell, *The Intimate Marriage*, p. 120.
30. Ellen Galinsky, *Between Generations: The Six Stages of Parenthood* (New York: Times, 1981), pp. 178-94.

like in the home is as imperative for the Christian as it is challenging (Deut. 6:1–9; Eph. 5:22–6:4; Col. 3:18–24). In today's troubled homes, it is not always easy to incorporate scriptural precepts into life behind the front door. The church should encourage personal maturity by fostering family growth, because individual stages are intricately interwoven with family stages.

The church can teach adults Christian truth that relates to their particular parental role. One adult course on discipline or a few sermons on the Christian home are not enough. Distinct stages confront parents with different issues. The nature and means of parental control, for instance, change as the child moves from pre-school to school age and then to the teenage years. Practices that worked in one period aren't effective in another. Problems change, and that causes confusion and inability to cope for people who in earlier years had things under control. Family transitions and crises sometimes become oppressive. "When I look at faces when I preach," one pastor told me, "they sometimes show so much hurt and bewilderment that I know they are not even listening to my sermon. If they are to grow as Christ's disciples, I must help them be winners at home."

Thankfully, more and more churches are sensing the need to train disciples by training parents. Publishers are producing elective adult courses and seminar materials, such as David C. Cook's new series of Sunday school materials based on family stages. Larger churches are adding family life ministers to the staff. In some cases, the job of the Christian education minister is modified to include more family life education and family counseling.

Courses and classes are not enough, for marriage and family skills are best learned outside the classroom. Just as a person cannot learn to swim by listening to an Olympic swimmer lecture, a father and mother cannot learn to communicate by hearing someone talk about it. Family dynamics are best learned in a family context. The church can "grow" family members by being a family itself.[31]

If church relationships are mostly *secondary*—that is, relationships that confine people to certain roles and rules and so inhibit closeness—adults will not learn the art of living in a *primary* group—one that is intimate and flexible. Unfortunately, some people try to make the home like a secondary group: rigid roles and strict rules replace love, honesty, patience, and gentleness as the means of avoiding conflict. Although a strong case for family member roles can be made from Scripture, that approach is too one-sided. Roles and rules need to be held with flexibility and love. When secondary roles and rules break down, group members often are stymied: a wife whose husband will not lead does not know what to do, and the family stagnates while waiting for the father to take up his role. However, the family that builds its life on love and understanding knows what to do. Acceptance, forbearance, sympathy, and patience will work in any situation. Christian virtues can triumph.

There is some evidence that those who usually function in secondary groups do not

31. Many have described the educational basis of this. Dennis B. Guernesy's *A New Design in Family Ministry* is the most recent book on the subject. I have made a defense for this type of ministry in *Family Ministry: The Enrichment of Family Life Through the Church.*

learn solid family communication skills. Two researchers discovered that first grade children who were from strongly role-oriented families did not have the ability to listen and communicate, while children from person-oriented families could.[32]

When families are hurting and breaking because they lack the art of relating, their members badly need a context where they can learn to relate. Empowered by God's Spirit, the church can be that place.

32. D. J. Bearison and T. Z. Cassel, "Cognitive Decentration and Social Codes: Communication Effectiveness in Young Children from Different Family Contexts," *Developmental Psychology* (1975):29–36, as cited by Galvin and Brommel, p. 219.

6

Strolling Single Street: Singlehood and Divorce

THE NEW MAJORITY

"There aren't any conditions under which I would consider getting married ... I want freedom of choice, freedom to do what I want."[1] More adults may be making that statement than ever before. Singleness is in!

That is in stark contrast to the thinking of a few decades ago. In the fifties, singles were talked about as being those who failed to marry. Marriage was normal; singleness was not. A study done in the early fifties concluded that only negative reasons kept singles from getting married. Those who did not marry had a high rate of personal and social problems like hostility toward marriage or toward persons of the opposite sex, or were homosexuals, in poor health or unattractive. Because of those and other reasons, they were passed over—unmarried because unselected. There was little suggestion in that study's findings that such persons might be making a positive decision not to marry, because it was assumed that any right-thinking person desires marriage.[2] Today's attitude toward singleness is not transformed, but it is in the process of changing.

Both married and single harbor hostile feelings about the issue. Married people get the impression singles are more anti-marriage than they are pro-single. And singles complain of being misunderstood and even maligned. They talk of being ignored and neglected; made to feel like the "fifth wheel." Like minority groups, they are treated like misfits in society and in church.

---

1. Statement of a young man interviewed by Peter Stein, "Singlehood: An Alternative to Marriage," *The Family Coordinator,* October 1975, p. 494.
2. Manfred Kuhn, "How Mates Are Sorted," *Family, Marriage and Parenthood,* as cited by Stein, p. 492.

In reality, they are not a minority group and must no longer be made to feel that they do not belong. Over half of all American adults are single—married adults are in the minority. Not all of those are widowed elderly people or adults in their early twenties. One-third of all adults between the ages of twenty and fifty-five are single— and the majority of those are over thirty. Although most of those are single temporarily, planning to get married or remarried, the shocker is this: one-third of the single men and one-fifth of the single women choose to be single because they like the life-style.[3]

Since singles tend to cluster in large urban areas, many individuals and churches are not aware of the mammoth size of the problems and potentials in the new wave of singleness.

NO SINGLE STEREOTYPE

Within this wave are all sorts of singles. Few of them fit the stereotype of "swinger" or "loser." One study, in fact, found them to be so diverse that it recommended relinquishing any stereotype about single living.[4] Including the never-married, divorced, and separated, some are single by choice, some by circumstances. Some are hurting badly; others are blissfully happy. Many of them have children to care for. Sociologists classify singles into four types: the voluntary temporary single; the voluntary stable single; the involuntary temporary single; and the involuntary stable single.[5]

Experts argue whether singleness is a normal state. To some, persons who never marry come from families that have damaged their ability to relate. But the Bible confirms that singleness is not abnormal. Jesus indicated that some would be born to be single (Matt. 19:12). Without defaming marriage the apostle Paul gave persuasive reasons for being single (1 Cor. 7). Affirming the single state does not negate the statement in Genesis 2:18 that it is not good for the man to be alone. That statement does not merely support marriage, but it more broadly insists that God created persons to be related to others. Persons receive their identity and fulfillment through a sense of belonging. Besides marriage, belongingness can be found in family, friendships, and church. Singles are not incomplete or abnormal because they are not married. A married person may be more alone than a single. Genital sex does not guarantee an escape from isolation. Married people can have sex without intimacy or have a marriage without satisfying belongingness.

Singleness needs to be treated less like a problem to cope with and more like a life stage to adjust to. The description of the developmental process of singlehood is limited because the research is scarce. Data is lacking to answer such basic questions as: When do singles who never marry decide to remain single? What are the

3. Jacqueline Simenauer and David Carrol, *Singles, The New Americans*, pp. 322 and 324.
4. Barry W. Reister, Alan L. Gordon, and Serena B. Strieby, "The Boston Single Life Study: Implications for the Helping Professions," *Journal of College Student Personnel* 22, no. 5 (September 1981):446.
5. P. J. Stein, "The Lifestyles and Life Changes of the Never-Married," *Marriage and Family Review* 1, no. 4(1978):3.

milestones in the single's life? What are the crises points for those who desire marriage and yet continue to be single?[6] One noted expert on singles states flatly: "Serious research about singlehood is notably missing from the field of family sociology."[7]

CREATIVE SINGLEHOOD

Creative singlehood is a term applied to those who carve out a special life for themselves as singles, either because they just never marry or because they never intend to.

Looking in on them near the end of their life, older singles are found to be quite content. A significant study of singles over age sixty-five proved they were more stable and less lonely than widowed elderly people. Changes for them were fewer in that they never had to adjust to being a grandparent or losing a spouse. Valuing their independence and having to live by themselves throughout life, they report that they are isolated but not lonely. They tend to see nothing peculiar about being unmarried; it's "just another way of life," they say.[8]

It is not known precisely why persons remain unmarried and when they decide to do so. Some, of course, do so for religious reasons. Studies confirm that the majority of singles hope to marry, but many just never find the so-called Mister or Miss Right. Others enjoy the benefits of the single life-style. A few do not marry because of homosexual tendencies. Homosexuals do not make the decision not to marry early in life. One study concluded that the "gay" identity takes longer to develop than the heterosexual one, usually not becoming set until the late twenties.[9] Homosexuals often marry heterosexuals. In one survey 20 percent were married and half of them had children.[10]

SINGLES WHO NEVER MARRY BUT ALWAYS HOPED TO

What is life like for persons who are single and want to marry? We can speculate that they grew up planning to get married, with all the usual boy-girl dreams of a wedding, home and family. Somewhere along the way, hope was mingled with disappointment and anxiety. Some years after high school, perhaps, the first inklings of possible future singleness occurred. The longer marriage is postponed, the more likely the person will remain unmarried throughout life.[11] Each year that passes becomes a stepping stone towards what they suspect will happen. Probably, it is not the years, but certain events, such as college graduation, that create milestones for

6. Douglas C. Kimmel, *Adulthood and Aging,* p. 223.
7. Stein, "Singlehood," p. 489.
8. J. F. Gubrium, "Being Single in Old Age," *International Journal of Aging and Human Development* 6, no. 1 (1975):29–41.
9. Dorothy Riddle and Stephen Morin, "Removing the Stigma from Individuals," *American Psychological Association Monitor* (November 1977):16 and 29 as cited by Kimmel, p. 232.
10. Alan P. Bell and Martin Weinberg, *Homosexualities: A Study of Diversity Among Men and Women,* as cited by Kimmel, p. 230.
11. Dennis Guernesy, *A New Design for Family Ministry,* p. 116.

them. *By the time I am through college, I will be engaged,* the person whispers to his optimistic self. With no marriage prospects at graduation, does the person have a difficult time? Since young people are choosing to marry later, that may not be a time to panic. Graduation from graduate school, however, does become a crisis time for many singles. Women who continue their education are more likely to remain single.[12] Graduation is forboding because it terminates what they hoped would be a golden opportunity to find a mate.

Disappointment and depression sometimes set in at that point. Confusion about the future is normal. "Should I settle down in some career and forget about getting married, or should I go somewhere where the chances of finding a partner are greater?" is a demanding question. Christians grope for God's will. Apparently, many concentrate on career building and service, and along with it, personal growth. "While singles depend on romance for much of their happiness, an even greater source of fulfillment comes from the development of personal skills, values, ideals, and potential. Seventy-five percent of the men and 84 percent of the women say personal growth is very or somewhat important."[13]

Do they ever go through stages of grief, not only for the loss of the dream partner but for the dream children? Passing through the thirtieth year is a critical time. "The single feels a push to find a partner," Gail Sheehy says.[14] Sheehy puts the single person into the total developmental picture. In other words, something can be known about the single voyage because the adult trip has been charted. Assuming that to be true, then it can be guessed that menopause is the next crucial marker event for the single woman. Most single women may come to terms with their single life by the time menopause comes.

I do not mean to suggest that the single life is dire and forboding. Apparently there are many singles who at first want to marry but, by a certain age, decide they like being single better. Perhaps they go through grief and struggle to come to that decision; perhaps not.

SINGLES WHO DECIDE TO REMAIN SINGLE

Some singles have no marriage plans in their future. Their reasons are as divergent as their life-styles. Peter Stein discovered that the singles in his study remained single because of negative attitudes toward marriage and positive attitudes toward the single life. Most of those studied were previously married, and most were planning to have sexual experiences as single persons. Therefore, they represent the growth of a rather distinct group in contemporary society. Some shun marriage because they think it limits the choice of friendships. Those see marriage as a sort of "flight from other people." Also to them, marriage is boring—an entrapment that requires compromises that cut them off from varieties of experiences. Remaining single instead offers

12. Elmer Spreitzer and Lawrence E. Riley, "Factors Associated with Singlehood," *Journal of Marriage and the Family* 36, no. 3 (August 1974):533–42.
13. Simenauer and Carrol, p. 334.
14. Gail Sheehy, *Passages*, p. 41.

freedom, enjoyment, opportunities to meet people and develop friendships, economic independence, "more and better sexual experiences," and personal development. No doubt, such creative singlehood is more likely today because of the change in moral thinking. Both men and women in Stein's study mentioned that sexual availability of other persons was an important motivation for remaining single.[15]

Not all those who choose creative singlehood are sexually active. The powerful pull toward singlehood for many is embodied in the opportunity for personal growth, service, and fulfilling relationships with others.

SINGLE STRUGGLES

Overall, it is known that the vast majority of singles wrestle with some distinct struggles. Of the 3000 asked in one survey 85 percent said loneliness was a major problem. Other problems were fear (mostly women), lack of money, lack of sexual activity and personal contacts, a tendency to become self-centered, and social pressures.[16]

Most successfully adapt to their singlehood. Many seem to end up with a family, one way or another. In the early years, most live with parents and in the later years with parents, siblings, or other relatives. In 1978 only 11 percent lived alone. But, the proportion of those living alone increases with age (over one-half in late life).[17]

DIVIDED HIGHWAY: SEPARATING

No matter what our views about divorce, no view justifies saying, "We don't work with divorced people." Rejecting divorced persons will not lower their number. A negative attitude toward them will keep us from understanding this stressful life transition—and as many as one out of three American adults go through it. Sooner or later we will be asked to slosh along the divorce trail with a friend or relative.

Divorce is most likely to occur during marriage's early years. Two-thirds of women whose first marriage ended in divorce in the U.S. by 1975 divorced before age thirty.[18] Divorce seems to be more stressful for them than for older women.[19]

The divorce transition, rather than its theology, will be examined here. The goal is to find ways to help divorcees as well as prevent divorces. Divorce will be the main arena of discussion, although there are other ways to dissolve a marriage, such as separation, legal separation, and annulment.

Although no one knows for certain what the road is like for all divorced persons, it is possible to divide the divorce journey into three stages. The stage leading to the decision to separate or file for a divorce can be called the *distancing period*. The *transition period* covers the time between filing for divorce and the eventual emotional detachment. This is the major phase, including the divorce and recovery.

15. Stein, "Singlehood," p. 494.
16. Simenauer and Carrol, pp. 242–46.
17. U.S. Census, 1979, as cited by Kimmel, p. 229.
18. David A. Chiriboga and Loraine Cutler, "Stress Responses Among Divorcing Men and Women," *Journal of Divorce* 1, no. 2 (1977):95–106.
19. U.S. Census, 1977, as cited by Kimmel, p. 224.

During the period of *redirection,* the detached person builds a new life. Charted, the passage looks like this:

Marriage	Separation	File for divorce	Divorce granted	Detachment
DISTANCING		TRANSITION		REDIRECTION
		(up to 2 years)		(up to 1½ years)

DISTANCING

It is difficult to put together a general description of how a marriage relationship breaks down. It may be fair to say that few appear to be doomed from the start. Perhaps some couples have some sort of conflict the first few weeks that eventually makes them call it quits. But more likely, the relationship deteriorates slowly, as a study of middle adults who divorced, clearly shows. Of 138 who returned a questionnaire, only one out of four said their marriage was wrong from the beginning.[20] However, because that study dealt with those divorced later in life, it may or may not apply to those who divorce in the early years of marriage.

If engineers were investigating the collapse of a bridge, they would first check the blueprints to find out what bolts, welds, and parts kept it intact; and then they would see which of those broke down. We can partly describe how a marriage comes apart by studying what keeps it together.

Love's elements. Robert Weiss of Harvard Laboratory of Community Psychology has described the love features that are part of a marriage relationship. He holds that most marriages begin with partners in love. Calling love "positive regard," he insightfully distinguishes its components. *Idealization* describes how a person projects onto the other person the aspects one wishes to see. The man, for instance, is seen as decisive and strong in stress situations, because that is something the woman wants in a man. *Trust* is an unquestioned belief in the other's commitment. *Identification* occurs whenever a person associates himself with the loved one, for example, a man may gain a feeling of *self*-esteem for himself because his wife is lovely or intelligent. The *complementary* sense comes when a person recognizes that the partner has strengths and capacities that he does not have. *Attachment* is the bonding that takes place. There is a feeling of at-homeness and ease when the other is present or felt to be near.[21]

If each of those five features is seen as a strand in the rope that ties the couple together, it is possible to understand that if one breaks, the others will be under severe strain. If a man does not live up to the wife's ideals, for example, tension is created. If he does not turn out to be as strong or sexy or loving as she idealized, she fights disappointment. Trust can begin to fade when a husband, for example, permits his job to interfere with his pledge to be an intimate partner. If any one of the five features

---

20. Maggie P. Hayes, Nick Stinnett and John Defrain, "Learning About Marriage from the Divorced," *Journal of Divorce* 4, no. 1 (Fall 1981):pp. 23-24.
21. Robert Weiss, *Marital Separation*, pp. 36-40.

becomes a trouble point, all may eventually be weakened. Weiss maintains that the last element, the feeling of bonding, seems to persist long after the other elements have faded.

Rewards. Another way to look at what holds a marriage together is to examine its rewards. George Levinger classifies rewards as *material* (house, income, etc.), *affectional* (sex, companionship, etc.), and *symbolic* (status from husband's or wife's career, etc.).[22] Conflict can occur in one or more of those areas. If the conflict is not properly resolved, negative feelings are aroused and possibly held inside. Other areas of the marriage deteriorate. Perhaps, instead of open conflict there is growing disenchantment about marriage itself. The relationship means little, not because there are problems, but because the rewards are not significant to one or both. In some marriages degeneration occurs slowly. One or both of the marriage partners invests less and less in the marriage as the years pass.[23]

Reasons for not breaking up. Of course, deterioration occurs in many marriages that do not end in divorce. That is because other types of bonds exist. These bonds consist of the reasons for not breaking up. Social pressure is one of those: "What would my mother think if we separated?" Religious reasons often keep people together. A feeling of obligation to the spouse or the children may also make a person stay in a marriage.

Christians should stress both the rewards of marriage as well as the sanctions against divorce. Not only should we teach why people should not divorce, but also how they can build strong marriages. Marriage preparation and enrichment training may be the best preventives against divorce. Those who divorce are often those who were poorly prepared for marriage.[24] If marriages start out well and end up bad, something is happening in the middle. Apparently people not only need premarital counseling, but periodic check-ups in the form of marriage enrichment sessions, interviews with counselors or pastors, reading, and marriage evaluation sessions.

Preparation for marriage should begin long before the engagement. Children and teens need to be told of the dangers of teen marriages. The divorce rate for those who marry young is much higher than the national average.[25] They should be warned against marrying for the wrong reasons. Those who marry to escape parents, for example, also have a high divorce rate.

The breaking point. Couples may continue to live in a relationship long after it has all but died. *Emotional divorce,* wherein little affection is left between a couple, can take place before the legal separation. Somewhere in the distancing period, one of the partners may make a decision to divorce. He sort of "clicks off."

Although each situation is unique, two factors often form the springboard for emotional divorce. Discovering an alternative is one. Levinger maintains that a relationship will continue, no matter how little its rewards or how little opposition

---

22. George Levinger, "A Social Psychological Perspective on Marital Dissolution," in *Divorce and Separation,* ed. George Levinger and Olver C. Moles, pp. 37–60.
23. Hayes, Stinnet and Defrain, p. 28.
24. Evelyn Millis Duvall, *Family Development,* p. 242, as cited by Kimmel, p. 223.
25. Kimmel, p. 223.

there is to breaking up, until a sufficient alternative becomes possible.[26] A woman, for example, may discover she can indeed get a job that will give her the income she will need to live alone. Or else friends will convince a person it would be better for him or her to live alone or to come live with them. An extramarital affair is often behind the decision to divorce, because the individual has found another source of sex and affection.

A second element in the decision to divorce is a life crisis or event. The age thirty transition seems to inspire decisions to divorce. So does the mid-life crisis. Sometimes the crisis is the death of a child, financial loss, an affair, or a major fight. If the crisis comes after fifteen or more years of marriage, the couple may try to rebuild. But by that time, many couples have little left in the marriage and they do not seem to feel it is worth saving.

When a person decides to divorce, he may not inform the spouse. In his own mind, the marriage has passed a point of no return, even though the spouse may not share that viewpoint or even be aware that the partner believes it. Marital life can become especially difficult when that happens. The one who secretly wants a divorce may provoke one conflict after another; or else he may reduce contact and communication to the bare minimum. Interestingly, those who study mid-life couples who divorced find they had little conflict before the divorce, because they hardly talked to each other at all by that time. The one who wants to save the relationship may go to great lengths to accommodate the other. One partner gives in, sacrifices, changes. The other provokes and sabotages. It is like one child constructing a house of dominoes while another keeps pulling out the bottom blocks.

Counseling can be effective at this time. The distancing party may come to see the potential of the marriage and the illusion of the option. But, counseling may be ineffective, for couples often come for help after one has already made the decision to leave. Such counseling is not unlike talking to a child about the cauliflower on his plate while his eye is on the cake on the kitchen counter.

The period between the separation or decision to divorce and the actual filing may be as long as two years. The partner who wants out may continue to look for reasons to end the marriage. He or she may try to sabotage the relationship to make it unbearable in order to justify terminating it.

TRANSITION

When one spouse leaves or files for divorce, the action precipitates the transition phase, which extends to the granting of the divorce and until the person has practically and emotionally recovered from the separation. It should be viewed as a crisis. Divorce ranks the highest of all life's stress-producing transitions.[27] Women tend to report greater emotional turmoil during the period prior to divorce and the divorce

---

26. Levinger as cited by Naomi Golan, *Passing Through Transitions*, p. 145.
27. Bernard L. Bloom, Stephen W. White and Shirley J. Asher, "Marital Disruption as a Stressful Life Event," in *Divorce and Separation*, ed. George Levinger and Oliver C. Moles, pp. 184–200.

proceedings, while men report greater difficulty afterwards.[28] Most people do not foresee the troubles divorce represents, even though enough information is available to describe the experience.

The emotional wounds caused by divorce are not simply due to the loss of a love relationship. Divorce is not like being jilted or breaking up. A divorced woman may be more upset over the lack of money than the absence of her man. The divorce experience has a spectacular height, depth, and breadth. Along with grief and stress, practical problems loom large. Divorced women report being overwhelmed by the quantity of tasks that face them. They say they do not have sufficient time or physical energy to deal with household maintenance, financial tasks, child care, and job and social demands.[29] Men say they experience the same feelings of chaos. Social relationships are a problem. Friends the couple shared are not available as before. The stigma that goes with divorce makes the divorced feel isolated. Relations with family members also become quite complex. The relationship with the former spouse is tension-producing. Caring for and relating to children may be difficult. Some researchers found that the divorced mother may find relating to a male child to be particularly stressful.[30] Contact with in-laws may present some problems, as does relating to one's own mother and father. Women, for example, who moved into their parent's home reported conflict within only a few weeks.[31]

Another facet is the change of roles. Seeing oneself as single again is a major adjustment. Also, the loss of each of the roles of father, mother, husband or wife, and so on must be handled. If children are involved, the spouse who gets custody takes on other roles. A woman becomes a producer, decision-maker, and sole disciplinarian.

William H. Berman and Dennis C. Turk catalog the six major divorce stress areas as follows:

- *Former spouse contacts:* talking about money matters or about the children with them, visitation of children
- *Parent-child interactions:* talking with child about life, about the divorce, expression of feelings
- *Interpersonal relations:* making new friends, getting involved in social activities, having some degree of intimacy with others
- *Loneliness:* being depressed, being alone, feeling inadequate as a person
- *Practical problems:* cooking meals, cleaning the house, having enough time with the children
- *Financial Concerns:* having enough money, balancing the budget[32]

---

28. David F. Hultsch and Francine Deutsch, *Adult Development and Aging*, p. 272.
29. E. M. Hetherington, R. M. Cox and R. Cox, "Stress and Coping in Divorce: A Focus on Women," in *Psychology and Women in Transition*, ed. J. E. Gullahorn, as cited by Hultsch and Deutsch, p. 273.
30. William H. Berman and Dennis C. Turk, "Adaptation to Divorce: Problems and Coping Strategies," *Journal of Marriage and Family* 43, no. 1 (February 1981):179-89.
31. Weiss, pp. 139-42.
32. Berman and Turk, pp. 179-89.

Apparently the problem areas do not contribute equally to distress. It is difficult to maintain satisfactory contact with people who were friends while one was married. Unhappiness seems to be closely associated with difficulties in peer and social relationships. Making up for the lost relationships seems to be especially stressful. Also, the person's mood seems to be dampened most by family interactions. There is great sensitivity to how one is communicating to the children, for example. In contrast, family problems the person has with the former spouse or the children do not seem to make much difference to overall life satisfaction. Causes of dissatisfaction are the financial and practical concerns.[33]

Legal problems. Legal hassles can be a problem. Though there are no-fault divorce laws in many states, in others one must prove the spouse is guilty. The division of property and the care of the children all become issues. Anger and bitterness often grow out of the legal fighting even if they were not there before. One spouse, prompted by guilt or hurt feelings, may surrender all the possessions to the partner. Sometimes one partner will take advantage of the other, insisting the spouse give in to his or her demands.[34]

The emotional upheavals. It is impossible to name the many emotions flooding a divorce. One's self-image is first of all disturbed. The feeling of failure threatens one's feeling of competence. A man or woman, highly successful elsewhere, may feel a tremendous blow to their feelings of worth. A sense of rejection may also exist.

Some theorists believe divorce triggers severe grief reactions such as depression, anger, sorrow, and anxiety.[35] Depression, nervousness, and other signs of stress are usually present. After studying people in various stages of the divorce transition, two researchers concluded that "clinicians dealing with people going through divorce could justifiably expect to be faced with a highly depressed population."[36] Divorced people may need assistance through the grief process.

Anger is often present and is generally leveled at the spouse. However, it may be transformed into self-blame. Self-pity, sorrow, and self-doubt all make their appearance. A person's competency is called into question, not only because of a feeling of failure in the marriage, but because of difficulties that arise in dealing with day-to-day things. A woman who has to struggle with a new job, fixing a furnace or a faucet, or handling the finances may be overcome by a sense of inadequacy.

Fear and anxiety relate to separation as they do when a loved one dies. A general feeling of fear may create a sense of panic.

Recovery strategies. Apparently, many go through the divorce transition with support from friends and others and without the need for counseling. However, others find their way into counselor's offices and seminar groups. They are confused and overcome by the multiple responsibilities and moods thrust upon them.

33. Ibid., p. 187.
34. Golan, p. 153.
35. G. Jacobson and S. Poruges, "Marital Separation and Divorce" in *Emergency and Disaster Management,* as cited by Joan C. Dasteel, "Stress Reactions to Marital Dissolution as Experienced by Adults Attending Courses on Divorce," *Journal of Divorce* 5, no. 3 (Spring 1982):37–47.
36. Ibid.

Divorced people face a major hurdle in their recovery. The church and community usually have certain built-in support mechanisms for people in distress; for example, a widow will immediately be surrounded by a network of support. The passage to widowhood is not only acceptable, but social norms and patterns exist to give direction to it. Not so for the divorce transition. There are almost no normative guidelines, and one's social network breaks down instead of rallying to one's aid. Friends are apt to feel divided in their loyalties and threatened by what is happening to their divorcing friends. Guilt and a sense of failure may make the divorced person turn from the church, which had once been a support in a time of crisis. The divorced person then gravitates to a small network of individuals who help him through the experience, while the person may feel some estrangement from society at large and the former social system.

Coping will include a number of things. First, divorced persons will need spiritual guidance to help them with biblical truths relating to divorce, guilt, failure, and remarriage.

Second, they will need to continue to function on their own. They will regain their sense of competency by facing their problems and working them through. Above all, they must maintain control.

Third, they will struggle to handle loneliness and intimacy problems. For many of them, sexual temptation and tension will be extremely intense. Many of them seek sexual encounters outside of marriage. The temptation is more than for physical release. They feel a great need to prove themselves, to convince themselves that they are still sexually desirable. Because they are not yet ready to commit themselves to another marriage, some of them have sex with a series of partners.

The Christian who is so tempted may need help dealing with the nature of temptation. While not denying that temptation comes from the sinful nature and satanic influence, it is possible to show a person that unusual temptation in a certain area has certain psychological and circumstantial roots. The divorced will need social contact to help overcome the loneliness and temptation that will assault them. They should not think that contact with friends will be a replacement for the intimacy marriage afforded, but such contacts will give them a sense of belonging and closeness necessary for living as a whole person.

REDIRECTION

Life goes on after divorce. Though divorce leaves its scars, the overwhelming number of divorced people say they are glad they went through it. One of the most recent studies of the welfare of divorced people concluded: "There is considerable evidence in this study that divorce was highly beneficial for many of the adults."[37] However, five years after the divorce one-fifth of the adults still felt it was ill-advised.[38] It seems clear that some divorced persons eventually restructure a new life with a

37. Judith S. Wallerstein and Joan Berlin Kelly, *Surviving the Breakup*, p. 306.
38. Ibid., p. 305.

great deal of success while some do not. Their redirection takes various paths.

Remarriage. Most divorced people cope with the problems of the solitary life by remarrying. Three-fourths of men of all ages will remarry, two-thirds of the women. Some remarry soon after the separation. Fifty percent of men under thirty-five remarry within one year after a divorce is granted. Half of divorced women under age thirty-five remarry within fourteen months of divorce.[39]

When children are involved, remarriage spells some special problems. The resulting "blended family" is not always a happy one. Without doubt some divorced people succeed in creating a happy home life for their children. However, in the Wallerstein and Kelly study, five years after the divorce over one-half of the children did not regard the divorced family as an improvement over their predivorce family. Despite the failing of the predivorce family, those children would prefer to turn back the clock and return to it.[40] Those findings clearly contradict previous studies of children of divorced families. The authors are quite dogmatic: "There is, in fact, no supporting evidence in this five-year study for the commonly made argument that divorce is overall better for children than an unhappy marriage, or, for its opposite argument, that living within an unhappy marriage is by and large more beneficial or less detrimental than living in the divorced family."[41]

For the person in a blended family, there is enough evidence of success to give them hope and sufficient evidence of struggle to give them concern. Divorce and its aftermath are sufficiently traumatic to make people think more than twice about it.

Obviously, those of us who minister to blended families should encourage their future instead of judging them by their past. Our task is to help build Christ-like harmonious homes, whether blended or not.

Remaining single. The minority of divorced who remain single become like the unmarried we studied in the first section of this chapter. Personal growth and achievement replace the fulfillment found in marriage. Close friends and involvement in groups help them cope with loneliness. The divorced person may also need some practical help, like being shown how to fix a faucet or cook a meal. Financial aid may be important to them, especially to women who are often put in a bad economic position by divorce. Those who have children have the special challenge of the single parent.

Single parent woes are many: financial problems, lack of a role model of one parent, lack of freedom for social life, dealing with children's problems alone. Compounding the difficulty is the possible negative reaction of the child to the divorce. Parents and others tend to blame any of the child's problems on the past.[42] "My daughter's stomach is constantly upset because of our breakup. My son isn't getting along with the other boys at school because of our divorce. My son was caught stealing at the drug store; if we hadn't separated this would not have happened." The problem with that analysis is that many children have stomachaches, are socially maladjusted, or

39. Hultsch and Deutsch, p. 272.
40. Wallerstein and Kelly, pp. 305–6.
41. Ibid., p. 306.
42. Lynne Carol Halem, *Separated and Divorced Women*, p. 4.

steal even though their parents are still together. The divorced parent may be too quick to blame normal growing up problems on the divorce. Children of divorced parents tend to blame personal inadequacies on the parent's broken marriage. They might heap on their parent's heads everything from C grades to sick headaches. "I can't relate to girls because my Dad divorced my Mother," said one solemn young man. The divorced couple and their children can easily slip into self-pity. The Christian message is to forget the things behind (not in the sense of failing to realize their influence, but in the sense of using them as an excuse) and press toward the future.

SOLOS IN THE CHURCH

That the vast majority of singles reject the church may be a sign that the church has not responded to them with much zest. Only 30 percent of those who never marry attend any kind of religious service during the week, according to one evangelical study. Attendance for the separated and divorced was even lower at 28 percent. Those figures compare to 40 percent of married adults—and the difference in percentage stands for millions of people.[43]

If the church continues to ignore single adults as some people accuse it of doing, it will be slighting the majority of adults. To boil down all that is being said about singles ministries without losing some of the prime ingredients is an impossible task. Some writers suggest revolutionary changes because they say the church is too heavily geared to married adults. Others suggest that a mere tinkering here and there will suffice. The following guidelines are not complete, but they touch on urgent matters.

ESTABLISH PARITY

The outcry of singles is that they are made to feel peculiar. Equality as adults is what they want. The New Testament affirms singleness—permanently and temporarily—as a legitimate way of life. Two evangelical seminary professors affirm, "There is no basis for assigning the single person an inferior status in the church."[44] The church must affirm its singles. Sermons, bulletins, announcements, and programs must tell them that singles are important in the family of God.

OFFER INVOLVEMENT

Part of bestowing equality will be done by opening up all parts of the church and ministry to them. J. Brittain Wood expressed that need in the title of his excellent book on singles and the church, *Single Adults Want to Be the Church, Too.* Some feel that when the church establishes special "singles' groups" it is segregating and not including them in the overall life of the church. Some write accusingly: "Singles groups in churches are little more than baptized 'singles bars'—incongruous reminders

---

43. J. David Jones, "Singles in America," *Solo Magazine,* March/April 1982, p. 38.
44. Hendrika Van De Kemp and G. Peter Schreck, "The Church's Ministry to Singles: A Family Model," *Journal of Religion and Health* 20, no. 2 (Summer 1981):152.

of how limited belongingness can be within the church."[45] Whether true or not, the point should be well taken: singles want to belong.

PROVIDE FAMILY-LIKE INTERACTION

Whenever they are asked, singles point to their need for fellowship. They not only want involvement, but close involvement. Chris Thomas saw that clearly through his survey of a large singles' group in an evangelical Wisconsin church: "Sixty percent said that their greatest need was to have fellowship with others, both single and married people, within a Christian context."[46] Intimacy and belongingness go together. As one increases, so does the other. Most people in singles' ministries maintain that the greatest thing the church can do for singles is to become more family-like. Singles, like other adults, will be untouched by a church that is highly institutional, where personal contacts are superficial and formalized. "Without access to intimate inclusion, the church's response to the single who is lonely, disconnected, and unsure of his personal identity and worth is hypocritical,"[47] say Hendrika Van de Kemp and G. Peter Schreck. Knowing they are asking for some substantial changes, they urge the church to have more cross-generational activities and community forms of the church. They urge families to invite singles into their homes to participate in non-single life experiences. Such "heterogeneous" interaction will also benefit single parents, whose children need warm fellowship with Christian adults to help make up for the absence of one parent. That is no small ministry: over half of the nation's children will spend a portion of life with a single parent.

PROVIDE HOMOGENEOUS INTERACTION

Though some believe singles' groups are a poor substitute for a single's involvement in the total family of God, others disagree. Those with long experience in ministry to singles maintain that singles need both types of involvement. They need status as equal, full members in the body of Christ, but they also need programs that focus on their special needs. The varieties of single adults and the difference in their ages will often dictate that there be more than one singles group. Most churches who minister to singles have numerous groups, usually divided by age. They should be led and developed by the singles themselves. Married persons can be successfully involved, but singles' groups thrive when singles are taking the initiative. The groups should focus on fellowship, but unless they revolve around personal growth, they become "match factories," where singles compete to find a mate. This problem is at the heart of singles' ministry: how to meet social needs without degenerating into just another meeting place.

45. Ibid.
46. Chris Thomas, "An Approach to the Problems of Single Adults from a Positive Perspective," p. 5.
47. Van de Kemp and Schreck, p. 153.

MAINTAIN AN EDUCATIONAL THRUST

Perhaps one of the best ways to keep singles groups healthy and productive is to highlight the study of God's Word. Although single adults, like others, desperately need fellowship, they also need truth on which to build a vigorous, vital life in Christ. In addition to direct Bible study, seminars and classes can focus on their particular transitions and tasks: recovering from divorce, living the single life, being a single parent, living as a widow, and so on. Or else, elective classes and special conferences can deal with issues and crises: depression, loss of friendship, grief, financial management, witnessing at work, sexuality and singlehood, and personal relationships. Formats for handling those subjects are legion: lectures, seminars, Sunday school electives, retreats, conferences, field projects and trips, and small group studies. Singles can be exposed to books on those subjects through a church bookstore or library.[48]

This discussion shows that the church's answers to singles' needs are no easier than the problems singles face. But making the changes may not be as dramatic as might at first be supposed. A small church with little special programming can provide a warm family context where singles can grow and feel they belong. Programming is not the key; attitude is. When married and single people begin to accept each other, a singles' ministry will follow. Scores of concerned and effective churches will be needed on the corners of Singles Street.

---

48. See John K. Landgraf, *Creative Singlehood and Pastoral Care*, p. 60.

7

The Valley of Decision: Establishing Individual Identity

Young adulthood is the valley of decision. Marriage and career choices lie, big as boulders, on the path; but important as they are, they are not the critical decisions. In the crevices and caverns of decision valley lurk the deeper questions: What values shall I own and what faith shall I claim as mine?

All developmental studies point to the period between eighteen and the late twenties as the time when the individual should become his own person. Dag Hammarskjold, the stalwart Swede who amazed the world as leader of the United Nations, described his own pilgrimage in these terms:

> I now recognize and endorse unreservedly those very beliefs which were handed down to me.... When I finally reached that point, the beliefs in which I was once brought up ... were recognized by me as *mine in their own right and by free choice* [italics added].[1]

Young adults crave the freedom to be themselves. They do not want their choices to be the results of someone else's programming. It is as if they are asking the world to stop for a moment so they can get off and decide about the beliefs, values, and commitments that have been injected into them by family, church, and nation. They will refuse to absorb those second hand. They want to compare them with other viewpoints and then possibly get back on the planet in about the same place. The resulting person will not be the same after such an evaluation.[2]

---

1. Quoted by John R. Hendrick, "Opening the Door of Faith: Criteria for Evangelism," *Austin Seminary Bulletin*, March 1973, p. 28.
2. Jack Renard Pressau, *I'm Saved, You're Saved. Maybe*, p. 48.

YOUNG ADULTS IN TRANSITION

Researcher Daniel Levinson describes two movements in the young adult's transition period. "Leaving the pre-adult world," is the first; "entering the adult world," the second.[3] It is the first movement, which I will now concentrate on for several chapters, that is so unnerving.

Young adulthood means raising questions about the nature of the world and one's place in it. It includes modifying or terminating the relationships with parents, peers, and groups that were part of one's earlier life. In the process, the young adult reappraises the self that was formed in that past and modifies it accordingly.

It is not merely that the young adult leaves home physically (many, in fact, do not), for, the leaving is primarily internal. Most of the men that Levinson interviewed did leave home at this time, but they said they felt the need to differentiate themselves from their families. A sort of psychological distancing was taking place, leaving them with less emotional dependence upon the family of origin.

Levinson's data is quite limited, dealing as it does with middle-class men, but his findings are significant when added to other studies. Of the forty men he interviewed, only seven stayed close to parents geographically and personally. Eight had major conflicts with parents, at least for several years. Twenty-five separated without bitter conflict. Levinson concludes that for most, the ties to parents eroded steadily during their twenties. "The great majority of the forty men formed a life in early adulthood quite different from that of their parents."[4] Only a small percentage of the men around age forty lived in a world that had much in common with their childhood world. Even in the area of religious and ethnic tradition, the great majority had only tenuous ties to their families' views and practices. To support that, Levinson cites the fact that eighteen of the forty men married women of other religious or ethnic groups.

That view of young adult passage arouses as much emotion as it does questions. Every parent leaving his son or daughter at the college dorm or in the newly furnished apartment, marking their entrance into this transition period, knows the mixture of emotions it can bring. The young adult, though excited by new freedom, may also have a haunting anxiety.

The evangelical church and its families have mixed reactions to young adults in transition. They worry about whether the products of their environments will jettison the Christian faith they have tried to nurture. At the same time, they look for strength and maturity to emerge. And it must be admitted that evangelicals do capitalize on the instability of this period by evangelistic efforts to college-age people.

Questions surround this transition phase. Do inner forces act upon the young adult to make the distancing happen? Is "leaving the pre-adult world" necessary for all mature development? If a young adult does not evaluate and choose for himself during

---

3. Daniel J. Levinson, *The Seasons of a Man's Life*, pp. 71-90.
4. Ibid., p. 74.

this time, will the process occur in a later period, say, mid-life? How are young adult choices related to previous ones? Must a young adult remake his decision to be a Christian? And if he merely continues, without struggle, to believe the faith he held prior to this, has a young adult come to a mature and true faith? It is said that God has no grandchildren, meaning that faith cannot be received from parents. Beliefs must be decided for oneself and made one's own. Does that necessarily occur in young adulthood, or might it occur much earlier? In light of that, how should young adults be treated? Should we, like Bill Gothard, tell them to conform to their parent's wishes even into their twenties, until marriage? Or should freedom be spread upon them as if it were a kind of psychological fertilizer containing necessary ingredients for growth?

TRANSITION AND CHRISTIAN FAITH

It is important at this point to discover what happens in the young adult's internal development. Developmentalists affirm the importance of "inner happenings." Unlike the behaviorists, they do not believe that all thought, feeling, and behavior is shaped by experiences and circumstances. Instead, they contend that there are inner forces shaping the way a person thinks, believes, and behaves, and that inner development is crucial. From the Christian perspective, inner development is often referred to as spiritual growth. But, inner development is not just spiritual if, by using the word *spiritual,* thoughts and feelings are excluded. There is an inner core of the person that needs to develop, and behavior will develop in parallel.

Therefore, at the outset, let it be clear that the purpose of this study is not to find out how to arrange the environment so that the young adult can be made to conform to the Christian faith. Nor is it to discover how to successfully put a fence around them to keep them in the fold. The purpose is to find out about the kind of atmosphere and circumstances we can create to foster their internal growth. A growth environment may contain fences of some sort, but those limitations will be set in place with sensitivity and the intent to allow growth to happen, not in order to restrict growth. Constricting peoples' movement must never be permitted as a substitute for internal growth, as if Christian growth were equal to outward conformity to others, or even to God. Believing that outer forces alone make us what we are is far too deterministic. Whenever *restricting* is the essence of Christian living, legalism follows. If, instead, we view Christian maturing as *restructuring,* genuine freedom ensues.

DEVELOPMENT OF PERCEPTION

One of the first aspects of inward development is the changing capacity to perceive. It has already been noted that the young adult sees the world differently from the teenager. Before young adulthood, a person looks at the world in an attempt to find who he is. Once identity is somewhat formed, he looks at the world to see what place there is for him. Whereas the world impacted the teenager, the young adult impacts the world.

In order to fully understand the young adult's difference in seeing and the difference it makes, the teenage years must first be examined. During early adolescence, around the ages of twelve to fifteen, an amazing human capacity develops, according to the developmentalist Jean Piaget. Piaget studied how thinking structures develop. By structure, he means not *what* is thought about, but *how* it is thought about. By observing children and youth, he developed a picture of how thinking capacities unfold, one follows another, and a person cannot leapfrog over one rational capacity to a higher one. The capacities are in a hierarchical arrangement, meaning that the later ones are better.

Piaget maintains that one of the rational capacities appearing at early adolescence is the ability to look at oneself from a spectator's point of view. Until then, a child cannot actually stand back and take a look at himself. At first, that seems difficult to accept. Those of us who are adults can hardly remember a time when we weren't reflecting on ourselves, constantly introspectively examining and wondering. But compare thinking to floating down a river. A child, carried by the flow of his life, reflects on the events and relationships from within that flow. The adolescent, however, mentally stands on the bank and watches himself as he floats along.[5]

That explains why the young adolescent becomes so self-conscious. For the first time seeing himself in that way, he is acutely aware that everyone else is looking at him. It plunges the young person headlong into introspection and inner probing. Most of us can identify with the young person who remarked, "I found myself thinking about my future and then I began to think about why I was thinking about why I was thinking about my future."[6] The youth is sometimes troubled by painful self-awareness as he attempts to establish some idea of who he is.[7]

The youth also develops another thinking skill: the ability to think about possibilities. That, like the other ability, is part of what Piaget calls *formal operations*. The child was able to think only about the actual. If someone asked him, "If coal were white...?" He might typically respond, "But it is not." The teenager has the ability to handle that now, because he can think logically about what might be. Parents may be the first to feel the brunt of that new development. The child, more or less, accepted his parents as they were. The teenager can think of what life might be like if parents were different. He has tremendous talent for criticizing his school, church, and all others. Reality is found wanting. The relentless criticism of self and others will take a more positive turn in young adulthood when he becomes more aware of his power to change things.

In the meantime, he will use his new faculty to point out the hypocrisies of parents and the deficiencies of school and society. Thinking about possibilities is necessary for growth. It is a crucial tool that allows adults to analyze problems and creatively

5. James Fowler, *Stages of Faith*, p. 71.
6. CRM Books editorial staff, *Developmental Psychology Today*, p. 367.
7. John Janeway Conger, *Adolescence and Youth*, p. 183.

suggest solutions. It will help the youth unfold, because that kind of thinking is part of discerning what a person with his talents, abilities, and capacities might become.

"Second-order" thinking—the ability to reflect on reflecting—is another new capacity. Thinking takes on a new dimension, resulting in a different view of life's rules. A child learns to think about the world as having certain rules that just are. Yes, he questions and even challenges them. But while the child questions the rules, the youth questions his questioning. He can now think about rule-making.

All of that aids the youth in forming a clear, more adult-like perception of himself. The richer, more mature view, however, will not take place until the end of adolescence.

Gene Bocknek maintains that personal perception depends on the evolution of two processes—formal operation and identity realization—that are usually not complete until the end of adolescence. Identity development enables a young adult to distinguish between individual (part) characteristics and overall (whole) self. For the adolescent, every part influences the way in which he sees himself as a whole person. For example, if he is told he is shy or that his nose is rather large, he will think of his whole self as a lesser person. To discover a pimple on the forehead makes him think of himself as ugly. The young adult, on the other hand, can become aware of a total self image that is not so completely threatened by the part or parts. The "ego," the inner sense about who he is, is stronger. The large nose or pimple does not make the person. He can accept those, along with a poor singing voice, an inability to play ping pong, or other imperfect parts without feeling inferior or incomplete.[8]

As a result, the young adult is much more likely to be able to solve personal problems. He is ready to admit weaknesses and deal with them, because the admission is no longer such a threat. He can, in the words of Gordon Allport, "view himself with complacency."[9]

A person who attains this maturity of perception (i.e., not always judging the whole by the part) will have some distinct characteristics. First of all, he will be more open to personal improvement through counseling and education. Seeking help from others will be less threatening, because having a personal problem or weakness is now acceptable. People who work with young adults will be alert to their search for help. Peter Drucker, management expert, has urged executives not to select subordinates based on a lack of weaknesses, but rather to hire them for their strengths.[10] Someone with flaws can make a great contribution in their field.

Second, the mature way of seeing will be transferred to others. Such a person can accept others with their flaws. One or two blemishes will not contaminate the whole person or group in his eyes, and he will learn not to be too severe in judging institutions and groups. Churches and other groups will not be condemned as useless because of one or more faults. Tolerance and acceptance are marks of a mature perspective.

Piaget maintains that a large percentage of adults never reach formal operations,

8. Gene Bocknek, *The Young Adult*, p. 110.
9. Cited by Bocknek, p. 111.
10. Peter F. Drucker, *The Effective Executive* (New York: Harper & Row, 1967), pp. 71–80.

and Erikson suggests that identity problems may continue into later life. Caution must be exercised in adopting that conclusion, but it is possible that stunted psychological growth may make it difficult for a person to maturely see self and others. It is possible that bigotry and intolerance are at least in part developmental problems.

8

Climbing Kohlberg's Ladder: Moral Development

THE SIX RUNGS

Leading moral development expert Lawrence Kohlberg loves moral dilemmas. From his studies, he maintains there are six types of responses, revealing six stages of moral development. For example, imagine being in Corrie ten Boom's house. The Nazis who are occupying her country are standing in the doorway. They ask: "Are there any Jews here in this house?" Knowing that several are cowering under the dining room table, what would you say?

If you think, *I would tell the truth. If the Germans find them, I'd be beaten, maybe killed,* you show yourself to be thinking on stage one. Kohlberg calls this stage *Obedience and Punishment Orientation.* Right action is based upon who is bigger.

If, however, you think, *I would lie, tell them no Jews were there, because God will bless me for helping save some lives,* you are a stage two person. Kohlberg calls this *Naively Egoistic Orientation.* Right action is what satisfies the person's needs—and occasionally the needs of others as well.

A stage-three person might reason, *I would tell the Nazis the truth because good citizens do not lie. Good Boy, Nice Girl Orientation* is the simple title of this stage. Right action comes out of the desire to be approved by others.

A staunch fourth-stage person will relate more to rules than roles. He would perhaps think, *I would not lie because the Germans are now in control and we should respect their laws and wishes.* Right action, in this case, is determined by doing one's duty and showing respect for authority. It is dubbed the *Authority and Social Order Orientation.*

The fifth-stage person would elaborate a bit more, reasoning thus: *I would lie because I believe that our laws were made to save innocent lives. Those Jews have done nothing illegal. They should be protected. In this case, it is proper to lie to uphold the principles behind our laws.* Right action is determined by avoiding the violation of the rights of others. This is called the *Social Contract Orientation,* referring to the fact that the individual understands the principles behind laws. Laws are seen as man-made formulations, based on people contracting together to preserve the rights of others. Therefore, sometimes the laws can be broken, or even rewritten, to achieve what is behind them.

It is difficult to say in a few words what the stage-six person might think. Kohlberg calls it the *Conscience or Principle Orientation.* Right action is determined by principles of justice the person has dedicated himself to; a person acts consistently on those principles in a universal way. This person would without doubt oppose the Nazis' desire to seize the Jews. Kohlberg has not found many people who achieve this stage, but he mentions Martin Luther King, Jr., Abraham Lincoln, and Jesus Christ as examples.

Kohlberg's description of the final stage does reveal what he is all about. His stages are moving toward the principles of justice, particularly as formulated by Immanuel Kant. A person should act in such a way that if their action were adopted by all it would be best for all. In other words, one should treat every man impartially and respect every man's rights.[1]

You may have noticed that the answers were not classified according to whether or not you would lie. Kohlberg is not concerned with the *content* of a person's answers (whether or not a person would decide to steal or lie or cheat), but rather the *structure* behind the answer. Note that a stage-two person could tell the truth or lie for the same reason: "Yes, I would tell the Germans because my own life would be in jeopardy if I lied and they searched and found them." Or else, "I would lie because the people I am hiding might reward me handsomely."

Notice also that the structures deal only with thinking. Kohlberg's theory is based solely upon a person's rational self. Emotions and religious beliefs are irrelevant. He contends that the way a person thinks about morality most determines how he acts.

That thinking, he says, will change as a person matures. One never skips a stage, and they are hierarchical, each rung going higher.

Most young adults operate on stages three, four, or five. Not all young adults will reach stage four, but they should have the capacity to do so. Possibly some will begin to move to stage five. All of that is important, but it requires some explanation.

Stage three, *Good Boy, Nice Girl Orientation,* is typical of the adolescent stage. Morality means conforming to the expectations of others. The person thinks about what is consistent with being a good Christian, a good citizen, a nice person. It is a low level of morality because a person may more easily take the wrong action in situations where the threat of being discovered is low. A stage three person may, for example, more readily cheat on an exam than the person who thinks on level four. Recall that the level-four person believes that cheating is wrong because there is a law of honesty.

---

1. Lawrence Kohlberg, "Stages of Moral Development as a Basis for Moral Education," *Moral Development, Moral Education and Kohlberg,* ed. Brenda Munsey, p. 85.

What would happen if everyone broke the law? he might say to himself. Doing what is lawful motivates him more than the fear of being caught. The real reason level three is a lower level because it lacks the principles of justice contained in higher levels.

Because of his ideal of justice, Kohlberg suggests that churches and schools do everything they can to raise people to higher levels of thinking. A person needs to understand that the laws of our country are based on principles regarding human rights. Without that understanding, someone can be committed to laws that may not be just. For example, laws that discriminate against blacks actually betray the principles underlying the U.S. If a person did not think on level five, he might resist any changes in such laws. The person who is on the higher level will not only understand changes but press for them. Human principles of justice, not particular expressions of law, guide the stage five person's behavior. That does not mean that the stage five person does not respect or obey laws. Although he may at times disobey them because he has found such laws to betray higher principles, he will respect the laws because he is committed to the rights they protect.[2]

THE MORAL STRETCH

If we assume Kohlberg is correct (not everyone thinks he is) that one's moral thinking continues, through its own tensions, to reach for higher levels, we may get some insight into the young adult's leaving the pre-adult world. Stage three finds him tied into the approval of parents, peers, and institutions such as school and church. It is a period of social conformity. That may even be true of the delinquent, who, although he disobeys the wishes of parents and others in society, may only be conforming to the role expectation of the chosen group of peers. In the case of the Christian at this stage, the pattern is the same. Lying, stealing, and other moral matters are determined by what he thinks a group of Christians expects.

A person who moves out of stage three is clearly distancing himself from others who were associated with childhood and early youth. His perspective broadens and his ability to think abstractly improves. Loyalty shifts from others (concrete persons) to laws (abstract regulations). Previously, in a stage three viewpoint, actions were right if they conformed to the expectations of one's "significant others." He was motivated by the desire to please those persons and not to disappoint them. In stage four the perspective is widened to include society as a whole.

But the sameness of the two stages softens the distancing. Both stages require conformity to laws and rules of significant others, whether parents, peers, or society in general. Actions are considered by both to be right if a person complies with rules. Independence for the teenager does not equal freedom from the group to which he belongs. Rather, it means personally disciplining himself to comply with the given norms. The liberty to step back and judge those sets of values and laws will come at the transition to stage five.

The transition to stage five is stressful. In the Kohlberg scheme of development,

2. Ibid., pp. 37–39.

the movement from stage four to five is a sort of becoming one's own person.

At this fifth level people make a clear effort to define moral values and principles that have validity and applicability apart from the authority of the group holding them and apart from the individual's own identification with that group.[3] Kohlberg is quite clear about what causes a person to lose faith in the authority of his country or religious group. It comes about when the person's widening contacts make him see the relativity of his rules. He soon learns that laws, customs, and group experiences differ from one society or group to another. He must learn to deal with that relativism by grasping for some higher general principles that will be a basis for action and will verify his particular set of laws.

In other words, the person searches for some absolutes. Kohlberg does refer to principles of justice as absolutes. The wrong response to relativism, Kohlberg maintains, is to absolutize one's own norms, laws, and customs. The correct response is to recognize the universal principles of justice.

Evangelicals whose faith rests in a revelation of absolute truth and moral precepts are caught in the middle of the controversy. In fact, some persons relegate evangelicals to moral immaturity. If one is truly concerned about one's own growth, and young adult growth in general, that viewpoint must be dealt with.

STUCK ON STAGE FOUR

It seems that Kohlberg himself believes that religious groups that claim absolute laws and norms are stuck on stage four. Obeying the Ten Commandments is a stage four matter. Doing so, one has not developed a system based on principles of justice. In fact, Kohlberg broadens his theory to suggest that the way one thinks about morality is the same way one thinks about God. Therefore, at stage one, God is an authority who dispenses punishment and reward. At stage two a child may say, "You be good to God and He will be good to you." At stage three, God is a good person, as the carrier and protector of goodness. At moral stage four, divinity is first seen as lawgiver, bound by law and the ultimate ground of order. At moral stage five, divinity becomes identified with, or is the ground of, freedom, individuality, and responsibility.[4]

Building on Kohlberg, Jack Pressau uses the stages to judge the moral level of Christian groups. Young Life and Youth for Christ are placed on stage three because the Christian hero or group becomes the means of directing a person's commitment. Campus Crusade for Christ is on stage four. "It offers a stage four set of spiritual laws. . . . In other words CCC is a typical conventional morality movement because it demands adherence to a total system of beliefs (laws) and practices (orders) with which it (and the churches it judges to be 'spiritual') concurs."[5]

The young adult campus group InterVarsity Christian Fellowship does not rest solidly on stage four, Pressau says. It is less leader-oriented and formula-minded than

3. James Fowler, *Stages of Faith*, p. 83.
4. Lawrence Kohlberg, "Education, Moral Development, and Faith," *Journal of Moral Education* 4 (1974):13-14.
5. Jack Renard Pressau, *I'm Saved, You're Saved . . . Maybe*, pp. 39, 42.

Campus Crusade. Also, he affirms, "IVCF leaves room for students to move from stage four conventional morality to a post conventional moral orientation (stage five) without ostracism." But, he reminds his readers, some people cannot understand how a group can have intellectual and methodological freedom as well as evangelical passion.[6] That is true because Pressau clearly sees stage five as theologically liberal in its orientation.

He freely admits that the root of the conflict between the law and order people and those in stage five is philosophical. Most people have inherited a static view of the universe that may be found in Greek philosopher Parmenides. Heraclitus's concept of reality, on the other hand, stated that "no one ever steps into the same river twice." He meant that the underlying quality of reality was change, not consistency; becoming, not being. Belief in the process and its direction would be the ultimate loyalty. "Most conventional folk would find [that] difficult to understand," judges Pressau.[7]

Pressau is quick to point out that he is not putting anyone down by shelving them on a lower level. Such persons are not wrong, just immature. He has even learned to gladly accept those whose immaturity causes them to confide in a theology different from his own. *Good* and *bad,* when applied to ordinary theologizing, is a false dichotomy. One's theology may be "earlier in moral stage development," but not *bad.* Everyone has gone through stages of faith-development that were once meaningful but have been outgrown.[8]

THE LADDER THAT FALLS SHORT

Before permitting Kohlberg's system to judge evangelicals as immature, his system must first of all be examined, as it has been by many researchers. Kohlberg claims his system is scientific. He contends he has found the natural process of development. As a first objection, some investigators say that Kohlberg's method is too subjective and point to the fact that he has repeatedly changed his interpretations of the data. At one time, for example, he said that young adults could reach stage five. Later, he said that most young adults only achieve a false stage five, and actually revert back to something approximating stage two. Eventually, he described their thinking as stage four and one-half. That apparent freedom to interpret the data makes some call into question the objectivity of his research.

Second, Kohlberg has limited his research to the study of people making decisions about hypothetical dilemmas. Gabriel Moran, for one, objects to that; people should be studied when they are emotionally involved in real-life ethical decisions. He points to Carol Gilligan's research on the thinking of women who were considering abortion. "Their moral judgment was not directed toward a hypothetical problem of someone else but to a painfully real problem of their own."[9] Kohlberg does not consider the impact emotions have upon moral thinking.

6. Ibid., pp. 42–43.
7. Ibid., pp. 55–56.
8. Ibid., p. 118.
9. See Gabriel Moran, Religious Education Development, pp. 83–84.

Third, Kohlberg limits his study to a certain way of thinking about moral questions. He claims to be discovering natural thinking. His theory is supposed to avoid any moral judgment, but it is apparent that such judgment does show up in stages five and six. The Kantian categorical imperative is the principle followed. In other words, the only maxims to be acted upon are ones that can be made into universal law. Thus, the only genuinely universal, comprehensive, and consistent rule is one that everyone adopts the same *reason* for following.[10] Critics of Kohlberg show how he has indeed introduced a value system into his research. He has not only limited his research to rational thinking but to a certain type of rational thinking.

But suppose something other than a rational approach to justice guides a person's moral behavior? Then Kohlberg's stages would no longer hold up in all circumstances. Craig Dykstra, James Loder, and Gabriel Moran all contend that there is something more: religious experience. From their liberal religious standpoint, they hold that certain virtues that come out of the religious experience dominate moral behavior. Those ultimates are not the result of rational thinking but of religious experience.[11]

USING THE KOHLBERG SYSTEM

Those criticisms, along with others, make it clear that Kohlberg does not have the final word about how people make moral choices. Nonetheless, some of his insights may still be useful in discovering how young adults develop.

First of all, it is clear that evangelicals should not demean expressions of moral behavior at levels three and four. Kohlberg maintains that most of the population is on those levels. Initially, he was optimistic that he could design methods that would raise the level of moral thinking to stages five and six. However, Moran points out that Kohlberg's hope that levels would be raised has been fading. He has all but abandoned his stage six, maintaining that his empirical research between 1968 and 1976 did not confirm his theoretical statements about a sixth and higher state.[12] Now, he speaks of a retrenchment to stage four goals as the end of civic education.[13]

Stages three and four were always higher levels in the Kohlberg scheme, but because of his emphasis on the principled thinking of stages five and six, the earlier

10. Ronald Duska and Mariellen Whelan, *Moral Development: A Guide to Piaget and Kohlberg*, p. 77.
11. The title of each of these men's books indicates their perspective. Dykstra's *Vision and Character* locates the absolutes that guide behavior in the broader religious perspective that comes from the religious imagination as one participates in worship and community interaction. *The Transforming Moment* by James Loder locates moral behavior in religious experience. Gabriel Moran's *Religious Education Development* follows Pierre Teilhard de Chardin and locates morality in God's imminent activity in human life. In religious experience, certain virtues and values stand out, leading in an evolutionary development of the individual and the human race toward unity.
12. Lawrence Kohlberg, "Educating for a Just Society: An Updated and Revised Standard," in Brenda Munsey, ed., *Moral Development, Moral Education, and Kohlberg* (Birmingham, Ala.: Religious Education, 1980), p. 457.
13. Ibid., p. 459.
14. Gabriel Moran, *Religious Education Development*, p. 82.

levels were cast in a negative light. Stage three actually represents interpersonal love. Stage four shows a respect for social order.[14] Both are admirable qualities. For Christians, however, stage five is not the desired goal; nor is strict stage four thinking the most mature.

TOWARD A PROPER VIEW OF GOD

An evangelical view of God can contain much more freedom than Kohlberg's stage four (God as a lawgiver who is bound by law and the ultimate ground of order) suggests. Christians have both law and freedom in Christ. God deals with men as persons whom He loves.

The Christian must come to realize that order, peace, and harmony within oneself and with others does not come through absolute compliance to a law. God brings those things by grace through salvation, because He is not commander-in-chief; He is our Father.

A PROPER ATTITUDE TOWARD OTHERS

Another corrective of stage four thinking is related to the Christian view of morality. Kohlberg uncovers the process by which people think about their responsibility to other people, not necessarily to God.

His so-called Heinz dilemma illustrates this. A brief version goes like this: Heinz's wife is dying of cancer. A special form of radium costing two thousand dollars might save her. After frantic efforts to raise the cash fail, Heinz pleads with the druggist to let him have it at a lower cost or on credit. Though it cost the druggist only one tenth of the selling price to make it, he refuses the plea. Desperate, Heinz breaks into the man's store to steal the drug for his wife.

Interviewees are asked eleven questions, including: Should Heinz steal the drug? Why? Which is worse, letting someone die or stealing? Why? What does the value of life mean to you?

A Ten Commandment-oriented person might tenaciously oppose any stealing. But the stage four person could not do it thoughtlessly. Another moral obligation competes with the command not to steal: the responsibility for his wife. The tension will compel him to define those opposing responsibilities and to get behind them in search of reasons in order to resolve the tension. In other words, it will not be easy for the stage-four person to say, as he might in situations without a dilemma, "I will not steal because God says I should not." He will now begin to ask, "Exactly what is stealing?" and "Why did God say it is wrong to steal?" He is then pressed to think not only about God but about others as well.

It is here that Kohlberg's theory and practice may be most helpful to us. Evangelicals, among others, may be underdeveloped in the area of moral thinking that is oriented toward others. That falls short of the biblical view of morality, which is other-oriented even though dominated by its Godward aspect. Half of the Ten Commandments are oriented to the general principle "love your neighbor as yourself" (Lev. 19:18). Adultery, murder, stealing, and even coveting are wrong not merely because God said they were, but because they violate the rights of others who are made in the image of God.

Clearly, then, there are broader principles behind the particular biblical regulations. Paul attempted to teach that truth to the law-oriented Galatians: "The entire law is summed up in a single command: 'Love your neighbor as yourself'" (Gal. 5:14). Paul is not advocating situation ethics, where all moral decisions are reduced to judging what it means to love in a particular situation. The particular commands (thou shalt not steal, for example) still stand. Paul was stressing the importance of understanding what lies behind the commands.

STAGE FOUR DEFICIENCIES

There are major emotional and moral deficiencies when an adult fails to think in terms of principles that deal with responsibilities toward others.

LACK OF EMPATHY

A stage four person may be weak in compassion, empathy, caring, understanding, and other virtues that comprise sensitivity toward other people. It is possible that human warmth may be all but lacking in a law-oriented individual, even when that person is thoroughly dedicated to God.[15] Critics of Kohlberg, such as Moran and Dykstra, have shown that human sensitivity is crucial to a Christian concept of ethics. Take, for example, the commandment about adultery. A man or woman may obey that in the strict sense because God commands it, but not understand that a reason behind it is to avoid hurting the parties involved. The commandment was also given to encourage the cultivation of an intimate relationship with one's spouse as well as to keep relationships with members of the opposite sex wholesome. It is true that David, in typical Jewish hyperbole, agonized to God: "Against Thee, Thee only, I have sinned" (Ps. 51:4). But it is clearly established that people can and do sin against one another: "Moreover if thy brother shall trespass against thee, go and tell him his fault between thee and him alone: if he shall hear thee, thou hast gained thy brother" (Matt. 18:15, KJV). The stage four person may be in danger of missing that.

INABILITY TO FACE ETHICAL PROBLEMS

If a person cannot see the human dimension behind rules, he will be unable to adequately handle perplexing moral issues. As the world opens up to idealistic young adults, major social and political issues call for careful ethical thinking. Sooner or later, they will discover that there is no particular verse of Scripture for every human problem. Moral principles will need to be extracted from Scripture and thoughtfully, often painfully, applied to life. Not all issues will be in the larger political or social

15. Others have shown us that it is also lacking in stage five, since Kohlberg's concept of justice is not equal to the biblical one. See Craig Dykstra, *Vision and Character,* pp. 13–15.

arena; many will be distressfully personal. A Christian man who works in a nursing home for the severely ill told me that he is faced daily with life-and-death moral dilemmas. For example, it is an established practice to give drugs that relieve the suffering of terminally ill persons but at the same time hasten their death. Situations such as that cause us to reach for the broader principles behind biblical injunctions.

INABILITY TO RISE ABOVE NATIONALISM

A stage four person's ethics tend to be oriented to his own group or nation. Higher levels of thinking are international in scope. Pressau may be correct when he claims that legalists could not participate in the Underground Railroad during the Civil War because it was illegal, whereas those at stage five appealed to a higher law and took the risk. Biblical principles drive us toward a higher, universal stance. Stage-four thinking may be a factor in the practice of linking Christianity too closely to one's nation. Although there are biblical reasons for national loyalty, they are by no means absolute. In a democratic nation, the Christian is not only governed, but one of the governors. He is obligated to morally approve national laws and policies. Unless a Christian's thinking is stretched to consider and adopt the principles of human rights behind those laws, no such judgment will occur. When human rights are seen to extend to all men, not only one's own nation, there is a major safeguard that keeps Christians from turning Christianity into a civil religion. But because Kohlberg has shown that the majority of adults operate on either stage three or four, it logically follows that the tendency of most people is to link religion and patriotism. God is *always* on your country's side. Persons who move in the law and order sphere can be expected to have a large following.

MOVING UP

Facilitating development beyond stage four, according to Kohlberg, is not easily done, and persons will not establish a stage five morality until their thirties or later, if at all.[16] Internally, the development is prompted by the tension that usually comes from broader experience.

ARRANGE CHALLENGING EXPERIENCES

Churches and schools can help persons have experiences that challenge their neatly ordered systems. Of course, that does not mean that we should not teach a system of truth, for if we teach the Bible we will surely do that. But our teaching should not be in a sheltered, aseptic context far removed from the perplexities of life. Young adulthood is the time to face matters and test one's system. Forums, panels, small group discussions, and field trips will provide the interaction needed for growth.

16. Kohlberg, "Educating for a Just Society," pp. 456–57.

GIVE RESPONSIBILITY

Besides discussion, we should encourage young adults to take responsibility. Kohlberg has found no true stage-five person in his longitudinal sample until age twenty-four.[17] From that, Kohlberg has conjectured that there are two kinds of experiences necessary to the development of stage-five thinking. First, the young person must leave home emotionally and perhaps physically, and encounter experiences of conflicting values in a context where there is substantial freedom to decide. Second, the young adult must have sustained responsibility for the welfare of others.[18] Young adults need to be in responsible leadership positions where they make significant decisions.

OFFER MORAL DILEMMAS

Kohlberg claims that challenging people to think about dilemmas is the best method for stimulating moral development.[19] Books full of dilemmas are available for classroom and small group discussion. Discussions of the moral dilemmas found in Scripture, such as David's eating the show bread and Rahab's lie to save the spies, can be started.

STIMULATE THE SEARCH FOR REASONS

Scripture and theology can be taught with a view toward looking behind the biblical injunctions for reasons. We can always be asking adults *why*, in order to sharpen their rational skills and point to the human element in moral decision making.

I suggest these practices for improving the way we think about morality. In doing so, I am not approving of Kohlberg's conviction that it is the sole way to influence right behavior. Many other factors play a part. Right living comes by faith, according to Scripture. Growth in faith is what we turn to next.

---

17. Fowler, p. 82.
18. Ibid.
19. Lawrence Kohlberg, "Stages of Moral Development as a Basis for Education," in Munsey, pp. 75–76.

9

The Road of Faith Development:
Freedom, Relativism,
and Internalization

FREE TO WANDER

Imagine a tribe of people cut off from the rest of the world by a dense rain forest. Highly organized taboos and rules govern every part of their life. Religious practices quench some fears, arouse others. Rituals and beliefs are enforced: if a member fails without reason to show up for a ceremonial dance, he may be punished or ostracized for a time. Shame and ridicule make everyone conform.

Suppose an ostracized member wanders around until, finding himself at the edge of the thick jungle, an opening allures him. He stumbles upon another tribe with practices he has never seen before. They do not perform the same rituals, yet they still prosper. They eat foods he was told would poison, but no harm comes to them.

Formerly, he had thought his tribe's rules were the only right ones (i.e., absolute) and were for all (i.e., universal). If he found more tribes with different views, would he not begin to doubt the universal and absolute nature not only of his tribal ways but those of any tribe? Would relativism seize control of his thinking? How would he feel? What values and rules would he now choose to live by?

Were he to return to his home, what would happen? He could not keep quiet about the wasteful and useless practices of his people. The authorities would reject him in order to protect their homeland's beliefs and customs, and he would probably be punished or banished. He would suffer because he would still yearn for the warm emotional attachment and the sense of belonging he had with his family and community. But his intellectual awakening has cut him off.

He might return, conform to the tribe's ways, but at the cost of denying himself. Or he might become embittered, cynical about society and truth and turn wholly inward.

He would have no one to trust, nothing to believe in, but himself.[1]

Developmentalists contend that the early young adult, particularly the college student is a "tribal wanderer". He has not been physically isolated from other groups but during high school he encountered those of other faiths and ideologies. Perhaps there has been somewhat of a psychological separation. Awareness of the challenge of other systems does not seem to solidify until early adulthood, though it is possible for it to come earlier for many. The young adult possesses two things that bring on the awareness: *freedom* and *personal identity.*

Like the tribesman in our analogy, the early young adult is somewhat free from his pre-adult group. The *freedom* may result from living away from home, where he is able to make choices about life-style and beliefs without pressures to conform. The sense of *personal identity* is similar to the tribesman now being on his own. Cut off from the tribe, he is somewhat alone in the world. What he does, he does as an individual and not as part of his group. The early young adult is alone in the sense that the identity he has formed makes him more secure as an individual. Though the identity is still tied in with the group, it is not as dependent upon the group as in adolescence.

The freedom of the emerging young adult gives him an opportunity for seeing beyond his adult group. The sense of personal identity that takes away some of the internal pressure to conform to his peers, family or church, gives the young adult some security to look more closely at other beliefs, in order to test and to experiment. He strikes out on his own in a new way.

What concerns us now is what happens to faith when the striking out on one's own takes place. Does a dedicated Christian youth's faith just continue, uninterrupted? Or is there some necessary unsettling passageway filled with doubts, disbelief and confusing relativism? Gabriel Moran insists that disbelief is a necessary step toward maturity. "There is a conversion of disbelief. . . . An individual who begins to disbelieve that his or her beliefs are adequate will then have to ask: What do I really believe in?"[2]

It seems clear that young adults undergo a special struggle to grasp a personal perspective of life's meaning. No one knows exactly what the nature of that struggle is. Like other areas of developmental psychology, the studies are inconclusive. In fact, the study of faith development is the most recent and is, therefore, even more subject to criticism and eventual modification.

STAGES OF FAITH

James Fowler is the most prominent faith development expert. After analyzing the substance of scores of interviews, Fowler outlined a six-stage faith development scheme. Like Piaget and Kohlberg before him, Fowler is looking for structures. Therefore, he is not studying *what* a person believes, but *how* that person believes.

1. Ronald Duska and Mariellen Whelan, *Moral Development: A Guide to Piaget and Kohlberg,* pp. 71–72.
2. Gabriel Moran, *Religious Education Development,* p. 151.

The faith that he is studying is what he calls *human faith.* Fowler's definition of faith is not a belief in doctrines or creeds but a trust and loyalty placed in some center of value and power (a career, God, a church group).[3] Although granting the possibility of the supernatural aspects of faith, Fowler studies faith as a natural development. His aim is to discover ways faith can develop in anyone of any persuasion: atheist, Jew, Muslim, or Christian.

Fowler's findings could be immediately dismissed at this point because his view of faith is not consistent with Christian faith, which does have supernatural cause (Eph. 2:8) and includes specific doctrine. Nonetheless, Fowler's findings may still be useful, starting with his premise that all people have some sort of faith. The biblical view of idolatry supports that. In both the Old and New Testaments it is clear that people have a capacity to trust in things, persons, and values other than in the God of Scripture. For example, Paul warned the rich not to fix their hope on the uncertainty of riches but on God (1 Tim. 6:17). It is decidedly unbiblical, of course, to equate Fowler's faith with the faith of the Christian—"Not all have faith" (2 Thess. 3:2).

Fowler's developmental theory may shed light on the human side of Christian faith as it progresses from childhood through adulthood. The difference does not seem to lie in the supernatural working of God, but in the natural development of the person, rationally, emotionally, and socially. Fowler's is the first major attempt at understanding that progression.

Fowler's stages three and four are most relevant to the discussion of young adult development and will be the only ones discussed here.

FROM STAGE THREE TO FOUR

The stage three to four transition is significant because it signals the transition to "making your faith your own." Stage three, which Fowler terms *Synthetic-Conventional* is a "conformist" stage. The person is tuned to the expectations and judgments of significant others. Stage four is grounded in one's own judgment. Until stage four, the individual has not grappled with his basic beliefs in a critical way. He does not have a sure enough grasp on his own identity and autonomous judgment to construct and maintain an independent perspective. About stage three, Fowler writes: "While beliefs and values are deeply felt, they typically are tacitly held—the person 'dwells' in them and in the meaning world they mediate. But there has not been occasion to step outside them to reflect on or examine them explicitly or systematically."[4]

The stage four person goes beyond that conforming kind of faith. Fowler sees the move to *Individuative-Reflective Faith* (stage four) as particularly critical. "It is in this transition that the late adolescent or adult must begin to take seriously the burden of responsibility for his or her own commitments, lifestyle, beliefs, and attitudes."[5] Fowler is particularly helpful because he brings together numerous developmental studies to describe this trek of faith.

3. James Fowler, *Stages of Faith,* p. 14.
4. Ibid., p. 173.
5. Ibid., p. 182.

Fowler speaks of the *locus of authority,* which is "the way persons at each stage interpret and rely upon sources of authoritative insights of 'truth' regarding the nature of the ultimate environment."[6] *Locus of authority* defines the criteria a person employs, consciously or unconsciously, at each stage for determining what is a reliable authority among competing sources.

THE SHIFT TO INTERNAL JUDGES

The stage three conformist's authority is located in others. Those may be persons of authority, such as parents, pastors, or teachers, or a group such as one's peers. Sharon Parks refers to the "tyranny of the peer group," where adolescent faith is placed in "those who count," who may be as few as one—a friend or spokesperson.[7] This is the era of "heroes." Such authority will usually "look the part, possess a conventionally expected style and mannerisms, have the approval of some personally valued institution or institution-like group, and come across as sincere, genuine, and truthful."[8]

The stage four person has a quite different view of authority. Whereas stage three was external, stage four is internally oriented. Fowler explains: "When the Stage 4 person looks at potential authority figures from authoritative ideological perspective, the criteria of acceptance or rejection are based on a complex comparison of 'reality' as seen and experienced through his or her own outlook, with the truth or reality claims of the person or perspective in question. This means that authority for Stage 4 is validated by internal processes."[9]

In a genuine movement from stage three to four there must be an interruption of reliance on external sources of authority. The tyranny of the group must be undermined, relocating authority within the self.[10]

BECOMING A RELATIVIST

Lawrence Kohlberg, James Fowler, Jane Loevinger, and William G. Perry have observed that young adults go through a period of relativistic thinking. Fowler describes the experience as "an unavoidable tension: the question of being committed to the relative versus struggle with the possibility of an absolute."[11]

Loevinger defines the period as a transition rather than a stage and suggests that most adults are at this level. "The self-aware level is characterized by increased consciousness of self and one's inner life. There is also an awareness of 'multiple possibilities' in situations, rather than holding to a belief that there can only be one right answer."[12]

6. James Fowler and Sam Keen, *Life Maps: Conversations on the Journey of Faith,* p. 14.
7. Sharon Parks, "Faith Development and Imagination in the Context of Higher Education," p. 131.
8. Fowler and Keen, p. 63.
9. Ibid., p. 72.
10. Fowler, p. 179.
11. Ibid., p. 182.
12. Jane Loevinger, *Ego Development,* p. 19.

Perry and his colleagues have done the most thorough study of the transition to relativism. Perry uses the term *relativism* as a label for the middle stage of intellectual and ethical development. A person procedes from *dualistic thinking* to *relativism* and then to *commitment.*[13]

Students arriving at college are usually dualistic thinkers. They believe that there are absolutes of truth and rightness, and because they have a high regard for authorities, they are unable to understand professors who do not give them the right answers. Their views of right and wrong are related to the group from which they came. The words of one student typifies their position: "I came here from a small town. Midwest, where, well, ah, everyone believed the same things. Everyone's a Methodist and everyone's a Republican."[14]

Soon, however, many of their views are challenged in and out of the classroom. Students begin to move from their absolutist stance. Says one student: "Before, I used to think that Christianity was the only religion in the world—the religion—but when you talk things over you find out the Catholic view, the Unitarian view, different views on religion; why they believe there is a God and why they don't . . . I never had been exposed to this kind of thing before."[15]

Eventually, many students come to believe that there is no absolute or ultimate authority to which they can appeal. But, after a while, the student realizes that he must make some commitments in life. "He must affirm his own position from within himself in full awareness that reason can never completely justify him or assure him. In affirming his values, reason may help, but it will not in itself convince him that these values are better than any others; he must commit himself through his own faith." That leap of faith extends to all areas of life. "In choosing his career, he must risk his life to his own best guess; reason can never tell him fully about the roads not taken. Yet in the nature of the world as he has come to see it, he must commit himself or abrogate responsibility."[16]

That commitment is made on the basis of one's own experiences; it includes an awareness that authority, as part of the pluralistic world, has no special access to rightness. Thus, it is a commitment within relativism. Commitment requires that one integrate ideas and commit oneself to a position based not necessarily on the discovery of an ultimate truth, but, more likely, on personal relevance.[17] One's own viewpoint becomes the standard for decision-making. If a student goes back to some outside authority, Perry considers him to be regressing. Thus, even one's religion does not provide any absolute authority in the old sense. "There is a criterion which reveals that this commitment has been made in the context of a relativistic world. This criterion is one's attitude toward other people with a belief or a faith in a different Absolute. They cannot appear as alien, as other than human; one must, however paradoxically, respect them. In one sense they 'must' be wrong, but in another sense,

---

13. William G. Perry, Jr., *Forms of Intellectual and Ethical Development in the College Years.*
14. Ibid., p. 100.
15. Ibid., p. 142.
16. Ibid., p. 184.
17. Gene Bocknek, *The Young Adult,* p. 131.

no more so than oneself. The moral obligation to convert them or to annihilate them has vanished."[18]

Many developmentalists contend that going through a crisis such as divorce, the death of a parent, moving, or changing jobs is necessary for attaining adult faith.[19] Richard G. Young, an evangelical, suggests that Christian youths also need to go through some crisis period. "Every individual who arrives at stage six (Kohlberg's highest level) must go through a process of rebellion and experimentation."[20] However, evangelicals, adhering to biblical absolutes, cannot condone the need for Christian young adults to become relativistic in their thinking. Young's recommendations may be based on a misunderstanding of the nature of the relativity that Fowler and Kohlberg are espousing.

Why, then, have developmentalists linked faith with a progression into and through the relativity stage? Simply because they side with those whose philosophy and theology support the contemporary relative stance toward truth. Parks, for example, cites George Rupp to defend her position that a relativistic viewpoint is the normal one in today's world. "It is inadequate to form a commitment upon a position which can claim to be immune to relativism."[21] The pluralism that characterizes contemporary culture brings one to this viewpoint: modern thought has relativised every authority to which theology can appeal.

In contrast, our evangelical faith contends that absolute truth lies in Scripture not in our experience. "Evangelicalism rejects on principle all forms of dogmatic theological relativism, as the fruit of the fundamental mistake of not taking biblical instruction, as such, to be the Word of God."[22]

EVANGELICAL YOUNG ADULTS AND RELATIVISM

Though evangelicals do camp on biblical authority, that does not mean that they should be placed on a stage three level, where authority is located within an unquestioned group. A young adult may go through some distancing from his pre-adult world if that means that he must come to see the relativity of that group. Evangelicals affirm some degree of relativity in all sources of authority, including our own interpretation of the Bible. J. I. Packer notes that "Evangelicalism recognizes that all the church's formulations of God's truth, being to some extent culturally determined, are bound to lack finality and to need augmenting and qualifying from time to time."[23] Faith should not be placed in one denomination or group. While admitting that biblical

---

18. Perry, p. 179.
19. Perry, p. 34; Parks, p. 107.
20. Richard G. Young, "Values Differentiation as Stage Transition: An Expansion of Kohlbergian Moral Stages," *Journal of Psychology and Theology* 9, no. 2 (Summer 1981):173.
21. George Rupp, *Beyond Existentialism and Zen. Religion in a Pluralistic World,* p. 4, as cited by Parks, p. 369.
22. J. I. Packer, "Infallible Scripture and the Role of Hermeneutics" in *Scripture and Truth,* ed. D. A. Carson and John D. Woodbridge, pp. 327-38.
23. Ibid., p. 327.

interpretations may not be absolute, we still maintain that we can let the Bible speak for itself, and when it does there is absolute truth.

Young people growing up in an evangelical environment will no doubt go through a stage three to four transition. In order to establish their own identity and be true to their own judgment, they should be called upon to be critical of their pre-adult formulations of faith. Their churches and schools should help them transfer any authority they may have invested in their group to the Word of God by encouraging them to question doctrines, beliefs, and values and to make them their own. Young adults should be offered a rich Christian educational experience, supplementing Bible study with theological studies, church history, the study of contemporary religions, and apologetics.

It is that sort of experience of relativism that Young rightly suggests is good for young adults. The authorities they should relativise are groups, authority figures and parents. "It seems imperative that we as Christians begin to distinguish between our own relative and absolute truths if we are ever to break down the petty differences between ourselves and our Christian brothers and arrive at a clearer understanding of God's truth."[24]

That, however, is different from the sort of relativism advocated by many developmentalists. Liberals see no dangers in pluralism because they build on a philosophical and theological relativism. Their foundations of truth lie in individual existential choices, not in biblical authority. Still, Fowler is no doubt correct when he insists that most people feel comfortable at stage three, where they can simply believe what authority figures tell them.[25] Through reading and dialogue, young Christians can be exposed to those who have non-Christian viewpoints. Small group discussions can stimulate them, enabling them to come to their own decisions about what they believe under the umbrella of biblical authority, and ultimately make their faith their own.

It may be necessary for persons to also come under the authority of the group. Discipline for serious transgressions is a New Testament concept, but it would seem best to always distinguish the group's authority from Scripture's. Fowler properly warns of the developmental dangers that come to individuals who are not permitted to think for themselves and challenge the group's thinking. Appeal must constantly be made to Scripture.

In summary: stage four requires distancing oneself from one's group. Evangelicals do not call for blind, or even enlightened, alligence to a group. The young Christian adult should be helped to shift authority from the group to the Scriptures. That, of course, does not mean an uncritical acceptance of Scripture, but a growing understanding of why and how Scripture provides ultimate truth. Fowler agrees that that is consistent with his stage four level, because he puts the evangelical apologist C. S. Lewis there.[26] A young adult should have freedom from group coercion to think through his faith and come to his own conclusions.

24. Young, p. 171.
25. Fowler, p. 163, 173, 264–65.
26. Ibid., p. 301.

DANGERS OF BEING STOPPED AT STAGE THREE

Fowler maintains that people often prefer to stay on stage three because moving from one's conventional moorings can be frightening and disorienting, and also because the character of the group to which one belongs can inhibit such a movement. Social fraternities or sororities in colleges often perpetuate the pre-adult group's values, in effect substituting one group for another.[27] Many religious groups also sanction an individual's dependence on external authority.

Failure to *internalize* one's authority, staying on stage three, has some negative results. First, the stage three person is always subject to the despair that comes when his faith sources betray him or break down in some way. If faith is in some television preacher, friend, or church, the danger of disappointment is very real.

Second, there may be problems related to ego development. Fowler shows how cultists, in particular, force people to conform at a stage three level, often in the name of denying themselves. His lengthy research interview of a person he calls Mary illustrates the destructive results of reliance on *external authority*. Mary's pilgrimage took her from one religious communal group to another, where individuals' decisions were made by the group. Though Mary was learning Scripture and gaining some personal identity, she was extremely group-oriented. Many of her remarks are filled with confusion and pain: "I still wasn't completely out of the Followers of God. It took me about three months after actually leaving to get over the withdrawal pains because I felt such fear and condemnation that I was out of God's will by even leaving that I didn't know where to go from there."[28]

The communities Mary was a part of did little to strengthen her personal identity apart from the group. Instead of supporting her personal growth in understanding of Scriptures and her ability to make judgments for herself, they became a substitute for her ego. Fowler writes, "Mary's conversion, genuine and powerful though it was, was seriously affected by the failure of the communities in which she found fellowship to sponsor her in the transformation, rather than the negation of the willful self."[29] Granted, Jesus calls believers to deny themselves in following Him, but those who attempt to make that mean the denial of our critical faculties or our own ego identity cause great distress to their followers.

Commitment to Christ means the surrender of one's ego and the transformation that follows. Paradoxically, it is only as an individual ego develops and grows that there is something to surrender to be used for His glory. Denying self must not make a person feel obliterated, as if past and present self were no longer in existence. A person must continue to explore who he was and is in order to allow the continual transformation to take place. Fowler warns that often people with painful pasts are glad to consider them dead and gone.[30] A Christian must be aware of the past and consider its influence upon him if he is to experience continued new life.

27. Ibid., p. 178.
28. Ibid., p. 227.
29. Ibid., p. 264.
30. Ibid., pp. 264-65.

A third danger in not proceeding to stage four is this: the expectations and evaluations of others can be so compellingly internalized that it may be difficult to make decisions for oneself. In order to adapt to young adult stresses, the individual gives in to the demands of others. A young man, for example, takes a secure job in the family business instead of pursuing an interest in biology. A married woman takes on the role of full-time housewife instead of following a deep desire to be a teacher. That method of coping is termed *identity foreclosure*. While not a serious mental or emotional problem, it can lead to a blunting of personality and deep dissatisfaction in later life.[31]

The task of the Christian community, then, is to support the individual young adult in making his own decisions. It should encourage his conforming to Christ, but not coerce conforming to the group's expectations. The church should help Christians find reasons for faith that make sense to them as individuals. The lyrics "it was good for my father, it was good for my mother and it's good enough for me," do not provide a legitimate basis for faith. Even the testimonies of celebrities and other influential persons should be used carefully. Their own example must not be the primary basis of faith. Faith grounded in such externals may suffice for awhile, particularly for those oriented in that way during adolescence, but it will not sustain throughout adult life.

THE ROLE OF THE GROUP

Stating that the Christian must develop faith for himself does not imply that a Christian has no need for group support for his faith. The portrait of the young adult painted by developmentalists turns out to be that of a rugged individualist. He crawls out from under the burden of his family and group beliefs, looks over the landscape and finds no absolute truth—but somehow must stand up like an adult to face the world. The only thing left to bring the young adult to his feet is a choice he must make by himself, with himself. Developmentalists maintain that standing on one's feet by grabbing for anything other than one's judgments is picking up the proverbial crutch. If one leans too strongly on significant others, one will be psychologically crippled.

That picture of the young adult distorts the very process of individualization or differentiation that developmentalists are studying. Maturing involves critical judgment of one's pre-adult group and deciding whether to continue to hold its values or to reject them. The juvenile delinquent becomes aware of the gang's power over him, and he leaves it, for example. But an individual is not entirely dependent on his own judgment and resources.

When Fowler speaks of the locus of authority shifting from external to internal sources, he is not necessarily talking of a complete break with any social context. Yet Fowler is a bit unclear as to how much he expects the stage four person to have broken with the group. Parks notes his tentativeness about how much authority is *external* at stage three and *internal* at stage four. The locus of authority does not shift in one simple movement from "out there" to being internal to the self, but rather, there are a series of movements. What happens is simply this: at first, the adolescent believes

31. Bocknek, pp. 189–90.

what his group believes, and he is not aware of how the group has such an influence upon him. Later, he develops a self-awareness that enables him to see the group's influence. He then turns to his own judgment. But as a young adult, he cannot fully trust that judgment. The new-found self with its ability to judge is now used to find an authority figure or group that fits his internal judgment. The locus of authority becomes the person or group chosen, although it is validated by the self.[32]

If that account is accurate, it underscores the rightness of some of our evangelical practices. Scripture affirms that the church, as Christ's body, is an important faith support group. Although it is possible to trust in one's group to a fault, it is still a human necessity to identify with a group. That does not negate individual choice.

The need for a group affirms the practice of having Christian groups on college and university campuses where Christian youth can be discipled. If those groups allow for individual freedom, they will not hinder the young adult's development, but be a necessary part of his progress. Leaders in those groups must resist the temptation to pose as authorities in order to protect the individual from the struggle of making his own choices. If the emphasis on modeling is too strong, individual development can be thwarted. Parks maintains that modeling by professors on college campuses is ineffective because students are trying to forge their own identities and not merely copy someone else. Teachers therefore should put more energy into helping the student's self emerge than into "pouring" themselves into students. Peer models seem to be more effective, however. But even here there needs to be some caution exercised. Sometimes groups that emphasize imitating the leaders encourage it in terms that are too specific. Followers merely conform to practices and behaviors instead of developing their individual gifts and expressions of faith.

Christian groups that minister to young adults are in a crucial place. They represent the stepping stone between a young adult's past and future commitments. Those groups can provide a great service if they are aware of the pain involved in distancing oneself from the past. Leaders of those groups can help young adults lovingly handle the conflict they will inevitably have with their parents.

Too often, young adult group leaders side with the young adults against parents, taking advantage of the rift that develops. Visits home from college are marked by endless rounds of arguments fostered in part by teachers and group leaders who win students over by provoking their rebellion. Parents deserve greater respect, particularly because they are filled with anxiety about where their child's new-found freedom will take them. Christians who stand in the middle of this rift between parent and young adult have a chance to be the badly needed peacemakers. Evangelical groups that win young adults from non-Christian backgrounds can help their converts appreciate and respect the good in those backgrounds as well as communicate the values of their group to parents to assure them that their child is not caught up in some stultifying cult.

The young adult faith passage can sometimes be a crisis as well as provoke crises. Blessed are those who understand and help them through it.

32. Parks, p. 133.

10

The Loss of a Little One: Infertility and the Death of One's Child

ACCEPTING INFERTILITY[1]

Brutal shock and *crisis* are words used by couples who have had to face the fact that they cannot give birth to a child. As many as one out of five couples may be infertile.

Like other married people, those couples live with the usual expectations of bearing children. They decide they are ready to have a family and discard the contraceptives. Time passes. Slowly the possibility of infertility arises. Concern mixes with alarm. In the beginning, they may avoid any diagnosis or treatment thereby denying the truth. In most cases, they eventually decide to seek a physician's help. When the medical data confirms their suspicion, the possibility of treatment still keeps their hope alive. But the treatment may be expensive and ineffective.

Only about half of those who are treated for infertility eventually conceive a child. Five percent will eventually conceive without medical attention. But nearly 45 percent will have to face the inevitable conclusion that they are unable to conceive. That amounts to one out of ten couples. Barbara Menning considers the situation to be a major life crisis.[2] Developmentalists consider adjusting to parenting to be one of the prime tasks of young adults. The infertile couple must adjust to being a nonparent, at least in the natural sense.

Only recently have the crisis dimensions of involuntary childlessness begun to be seen. It has been a neglected field of study. People around the infertile couple are quite insensitive to their trauma and can become a part of the problem when the couple is made to feel badly about their emotional reaction to the whole matter. Some mistake the couple's childlessness as self-indulgence and selfishness. Those who know the real

1. This section is based on a research paper by David Bredfeldt (Trinity Evangelical Divinity School)
2. Barbara E. Menning, *Infertility: A Guide for the Childless Couple*, p. 5.

reason often make suggestions on how to solve the problem. Friends and family suggest that it is psychological; the couple is told to relax and enjoy their sexual relations. Still others laugh about their own fertility, making light of the ability to conceive, and turn the infertile couple's problem into a joke.

The infertile wife may struggle with her self-identity. Many women include motherhood in their idea of being a complete woman. Says one,

> When I was young and impressionable, I heard a neighbor of ours tell my mother that a woman was never truly complete until she conceived and bore a child. She certainly must have felt complete, since she had five children by three different husbands. I never questioned this idea. Later when I was going through the worst pain of my infertility struggle and conception looked hopeless, I learned that she had committed suicide . . . and my first thought was—at least she died complete.[3]

The husband, too, may struggle with his personal identity. Though he fights it, he may sense he is a failure because he cannot reproduce. His dream of playing ball with his own son or taking his daughter to the zoo is crushed.

> I found it hard to believe our problem was my fault. But the test showed it to be me so what could I say? I felt like a total failure as a man . . . for a long time, I became depressed. I even thought of offering to divorce my wife so she could marry someone else who was more of a man. Now I realize that it has nothing to do with how masculine I am. It is purely a medical problem which we've accepted now.[4]

COPING MECHANISMS

It is quite likely that the response to infertility follows a pattern closely akin to the Kübler-Ross stages of grief. Because the childless couple faces a death—the death of their dream for a child—it is quite reasonable the following responses may result.

Denial. After examinations and tests, the infertile couple may say to one another, "Maybe the doctor is wrong. Let's get another opinion." For some couples the use of denial by one or both partners has the effect of prolonging their search for medical help, as they go from doctor to doctor hoping for a more favorable prognosis. It also keeps them from moving forward in the "mourning" process.[5] They may involve themselves in careers or make excuses to others like "after the mortgage is paid." All the while they are hurting and hoping. Denial is even more of a problem with those couples who are diagnosed as "inconclusive infertile couples," meaning that there is no cause for their infertility. They find themselves in a hope/despair cycle, as each month brings more disappointment.

3. Ibid., p. 99.
4. Case study from the files of Adoption Center of Delaware Valley (1218 Chestnut Street, Philadelphia, Pa. 19107).
5. Constance Hoenk Shapiro, "The Impact of Infertility on the Marital Relationship," *Social Casework: The Journal of Contemporary Social Work* 63, no. 7 (September 1982): 387-93.

Anger. Any number of persons provide targets for the anger that may swell the hearts of the grieving couple: the doctors, who seem cold and impersonal about the matter; themselves; or even God. Scriptures tell them of women who conceived when God heard their pleas, but the God of Hannah and Rachel does not seem to hear them.

Anger, like water, seeks its own level. Thus, if denied or improperly handled, it can pop through in unsuspected areas. It may surface in the marriage causing tension over issues and problems the couple would otherwise handle with ease. As a result, they may expend more energy on false issues than on coping with their shared problem of infertility.[6]

When the anger is directed against the self, it may produce a condition of *learned helplessness* and depression. The individual comes to believe that no effort can result in a favorable outcome. The helplessness is a logical result of the couple's feeling that they have lost control over their carefully laid life plans.[7] Feeling cheated, they struggle for control—giving all of their attention to the effort to conceive. Vacations are postponed, job opportunities are passed up, and business trips are arranged around doctors' appointments. The depression that causes the frantic, obsessive struggle is also likely to have an unhealthy impact on the marriage. The best defense against the sense of helplessness is information. Attempting to understand infertility and what is happening to them emotionally will help the couple regain a sense of control and overcome their feelings of helplessness.

The couple will find serenity ultimately in resting in the will of a kind heavenly Father, although it may take months or even years to live down the feelings of resentment toward God. An infertile woman in one of my classes had that experience. Though then over fifty years of age, she was deeply disturbed by a film I showed on the development of a fetus and eventual birth of the child. After watching it and being reminded once again of what she had missed, she was surprised by the return of anger. Though a very dedicated Christian, it took her several days to work through those troubled feelings.

The couple may also feel anger toward society in general. Other people do not seem to understand. People who can be supportive and kind to those who have lost a loved one do not always understand why the infertile couple's loss is so great. As one infertile person said to me, "There is no avenue to mourn our loss openly." Thus, anger grows.

Bargaining. It is easy to see how a couple in this situation could begin bargaining with God. They may offer their lives in exchange for a child. Church attendance, Christian service, or regular personal prayer may be used to somehow merit God's favor. When the bargaining fails, however, they may once again become depressed.

Those near the couple at this time should respond as they would to any grief. They should listen carefully and avoid glibly quoting verses that make the couple feel guilty. Words of assurance, such as "I know you will, by His grace, handle this," should be

6. Ibid., pp. 8–9.
7. Ibid.

mixed with realistic statements, such as "I know how tough it must be, but reality will have to be faced." Reminders of God's faithfulness and personal will for each of us need to be given gently, without condemning the couple for emotions and thoughts that they are dealing with. "It's OK to be angry with God. All of us feel that way sometimes. But you'll get through it."

Depression. Depression, sometimes brought on by false guilt, is the most difficult stage. Most couples will easily find a reason to feel guilty because they cannot conceive a child: past sins, poor church attendance, use of contraceptives. While they must deal with past sins, they will also have to come to terms with the false guilt that plagues them. They will have to recognize that infertility is not a form of punishment God hands out in special cases.

Although guilt usually falls on the infertile partner, it may also overcome the fertile partner, who fears that his or her grief may cause the spouse to bear a double load of guilt.[8] If not managed, it can often cause a serious rift in the marriage. Constance Shapiro, who has made a major study of infertility, claims, that "it is not uncommon for the infertile spouse to encourage, either directly or subtly, the fertile spouse to seek a partner with whom he or she may bear children."[9]

If their grief follows a regular pattern, they may experience physical distresses, such as headaches, upset stomachs and disruption of sleep. Sexually, they may have problems of impotency and disinterest. They may become preoccupied with the image of their lost "dream child." They fantasize announcing their pregnancy or what the child would have looked like.

Couples at that point need to know how normal their reaction is. They also need to be alert to what their emotions are doing to them as a couple. Their relationship might be strained, but they should be careful not to allow their emotions to separate them. They must come to realize that those emotions will pass and that they will emerge from the disappointment.

Acceptance. Acceptance, the last stage, comes in discernable steps. First, the couple must decide to decrease their hope of conception. That may be very difficult because it involves making choices related to the medical assistance they may have been receiving. Tests may be stopped, or a time limit may be established, after which they will stop medical attempts to resolve their infertility.

The second step is increased life control. They will move from the sense of helplessness to some sense of control. For a long period of time doctors, temperature charts, and ovulation periods dominated their lives. It is essential that they make some clear choices that indicate that they are once again taking charge.

Growing acceptance of the situation will give them a chance to work through the grief period as well as begin to see that there are different types of parents and that options are still open to them. They may not be able to a *birthparent,* but they can be a *parent parent.* Giving birth to a child is little compared to giving a child the love, discipline, and care that follows the birth. They must, however, decide which they

8. Ibid., p. 390.
9. Ibid.

most desire. If it is parenting, they can seek other options, such as adoption. If it is birthing, they will have to continue infertility treatment or give up completely.

The final step of acceptance seems to involve the actual death of the dream child. One woman beautifully tells of her experience:

> Erin, the little girl with the musical talent from her father's side of the family, her mother's love of books and reading and curly auburn hair from both sides of her family, died in the doctor's office. Her death was not particularly sudden or unexpected. The results of the numerous tests were not good and yet her family was not prepared for her death.
>
> Erin was a dream-child whose creation began sometime in the long-forgotten past when her mother was given her first doll. Erin's development continued and really took a definite form when her parents met and married. "Death" came when they, and the doctors, came to the conclusion that they were an infertile couple.
>
> Erin was my dream-child. I am now the mother of a three year-old Vietnamese daughter, Kia. Kia is a child different from and yet exceeding all my dreams.[10]

ADOPTION

One out of three couples who are proven to be infertile eventually adopt a child. The other two choose to remain childless or delay their decision until they are too old to meet the standards of adoption agencies. Couples need to face the forces that either encourage or discourage them from deciding to adopt. They need to look within themselves to ask why they want to be parents. If the marriage is strong, they will be more inclined to adopt in order to share their good home with a child. Sometimes they will seek adoption because of an intense desire to parent. Not all the factors may favor adoption. Friends and relatives may not encourage them or may even be openly negative about it. Adoption is expensive; fees range from several thousand up to ten thousand dollars—which is neither tax deductible or covered by insurance.

Aid in coming to a decision as well as for facing infertility can be found in the services of adoption agencies. Groups like Resolve, Inc. offer information to childless couples and help them cope with their situation through meetings with other couples.[11] In Delaware, a group of adoptive parents who call themselves AFIS (Adoptive Families with Information and Support) provides regular meetings and positive support.

Once the decision to adopt has been made, the couple moves into another phase that has its own unique pressures. H. David Kirk identifies several of those. They will face, first of all, the grim reality of the shortage of available babies. That leads to the second, most difficult part of the process: waiting. Unlike a pregnant woman, those

10. Cathy Cheleen, "The Real Dream-Child Comes at Last" (Available from Resolve, Inc., P.O. Box 474, Belmont, Mass. 02178).
11. To contact this organization, write to: Resolve, Inc., P.O. Box 474, Belmont, Mass. 02178.

who wait for the arrival of the adoptive child have no known timetable. The unpredict-able nature of adoption brings its own distress.[12]

The uniqueness of their experience may also make it more stressful. Their close friends may have gone through several pregnancies, but none of them may have gone through an adoption. Most likely, the couple will need to find others who lie outside the circle of their present friends. The financial strains will mix with anxieties about what the child will be like, whether or not they will learn to love each other, and how well the child will adjust.

But when adoption occurs, it provides a resolution to the infertility crisis. For many couples, their need to parent is fulfilled and their joint venture of service to another gives them an opportunity to grow as a couple as well as individually.

LIVING WITH A CHILD'S DEATH

"I can't sleep, and I don't know anyone else to call. Will you talk to me?" The despair in those words reflects the feelings of a mother who only days before saw her son die.[13] Though desperate, that parent's plea is not totally hopeless. She knows she is going through something unbelievably painful, but she also senses that she will somehow survive. She needs what people in grief seem to need most: someone to talk to.

THE HARD PLACES

The peculiar torment of those who lose a child places them into a special group of grievers. Along with God's comfort, they need the comfort of others who have gone through the same ordeal as theirs. Hospital chaplain R. Wayne Willis formed a support group for such parents. Not only did he learn about the rough spots they encountered, but he also discovered what helps them through grief's valley. In addition to the normal grieving process just discussed, bereaved parents have special concerns.

Last Things. Bereaved parents relive the final hours of their child's life and judge themselves by how they behaved. Were they with the child when he died? Did the child know they were there? Did he die wondering if Mom and Dad really loved him? They sometimes feel they have failed the child if, for any reason, in the final moment of death they are not sure their child felt their nearness and love. They need to work through other matters: whether or not the child had the best care; how the staff acted; how the question of autopsy was handled.

Anger. Parents ask "Why did this happen to my child?" not so much for an answer as for an empathic response. Months later, a parent may be as confused as ever. Some may focus anger on physicians or themselves or other members of their family. Christians will call on their spiritual knowledge and their relationship to God to help

12. H. David Kirk, *Shared Fate,* pp. 1-15.
13. R. Wayne Willis, "Some Concerns of Bereaved Parents," *Journal of Religion and Health* 20, no. 2 (Summer 1981):133-40.

them understand their anger and cope with it, although they will undoubtedly endure a struggle of faith.

Guilt. Because parents feel responsible for their children, they may feel guilty even if the death is from something entirely beyond their control, such as from leukemia. They may think up illogical explanations as to why the child got sick, such as recalling times when they fleetingly wished they had no children, somehow thinking that they had wished for their child's death.

Surviving children. Helping their other children, if there are any, to grieve becomes a problem to them. They may not understand when the dead child's brother or sister makes angry statements about God. They will need help in understanding how children handle bereavement, and they will need to help their children work at it. They must fight a tendency to overprotect the surviving children.[14]

Restructuring life. Parents in Chaplain Willis' support group tell each other that there is no right or wrong way to grieve. They comfort each other for doing things others might condemn or think unwise. Some people seal off the child's bedroom, leaving it just like it was the day he died; others immediately clear out the room, trying to get rid of reminders. Some couples try for a pregnancy as soon as possible; some determine not to have any more children. Couples coping with the loss of a child need acceptance and understanding more than advice. They should be urged to decide for themselves what is best instead of permitting them to lean on others for what is right or wrong.

Yearning for reunion. Some parents worry because they have such a strong desire to make contact with the child. They report hallucinations—visions, hearing voices, having conversations with the child—and worry about whether they are losing their minds. Yet, instead of a sign of breakdown, it seems that the desire for contact is normal and fulfills some purpose. Those parents seem to be seeking some reassurance that the child is all right.

Anniversaries. There are three days of the year that bereaved parents find most grievous: Christmas, the child's birthday, and the child's death day.

SUPPORT SYSTEMS

Relatives and friends will be needed to support the grieving parents because God ministers through people. Like other grievers, they most need from others "a touch, a facial expression, a tear, a word that somehow lets us know you are with us."[15] While some have good experiences with relatives and friends who help them get through their grief, others feel neglected and even avoided. Some have experienced people literally crossing to the other side of the street. Members of Willis's group reported that no members of their church called or visited after their child's death. When people do try to support them, they often do not know what to do. Supporters fail

14. See Marlee Alex and Ben Alex, *Grandpa and Me: We Learn About Death* (Minneapolis: Bethany House, 1982); Earl A. Grollman, *Talking About Death: A Dialog Between Parent and Child* (Boston: Beacon, 1976).
15. Willis, pp. 133–40.

to mention the dead child, even though the bereaved want to talk about him.

Husbands and wives have trouble supporting each other. "My wife feels so sorry for herself that she can't see how badly I am hurting," said one husband.[16] If grief is not properly worked through, it can create severe marital discord.

Eventually, Christian parents will discover solace in God. Comfort may come from the knowledge that ultimately all things, even the tragic, work together for good.

16. Ibid., p. 139.

PART 2

MIDDLE ADULTHOOD

11

The Churning Point: Mid-Life Crises

WHAT'S IN A MID-LIFE CRISIS?

At first I thought I was suffering from a dragged-out case of that season's flu. Christmas was a burden. I didn't feel like celebrating my January birthday. Whether or not the ground hog saw its shadow on February 2 was irrelevant. I wasn't sure I would live until spring. Tired blood—maybe, that's it, I thought. My doctor ordered some lab tests, which showed that there was nothing physically wrong; I just had a case of middle-age melancholia.[1]

Does life, like a cross-country marathon, really have a middle? If so, what does being there do to a person?

Mid-life as a concept is comparatively new. Before 1900, when the average life expectancy of Americans was still less than fifty years, old age was thought to set in about forty. "People thought of being little and then of being old,"[2] observed social historian John Demos. The middle part of life was not thought of as a distinct stage. Now, mid-life is certainly a life period, but is it a crisis? Some say no. Harvard psychologist Jerome Kegan says it is more a part of culture than of personal development. "If the culture says you should go through a stage, then you expect to go through it. It's a middle class phenomena."[3]

No one knows for sure that a crisis must happen in life's midstream, but it does happen—and to many people. It often shows up in a powerful desire for change. Extroverts want to be more introverted, turning to reading, gardening, or painting. Introverts may want to pop out of their shell more, sharing feelings and thoughts

---

1. Vergie Gillespie, review of *Mid-Life: A Time to Discover, A Time to Decide*, by Richard P. Olson, *Baptist Leader*, June 1981, p. 8.
2. Kenneth L. Woodward with Paul Brinkley-Rogers, "All of Life's a Stage," *Newsweek*, 6 June 1977, p. 83.
3. Ibid.

more openly. A man or woman may be compelled to jog or join a health club, as if suddenly discovering he or she has a body. Some explore the sensual side of their nature, appreciatively touching the spouse in profoundly romantic and sexual ways. Others disastrously look outside of marriage for new sensual "highs." There is a new serious look at life. Vocations and marriages are scrutinized soberly, with the intent of improving or abandoning them.[4]

THE CRITERIA FOR CRISIS

All of that changing may not amount to a crisis. To be considered a mid-life crisis, two criteria must be met. Trauma is the first. Emotional upheaval occurred for over half of the men Daniel J. Levinson interviewed.

> For the great majority of men—about 80 percent of our subjects—this period evokes tumultuous struggles within the self and the external world. Their mid-life transition is a time of moderate or severe crisis. Every aspect of their lives comes into question, and they are horrified by much that is revealed. They are full of recriminations against themselves and others. They cannot go on as before, but need time to choose a new path or modify an old one.[5]

The second criterion of a crisis concerns possible outcome. Forces (external or internal) are sometimes so great that a mid-lifer is in danger of responding in a destructive way. They teeter on a point of time, in jeopardy of falling to the wrong side. The "fall" seems to happen all too often. For example, I know of a man, an elder in a church, who clearly plummeted in the wrong direction. After twenty years of model service in the church, he turned to another religion, changed jobs, divorced his wife, and married another woman, rejecting everything touched by his past. Lying in his wake were scores of hurt, disillusioned people.

Some respond with the severest form of rejection: suicide. "Staffs of crisis centers and mental health clinics are trained to be alert to the middle-aged businessman who signifies suicidal intentions."[6]

Only a few get to that place, and not all mid-lifers undergo a crisis. Levinson reports that for some, the transition was rather mild. In a recent major research project, Michael P. Farrell and Stanley D. Rosenberg found no evidence that the mid-life crisis is universal.[7]

Researchers have grouped themselves on two sides of the mid-life issue. A cadre of writers argue that this period is the most stable and satisfying of all. Others argue that somewhere within the late thirties to early forties there is more or less a universal crisis period.

---

4. John R. Landgraf, "Career Development in Mid-Life," *Baptist Leader* 43, no. 3:16 (June 1981): 16–19.
5. Daniel J. Levinson, *Seasons of a Man's Life*, p. 199.
6. Naomi Golan, *Passing Through Transitions*, p. 136.
7. Levinson, p. 198; Michael P. Farrell and Stanley D. Rosenberg, *Men at Midlife*, p. 206.

THE RESPONSES TO CRISIS

Michael Farrell and Stanley Rosenberg have had the latest, but certainly not the last, word on the subject. Using questionnaires, tests, and interviews, they conclude that there is no universal crisis. Mid-life is not a time of severe emotional upheaval or a dangerous turning point for all men.

Instead, they found that just as all people do not react in the same way to the World Series, so not all all get upset over mid-life. Some men, especially professionals and middle class executives who have the greatest opportunities for personal development, find mid-life to be a peak period. They report satisfaction with work, family, and their positions in the community.

Unskilled laborers, on the other hand, have the most mid-life trouble. Those men began adulthood feeling alienated. They never had opportunities to fulfill themselves, or they failed to take advantage of chances they had. At mid-life, they feel somewhat hopeless and show signs of stress. A report entitled *Men at Midlife*, says: "They suffer from anxiety, depression and physical illness and they are very much aware of not having found gratification in the spheres of work, family, or community."[8]

A third type of response is typical of the bulk of lower-middle-class men, such as skilled workers, clerical workers, and small businessmen. Their reaction is quite subtle. On the surface those men report they have adjusted well, but when the researchers looked closer, they found a protective coat of denial. Those men fail to see any problems with themselves and instead project a variety of faults onto minority groups. They avoid any surprises and risks in life by adopting a rather narrow world for themselves. An "even, regular life" is what they want. They are likely to be authoritarian in raising their children. Unlike those who are more satisfied with life, they are depressed and they try to hide it. Of all men, they are the most likely to report unsatisfying sexual relations, even though they are least likely to have trouble with their wives. In some cases, the wives did not look at it the same way. Some of them said they were "fed up" with their husbands and if it were not for the children, they would leave. The men cope by playing ostrich, refusing to see their own failings and distress as well as the unhappiness of those around them.[9]

Farrell and Rosenberg help a great deal with clearing up the confusion over the mid-life experience. Although only 12 percent of the persons they studied really had what might be called an overt mid-life crisis, another 56 percent were hiding it. That means a majority are experiencing a distinct crisis during those years. Yet if 56 percent are wearing a mask, they may not come out looking too bad; thus, some writers see mid-life as a fairly tranquil or happy time. In other words, depending on how you look at them, you can put the 56 percent in either category.[10]

Farrel and Rosenberg offer one more important insight. They found that the candidates for struggle in mid-life are those who all along have been insecure. If a person does not successfully navigate the transitions of young adulthood, he will have

8. Ibid., p. 87.
9. Ibid., pp. 83–88.
10. Ibid., pp. 88.

a difficult time later. If a person has not really found himself, has not really had expectations met in marriage or in a job, he naturally expects to overcome those shortcomings in the future. When such a person moves into mid-life, that hope is likely to fade and he will feel trapped in unfolding events he cannot control. With hope gone, bitterness sets in. Depression and physical illness might result. He has been going along in the same old insecure, uncertain self, but in mid-life he comes to a difficult intersection. When many issues converge, some men crash. It is not the fault of the intersection as much as the fact that the person is bringing along unresolved issues of earlier life, such as lack of trust, an inability to be intimate, or a shortage of self-esteem.

Whether a person is secure or not, all researchers tend to agree that there is something distinct about mid-life. A complex set of forces is acting upon a married man or woman. Issues concerning the spouse, the children, health, and career matters; all those are changing. Understanding the complexities may help a counselor in his own mid-life passage as well as help others face theirs.

THE BEGINNING OF THE MIDDLE

"Jane is Forty" were the words on a huge sign draped across the yellow siding of the house. Black crepe paper hung from the trees to the house, shrouding the cardboard tombstone, direfully bearing the name *Jane*. Jane's friends were "helping" her deal with turning forty.[11]

Entrance to mid-life is not always marked by a certain birthday, even though the fortieth is a popular doorway. Louis Argon, the French novelist and poet wrote: "When I was only forty I still could not believe it when I stood there in front of the looking-glass and said to myself, 'I am forty.' " Mid-life is not necessarily a numbers game. Therefore, Levinson places the mid-life transition between forty and forty-five, but adds, "give or take a few years."[12] Some researchers would say "give or take a lot of years," because they contend life span events are not the same for all people. Working-class persons may hit mid-life issues earlier than people of the middle and upper classes because they tend to get started earlier in marriage and vocation. Gail Sheehy believes that the transition is earlier for women, beginning at about age thirty-five.[13] Not necessarily a birthday but a combination of things makes a person aware that he is in some new phase of life. The biological, psychological, and social all seem to combine to have an effect.

BODY LANGUAGE

The body may give the first signals that something is happening. At about forty, physical and mental powers are somewhat diminished. General biological changes are gradual and unnoticed, but several small changes at this time bring about a major drop

11. The name has been changed in this otherwise true account.
12. Levinson, pp. 18–19.
13. Gail Sheehy, *Passages*, p. 377.

in the quality of physical stamina. In such a youth-oriented culture, the loss of youthful vitality comes as a basic threat. "It is as though he were on the threshold of senility and even death."[14] A person is suddenly struck by his own mortality. The physical loss (unable to run as fast, lift as much, or for a woman, unable to have children) triggers a sense of helplessness in general. The reaction is deeper than the mere feeling that one will have to take it a bit slower and rest more. Sheehy sensed this as the start of her own crisis. As a reporter caught in the cross-fire in Irish street warfare, she was struck by helplessness: "No one is with me. No one can keep me safe. There is no one who won't ever leave me."[15] UCLA psychologist Roger Gould describes it this way: "By middle life adults must confront the last illusion of safety, there is now death in the world."[16]

STARTING TO COUNT BACK

A person begins to look at his life differently. Peter Weaver's description is graphic:

> You may not realize what is happening. There is no band playing, and no speeches. But, somewhere in your forties, you pass the second half of your life. You are probably too busy working, raising a family, coping to think about it or even recognize it. You might notice some subtle changes in the way you look at your life. Instead of counting from the day you were born, or the first day you can remember you almost imperceptibly begin to count back from some vague, future end of your life. Sometimes you count the years, usually giving yourself a full measure, and come up with figures that add up to 75, 80 or 85. You pick some ripe old age you think you might live to and then subtract your current age. This gives you the Number of Years You Have Left, which usually ranges from 25 to 30 years or more, depending on your current age and your optimism-pessimism quotient. . . . When you start thinking this way it's official: you're in the second half.[17]

BECOMING ONE OF THE WRONG GANG

In addition to looking at one's life span differently, there is another change in perspective. Levinson maintains that people begin to see themselves differently in relationship to the generation below them. Levinson says that a "sequence of generations" forms in the mind. People develop a way of determining who are or are not their peers as adults. If people are five to seven years older or younger, they are included as roughly the same age. Whenever the difference goes from eight to fifteen years, it is regarded as a half generation. When the difference increases to twenty and beyond, a full generation separates the two—the older one is more like a parent than a brother or sister.

14. Levinson, pp. 213–14.
15. Sheehy, p. 5.
16. Woodward with Brinkley-Rogers, p. 83.
17. Peter Weaver, *Strategies for the Second Half of Life,* pp. xi–xii. See also Bernice L. Neugarten, "The Awareness of Middle Age," in *Middle Age and Aging* (Chicago, U. of Chicago, 1968).

A man or woman of thirty or thirty-five is likely to be regarded as one of the gang with persons in their twenties. But when the person hits the forties, something happens. Even though the forty-year-old may still regard himself as quite young, the younger adults tend to see him as older. The man, for example, is more like a "dad" than a "buddy." A woman may feel this at work when her youthful male colleagues start treating her with a distant respect rather than as a comrade.[18]

WRITING YOUR OWN REVIEWS

THE NEED TO REVIEW

The middle adult is in the middle, neither young nor old. He is at the point where the past and future close in. The past calls for reevaluation; the future demands restructuring.

Some event may set a review in motion. Here is one man's story: He went to the doctor with a few complaints. Upon examining him, the doctor suggested some testing be done in a hospital, and the next day he was lying in bed "connected by wires to every outlet in the hospital. Watching the screen with its blips and modulating lines representing my life, I began to take stock of myself, not just my career, but my whole life: the spiritual—how I had let my quiet times become fewer; the physical—how my body had been neglected; my family life—my seventeen-year-old daughter's struggles; my financial—how I had not been planning for retirement."

The reevaluation had begun. Was it the interruption to life's routine that triggered it? Or was it the reality of a physical examination? With body functions portrayed on a screen in front of him, he was forced to stop and think. Did the biofeedback produce the courage or the anxiety that pressed him to total self-examination?

The term *middlescence* is designed to compare this time with adolescence. Like adolescence, this middle transition comes with a good supply of questions, as well as fluctuations and instability. Raising questions and making landmark decisions permeates the whole period, as in adolescence.[19] Nonetheless, there is a major difference. The adolescent is just starting: much can still be done later. But, there seems to be little "later" left for the mid-lifer. The young adult is like the team at the start of the game; the mid-lifer is coming out of the locker room after half-time. There is an urgency to make the second half count. Unlike the adolescent who struggles to forge an identity, the person in mid-life wonders about who he has become.[20]

Recently, I had supper with a man who was at his "halftime." Noting some depression, I asked if something was wrong. Wistfully, he told me of how he always dreamed of owning a gift shop in some resort area. He said, "Perhaps someday I will be able to do that." Now he was bored and discouraged, a slave to the successful

18. Golan, p. 125.
19. Jan Chartier, "The Mid-Life Load: A Challenge for Creative Ministry," *Baptist Leader* 43, no. 1 (June 1981):27.
20. Sharan Merriam, "Professional Literature on Middle Age," in *Programming for Adults Facing Mid-Life Change*, p. 25.

television repair shop he owned. He was sick of complaining customers. Responsibilities and past choices now made freedom to do what he really wanted virtually impossible.

THE DREAM YARDSTICK

It is the dream that is the yardstick for evaluation at this time, says Levinson. Sometimes, the dream is the goal that has been pursued in the first half; at other times, it is not. The dream may have been pushed back into the subconscious—an idea that might somehow happen someday. Attaining it does not always bring satisfaction. "There are two tragedies in life," wrote Bernard Shaw. "One is not to get your heart's desire. The other is to get it."[21] If one attains his dream, he may ask: "Would there have been a better one?"

Those who do not reach their dream may be like Wally, who surprised me one morning.[22] A pleasant, middle-aged man, he told me, "I have a Master's degree in the classical languages." That revelation came while he was taking my yellow and white credit card to charge me for fifteen dollars worth of gas. Wally, the owner and operator of a service station, loved languages and had studied Latin for seven years, Greek for five. Sandwiched between "How much gas did you pump?" and "Your license number?" he recited a short biographical sketch explaining why he had not ended up teaching. Reading regret on his face, I watched him press his thumb to his chest and say "I have an empty spot here that is always with me. But that's life." Having known him for two years, I never guessed what he was carrying in his heart. He, however, has come to terms with it and is not a defeated man.

Women, apparently, experience reassessment, but perhaps not as much in regard to the "dream." Sheehy maintains that woman's questioning is associated with her role as a caregiver instead of a career. The imminence of menopause, when her ability to procreate is gone, hits her. Naomi Golan says, "In general, we find little evidence that women undergo the same type of existential soul-searching as men do."[23] She thinks about what she has contributed and how she will continue to do so. The reassessment may include vocation, of course, if she has been a career woman. Even if not, a woman who gave up a career for her role as homemaker may begin life review when her children are close to leaving home. She knows her role as caregiver cannot last forever. She may wonder about earlier dreams she laid aside. She may ask if it has been worth it all. *Was my husband to blame,* she may wonder, *for my giving up an opportunity to be a musician? a writer?*

The mid-life thinking may go like this: I'm not all that I hoped or dreamed I would be. I'm not even all I could have been. If only . . . I'd gone to college . . . taken a different job . . . lived in another part of the country . . . [24]

---

21. Bernard Shaw, *Man and Superman,* Act 4, as cited by Sheehy, p. 402.
22. The name has been changed in this otherwise true account.
23. Sheehy, pp. 396–97; Golan, p. 126.
24. Chartier, p. 27.

EVERYTHING BROUGHT TO THE LIGHT

The reassessment will touch other things as well: values, attitudes, religious and moral views, human relationships. All is up for grabs, to be kept or jettisoned.

In general, there is a value shift for both men and women in this period. As a young adult, the person set out to master the environment, perhaps through science, social work, or missions. Stopping and looking, the individual now sees the importance of other values besides accomplishment. Enriching human relationships become more significant, as does cultivating one's internal self. Those who come through this period successfully will see there is more than one brass ring to reach for.

The shift in thinking may lead to a change in living. For some, old life patterns are subtly reshaped (more volunteer social work may make life meaningful). A major upheaval erupts for others, leading to changes in career, close relationships, and living habits. Feelings of fulfillment are crucial. Those emotions are primarily tied to the search for life's meaning.[25]

INDIVIDUATION

Where is life's meaning to be found: within the self, or somewhere in the externals of society and circumstances? Levinson, following Jung, points to the inner man.[26] *Individuation* is a process in which the individual person becomes more and more separate from environmental direction. It begins at birth: now separate from the mother, the infant begins the pathway toward personal individuality.

Mid-life is a time for determining how much one's life has been determined by the inner self and how much it has been shaped by conformity to the world around. The self is a growing plant, programmed to become full grown in its own special way. But the environment presses in upon it, inhibits, demands, boxes in, until the plant is no longer true to its own self. In mid-life, a person asks how much he has been permitted to grow and blossom. Have the expectations and demands of others been too influential?

One of Sheehy's examples personifies the struggle. Explaining why he chose the ministry as an occupation, Reverend Raines said: "All three boys in our family went into seminary, which indicates there was a quiet, but pervasive pressure on us. I bought it all. It was like carrying the family mantle. I never did disestablish myself from my father in adolescence, so I've had to do it in middlescence." Sheehy observes: "At 40, Reverend Raines felt as though his person had collapsed inside his profession."[27]

The real inside you. The mid-life challenge is to remedy that "collapse," and regain the self. Abraham Maslow calls the process self-actualization. Sheehy speaks of it as "gaining our authenticity."[28]

25. Ibid.
26. Levinson, p. 196.
27. Sheehy, p. 373.
28. Ibid., pp. 48–49.

Carl Jung was one of the early voices calling mid-lifers to be true to themselves. He leaves no doubt that life's meaning lies within. Following Jung, two religious writers, Janice Brewi and Anne Brennan, urge adults "to turn our attention to the voice from that inner world that has been speaking to our self from the first moment of conception. . . . The forces of the first half of life . . . have called forth certain potentials of our personalities and left others untouched. . . . Individuation is the task of the second half of life. It means becoming one's own true self."[29]

Is this the treacherous, alluring, sweet song of the Siren? One thing is certain: it is alluring. Sheehy's title appealed to confused moderns looking for some chart to map out life's course. Quoting the philosopher Nietzsche, she claims direction comes from within. "This is my way; what is your way? The way doesn't exist."[30]

For Jung, the mid-life crisis is unique because he saw life having only two periods. Young adulthood, he believed, was too soon to ask a person to adopt major life values and personal ideals.[31] That is a task for mid-life. Having lived through adolescence and young adulthood one now has the experience to separate the true from the false, the real from the mythical.

Jung saw development in terms of a conflict between two realities: the *persona* and the *shadow*.[32] Using the image of the masks of the early Greek theatres, the persona stands for the masks persons put on according to life roles. The adolescent chooses a mask that makes him an acceptable member of a family, church, or group. His persona is mostly constructed out of cultural expectations associated with success and social acceptance.

Constructing the persona, the adolescent represses the shadow. That is the dark, neglected side of self. For example, to make a living, the young adult gives up his deep yearning to be an artist.

A raging battle. In mid-life, the conflict between the persona and the shadow rages. After lying submerged and quiet for a long time, the shadow self emerges; the inner voices become louder. But in the agony of the battle lies opportunity. The conflict is not an easy one. Calling it a rebirth, two of Jung's followers speak of it almost poetically:

> This is a lonely time, solitary moments piled up, a spirituality dictated from the depths of the psyche, a struggle and a warfare, a tearing and a wrenching, a loving and a hating, a despair and a hope, a letting go and a holding on, a death and a rebirth, a sameness and a newness, that no one can escape unless he deny himself entrance into the second half of life, and thus the continual ongoing creation of the self.[33]

29. Janice Brewi and Anne Brennan, *Mid-Life: Psychological and Spiritual Perspectives,* pp. 31–32.
30. Sheehy, p. 372.
31. Cyril D. Garrett, "Middle-Age Shadows and Adolescent Personas," *Baptist Leader* 43, no. 3 (June 1981):2–4.
32. Ibid.
33. Brewi and Brennan, p. 47.

Besides the inward forces, social pressures escalate the ferocity of the conflict. "Although individuation is a natural process, our culture and society does not foster it; rather, it almost denies it."[34]

Yet Jung speaks of the crisis in spiritual optimistic terms: "It is a veritable gold mine if the middle aged person sees the struggle as God's way of giving us another chance to rethink as middle-aged persons the decisions we so easily made and accepted in adolescence."[35] For Jung and his followers, life begins at forty, because only then can one find true life. It is no wonder that so many writers paint the mid-life period in radiant colors and speak of it in upbeat terms. It is a once-in-a-lifetime opportunity to become the new, authentic person one was meant to be.

MIDDLE OR MUDDLE

Is mid-life so great? Is it a curse or a chance? A time to cut loose or settle down? Are the inner yearnings God's call or the flesh's temptation? How should the Christian respond to mid-life turmoil—if it comes?

The evangelical cannot respond to it with the same gusto of many of our contemporaries. Scripture does not permit us to place such confidence in those inward voices. We have a Word from outside ourselves to guide our lives. It, not self, is a lamp to our feet and a light to our path.

Those who cut themselves loose from the authority of Scripture are quick to reach for authority in the self. Those who do so in the name of Christianity are not too convincing when they try to undergird it theologically.

> Responding to the increased awareness and consciousness is responding to the reality of the coming Kingdom of God. . . . Can we say that John's baptism of Jesus and the temptations of Christ sacramentalize for us this mid-life crisis and transition? Jesus refers to spiritual rebirth often and that is what the mid-life transition is. Jung tells us that every mid-life crisis is a spiritual crisis. We are called to die to the self (ego) and the fruit of the first half of life and liberate the new man or woman within us.[36]

Brewi and Brennan's theological position permits them to be very loose in interpreting and applying Scripture.

Evangelicals believe that Scripture commands conformity to Jesus Christ. His example is the authority. Though certain inner desires and values are true to God's purpose, the true guide is external, found in the revelation of God's Word and Son.

Therefore evangelicals recognize the peril of locating authority within the self. Although created in the image of God, man is also plagued by a sinful nature. God's truth enables man to discern what is right and wrong about himself. Talents, ambitions, desires, and yearnings must be sorted out, not surrendered to.

---

34. Ibid. Their comments are based on C. G. Jung, *Modern Man in Search of a Soul,* p. 108.
35. Garrett, p. 4.
36. Brewi and Brennan, p. 19.

Even some non-Christians are critical of those developmentalists who want to make self the measure of all things. Critics of such extreme individualism call it selfishness. Self-fulfillment and self-actualization are, according to one, a new form of narcissism.[37]

The Christian cannot recklessly abandon the first half of life. He will not be convinced that his earlier life was built on a betrayal of the self. The Christian knows that God guides through circumstances as well as through inner consciousness. Granted, it is not always a simple matter to judge what God's will is. Yet a Christian cannot condone deserting commitments made in the past in order to pursue some inner part of oneself. Mid-lifers—as has already been seen—often leave a lot of havoc in their path when they make radical changes on that basis. The Christian will weigh the risk to others as well as examine such changes in the light of God's Word.

The man who has judged his wife inadequate to fulfill his dreams must think carefully about separating from her. The woman who has sacrificed a writing career to be a parent will need to be cautious about deciding the parental role was something forced upon her. Behind life's circumstances is a sovereign God who works all things after the council of His own will. We cannot agree with those who say that the power and direction of life is resident within us.

THE OTHER SIDE OF THE MIDDLE

On the other hand, it would be wrong to ignore the potential of mid-life. For a believer, it offers new horizons. God gives us a new vantage point from which to see life. Scripture tells us to review life constantly. "So teach us to number our days," said the Psalmist (Ps. 90:12). We should count our days because our days count. The halfway point is a chance to reassess, readjust and renew. The Christian looks back with gratitude, ahead with hope. "Act like men, be strong," said the apostle Paul (1 Cor. 16:13). Life is a challenge. Though we are subject to its limitations, demands, and pressures, we are still, as Christians, in possession of some control. Although we do accept certain circumstances, we must not so easily submit to being unnecessarily hedged in, excusing our unwillingness to change by appealing to God's sovereignty or predestination. Whatever our lot, Some potential for change lies in it. We can grow and not allow ourselves to stagnate. "Afflicted . . . but not crushed; perplexed, but not despairing; . . . struck down, but not destroyed" (2 Cor. 4:8-9), we should take life head on.

Renewal. Mid-life offers a chance to change. If Jung and others are correct, the mid-life person is more in touch with all parts of himself than at any other time. Instinct, values, and feelings repressed in young adulthood now have a chance to reassert themselves. Some of those had been laid aside for selfish or ambitious reasons. The love of people may have given way to the love of possessions, and entanglement with a job, for example. Some of the repressed values may be priceless: the desire to love others, to appreciate life, to serve God. With a new capacity

37. Christopher Lasch, "The New Narcissism," *The New York Review of Books* 13, no. 15 (30 September 1976), pp. 5, 8, 10-13.

for discerning the true from the false, the mid-life person can launch out in new directions.

The will of God might be found in drastic changes. Mid-lifers sell their businesses or quit their jobs in order to trek off to other countries and inner cities to serve people and share Christ. The inner voice they repressed before can no longer be silenced.

Less drastic moves can be taken towards God's will. Renewal can be sought within a boring marriage or job. That too takes courage. New ventures can be added to continue commitments. Some mid-lifers add spark to life by serving others in volunteer ministries.

Authenticity. Along with change, mid-life doles out a chance for authenticity. Phoniness can be shed. The self can be faced more totally and honestly. Some studies, however, show many mid-lifers fearfully reluctant to face themselves.[38] They deny any change of perspective. They baptize the past and want to freeze time by making their own narrow world into the best possible place with as little change as possible. The path of least resistance they take is purposeless. All that matters is survival, even if mere survival has no meaning in it. The Christian ought not to stagnate. He knows God is ever transforming him into the image of Christ (2 Cor. 3:18).

Missing the opportunity to be authentic, some middle adults also fail to be intimate. Genuine relationships with others are impossible for them. Unable to be true to themselves, they cannot be truly themselves with others. They cannot even admit their own depression and disappointment because their review of the past is too painful to face. Being open with others is not possible because such a person is not open to himself. He lives within a smokescreen. Others are rarely allowed in and there is little reaching out.

The church at the crossroad. The church on the corner of this mid-life crossroad has an important role to play. Middle adults who stop there need to be alerted about the perils of haphazardly yielding themselves to repressed desires, dreams, and interests. Panic may overcome some of them. *If I don't seize the chance now, I'll never be fulfilled,* they may tell themselves. Yet while being warned about their dangers they can also be taught about the possibilities in the inner voices. We can help them maintain a continuing, exciting search for God's direction. First-half commitments need not always prevent them from launching out in new ventures. Whatever the will of God is, it is not a trap, even though many middle adults feel little freedom.

Lower class workers with little chance for new vocational ventures may especially feel that way. Their plight is a hard one. Perhaps creative fulfillment for most of them will have to be found outside their employment.

Authenticity and intimacy can comprise the most noble gifts the church can give its adults. Above all, Christians should be willing to face the truth. God's forgiveness allows them to admit past mistakes. God's grace fosters a willingness to be honest with oneself and others.

38. Farrell and Rosenberg, pp. 19, 71–72.

Being genuine means being willing to admit a mid-life upheaval if it occurs. Apparently, many members of Christ's church are embarrassed by the mid-life confusion.[39] They equate maturity with stability. When they get destabilized they wonder where their faith went. The tragedy is that they end up disguising what they are going through, pretending all is under control when inside they are seething with anxiety. Such pretense of maturity prevents maturity from happening. The person who is in the best position to grow is one who admits what is happening inside and shares the struggle in order to understand and overcome forces that might otherwise overwhelm.

Too often the Christian thinks he is to look like a victorious prize fighter. Arms and hands raised in gestures of victory, he jumps up and down amid cheering, dancing friends who crowd the ring to celebrate with him. The picture is true only insofar as it compares the Christian to a boxer (1 Cor. 9:26). But it misses the point because the Christian is still in the ring. He will be battling until Christ returns or he is taken to be with the Lord. Until then, one round after another will be fought. The middle adult round can be a heated one. But, attuned to self and sensitive to the Lord's presence, the middle adult can grow stronger and move closer toward the "prize of the upward call of God in Christ Jesus" (Phil. 3:14).

---

39. Evelyn Eaton Whitehead and James D. Whitehead, "Retirement," in *Ministry with the Aging*, ed. William C. Clements, p. 159.

12

Changing Lanes:
Generativity and Polarities

GENERATIVITY

I am the kind that stops to help when I spot a stranded driver with a broken-down car. It is no imposition. It is fun. I really like doing it. When someone tries to pay me for a battery jump or some other aid, I say, "No, I'm just paying back my debt to humanity." Driving old cars while I worked my way through college and seminary, I hardly suspected a car could go between oil changes without breaking down. The scores of times I was stranded and then helped by some stranger are my "debt."

Now a middle adult, I look at a lot of what I do in that way. When my wife and I buy my son a watch, I remember when my Dad bought one for me. The checks we send to someone in need remind me of the ones that rescued us during seminary days.

Most middle adults think the same way. Researcher George Vaillant calls it a mid-life coping mechanism. Those he judges to have the "best outcome" in middle age are those who give themselves "back to the world." Those he judges to have the "worst outcome" are those who are less willing to assume responsibility for other adults.[1]

Generativity is the name Erikson gives to this "concern in establishing and guiding the next generation."[2] Remembering that Erikson's scheme is built upon the sexual nature of persons, it is not hard to see how logical his concept is. Producing a child gives way to a concern for its care (generativity). But it is also included in the broader psychosocial schedule (evolutionary for Erikson), since the continuation of human life depends upon one generation's teaching and caring for the younger one. Nurturing children is only part of the way generativity is expressed. Adults who do not have children may develop generativity; some adults who do give birth may not. Generativity

1. George E. Vaillant, *Adaptation to Life*, p. 350.
2. Erik Erikson, *Childhood and Society*, p. 267.

refers to the middle adult's acceptance of responsibility for serving and ministering to the coming generation. This can be expressed through vocation. Think of how some people refer to a creative project as "my baby."

Humanity needs the generative middle adult, but middle adults also need humanity. "Mature man needs to be needed, and maturity needs guidance as well as encouragement from what has been produced and must be taken care of."[3]

Competence and experience combine in middle adults to place them in positions of authority. The desire for responsibility, willingness to assume leadership and ability to take control are crucial motivators for them. The person who moves through the mid-life crisis successfully emerges as a caring individual. Who he is and what he is to accomplish must be determined anew. Adults who fail to face themselves (and subsequently do not develop generativity) become stagnant. Worse than merely feeling they are making no worthwhile contribution, they turn to an "obsessive need for pseudo-intimacy." They cannot be honest with themselves or others. A gnawing sense of personal impoverishment plagues them.[4]

Sheehy paints a tragic portrait of an executive manager who fails to reevaluate and adjust in midstream.

> A man in this familiar stage, feeling unappreciated and unutterably valueless, often keeps the tears inside; they are shunted into ulcers and covered by accumulations of overweight. He sits in restaurants eating and swelling, saying he shouldn't, 'but just this time,' and slowly committing suicide. Anyone who challenges him to reconsider his priorities—a wife, a friend, a management consultant—becomes the enemy. He may try every form of self-delusion, retreat into drinking or hypochondria, cast his wife as a monster, abandon his family, almost anything to forestall looking into the mess inside. For if he were to examine one-tenth of what is making him miserable, he would know too much to ignore the other nine-tenths. And that would mean changing so many circumstances of his old life structure, he might prefer not to look at all.[5]

Generativity includes a realization that there is "nobody here but us." The middle adult senses that *he* is now responsible for his world—not the older adults anymore, who have become dependent on him. It is fearful, that feeling of being in charge. During young adulthood he was aware of having a personal impact on the world. Now, the contribution is wedded to a heavy sense of responsibility. Both accountability ("I am responsible for what I have done") and care ("I have responsibility for what I have created") come into perspective.[6]

The creativity of young adulthood is distinct from the generativity in middle adulthood in another way. Generativity is not merely being productive or creative. It involves nurturing others. In other words, productivity and creativity must be directed toward the development of others. Earlier creative expressions were dominated by

3. Ibid.
4. Ibid.
5. Gail Sheehy, *Passages*, p. 408.
6. Evelyn Eaton Whitehead and James D. Whitehad, *Christian Life Patterns*, p. 128.

what others expected and the desire to prove one's adequacy. Generativity absorbs (but does not do away with) the impulses to prove oneself and express oneself into the capacity to give of oneself.[7]

It is surprising that this results in less desire to control those who are being nurtured. That is because the middle adult does not look at them as extensions of himself. The more generative person invests in others for their own sake. A certain respect for the life course of others is present. Nurturing is not done "in one's own image," but in the potential image of the one being supported and trained. Nobel prize winner Subrahmanyan Chandrasekhar typifies the sacrifice involved. "In the 1940's, Chandrasekhar drove to the campus [University of Chicago] from the Yerkes Observatory for weeks on end to teach a class of only two students. Some of his colleagues wondered why he bothered. Ten years later, both those students, Tsung Doa-lee and Chen Ning-yang, won Nobel prizes in physics."[8]

The mature adult often accepts responsibilities in situations and for people that he has not chosen. He becomes dependable because others depend upon him.[9] The young adult may lack such willingness to accept what he did not choose. A young professor may, for example, pour his life into his students because they represent the furthering of his own achievement. The older professor, less concerned about furthering himself, may offer assistance, guidance, and support to those he may not have chosen and who may never represent him in any way.

The parent of a teenager must develop such an attitude. The teenager must be supported to grow "according to his way," instead of shaped into an extension of the parent's identity, ambitions, and desires. That then, is truly nurturing for nurturing's sake.

Part of this ability to "let go" comes from the middle adult's realization that he cannot control the world—or even his own world. Though humbling, the realization also brings relief. One middle adult said in a discussion about security: "I feel most secure when in a difficult situation I suddenly realize I cannot control it. I get a sense of relief that there is nothing I can do but simply trust."

Such detachment is a mark of maturity according to Erikson. At its core is acceptance. While the mature adult often has mastery of situations, he also senses the "mastery" in accepting. Growing awareness of his own limits brings that on. "Often it seems that in the significant areas of adult life—in marriage, family, career, health, friendship—the demand for creative acceptance is as great as that for active choice."[10]

Generativity is, of course, crucial for both men and women. The generative task has many forms. Lowenthal and her colleagues found that problems of middle-age women cluster around this. Most of the women studied were experiencing "heightened marital dissatisfaction." They determined that was not due to the onset of menopause or the "empty nest" but rather because of the issue of generativity. If a woman only thought of her contribution in terms of the family, she was more apt to be upset by life

7. Ibid., p. 130.
8. "U. of C. Prof Wins Nobel Prize," *Chicago Tribune,* 20 October 1983.
9. Erik Erikson, *Identity, Youth and Crisis,* p. 138.
10. Whitehead and Whitehead, p. 135.

changes. For her the challenge was to discover new areas for her nurturing energies.[11]

The possibilities of this generative stage are enormous—for the individual, the church, and society. Leadership lies here. Vaillant puts it this way:

> Almost always, full leadership involves a shift in career focus. Instead of delving progressively deeper into their specialized careers and acquiring progressively more competence, in middle life the men's career patterns suddenly diverged and broadened; they assumed tasks that they had not been trained for. Being truly responsible for others was not the job for the specialist.[12]

These traits—unselfish creativity, acceptance, without the compulsion to control, and broader concerns—are marks of mature Christian leadership. The church should be a virtual greenhouse in which middle adults flourish.

To be such a place, clergy will need to permit middle adults to contribute. If the structure of the church and the understanding of ministry do not allow for generative participation, middle adults are stifled.[13] The apostle Paul warned against that in 1 Thessalonians 5:19: "Do not quench the Spirit." Early church leaders were apparently not permitting some people to speak, thus inhibiting the Spirit's work. Allowing adult participation and resisting being a dictator demands trust in the Holy Spirit. Ministers who fail to rely on Him believe they must keep things in hand themselves. Many apparently have not made their way to maturity. Because of that, others are a threat to their control and authority. Such a person may fail to negotiate the mid-life passage by not being willing to give up or share control. The Farrell and Rosenberg study showed the tendency for some men in mid-life to become increasingly authoritarian. Apparently, such persons have become stuck at the young adult stage. They are accustomed to the blend of care and control appropriate to their thirties. They essentially are ill-equipped to hand on adult responsibility to the next generation.[14]

A whole church can be characterized by such immaturity. Their only interest lies in reproducing the next generation in their own image. Young adults sense they are only being used, not nurtured. Their own creativity is all but smothered by being beaten and squeezed to fit the "mold."

A conservative pastor can easily fall prey to that. As defender of the faith, he justifies the extension of his control into all the life of the church. His loving and caring manner may mask his dictatorial ways. Biblical metaphors can even be employed to soften what is going on. The members of the congregation are referred to as "sheep" or "the children of God." He characterizes them as "dumb sheep" or "overgrown children." But, "while rejoicing in their status of children of God, . . . adults do not fare well as children of the clergy."[15] The dependency is a hazard to

---

11. Marjorie Fiske Lowenthal et al, *Four Stages of Life,* p. 226.
12. Vaillant, p. 227.
13. Whitehead and Whitehead, p. 153.
14. Michael P. Farrell and Stanley D. Rosenberg, *Men at Midlife,* pp. 83–84; Whitehead and Whitehead, p. 154.
15. Whitehead and Whitehead, p. 154.

adults' spiritual as well as psychological growth. Though the pastor may say he is doing it for spiritual ends, his motivation may be a yearning to reproduce himself.

The dependency risk is less for the young adult who generally is not ready for complete independence. Young adults are mentor oriented. That is, they seek out an older adult who will nurture and support them. The mentor, however, must be careful since the attachment can be quite tenacious. The young adult may imitate the mentor's capacities rather than develop his own, resulting in dissatisfaction with himself. Some discipling programs exploit the mentor relationship by insisting too much on conformity. The discipler is trying to develop little *Pauls* rather than *Timothys*. Evangelical groups sometimes talk of "reproducing yourself," conveying the wrong idea of what it means to disciple someone else. Certainly, it is not wrong to urge others to imitate positive characteristics as Paul did. But such imitation should involve the broader aspects of Christian character and behavior and not include too specific compliance to the discipler's practices and personality. Groups that urge leaders to "pour yourself into someone" may be in danger of treating the disciple as an empty vessel instead of a developing person. An effective mentor is one who can care for the young person without needing to manipulate. Generative care is coupled with detachment. Knowing that the young person's growth will soon lead far beyond the mentor's influence and care, the mentor who cares is prepared to let go.[16]

For that reason, programs and institutions that blossom among young adults may have trouble taking root among the middle-aged in most churches. Middle adults are not subject to the same approach that is successful with young adults. Internally, middle adults are being pressured to broaden their outlook, to lesson their control over others. Feeling less the need to make people after their own kind they also resist those who would do that to them. They will resist church and discipling programs that are marked by rigidity and conformity. Such programs flourish among young adults. Parachurch organizations like the Navigators and Campus Crusade for Christ have discovered that. The methods and materials effectively forged in young adult ministry do not work well with middle and older adults.

That may also account for the fact that many leaders do not remain in those groups after reaching their middle adult years. They no longer have the inner capacity for the leadership style demanded by the inflexible approach to disciple making. They yearn for a climate of freedom for themselves; but they also want to bestow on others the freedom to mature in Christ according to His image, not theirs.

It may also be possible that the difference between young and middle adults may explain another phenomena. Young adult parachurch groups tend to criticize the church. Although many reasons may underlie this, the different perspective in regard to control may be a cause. So much of their criticism boils down to the statement "The church is not like us." The church does not witness (the way we do); it does not pray (the way we do); it does not teach its members to memorize Scripture (as we do), and so forth. Those groups often fail to recognize the many forms Christian maturity takes, being convinced that conformity to its way of life is true discipleship.

16. Ibid., p. 146.

FOUR POLARITIES

When I went to Sunday school, the junior high class was called the *intermediate* class. Since then, someone realized how unfair that title was. An intermediate is someone "in between." In that case, between being a child and being an adult. It rightly puts a person in the middle, but it wrongly leaves the youth without any sense of identity. And since identity is such a major problem of that age anyway, some kind person said, "Let's not add to their problem by calling them intermediates."

Middle adults are somewhat in the same position. No longer young, they are also not yet old. Possibly, they are at the best stage of life. But some theorists contend that they sometimes feel their "in between" status.

Jung portrayed the middle adult in a state of tension. Old and young, for example, are polarities. Throughout the middle years, the adult somehow puts the two together to form some sense of self.[17]

Levinson acknowledges that polarities exist during the entire life cycle. They are worked on in all stages of adult life although they can never be fully resolved. Though not specific to the mid-life transition, they operate here with special force.[18]

YOUNG/OLD POLARITY

> At mid-life a man feels young in many respects, but he also has a sense of being old. He feels older than the young, but not yet ready to join the generation defined as *middle aged.* He feels alternately young, old and 'in between.' His developmental task is to make sense of this condition and become young/old in a new way.[19]

As early adulthood comes to an end, new fears regarding the loss of youth grip a person. Physical decline signals this most markedly. A doctor may detect a slight loss of hearing. An optometrist may explain the need for eye glasses is now due to changes in the eye ("old lens just isn't as elastic as it was"). Tennis games may produce new and more aches and pains. A major illness may threaten life, causing an increased awareness of eventual death. The new perspective may alarm the mid-lifer. He is coming to grips with aging, which means coming to terms with mortality.

The sense of aging is not just a physical matter. Actually, physical decline is normally quite moderate. Capacities are quite adequate for successful living. The *reaction* to the physical loss is what is troublesome. "He feels that the young— variously represented as the child, the adolescent and the youthful adult in himself—is dying. The imagery of old age and death hangs over him like a pall."[20]

The reactions may turn the person in a number of directions. Concern for success and contribution may overwhelm. Fear of death may become gripping. Levinson theorizes that those reactions are due to the wish for immortality. It may drive a

17. Daniel J. Levinson, *Seasons of a Man's Life*, pp. 209–13.
18. Levinson, p. 227.
19. Ibid., p. 197.
20. Ibid., p. 213.

person to be overly concerned about leaving a mark on the world. Or it may turn a person to a search for meaning in life. "He often feels that his life until now has been wasted. Even if in cooler moments, he finds some redeeming qualities, he is still likely to feel that his life has not enough accrued value."[21]

Little inner fire may be left for the rest of life if the middle adult does not deal adequately with this tension. Such men often die in their forties or fifties. Illness, accident, or alcoholism may be the immediate cause. The basic cause is that one finds no spice to life—"he just withers away."[22]

Howard Hughes was a dramatic example. From a small fortune, he built a fantastic empire. At the end, with all his power, he died of starvation, disease, and emotional isolation. He could invest his money with great profit, but he could not invest his life in any enterprise or obtain psychic income from it. "He finally suffocated within the cocoon he had built around himself."[23] Novels also provide examples of middle adult decline: Eugene O'Neill's *The Iceman Cometh;* Lillian Hellman's play *The Autumn Garden;* Saul Bellow's *Herzog.*

Resolving the young/old polarity is mainly the painful process of coming to terms with one's mortality. At first blush, it may appear that the Christian would have little trouble with this. Hebrews 2:15 assures that Christ came that He "might deliver those who through fear of death were subject to slavery all their lives." The promise of immortality should put an end to the fear of death and mortality.

Mortality might not concern mid-lifers if their fear were only centered in eternity. Their anxiety, though, relates more to this life than the next. Confronted by the stark reality that one's life may soon be over, they are pressed to think not only of the next life but of the rest of this life.

On Christians facing death. Annie Dillard knows how the promise of eternal life does not remove death's threat.

> Agnostics don't know what in the world is going on. They think religion is safety when in fact they have the safety. To an agnostic you have to say over and over again that the fear of death doesn't lead you to love God. Love of God leads you to fear of death.
>
> Agnostics often think that people run to God because they are afraid of dying. On the contrary, the biblical religion is not a safe thing. People in the Bible understood the transitory nature—the risk—of life better than most people. They weren't using religion as an escape hatch. Faith forces you to constant awareness of final things. Agnostics don't remember all the time that they're going to die. But Christians do remember. All our actions in this life must be affected by God's point of view.[24]

Whether one has hope of eternal life or not, one still asks, "What have I made of this life?" In fact, the Christian who must someday stand before Christ may be even

---

21. Ibid., pp. 215–16.
22. Ibid., p. 216.
23. Ibid.
24. Annie Dillard as interviewed by Philip Yancey, *Open Windows,* pp. 143–44.

more concerned about that question. The middle adult could be haunted by the couplet

> Only one life, 'twill soon be past;
> Only what's done for Christ will last.

To resolve that issue, middle adults will first need the assurance of forgiveness for failures and sins of the first half of life. Second, they will need to take advantage of the opportunities of the second half. They will learn they can still function effectively with all the youthful assets they had earlier. Third, they will need to use Christian values in their personal assessment. Levinson notes that the "image of legacy" tends to flourish during the mid-life transition as part of the work of the young/old polarity. Legacy is what one passes on to future generations: material possessions, creative products, enterprises, influence on others. Because people differ greatly in their views of a legacy, Christians will need to formulate views in accordance with biblical standards. Personal circumstances and gifts will be taken into account. God's will may include passing on material things; an estate may be parceled out to Christian institutions. More than just material goods, a legacy is also found in children, in people won to Christ, in faithful support of missions, in social ministry. If Levinson is right, the middle adult who thinks rightly about a legacy could experience a new-found altruism. The middle adult cares more about the well-being of his community, religious organization, college, union, or professional society. . . . "The altruism is, in part a vehicle for the search for immortality."[25]

Mid-lifers will need to be realistic about the legacy matter. The heightened sense of responsibility may not be coupled with greater opportunity or ability. Working-class men and women may feel trapped, unable to break out, or to have much energy left over for extra service. A middle adult may be struck with an acute need to evangelize but discover he has little gift in winning others to Christ. Leaving fine Christian offspring to the world may also be a burden. Parents may become too preoccupied with "how the children are doing" because those children are part of the legacy. "No man who truly cares about his fatherhood can be without those feelings," Levinson claims. The realization that one continues to live through the children enriches life. But if one concentrates too much on that, it can lead to extreme disillusionment since children do not always live up to parents' expectations. If a middle adult pressures his adult children in order to resolve his own feelings about immortality, the results can be disastrous. "They [the feelings] become an albatross around the neck of both parent and offspring."[26]

DESTRUCTION/CREATION POLARITY

Some people in middle age may go through intense periods of suffering, confusion, and rage against others or against themselves. Those are reactions to the acute

25. Levinson, p. 218-19.
26. Ibid.

awareness of the destructive side of life and of themselves. Everyone, even a child, recognizes that there is a painful, ruinous side of life. In nature, animals survive by capturing and killing. Religions and philosophies try to reconcile those seemingly disparate forces of nature: creativity and destruction.

Middle adults, however, seem to face the tension between those two in a new way. Part of the pressure is, no doubt, brought on by the urgent drive to create, to produce. The newly awakened desire is met head on by the forces of life that are there to blot out, to annihilate. Or it may be the other way around: the new awareness of the destructive may produce the desire to create. Both seem related to concern over the impending end of life.[27]

Perhaps it is the middle ager's own physical ills and limitations that make him more attuned to this side of life. Those close to him are more likely to experience loss. Parents, now in their sixties or seventies, are subject to disease and death. Many more people, it seems, are dying or becoming seriously ill. There are more accidents and heart attacks, more divorces, depressions, alcoholism, job failures, troubles with children or parents, suffering of all kinds. It is not suffering, however, that has increased but the middle adult's awareness of it.

He may aim resentment and anger at himself as his sensitivity sheds light on his own destructive impulses and actions. Harmful and painful results of past actions involving parents, children, friends, and colleagues who have been hurt by his mistakes, failure, and anger will come to mind. He may need a great deal of forgiveness. Believing by faith that God has forgiven, the mid-lifer will still probably struggle with forgiving himself.

Forgiving others will also be on the agenda. The new consciousness unveils how others have harmed him. "Vaillant found many of his subjects reworking their relationship with their parents during the mid-forties."[28] Part of that included becoming aware of their own animosity toward them.

Not all middle adults will be conscious of the struggle. Much of the reworking of painful feelings may be done at an unconscious level. "Many men have no awareness that they have done harm to others or might live to do so. Others feel so guilty over the real or imagined damage they have inflicted that they cannot see the issue of destructiveness in its true perspective."[29]

Ministry at this time must be realistic if the church is to help adults with this tension. Preaching or teaching that ignores the tragic will not help. Many apparently cope with this mid-life awareness of the destructive by denying it. They build an unreal world around themselves that becomes a narrow, confined prison they fear to leave. The Christian has an advantage. He can face the evil and ugly in life knowing Christ will some day bring victory. The church must preach victory but also be honest about suffering and defeat. Trying to foster faith, a good balance between stark honesty and encouragement is not always achieved by the church. Attention is called to dramatic

27. Ibid., pp. 222–23.
28. Whitehead and Whitehead, p. 143.
29. Naomi Golan, *Passing Through Transitions*, p. 121.

answers to prayer: a sick person gets well or a family is saved from a serious accident. But the fact that some we pray for die and others perish in fiery crashes is often not adequately handled. Theology for the middle adult must reckon with both sides. No power of positive thinking that ignores life's suffering can suffice. The inward raging must be dealt with. The middle adult must emerge with a new desire to continue creative involvement despite the evil within and outside himself.

MASCULINE/FEMININE POLARITY

Although some explanation is given for the forcefulness of the other tensions, none is given for the presence of the masculine/feminine polarity. Levinson maintains that the middle adult must come more fully to terms with the co-existence of masculine and feminine parts of the self than with any of the other tensions.

The polarity is tied up with aspects of gender identity that prevail in this culture. The men in Levinson's study tended to distinguish masculine/feminine traits as follows:

Male	Female
Bodily power and toughness	Frail, weak, vulnerable to attack
Responsible for achievement and ambition	Responsible for home related activities
Logical, reasonable, analytical, repress emotions	Emotional, intuitive, makes decisions on basis of feeling, express feelings[30]

The meanings of masculinity and femininity will probably be rethought. A man learns to value and admit to the "feminine" traits: expressing feelings, being sensitive to others, admitting weaknesses. Formerly, these aspects were probably repressed in his drive toward achievement. A middle-aged woman, on the other hand, may exhibit more of the supposed masculine traits: more attention given to the external world and accomplishment, for example. She may be assertive in ways she previously thought were unwomanly.[31]

Integrating the male and female sides is not exactly equal to balancing them. One does not merely drop masculine traits for more feminine ones or vice versa. A man, for instance, may express himself more forcefully in what he thinks are masculine ways as the result of being more comfortable with the gentle, more feminine, side of himself. He is more willing to be assertive because he is not afraid of losing control or of hurting people.

The tendency in middle age toward male-female role reversals is supported by much of the literature. Jung observes that the middle-aged husband discovers his tender feelings, and the wife her sharpness of mind.[32] It is the change in social task that

30. Levinson, pp. 228–29.
31. Whitehead and Whitehead, p. 144.
32. Carl G. Jung, "The Stages of Life," in *The Portable Jung,* ed. J. Campbell, p. 16.

causes the shift. Men's careers have plateaued; they have more time for deeper relationships. The children have left home, allowing the wife more time for independent activities. In a study of personality change with white urban men and women aged forty-seven, a researcher found that in later life men put more stress on self-control, friendly adaptation, and passivity; women become more egocentric, impulsive, and directly aggressive.[33]

Sam Keen notes a possible intellectual difference. In mid-life, a woman may move toward more order and logic in her thinking. A man may become more willing to live without explaining everything, becoming more patient with contradiction and paradox.[34]

A man may change his view of women, including his mother and his wife. Some maintain that in early adulthood a man normally carries within himself a little boy and a mother engaged in a complex relationship. The mother may symbolize a powerful source of care and protection; an enemy who can deprive, smother, or destroy; or even a weak figure who may abandon him or leave him open to assult from a vengeful father. During the mid-life passage, a man can partially free himself from those images and their anxieties. Less afraid of a woman's power to withhold, devour, and seduce, he can give more of himself, receive more from women, and accept greater independence on the part of women in his life.[35] A man may be more able to have true friendship relationships with other women, sexual differences neither attracting or repelling. He may function as a mentor to women in a more healthy, mature way. As pastor, elder, or teacher in the church, he may be in a better position to minister to women than in earlier years.

A woman in mid-life may become more inclined to control whereas previously she tended to surrender. Personal goals may replace the earlier care-giver role.

Something wonderfully rewarding may be happening to middle-aged married couples. Their personalities may be blending in a new and remarkable balance. The husband's new desire for the intimate (with the sexual) may stimulate his wife's awareness of her femininity, creating a virtual honeymoon during the early fifties. In turn, the wife's new assertiveness is not the threat to her husband's masculinity it once may have been. Her new interest in the world outside may make her more of a pleasant companion to him. She will discover that his new regard for dreams, sensation, and intuition makes him a better friend. Less a "knower, warrior, controller," he is decidedly a better lover.

The church can help mid-lifers in their struggle to deal with the masculine and feminine in themselves. It can hold up the complete view of male and female and resist the neat categories taught by Western culture. It can escape the worldly tendency to degrade traits that are labeled "feminine." Jesus, though fully man, showed some of those. He rejected the use of raw power, refused to repress His feelings, was gentle, sensitive, empathetic. He publicly wept—an act that might prevent election to public office today.

33. Sharan Merriam, "Professional Literature on Middle Age," p. 9.
34. Jim Fowler and Sam Keen, *Life Maps,* p. 115.
35. Levinson, p. 237.

Many men in mid-life refuse to accept their so-called feminine side. They entrench themselves in their masculine ways. One symptom of that is the fact that intimacy is such a major problem for them.[36] Because they refuse to be honest with themselves, they cannot be honest with others. Unable to squarely face their depression and disappointment, they lash out critically at others, while continuing in empty involvement with the externals of life. They live out the lyrics "Life goes on, after the thrill of living is gone." Sharing their grief, sorrow, and anxieties with others would enable them to cope with their emotions. The church can try to meet their need by making honesty and intimacy part of its life. Scriptural teaching and examples that urge Christians to "speak the truth in love" demand that whatever else the church is, it is to be real.

The masculine-feminine polarity of mid-life is part of another church issue: the closeness of male-female relationships. Caution is rightly exercised about fostering close contact between adults of the opposite sex that might occasion temptation. Yet there is a growing need for legitimate intimacy in male-female relationships, particularly where single adults are concerned. The number of single adults in the United States will soon surpass the number of married adults. Many singles are divorced or widowed. They (and their children when present) badly need exposure to Christian adults of the opposite sex. Mature middle adults, who have successfully adjusted to their own sexuality, can be spiritual brothers and sisters to such people. Many churches train elders to be shepherds of small groups. Elders and their wives support and serve single women and men in wholesome ways. The possibilities for such support ministries should not be lost midst our concern for avoiding sexual affairs. The tendency to stereotype middle adults as sexually immature because some fall into immorality should be resisted. Research shows that mid-life has the potential for genuine relationships with the opposite sex, less complicated by the sexual inuendos of previous years.

ATTACHMENT/SEPARATENESS POLARITY

This polarity sets the external world on one side, the internal on the other. Attachment refers to being plugged into the environment; separateness to being engaged in the inner world of imagination, fantasy, and play. In young adulthood attachment dominates the life pattern.[37] Life itself, for the man in particular, pushes in that direction. Family matters, occupation, and financial concerns make it difficult for him to find time for solitude, play, and quiet renewal. Goals are attained at the expense of the internal self. Perhaps it is the change in circumstances that makes some men sense the urgency of the internal. Goals are attained or changed, and family becomes less demanding. At any rate, the middle adult begins to fill up the *separateness* side of the balance sheet.

In her extensive study, Bernice Neugarten observed that, with certainty, one word can be written over middle adults: *interiority.* Assertiveness and mastery of the

36. Farrell and Rosenberg, pp. 76 and 215.
37. Levinson, p. 241.

environment creates that internalization.[38] Part of that involves spending time on re-examination, mentioned earlier. "To do the work of reappraisal and de-illusionment, he must run inward." He has to discover what turmoil is about and where it hurts. He wants to find and lick his wounds. Having been overly engaged in the worldly struggles, he needs to become more engaged with himself.[39]

In the process, self becomes as important as the external world.[40] As a result, the person may remove himself from group affiliations. He becomes more critical of those institutions and their traditions since he is more detached from them but can also appreciate the good in them without having a need for the rewards offered or the activities provided. Because of that, a middle adult may do something quite significant: he may attempt some reconciliation with family values or groups from which he broke away in young adulthood.

Separateness does not necessarily reduce the person's engagement in life. Rather, the external and internal worlds become integrated. A major developmental task of the middle adult is to find a better balance between self's needs and society's needs.[41]

The church's involvement in this tension is crucial. Theoretically, middle adults are ripe for evangelism. Internalizing may lead them to spiritual matters. The new appreciation of the past may make the middle adult take a second look at the church and values he rejected earlier.

Middle adults who are in the church may need lots of support in thinking through faith issues. Those who came to Christ out of a non-Christian background may be having second thoughts about their earlier decisions. They may be expected to be rethinking their past commitments and looking for answers. It must not be assumed that a Christian is settled in his faith merely because of long involvement in the church. Books, classes, and sermons that touch on church history, apologetics, and comparative religion may be crucial to them. In his preliminary study Cobble did not find many middle adults interested in the intellectual aspects of faith.[42] Theoretically, that is difficult to believe. What he may have uncovered is that middle adults may be questioning their faith but not looking for intellectual answers. They may be testing it in other more experiential ways. Such a pragmatic approach can be dangerous. Middle adults need to be prodded to go beyond the "Does it work?" question to the more theological "Is it true?" Above all, it is important to listen carefully to them to find out what they are asking or what they are afraid to ask. It is hoped that more can be learned about the patterns middle adults are following in their new search for meaning.

38. Bernice L. Neugarten, "The Awareness of Middle Age," in *Middle Age and Aging,* ed. Bernice L. Neugarten, pp. 94–96.
39. Levinson, p. 241.
40. Ibid., p. 242.
41. Ibid., p. 241.
42. James Cobble, unpublished manuscript, 1983.

13

In the Savage Woods: Faith Development

Dante, in his *Divine Comedy,* wrote:

> Upon the journey of our life midway
>   I came unto myself in a dark wood,
> For from the straight path I had gone astray.
> Ah, how is hard the telling what a drear
>   And savage and entangled wood it was,
> That in the very thought renews the fear!
> So bitter is it death is little more.[1]

Some middle adults, like Dante, stumble in the savage woods. Even their former faith fails to keep them on a straight path.

THE STAGE FOUR UPHEAVAL

Does middle age offer a special sort of spiritual challenge? Do mid-lifers discover a new way of looking at God? Because of this, is there a mid-life dropout phenomenon in our churches? Or are the changes mostly for the better? Levinson reports that the typical middle-aged man changes his spiritual outlook. "His spirituality may take the form of an explicit religious doctrine, but often he tries to free himself from formal doctrine in order to attain a personal understanding of what it means to be human."[2]

Fowler agrees that mid-life can occasion some dramatic changes in faith. It is usually not until middle age that a person can reach stage five in Fowler's six-stage faith

1. Jefferson Butler Fletcher, trans., *The Divine Comedy of Dante Alighier* (New York: Columbia U., 1931), canto 1, lines 1–9.
2. Daniel J. Levinson, *Seasons of a Man's Life,* p. 242.

development ladder. Controversial and not fully substantiated, Fowler's scheme includes a unique summary of mid-life faith. A discussion of stages four and five of Fowler's theory follows.

STAGE FOUR FAITH

Essentially, stage four represents an internalization of one's identity and world view, usually taking place during young adulthood. No longer does a person hold values and beliefs merely because of identity with some circle of significant others. Rather, faith is made one's own. That is due to a number of features in a person's development. First, he is able to think about abstract concepts in a logical way. (This ability, is comparable to Piaget's level of formal operations discussed on pages 76-77.) This makes it possible for a person to critically reflect upon himself and his group[3] and "to differentiate himself or herself from others and to hammer out an independent perspective."[4] In other words, the stage four person will give you reasons he believes in God; a stage three person might merely say something like, "Well, I have been a Methodist for many years and everyone in my church believes in Him."

The stage four person has the capacity to see that there are other systems of belief around and looks inside to make some judgment about which to accept. He is not content to live with a lot of mystery about why or what he believes; he wants some answers.

The stage four person's perspective of self and others also undergoes a change. He is not only able to concentrate on looking at himself objectively; he is conscious that others are also doing that to him and judging him in the process. Thus, he must examine his beliefs in the light of what others say about them.[5]

Change also takes place in the area of authority. Authorities are judged by whether or not they fit the stage four person's view of reality. The pastor is no longer an authority merely because his church ordained him. Rather, the pastor must prove what he has to say in a way that fits the stage four person's perceptions. In other words, the stage four person's authority is inside himself. "Truth must 'fit' with other elements of one's outlook taken as a whole."[6] Any act of judgment involves the whole person, the emotional as well as the intellectual.

As the stage four person defends his position against other groups, he may tend to caricature them. That is due to the fact that he has a psychological drive to justify and preserve the boundaries of his own and his group's truth perspectives. Fowler holds that that distortion of others' viewpoints is done unconsciously.[7] A person who believes in eternal security, for example, may not really listen carefully to another viewpoint.

3. James Fowler, "Stages of Faith and Adults' Life Cycles," in *Faith Development in the Adult Life Cycle*, Kenneth Stokes, ed., pp. 189-90.
4. Jim Fowler and Sam Keen, *Life Maps: Conversations on the Journey of Faith*, p. 71.
5. Ibid.
6. Ibid., p. 72.
7. Fowler, "Stages of Faith," p. 185.

UNSETTLING FACTORS

Most adults do not rise above stage four, according to Fowler. If they do, it is because certain unsettling things take place. For one thing, the stage four person becomes more conscious of the fact that he has been failing to evaluate other viewpoints carefully, without distorting them. When he begins examining them, his faith system does not look as neat as before.[8] Life appears more complex. Previously, he had ignored or compromised here and there to keep his system together. Now the person "finds him or herself attending to what may feel like anarchic and disturbing inner voices."[9] The problem with stage four is its excessive confidence in the conscious mind and in critical thought. There is a sort of self-centered faith in one's ability to organize reality and to make other people's views fit into one's point of view (by seeing them as false, for example). Fowler calls this logical defense of one position *dichotomizing*.

STAGE FIVE FAITH

Movement into stage five comes when the mid-lifer (usually older than thirty) moves to a style of thinking Fowler calls *dialogical*.[10] *That fits the title he gives to stage five: Conjunctive Faith.* The person on this level is able to be more open to the diverse ideas of others. Truth lies in embracing many positions, somehow even opposing ones. Ultimate truth lies in paradoxes. Fowler explains: "Stage five also sees, however, that the relativity of religious traditions that matters is not their relativity to each other, but their relativity—their *relativity*—to the reality to which they mediate relation." "Conjunctive faith," he continues, "is ready for significant encounters with other traditions than its own, expecting that truth has disclosed and will disclose itself in those traditions in ways that may complement or correct its own."[11]

Fowler insists that this does not mean that the stage five person lacks commitment to his own religious faith. Rather, he is open to other systems because he is confident of the truth of his own tradition. "The person of stage five makes his own experience the principle by which other claims to truth are tested. But he or she assumes that each genuine perspective will augment and correct aspects of the other, in a mutual movement toward the real and the true,"[12] The only example Fowler gives of a stage five person is "Miss T." When interviewed she was a seventy-eight year old widow. She had synthesized into her life and thinking elements of her Unitarian church background, the psychoanalyst Carl Jung, Krishnamurti, a "wonderful swami in California," and the teaching of the Quakers.

If all of this sounds like the stage five person has departed from an evangelical view of faith, that is probably right.

---

8. Fowler and Keen, p. 182.
9. Fowler, "Stages of Faith," p. 183.
10. Ibid., p. 185.
11. Ibid., p. 186.
12. Ibid.

Moran's explanation clearly shows this to be true. Speaking of the fifth stage of faith, he indicates that at this stage one no longer has a religion, one is religious in a particular way. He means, in effect, that a Christian, Jew or Muslim who arrives at this stage realizes that his doctrines, beliefs, and practices are relative. They are all on the way to something ultimate. "Someone religiously Christian recognizes someone religiously Jewish, for example, as sharing a common religious quest. Both quests can be seen as valid because the two groups are on the way even though the particularity of one's ways is what is most valued."[13] The word *particularity* refers to one's form of religion. In other words, a Catholic or Jew values his religion, but he now sees that its dogmas and practices are only symbols or parables pointing to the ultimate. "Religious language is now understood not to be a set of sacred words or a collection of texts or sacred objects but a process of using language to subvert our concepts of the ordinary world and reveal deeper truth."[14] Truth then lies in the non-rational, in the imagination, in the religious. The religious person is not irrational, but he knows that truth lies within the rational tensions or paradoxes. Truth is more multidimensional and organically interdependent than most theories or accounts of truth can grasp.[15]

In summary, truth lies in a person's religious experience. At this stage, Scripture is only symbolic, somehow pointing to ultimate truth. It does not contain cognitive statements of truth. If evangelical faith accepts the Bible's statements as truth, then Fowler's stage five is a non-evangelical rung of the ladder. That he judges C. S. Lewis, one of the most prominent defenders of evangelical faith, to be on rung four, a stage lower, shows that stage five contains a liberal viewpoint.

IS THERE A MIDDLE FAITH?

Fowler is a pioneer in his field. His stages will no doubt be used as a yardstick to measure people for years to come. Though he says his search is for educational purposes, to help people mature, he also maintains he is looking for some standard to judge the destructive features of religions. Evangelicals who hold to authority of Scripture will be considered "immature."

Though evangelicals differ with his scheme, it is still possible to learn from him. Fowler's analysis is complex and extremely insightful, using seven different subcategories to examine each stage. Perhaps something does happen to middle adults to test their firmly fixed rational faith system.

SEEING THROUGH A GLASS DARKLY

Perhaps it is the accumulated impact of half a life's experiences that causes ripples in the mid-lifer's faith. Life bats the middle adult around quite a bit, bruising his emotions and confusing his thinking. Christian friends who had great faith are killed

13. Gabriel Moran, *Religious Education Development*, p. 153.
14. Ibid., pp. 153-54.
15. Ibid., p. 186.

in a tragic accident. Stable, solid believers lose their jobs and struggle financially. Church leaders fall, without obvious warning, into immorality. All this has to be worked through. Maybe simple answers sufficed for simple times, but life no longer appears to be simple. Even if life is not more complex, it may seem to be. Perhaps Fowler is right in saying that the middle adult begins to see that truth is not so easily wrapped up into simple statements. The mid-lifer has faced paradoxes before. Now, perhaps he will apply the paradox concept to more and more of life and truth.

In one place, Fowler describes his stage five faith as "discovering that the rational solution or 'explanation' of a problem that seemed so elegant is but a painted canvas covering an intricate, endlessly intriguing cavern of surprising depth."[16] He may be on to something there. Truth, even biblical truth, for the mid-lifer may not seem so clear, so plain. He realizes that reality is not so easily bottled up in words. Fowler goes too far, though, in suggesting that the words are therefore not ultimate truth. Evangelicals believe Scripture is truth but that "we see through a glass darkly." Although the truth has been revealed, it is not understood in precisely the same dimensions as it will be known someday when "we shall see Him as He is." It is possible, therefore, that as a Christian goes through life, he becomes more aware of the reality beyond the words and concepts. He accepts more of the mystery and the paradox in life.

BACKING OFF

Perhaps, too, there is something of Erikson's concept of detachment at work here. Although the middle adult is involved in life, Erikson observes a certain backing off. Perhaps, part of that detachment involves the movement away from trying to explain everything and fit it into a neat system. Cobble found in his preliminary study of evangelicals that middle adults did not seem interested in the intellectual questions of faith. That lack of interest has been explained by saying that they have more practical matters to concern them. It may be that they are becoming somewhat detached from the frantic attempt to make rational sense out of life. They are more willing than younger adults to take it all in and live with a menagerie of ideas.

Granted, it has already been seen that this openmindedness is not typical of all middle adults. Working class men, according to the Farrell and Rosenberg study, for example, tend to deny mid-life inner voices and thus become highly prejudicial toward others. Instead of exposing themselves to potentially threatening viewpoints, they retreat into their own little world in order to protect their established mindsets that give their lives meaning.

UNREPRESSING

The concept of repression may also help to explain what is happening to the mid-lifer. If Erikson and Jung are correct, the young adult sets aside a large measure of

16. Fowler, "Stages of Faith," p. 184.
17. Michael P. Farrell and Stanley D. Rosenberg, *Men at Midlife*, p. 35.

himself in pursuit of life's practical, demanding tasks: career, marriage, attachment to social groups. The freedom from life's demands that mid-life brings to some may allow repressed thoughts, feelings, and impulses to come to the surface. Some of those may be in the form of doubt or inconsistencies. The mid-lifer begins to face the fact that all along he has not been honest with opposing points of view. If, as a young adult, for example, Calvinists had been written off, there is now a gnawing sense that one has not treated them quite fairly. The mid-lifer may plunge into an examination of Calvinism and either reconcile himself to it or come to tolerate it. There is a new willingness to concede some truths, to become more tolerant.

Certainly, seeing the complexity of life and believing that a part of the self has been denied may lead some mid-lifers in dangerous directions. It seems that some abandon their faith entirely, their newly discovered inner voices convincing them that they have been deceiving themselves all along. "To thine own self be true" becomes their test of truth.

LOSING ZEAL

Is it possible that mid-life may produce indifference in some people? Zeal fades; church attendance may be sporadic; church positions are parceled out to younger persons. Make no mistake: middle adults make up the backbone of most churches. But is it possible that the faith of some grows lukewarm? Middle adults who have invested years in a church and its faith system may not have the courage to leave and adopt a new faith. Some might—particularly when a geographic move offers freedom to do so—But others emotionally divorce themselves from church as sometimes happens in marriage. They "hang in," satisfied to be nominal church members. An inward pessimism about their own beliefs saps their vitality.

It is not hard to see how mid-life events test a person's faith. Life's complexities and perplexities combine with life's struggles. Faith counts more to them than in the past. Life changes make a middle adult lean hard on faith, perhaps as never before. For example, immorality becomes a new or renewed issue for some. Evidence shows that a wife is most likely to be unfaithful to her husband in her late thirties. Most of the women do not want to give up their marriages. They are looking for a clandestine relationship as Sheehy puts it "to be saved from the jaws of bodily rot and delivered from the threat of death...[by] seeing their youthful self-image restored in the untainted eyes of a new lover."[18] Some apparently are trying to replace their children or fill the vacuum left by a husband who is "always working." Their lives lack direction; they are looking for diversion. That is just one example of how faith becomes so crucial. Will it give them direction and hold them together, even when life sometimes seems to be falling apart?

Faith, too, will be related to the mid-lifer's church life. Church involvement is not, of course, the only sustainer of faith, but its importance cannot be denied. Only recently has the middle adult's church experience been examined.

18. Gail Sheehy, *Passages*, p. 262.

MID-LIFE DROPOUT?

Is it possible that faith development and struggle as described here is leading to a dropout phenomena? The adolescent dropout has long been studied. Is there a "middlescent" dropout? Richard P. Olson speculates that many middle adults do become dropouts.[19] From insight mined from pastoral experiences, he forges six reasons.

1. The empty nest plays a part. If parental responsibility motivated a person to attend church, for the sake of the children, that person is apt to leave church when the children leave home.
2. He cites "the still-to-be-developed faith." Still on a faith journey, middle adults want an "owned faith," a faith claimed, taken responsibility for, witnessed to, a growing faith within the context of great affirmations on which one will stake one's life.[20] This quest creates a dilemma for many. The church seems to assume the adult person is mature, fully developed, or at least ought to be. The middle adult may find little help or encouragement from his church to grow in faith.
3. Career quests may cause them to leave church. Some middle adults are still in hot pursuit of their dream. Like horses in the final stretch, they may let it all out, sacrificing all else. If the church hassles them, demanding more time, they stop showing up.
4. Some dropouts are burnouts. Those who have given so much of time and self to church ministry are especially subject to this. Like the electric circuit, they get overloaded for too long and simply burn out. "This happens to mid-life people more often than we church leaders are ready to admit yet."[21]
5. Some leave the church for "fun in the sun." Many mid-lifers have a new leisure that comes from less work, no children at home and more money. They ease into a new life-style, seeking adventure in hobbies or travel. They may think they have done enough at church. "Let the young people do it" goes with many a resignation.
6. "Typical mid-life problems" constitute the final reason mid-lifers abandon the church. Marital problems may top the list of stresses leading to the exit. Parents Without Partners claims to have statistics to back up their assertion that 95 percent of the people who get divorced quit going to church.[22] The report does not tell when or for how long those people fade from church life. Mid-lifers, as has already been seen, have their share of family plights. Embarrassment or shame over their family situation may play a part in breaking away from church. Feelings about God also may be involved. The problem-laden person, for instance, may wonder why

19. Richard P. Olson, "The Mid-Life Dropout," *Baptist Leader* 43, no. 3 (June 1981):32–36.
20. John Westerhoff, *Will Our Children Have Faith?*, pp. 89–99, as cited by Olson, pp. 32–36.
21. Westerhoff, p. 91, as cited by Olson, p. 33.
22. The study was cited by Richard Bennett, Executive Director of Lutheran Social Services of Northern Indiana, as repeated in "New Hope for Single Parents," *Wheat Ridge* (Newsletter of Wheat Ridge Foundation, Chicago), Spring 1979, p. 1.

God has not come to the rescue. Many are in a state of spiritual emergency. Apparently, the church does not always look like a trauma center to them. Treatment for spiritual shock will be only one feature of a church where middle adults are helped.

THE KIND OF CHURCH MIDDLE ADULTS NEED

AUTHENTICITY

If a middle adult is to grow in faith, he will need an authentic atmosphere. Like the critical adolescent, the middle adult will develop a nose for hypocrisy. Trying to be true to himself, he will be keenly aware of phoniness in others. He will not tolerate persons who try to manipulate him. Church leaders who demand loyalty to boring, purposeless programs test his patience. The maturing middle adult is groping for meaning, not empty activity. An authentic church is one that has good biblical reasons for what it does.

An authentic church also promotes openness in relationships. Only a climate of loving acceptance will foster this. For the middle adult, support comes from hearing that other people, too, have problems and struggles and from hearing how they have faced them. Discussion groups foster sharing of hurts, problems, and feelings. High ideals of what should be are mixed with the low-down way people sometimes behave and feel about themselves. This admission of reality is not merely a comforting way to accept our ways and stop growing. Rather, the real is laid out so that it can be grappled with. Victory comes from struggling with problems and immaturities, not from denying or ignoring them.

Authenticity also means that tragedy, evil, and pain are recognized in the world as well as in themselves. Phil Yancey chides Christians for not dealing squarely with the problem of pain. The disillusioned say things like: "I can't believe in a God who would allow Auschwitz and Vietnam. My teenage sister died of leukemia despite all the Christians' prayers; one-third of the world went to bed hungry last night—how does that fit in with your Christianity?" Christian answers sound too much like an apology, "not in the classic theological sense of a well-reasoned defense, but in the red-faced foot-shuffling lowered-head sense of embarrassment."[23]

Pursuing the questions that middle adults raise about pain, suffering and evil will drag them into mystery. For some, the discomfort and risk will be too great. On the other hand, life is dragging people there all of the time. Not facing the difficult questions may be the greater risk. Pulitzer prize winning Christian author Annie Dillard describes how she keeps being brought to those questions. "Every single thing I follow takes me there, to the edge of a cliff. As soon as I start writing, I'm hanging over the cliff again. You can make a perfectly coherent world at the snap of a finger—but only if you don't bother being honest about it."[24] Yancey questions her: "You seem driven to that mystery. You describe the beauty of nature with such

23. Phil Yancey, *Open Windows*, p. 73.
24. Annie Dillard, as quoted in Yancey, p. 138.

eloquence in *Pilgrim at Tinker Creek* but just as I'm exulting, you strike me with its terror and injustice."[25] Her answer is a challenge to all who minister to others.

> As I wrote *Pilgrim,* I kept before me the image of people who are suffering. They were right there in the room as I wrote the book. I could not write a cheerful nature book or a new version of the argument from design—not with a leukemia patient next to me. I had to write for people who are dying or grieving—and that's everybody. I can't write just from my safe position.[26]

Those are remarkable words of reminder for the church. True ministry cannot come only from moments of safety but from all moments, including the painful ones.

FREEDOM

Freedom may also be needed for middle adults to thrive. The strong call to conform characterizes many of our churches. This is not all wrong. "If you love Me, you will keep My commandments" (John 14:15), said Jesus. The church, however, will need to temper the call to measure up with the freedom to find one's own way of doing so. Doctrines that are taught and preached should not be accepted without explanation or understanding their basis in Scripture. Questions should be invited, doubts admitted. Middle adult renewal is built on asking old questions afresh. Emerging from the struggle, the growing adult will be stronger in faith, more resolute to follow the Lord.

Autonomous choice rather than group pressure will motivate the middle adult. Not that the group and its context play little role in what is believed and valued, but perhaps the middle adult's movement toward greater dependence on Christ grows out of less dependence upon others for his faith. To achieve that, he needs some room to explore in a church that offers respect for choice, questioning, and individual differences. Granted, a church has a right and necessity to insist its leaders have a certain doctrinal stance, but the members should not be coerced into faith through threat of expulsion or withdrawn love.

Fowler observes that few churches provide a climate for adult growth. Persons struggling to leave stage four end up either leaving the church or remaining because of social pressure. The ones who stay, withdraw, halfheartedly participating as little as necessary to continue their affiliation.

EMPATHY

Putting pressure on middle adults will be less effective than pouring on empathy. Olson tells us how to handle those close to dropping out. "Basically, I have been arguing for sensitivity to and support of the needs of mid-life people. For years churches have claimed the talents, time, energy, and money of mid-life people. Churches have done this with the accurate recognition of how much these folks have

25. Yancey, p. 138.
26. Annie Dillard, as quoted in Yancey, p. 138.

to give. But these same persons have needs also—needs that have too often been ignored. So take a mid-life person out to lunch. Take two. Even if you don't want anything from them."[27]

WHOLISM

If the middle adult's view of life is expanding, he will outgrow a narrow-minded church. A church that embraces all aspects of life will appeal to him. It will be a wholistic church, teaching and preaching about the social, political, emotional, intellectual, and spiritual realities of life. If only the spiritual is dealt with, the middle adult may be reluctant to integrate all of life into his faith. He may even feel guilty about it, thinking that concern for job, family, and temporal things is unworthy.

Positive wholism is based on the idea that man is more than a spiritual creature, for God has created him a physical, emotional, and mental creature. It will frustrate adults to be told all problems are spiritual and that all have spiritual answers. Emotional and physical stress may have a grip on them that praying simply does not remove. Problems with sex may be physical; social struggles may be caused by depression. A church that has a balanced view of life will support the middle adults who are facing problems in all areas.

THEOLOGICAL THEMES FOR MID-LIFERS

The areas of life mentioned above (spiritual, physical, emotional, and mental) as well as others should come under theological scrutiny. The mid-lifer may be eager for new truth as well as new insights into familiar truth.

Although many pastors and teachers would not agree, it is better to use the discussion method in addition to the inductive Bible study method with mid-lifers. When asked, adults prefer a mixture of lecture and discussion. Middle adults know they want to learn and usually know *what* specific subjects will interest them. The problem is that they sometimes do not know *how* to learn. Mid-life is an extended "teachable moment."[28]

They have much to offer to one another, if some able teacher can facilitate their sharing with each other. They need help in getting in touch with their accumulated wisdom and resources. Teaching them how to learn inductively and to study the Bible for themselves will equip them to face the issues peculiar to their own side of the street. A skilled discussion leader can gently prompt them to integrate God's truth with the most intimate personal matters.

The following doctrinal studies might hold special interest and importance for the mid-lifer.

27. Olson, pp. 32–36.
28. John R. Landgraf, "Career Development in Mid-Life," *Baptist Leader* 43 (June 1981):18.

THEOLOGY OF SUFFERING

Mid-lifers may be ready for a second look at Christian theodicy, an explanation for evil and suffering in a world ruled by a good God.

THE DOCTRINE OF MATURITY

Though many will be familiar with the Bible and the Holy Spirit's role in producing maturity, they may have renewed interest in some of the more complex aspects. Finding they are not as mature as they thought they might be, they may have many questions about how Christians grow in faith. They may be surprised and embarrassed by their mid-life struggles and have questions about them. They may grope for some standards of performance against which to measure themselves.[29] They may ask, "How is maturity manifested in mid-life? "How central is self-directedness? What types of commitment are right?"

THE DOCTRINE OF GRACE

A sense of failure and guilt may make a middle adult plunge into the refreshing pool of grace. They need to hear the words "My grace is sufficient for you" (2 Cor. 12:9).

THEOLOGY OF THE CHURCH

Middle adults who have resolved much of their inner conflict may, perhaps for the first time, become aware of and involved in the caring character of the Christian community.

THEOLOGY OF SOCIETY

Broader awareness of community and the world will make many adults turn to social issues. Biblical truths will be brought to bear in support of their new sense of responsibility in dealing with world poverty, war, abortion, and a host of social concerns.

THEOLOGY OF HOPE

Death and eschatology intrigue middle adults. Large attendance at prophetic conferences may signal a need for assurance and not just idle curiosity. In the study of last things, the acknowledgement of God's sovereignty allows the middle adult faith in ultimate order despite the destructive, chaotic, sinful surface of the planet.

If the mid-lifer finds himself in the dark woods, God's Word will be the light for his path to guide him through it.

29. Alan B. Knox, "Issues of Mid-Life," *Programming for Adults Facing Mid-Life Change*, pp. 125–26.

14

Vibrations and Tremors: Vocational Problems and Teen Troubles

CHIMES FROM THE CAREER CLOCK

Is there is "career clock" inside adults? Douglas C. Kimmel thinks so.[1] Each adult has a subjective sense of being "on time" in his career development. Levinson says that the starting point of concern about being on time comes during the late thirties in the settling down period. The young adult has looked at enough alternatives and made enough choices to finally feel that he has arrived at some more or less permanent direction in his life.

Levinson uses the figure of the ladder to describe the career expectations. In the early thirties, a man constructs a foundation for the ladder. The more he has accomplished by the time he begins constructing his mental ladder, the greater heights he envisions for the future. For example, assume a man is in middle management in his thirties. He may then hope to reach the top of his division or corporation. If he is on the top of a division, he may form his own small corporation in the settling down stage, aiming to become the giant in his field. The starting point for the settling down phase is the bottom rung of the ladder he creates in his head. The top rung may be clear or vague, but the aspiration to move up is definitely present.[2]

At mid-life, the adult clock and the ladder figures merge when the man asks, "How far have I come?" If in his own mind a man has not climbed far enough by

1. Douglas C. Kimmel, *Adulthood and Aging*, pp. 275-76.
2. Daniel J. Levinson, *Seasons of a Man's Life*, pp. 59-60, 141-43.

mid-life, he will have a greater awareness of his age.[3]

For some the clock-ladder intersection reduces their motivation. Having arrived, a sense of satisfaction sets in, although since most have reached an occupational plateau, the potential for strong dissatisfaction is present.

The concept of the ladder can be applied to other areas as well. Young adults begin their climb to success in the areas of family and spiritual life. Goals and dreams abound. Career assessment is, in that respect, part of a larger life reassessment. As such, it can be characteristic of both men and women, although studies show that women tend to be less concerned about measuring their lives in terms of achievement than men. Levinson found men that had plans for advancement, whether in work or nonwork contexts.[4]

The mid-life person will need to expand his definition of success to include areas other than career if he has not done so earlier. "Without losing all desire for accomplishment, power and excellence, he comes to be less driven by ambition. [Thus, he becomes] more aware of the magical qualities he formerly attributed to reaching the top of the ladder. It is no longer essential to succeed, no longer catastrophic to fail."[5] Success and failure are judged in more complex terms: the quality of experience, the value of the products, and the meaning of work to self and others.

ALTERNATIVES TO THE STATUS QUO

Four possible paths lie ahead for being reconciled to the dream created in young adulthood.[6]

De-illusionment. The de-illusionment approach deals with the distance between one's dream and one's achievement of it. This does not necessarily include abandoning the dream or admitting failure. Rather, it consists of modifying and personalizing it so that it better represents one's present hopes. Instead of anticipating becoming school superintendent, a teacher may hope to be a better history teacher, using his position to help his students cope with the world. The de-illusionment can result in a beautiful increase in self-knowledge and refreshing self-acceptance. It represents a mature look at one's abilities, energies and future decades.

Getting free. A second pathway leads to dealing with one of the pernicious traits of the dream: its potential tyranny. Adolescent and young adult dreams are by nature idealistic, lacking a firm grounding in experience and resulting from a partial understanding of self. If the adult continues to relentlessly pursue it, the dream can tyrannize. A single purpose controls life, while other matters, desires and goals atrophy. "By the early forties such a single-minded pursuit may well have produced some achievement, but the person may experience it as a hollow victory."[7] In hot

3. Bernice L. Neugarten, "The Awareness of Middle Age," in *Middle Age and Aging,* ed. Bernice L. Neugarten, p. 96.
4. Levinson, pp. 91–93.
5. Ibid., p. 249.
6. The following discussion is primarily from Levinson, pp. 245–50.
7. Evelyn Eaton Whitehead and James D. Whitehead, p. 140.

pursuit of goals, a man or woman may have pushed aside family, personal needs, joy, and God. The unachieved dream will have to be abandoned or at least changed, or it will lead to further betrayal of oneself and others. But achieved or not, the individual will need to let go and discover the neglected parts of life.

Recovering. A third means of reconciliation to the dream leads to recovering a dream that has been ignored. If earlier personal choices led a person in a life direction that ignored the dream, the person may say, in Levinson's terms, "I have climbed the wrong ladder." The mid-lifer's awareness of a limited future breathes a sense of urgency into that realization. Sometimes a radical change in life-style or vocation is called for.

Resurrecting. The last form of reconciliation seems to be what many women experience in the mid-life transition. Culturally, and particularly within the evangelical tradition, women have been expected to play a supporting role to their husbands. Her dream is tied up with his. Her personal dream is lost in the process. When the children are grown and leave home, the long supressed dream may make a reappearance. A career woman may experience something similiar, recognizing that she has been performing according to someone else's expectations rather than her own. She may have lapsed into striving for the appropriate level of creativity and responsibility, which could be considerably lower than her original dream.[7] Achieving peace with herself may demand reviving the dream and taking a second look. A married woman may choose to return to the abandoned career. The career woman may decide on a second career or changes in her vocational plans within her field. Women must also deal with the anger and hostility that may accompany that reawakening.[8]

Turmoil lies on all four pathways. Loved ones and a supporting community play an important role in getting through them. Counselors, pastors, spouses, and children should be aware that career changes may be sensible options for the mid-lifer. In the public sector, more programs are developing to assist men and women in career development at this time of life. In some cases, the change may be radical, like the man I recently met who was cleaning homes. One morning he simply decided not to return to the downtown skyscraper that housed the insurance firm he had devoted his life to. The pressure of that executive position gone, he was ecstatic over the fun and freedom he got from washing windows, cleaning carpets, and scrubbing walls. His wife was delighted by the happiness of her liberated husband. Persons close to such a mid-lifer may need to resist the tendency to criticize and constrict the mid-lifer's freedom.

In the case of women, career concerns may lead to a re-entry into the world of work. Two facts make that an emotional challenge as well as a practical one. Realistically, timing will make it difficult for many women in mid-life to begin new careers. It may be too late to start. Age bias along with lack of prior experience puts them at a disadvantage. It is more likely that women who have trained for careers in young adulthood will update their knowledge and skills. Some may take a part-time job to

8. Ibid., p. 141.
9. Ibid.

test their rusted abilities. Those who had part-time employment while the children were growing up may seek a more challenging full-time vocation.

CHANGING CAREERS IS RISKY BUSINESS

How advisable are job shifts, particularly for men and women who have established careers that no longer satisfy them? Middle adults may need to be reminded that changing horses in midstream is a risky business. Like adolescents, they may tend to think "everybody's doing it." Yet, most middle adults are not making big vocational changes. Expert Alan B. Knox says that "contrary to assertions about widespread career changes around age forty, the actual research data indicates that between thirty-five and fifty years of age career mobility rates decline sharply with no indication of enough people experiencing a mid-life crisis around age forty to result in even a ripple in the career change statistics."[10]

Dreams can be fulfilled in Christian ministry in and through the church or in voluntary services. While the mid-lifer may yearn for some adventure, he also needs a modicum of stability. Adventure might be found in community and church involvement that offers multifaceted opportunities for meaningful involvement without risky career changes.

TEEN TIME

MID–LIFE—ADOLESCENT CONNECTION

Some people have attributed to God a morbid sense of humor over the fact that whenever a parent reaches his mid-life passage he usually has a teen who is going through the adolescent transition. It is a case of the groping leading the groping. This is not the case with all parents, of course, since some will be younger or older than mid-life when their offspring are in their teens. It is a developmental irony, however, that most middle-aged people have a teenager to manage. It is not just that one person in transition is in charge of another person in transition, like two people each on different merry-go-rounds trying to keep in touch. Rather, the two transitions act upon one another.

The youngster moving into adolescence becomes a reminder to the parent that he is moving into old age. Ellen Galinsky describes the irony: "At a point when the parent may be confronting pain, may be feeling more aches and pains and witnessing the illnesses and the deaths of contempories or his or her parents, and thus thinking, 'I'm next in line,' the child is the very epitome of youth." The child surpasses the parents, possibly in height, in physical shape, even in the ability to run faster and work longer. As one parent said of her adolescent: "He makes my own mortality pretty clear to me."[11] Parents often report a modicum of envy or jealousy over their child's youthfulness.

10. Alan B. Knox, ed., *Programming for Adults Facing Mid-Life Change*, p. 3.
11. Ellen Galinsky, *Between Generations*, p. 260.

In fact, it may be the first signs of maturing in the child that trigger the middle adult's arrival at a different stage. No research confirms that children turning into teenagers actually creates a turning point for their parents, but observing the child's physical development may trigger the parent's awareness of arriving at another stage himself.

If the presence and appearance of the youth does not make the parent notice his own aging, the words of the teen probably will. Turning now to evaluating themselves, mid-lifers will get a boost from their critical adolescent sons and daughters. The penchant teens have for judging is tied to their search for identity. They form an ideal picture of what they and life ought to be. Reality, including parents, is held up to the picture for comparisons. Naturally, reality falls short, and the teen is often vocal in proclaiming where discrepancies lie. No one knows for sure how, or even if, such critical remarks serve as a catalyst for middle adults' self-evaluations, but there seems to be some connection.

Teens' actions are another way of reminding the parent to examine himself. Galinsky explains that when the children are in the pre-adolescent stage a parent is likely to have thought of himself as having improved a great deal as a parent. A mother, for example, may have finally begun to yell less at her child and is thinking she deserves a B+, if not an A, on the parental report card. But when her child becomes a teen and begins to challenge her by little acts of independence, she is surprised to find herself yelling as in days of old. Shocked, she grills herself with "What kind of parent am I?" If the rebellious actions are sizable and parental responses ineffective, the parent is now in for a greater jolt. "I thought I was doing a great job with my son. Now look at him!" The parental image and dream is in jeopardy. "Have I compromised my desire to be a good parent with my yearning to be a good mechanic?" is an awful question to have to ask.

THE NORMAL TEEN MYTH

Of course, not all teens give their parents that much grief. There is little empirical evidence that anything approaching rebellion takes place during adolescence. In two of the best-known studies of youth, the researchers reported that relationships between parents and teenagers were surprisingly harmonious.[12] Teens may be different but not necessarily rebellious. Experts distinguish between the two:

> There are indeed many differences between generations but they are apt to be differences in defining and implementing ideals, in roles, in responses to change, and in personal taste, which generally occur within a context of mutual acceptance, rather than differences that bespeak hostility and disrespect. The gap is largely between the general worlds of adults and young people rather than between parents and children.[13]

12. Judith Gallatin, "Political Thinking in Adolescence," in *Handbook of Adolescent Psychology*, ed. Joseph Adelson, p. 358, referring to E. Douvan and J. Adelson, *The Adolescent Experience*, and Daniel Offer, *The Psychological World of the Teenager.*
13. S. Coopersmith, M. Regan, and L. Dick, *The Myth of the Generation Gap*, pp. 316–17, as cited by Gallatin, p. 358.

Disagreements may not seem to be all that intense. Parental power is still at work in teen's lives. I know of no broad study of parental influence on teens, but a summary of research about youth's political views is germane. Parents rank above school and media in shaping their children's outlook on politics. Peers have relatively little influence in the political arena. Several authors have inferred that teenagers have a kind of dual orientation, relying on friends judgment for ordinary day-to-day decisions but consulting parents for more serious questions.[14]

Parent-teen relationships can be difficult. Lowenthal discovered that in both middle-aged and pre-retirement couples, teenage children were especially trying and about three-fourths reported conflict with them, although most of it was mild.[15]

There is little doubt that parenting teenagers is the hardest part of the parent's role as well as the most troublesome part of middle adulthood. Mid-lifers might benefit from knowing of the subtle connection between their transition and their teens'. Understanding may be what they lack most. Literature, friends, pastors, and others offer simple guidelines: "Limit 'em, love 'em, let 'em grow up." All the while, though, the confused parents are wrestling with puzzling inner voices: *Why can't I be more understanding? Why do I have a difficult time making limits and a harder time sticking to them? Why doesn't my daughter talk with me when she gets moody? What have I done wrong all these years? Why does parenting this teenager kindle so much inner turmoil? How and why does it seem to sometimes upset my marriage? Is it normal to be asking such questions?*

For parents of teenagers, grasping developmental understanding can be as welcome as a street light on a hazardous road. Some specific suggestions are also available to make the trip more pleasant.

REALITY RESKETCHING

The teenager's parents will have to allow preconceived images to give way to reality. Just as a person forms mental pictures of what a planned Caribbean vacation would be like, the parents form ideas about what being a parent of a teenager will be like. Galinsky says they mentally write a script and rehearse it so they will be ready. Those mental sketches are not the product of mere fantasy.[16] Parents look around at other teens and their parents, trying to determine just what works and what the venture promises. They decide how they will react when the teen complains about acne or when the length of his phone calls seem to test the limits of infinity. Just like the vacationers, many of those expectations will have to be modified or mutilated to make the most of the trip.

Awesome expectations. The first image to be shattered by the hammer of reality has to do with how bad they thought the trip would be. "The teenager years, in American

14. Gallatin, p. 362.
15. Marjorie Fisk Lowenthal, et al., *Four Stages of Life*, pp. 40–41.
16. Galinsky, p. 229.

culture today, have an awesome reputation. Even during pregnancy, parents-to-be have had foreboding fears. . . . Some parents, remembering their own teenage years, picture the worst—their children transformed, surely turning their backs on their parents, ungrateful, speeding dangerously down highways, drinking, metamorphosed by drugs, enmeshed in sex." When the children are young, parents are solemnly warned: "You think it's nice (or hard) now—well, just wait.[17]

If the waiting brings on a charge of negative feelings and even depression, it is quite understandable. Parents will need some assurance that it may not be all that terrible. Research can be summoned to their side to show that teenage years are usually not stressful for the teen or the parents. Mixing younger and older parents in Sunday school classes and small groups is also reassuring. Nothing will dissipate young parents' fears as much as good talks with middle and older adults who have a more realistic idea of what the adolescent period is like for a Christian family. Lacking such intergenerational contact, family life is like a hidden drama replete with mysteries and hints of tragedy and suffering. The tendency of the American family to hide family troubles as well as joys forces parents to base their actions on guesswork, hearsay, or often contradictory expert opinion. Parents could help each other a great deal if they just got together and shared what is happening and how they are handling it.

At the other end of the spectrum are parents who think they are prepared for their child's puberty and are shocked when problems arise. The images they have of their son or daughter and the one they have of themselves as parents must be retouched. "In my wildest imagination, I never believed my son would have a drinking problem," one father said. He was frantically searching for answers: What kind of person becomes an alcoholic? What kind of parent contributes to it, if there is any contribution? What kind of parent have I been? What kind of person is my son? He had to face the reality that Christian parents could raise a son with a drinking problem. Faith can enable such parents to face their problems and help their child cope with problems like addiction. The new image developed by a parent who had a child in a crisis situation and survived can also be used to help other parents. *Before* problems occur, a parent with an idealized view of parenting would have blamed himself for problems. *Afterward,* the parent knows differently. Therefore, he will have a new-found acceptance of other parents of teenagers in trouble, making him a valuable resource person to them.

Changing teens and their changing images. It is not just severe behavior that presses parents to change their images of their child. Any of the following will do nicely:

- A younger child tells her parents that her fifteen-year-old brother got off the school bus five stops before home. When he gets home two hours later, he refuses to tell where he has been. This takes place at a time when there has been a new outburst of drug use at his high school.

17. Ibid.

- A fourteen-year-old girl comes to her mother sobbing saying that she has just ripped a button off the blouse she was going to wear. Her mother says, "Oh, I'm sorry. I'll sew it for you." The daughter turns away, slamming the door, saying, "You don't really care."[18]
- A thirteen-year-old boy wants a transistor radio like everyone else. His parents refuse on financial grounds. Two days later he comes home with one; when asked where he got it, he reports that he traded it for something with one of the kids at school. He refuses to say more.

Episodes like those can stir strong feelings in parents' breasts. They wonder if they are not really the parents they thought they were. *Shocked, unexpected, surprised* are words parents often use when describing their reaction to ordinary teen-age behavior. Sometimes the shock is due to timing or not expecting their child to change when becoming a teenager. "We expected it later, but not now," they say. Neugarten has theorized that timing often turns developmental change into a crisis.[19] Some parents may not know that children mature earlier than in the past or that individual differences cause children to grow up on different, personal timetables. A mother is surprised to discover menstruation for her daughter is two years earlier than she anticipated. Her timetable is upset; her daughter has changed, bringing the foreseen responsibilities and fears to the family ahead of the anticipated schedule.

Surprise may be due to the simple fact of life that no one is ever fully prepared for change. "It is difficult to let go of one's image of a child, say good-bye to the child a parent knows, and get accustomed to this slightly new child inhabiting the known child's body."[20]

Sometimes the greater the emotional investment and attachment, the greater the difficulty in accepting change. There are losses involved. The child could be picked up in one's arms, tossed about almost any time, but not the teenager. The parent's hugs and kisses freely given before, need to be more calculated now. Timing must be watched, for the parent senses a change in his child's responses. Something has been lost. It is difficult to let go of the child and therefore of one's image. While I write this, my own son is changing rapidly, during his sixteenth year. Lately, I often feel a sense of shock when he speaks; his voice is decidedly different, not only the lower tone but the way he talks to me. I really do not want him to change. He is our fourth and last child. In a sense, by their growing up I have lost three children already. Sometimes, I try to remember what they were all like in their childhood, to conjure up past joy-filled days when they jumped in my arms as I came in the door and looked at me in a special way. But, reliving those days is not the same as living them. Those memories sometimes fill my eyes with tears. Now, I am losing my fourth child. He is hard to give up. Therefore I experience the grief reactions of shock, denial, and sorrow. That is the lot of middle adult parents. Of course, the joys of seeing children mature make it all worthwhile.

18. Ibid., p. 234.
19. Bernice Neugarten et al., *Personality in Middle and Late Life: Empirical Studies*, pp. 290–91.
20. Galinsky, p. 233.

No more super parent Sometimes parents are hurt by discovering they are really not measuring up to the parents they thought they would be. Before their child's teen years, they imagined what they would do when they had to cope with teen behavior. Their ideas were often fostered by their critical views of other parents. *I'll be a stronger authority* they say to themselves when it seems their neighbor's teen gets away with murder. Or they shape their images by reflecting on their own childhood. "My mother never talked to me about my problems; I will be open with my girl; she will always feel free to come to me."

When adolescence arrives, the expectations become fading apparitions. The father who was going to exercise control is wondering how to get Solomon-like wisdom to know when to say *no*. Should a parent insist on knowing every detail about his child's activity? How far does parental authority extend, and what does *trust* demand? The mother who was going to be open to her daughter finds her child just is not open with her. She is one of those teens who, for whatever reason, goes to her room, sad and sobbing, refusing to tell why.

Parents who thought it would be difficult to raise teens may not have been ready for all the perplexity and internal self-reflecting, although images and reality sometimes turn out to be one and the same (pictures on travel brochures sometimes tell the truth, don't they?). The reasonable person knows that he will have to modify present images for future realities; parents must change with their changing children.

COPING WITH CONTROL

Young children often make their parents feel like policemen, and teens surely create that feeling. Teens challenge their parents to think through their role as authorities. Both parents and teens agree there is no issue more prominent in the family than that one. Conflicts over money, the use of the car, and privacy revolve around the question: Who is in charge here?

Middle adults are in the process of dealing with control in a more generalized way. World events, personal setbacks, and tragedies have been instructing him that the world cannot be beaten into shape, not even his own little world. The mid-lifer learns to live with the inevitable—the unchangeable.

Teens do a lot to teach about the illusiveness of control even without rebelliousness or immoral acts. The teen's own right to be himself will defy the adult's sense of power. The teen might challenge the parent's own dream for him or her. A linguist I know taught his children Greek when they were little, consistent with his own vision that they would love the classics as he. But they soon resisted memorizing Greek words and verb forms. The professor learned he could not so easily control his children's lives.

CORRECT CORRECTION

Parents will, however, need to exercise control during their child's teen years, even while they see their authority diminishing. Experts say that teens still need guidance, bathed in love and kindness. Children not only grow older, they grow more autonomous. They come and go to school by themselves, stay at home alone, buy their own clothes, cook for themselves, go off with their friends to the shopping mall and to social affairs. The father of one fourteen-year-old says, "I feel like the circle of her life is widening away from us."[21] It is difficult for parents to regulate their teen's social life. If parents are too strict, the child may run away or rebel in destructive ways. Legal and social pressures to obey parents are diminishing. Society favors the youth's freedom.

The teen's parents learn to exercise control differently then when the children were younger. The church can help by affirming this. Too often, parents are given the impression that they are to exercise absolute control over their teens. Paradoxically, society reduces the parent's power, without discounting the blame. Youth leaders criticize parents when young people fail to show up in Sunday school or the youth group, failing to realize that parental control must be mixed with some freedom and that freedom is risky business. Church leaders need to show they understand that.

God's Word obviously addresses the matter of parental authority. Though its guidelines for disciplining children are quite clear, they are also quite general. Parents are to nurture their children through example, teaching, and discipline. Children are to honor parents, rendering them due obedience. But, both of those simple commands are qualified. Parents must discipline carefully so as not to make their children rebellious (Eph. 6:4) or discouraged (Col. 3:21). Somewhere between control and caution lies a lot of middle ground. The modern parent is hard pressed to know exactly where to stand on specific contemporary issues. It is not a simple matter of laying down the law. Sensitivity and love insist that parents care about how the child is reacting.

Even the teen's obedience is not to be understood in absolute terms. Teens are not under obligation to obey in areas off limits to parental authority. Parents cannot insist a teen conform to their religious beliefs or make a teen do an immoral act. It also makes good sense to allow teens some amount of freedom if they are to live in a democratic, highly individualized Western society. Parental discipline must be a mixture of control and freedom, of caution and trust.

Contract control. A noted expert on teen development, David Elkind, suggests that parent-teen linkage be viewed as a series of contracts.[22] There are three basic contracts. The first takes in freedom and responsibility. Parents grant freedom as the teens show they can handle responsibility—more liberty to the more trustworthy. Even if a teen can seize freedom in some areas that the parent cannot directly control, the parent can set limits. For example, use of the family car can be withdrawn until school grades improve. This is not a punishment but a limitation. Better grades signal the youth can better handle things that compete with study time. Therefore, using the family car again may not pose a threat to school grades.

21. Ibid., p. 241.
22. The following is from David Elkind, "Growing Up Faster," *Psychology Today,* February 1979, pp. 38–45.

The second type of contract deals with loyalty and commitment. Parents no longer expect teens to express the loyal affection they did as children because peers are gaining in importance to the teens. Nonetheless, parents expect them to remain loyal to values and beliefs the parents support. In turn, teens expect parents will be dedicated to those values in deed as well as word. Adolescents dislike hypocrisy. If parents insist on allegiance to a certain value system, they should set the example.

Achievement and support make up the third contract. Expected achievements, especially for middle-class situations, are academic, extracurricular (i.e., sports or music) and social (i.e., the right friends). In return for that, parents show approval for effort and performance, give financial support for uniforms, equipment, and instruments, and provide needed transportation.

Elkind argues that historical and social circumstances will determine which of the above contracts gets prominent place. In the sixties, loyalty was the issue. Adolescents thought adults did not live out their values, minority groups were mistreated, and the Vietnam war was morally unjust and dishonest. Societal hypocrisy led them to question American ideals in general. Feeling that loyalty to those standards was not deserved, many of them withdrew.

Today, Elkind thinks parent-child contracts should center on freedom and responsibility. Parents may be giving too much freedom to children without getting a show of responsibility back.

DEVELOPING COMMUNICATION

Communicating is at the core of any relationship. Many times, however, it is difficult to discern what parents should expect from talking with teens. At a minimum, parents should clearly explain rules and expectations and talk freely about them. One research project has shown that teens' conformity to rules is linked to parent's patience in discussing them. Three types of parent-teen interactions were studied: permissive, democratic, and autocratic. Researchers noted how often explanations were given when children questioned the family rules. Particularly, the researcher looked at a teens' compliance to parental disapproval of their friends. Teens were least likely to fall in line, it was found, whenever the parents were either permissive or autocratic, when explanations were scarce.[23] Apparently, the same rule applies to other areas of behavior. A parent should talk it over if he wants the teen to carry it out.

Parents of teens also will do well to communicate their interest in the child. A number of research projects have shown that parental indifference plays a role in just how much influence a teen's peers have on him. If parental interest and support are lacking, the teen has a high commitment to the peer group's values.[24] If that is true,

23. G. H. Elder, Jr., "Parental Power: Legitimation and the Effect on the Adolescent," *Sociometry* 27 (1963):50–56 as cited in John Coleman, "Friendship and the Peer Group in Adolescence," in *Handbook of Adolescent Psychology*, ed. Joseph Adelson, p. 417.
24. J. Conger, "Adolescence and Youth," in *Handbook of Adolescent Psychology*, ed. Joseph Adelson, p. 428.

then the peer group may be filling a vacuum more than it is provoking conflict between parents and teens.

Quality communication is obviously difficult for some parents and teens to achieve. A couple of generalizations might help. First, it is clear that individual differences in the personalities of parents *and* teens play a part. Some teens are as open as a twenty-four-hour corner store; some are not. The factors are many and complex. "Teenagers run the gamut from ones . . . who go off by themselves when in turmoil and refuse to talk, to ones . . . [who are] articulate and vocal about their feelings and problems."[25]

Second, parents of teens can help by exchanging old ways of communicating for new ones. They change with the child's changes. That may mean waiting for the youth to bring up the subject instead of pulling it out of him. Parents must try to understand the individual adolescent and respond accordingly. When the teen is secretive and incommunicative, the enlightened parent will wait it out, patiently, prayerfully, knowing the teen may need to work out a problem for himself.

Third, talking with other parents and teens may help parents communicate better with their own teen. From others, they may become better informed about their teen's school and world, giving them more insight into the teen's behavior. Parents will soon find, however, that keeping in touch with other parents and children is much more difficult than it was when their child was younger. The teen's friends and world are simply much more scattered. People who move into a new community during their child's teenage years will especially have to work hard at making connections.

Fourth, parents will need to try to be open to their teenagers. Open doors are made of heaps of affirmation. Research has shown that if even a small percentage of parents' comments are critical, the average teen will conclude: "My parent never listens and always condemns me." That shows how hard parents have to work at projecting a positive attitude toward the teen, whose yearning for affirmation and someone to listen to him seems to match his late evening appetite for snacks. Ed Seely confirmed that in 1979 by his survey of over fifteen-hundred teens in Youth For Christ clubs. His firm conclusion was that listening is ranked as the most important behavior performed by peer and adult leaders.[26] Teens also want parents who will listen attentively and work hard at understanding them.

Finally, parents will need to press for conversation at crucial times, especially in matters relating to discipline and control. As soap is to grease, so talk is to conflict. To clean up matters, parents and teens must express their feelings and thoughts. Middle adults need to learn acceptable modes of conflict management in order to teach their teens how to deal with conflict. Parents must insist on talking: about contracts, about rules, about anger, about distrust, about anything that threatens their tie with their teens. Sometimes, they must try to be available so that the teen can air his mind when he is ready. "You have got to develop a sixth sense about when they want to talk and

---

25. Galinsky, p. 251.
26. Edward Seely, "Behaviors of Peer Leaders," pp. 128, 130.

then leave the door open so if they decide to walk through it, they can. That, at least to me, takes an incredible amount of energy and time; just being there without being there. . . . You have to get rid of your agendas and just sort of lay back so the kids feel free to move in with theirs."[27]

SEPARATING AND SUSTAINING

Though the child's separation from the parents has been going on since birth, it becomes a paramount task during adolescence. Unfortunately, it is not so gradual and constant as might be supposed. Teens swing back and forth from dependence to independence. They go from family to friends and back again. Such swings of the pendulum unsettle the parent's emotions. Envy pops up when the teenager cuts himself off from a parent. *Almost everyone has a better relationship with my son than I,* the parent may think. A wife says of her husband and teenage son, "I see them watching television together and it's really lovely, but I guess I'm jealous that my husband has that and I don't."[28] Inner resentment can bubble up in a parent's heart over his teen's close relationship with friends. Fears also have to be fought. No longer able to protect children as before, parents easily become afraid of the teen's new autonomy. If the phone rings while the teen is out, parents report being struck fleetingly by fear. Might it also be assumed that that fear of danger is linked with the middle-aged person's new fear of his own mortality? The separation from the child "is a symbolic kind of death."[29]

Pride, hostilities, and regret, can all be products of the necessary separation of teen from parent. Pride can be a positive thing, signaling a sense of satisfaction over the direction the child is going on his own. Pride can also beget guilt and deep regret, however. If the child is going his way instead of the parents', pride can make them feel they should have done more to impose their will on the child when they had the chance.

Part of the answer to those negative emotions lies in the parents' willingness to let the child go. As the teen distances himself, parents must be careful not to give fear, anxiety, or envy a place. "God hath not given us the spirit of fear," said Paul (2 Tim. 1:7, KJV).

Youth's movement away from parents is a movement toward self-discovery. The process of discovering his identity means learning about how he is unlike his family. The identity task of the teenager determines the task of his parent. "Part of the redefinition of the parent/child relationships is the task of continuing the process of accepting the child's separate identity."[30]

Parents will need Job's patience. A teen vacillates in his opinion of who he is or what he is to become. Parents will need to live with the unpredictable. "When I think of Alexander, I cannot imagine what he will be like as a grown up," one confused parent exclaims.

27. Galinsky, p. 253.
28. Ibid., p. 277.
29. Ibid.
30. Ibid., p. 270.

If you had a crystal ball and told me he was going to be an astronaut, I would say fine. If you told me he was going to go to the Mojave Desert and be a monk, I'd say that's possible. I mean there's no way I could tell you what I think. I feel like he's going to peel his skin about five times and each metamorphosis will be one step along.[31]

This is not to say that the separation from parents is equal to severing. The distancing from parents that goes on in adolescence is not like losing a relationship as much as it is like modifying it. A new adult-to-adult fellowship can emerge from the adult-to-child union. Then the pains of the separation will finally slip from memory over joy that a mature adult is born. What was it Jesus said about labor pains?

31. Ibid.

15

Aging Lovebirds and Empty Nests: Physical Changes and Marital Matters

The doctor said he died of fright. There seemed to be no other explanation. He had been sitting upright in the hospital bed, a triple by-pass surgery behind him. Vital signs were excellent. His son said he was unsettled as they talked about his situation. The chat between father and son abruptly became their last when his head fell to one side: he was dead.

Fright! A strange term for today's sophisticated, knowledgeable doctors to use. My fifty-year-old friend just was not able to cope with what was happening to his body.

SYMPTOMS OF AGING

Adjusting to physical decline is a mid-life task. Signs of aging begin before then. During the thirties the balance between physical growth and physical deterioration begins to waver. But, it settles definitely on the side of degeneration after the fortieth year.[1]

The sense organs undergo change at an amazing rate of uniformity. Perhaps the most notable changes occur in the eyes. At about age forty-five, most adults have prebyopa, a reduction of the elasticity of the crystalline lens. The lens can no longer change its curvature to focus on things close in as easily as it once did.[2] I recall so well how helpless I felt the first time, driving alone at night, I was lost and unable to read the road map. *Old, you're getting old,* my inside voice shouted. As the eyes go, so go the ears. Hearing loss occurs, particularly the inability to hear high frequency tones.

The physical structure begins to decline about age forty-five or fifty. The head

---

1. W. A. Marshall, in *The Seven Ages of Man,* p. 99.
2. George Kaluger and Meriem Fair Kaluger, *Human Development: The Life Span,* p. 269.

continues to grow, but the rest of the skeleton begins to wane.

Muscles do not cooperate as readily with the brain. On average, by the age of forty-five, the strength of the back muscles in men has dropped to 96 percent of its maximum value. For men of fifty, it is down to 93 percent, and the decrease continues. Muscles balk at doing the same amount of work, simply because the body is giving them less oxygen—as much as 60 percent less between the ages of twenty and fifty. Recovering from hard labor is tougher for the older person. He needs longer rest periods between bouts of heavy work,[3] prompting the "you're always tired" line from the spouse. Though the average man or woman in the forties is able to maintain adequate standards of work, the physical decline does create some limitations. One out of twenty middle adults is subject to activity limitations, as compared to one out of one hundred younger adults.[4]

The weight gain of middle adults does not help their health, either. Yet, that too, is due in part to physical changes: metabolism slows down. The body is as cruel as a computer with what it does with what is put into it. "Eat less or else," it relentlessly says to the aging adult.

The role of disease will be more prominent than during young adulthood. "Old age diseases" begin to show up. Many middle adults learn firsthand about such physical ailments as diabetes, gall and kidney stones, and chronic bronchitis. Arthritis makes its appearance. Only 28.4 percent of Americans age forty-five to sixty-four were found to be without a chronic disease when a national health survey was taken.[5]

Most women will be concerned with something more normal than disease: menopause. The menstrual flow stops; the childbearing capacity ceases; sexual responsiveness may be reduced. Nervousness, hot flashes, and other symptoms are common. It is the psychological reaction to menopause and the hormone imbalance that usually causes the most distress, however.

Until very old age, men continue to produce sperm and are capable of producing children. But beginning about thirty years of age, a gradual decline in the secretion of testosterone and androgen begins. Those hormones can cause changes in sexual activity and physical strength as well as lead to loss of hair and teeth. Possibly there will be a shift to more sexual/sensual feeling through the whole body during intercourse rather than the more specific genital areas as in youth.[6] Though studies are incomplete, Golan claims that "biomedical changes . . . affect health and physical appearance, family relationships, attitude toward work, self-concept and personality."[7]

It is a fact that many men and women do struggle with symptoms that may have

3. Marshall, pp. 99–101.
4. David Moberg and Robert Gray, *The Church and the Older Person*, p. 20.
5. U.S. Public Health Service, *Working with Older People: A Guide to Practice*, vol. 22, pub. no. 1459, p. i.
6. Orville G. Brim, Jr., "Theories of the Male Mid-Life Crisis," *Counseling Psychologist* 6 (1976): 2–9, as cited by Naomi Golan, *Passing Through Transitions*, p. 135.
7. Ibid.

some physical causes. However, 90 percent of women today are not overwhelmed by problems of the menopause period, according to Sheehey.[8] Only 15 percent of men are candidates for a radical hormone shake-up, so the likelihood of great change for the majority is slight.[9] Some also maintain that struggles in mid-life, whether for men or women, remain more a matter of the mind than the body. And, happily for most, none of the changes need interfere with the middle adult's sex life. Some illnesses can affect sexual desire, even causing temporary impotency at times. But what matters most to maintaining sexual activity is sexual activity itself. Couples who enjoy their physical relationship on a regular basis, in the context of a warm union, may continue to expect its pleasures.

How badly a biblical theology of sex needs to be taught! Sex needs to be seen in all of its enriching and wholesome dimensions. Although God created sex for pro-creating children, He also intended it for instilling a sense of oneness between husband and wife. Sex is communication. Couples send powerful, warm nonverbal messages to each other in sex play and intercourse. As a person gets older and the childbearing years are gone, sex still gives a sense of belongingness, pleasure, and love.

Studies show that the one who gives up sex in mid-life is the one who has never enjoyed it. A man or woman now has an excuse to give it up.[10] If both husband and wife feel that way, perhaps there is no loss. There are other ways to create intimacy. But when only one partner cuts off that avenue of love, the pain and emptiness can be sizable and the adjustment agonizing. Younger adults need to build an enriching and intimate sex life that will not fade when their years increase. Middle adults can be helped to overcome sexual problems and even bloom where they have not blossomed before. Sexual counseling for middle adults is often quite successful.

Recently, a woman who read my book on marriage told my wife how a new insight changed her. Her sex life with her middle-aged husband had been nil for some time. "Why no desire?" she asked herself. "Menopause," she answered. After reading that sex was a form of communication, however, she asked herself the same question again. This time, she suspected the answer lay in the lack of warmth in her verbal exchanges with her husband. Family troubles prompted them to shout and argue instead of talk. Two days later, something changed that pattern. She and her husband sat calmly discussing their family situation in the early evening. An aura of unity enveloped them. Allowing herself to draw close, she made love with her husband, reminding her of vigorous, exciting earlier days. Her experience illustrates that sex is more a matter of the mind than the body. Theology can shape our thinking and crystallize right attitudes.

Perhaps the church can also play a part in what sometimes is not readily thought of as its concern: physical health. It can, first of all, join forces with those who are promoting good eating and exercise habits. In recent years, medical experts have noted

8. Gail Sheehy, *Passages,* p. 463.
9. Ibid., p. 462.
10. Judith Brier and Dan Rubenstein, "Sex for the Elderly? Why Not?" p. 200.

a sharp rise in the number of patients with heart attacks, strokes, cancer, and other degenerative diseases. American men have one of the highest rates of cardiac disease in the world. Much of it is directly linked to stress, tension, smoking, drinking, drugs, poor diet, obesity, and lack of exercise. It is sad that list could be a middle adult man's genuine obituary. Yet so many mid-lifers fail to take their doctor's advice on those matters.[11] Maybe involvement in the church will make them better listeners. Even more than that, some churches are starting exercise clubs or having aerobics along with Bible study times.

Attitudes and thinking about disease also need to be shaped in the church. As discussed, the church must explain the destructive in life. Diseases are not always healed. Aging and its pains do not go away. Yet, the church may sometimes give the impression that those things should not exist. The well-known German pastor and theologian Helmut Thielicke was once asked what was the greatest problem he observed in the United States. He replied, "They have an inadequate view of suffering."[12] Middle adults will need to learn to see the benefits of suffering and pain. "Although He was a Son, He learned obedience from the things which He suffered" (Heb. 5:8). Much of value lies beneath a surface understanding of pain for those who dare to explore.

IS THE EMPTY NEST EMPTY?

It is said that when the last child leaves home, the mother and father are now in the lonesome, depressive confines of the empty nest. However, tell this to some middle-aged couples whose last offspring has finally gone off to college, and they might challenge you. They do not seem the slightest bit down over the lost pitter-patter of teenage tennis shoes.

How empty is the empty nest? One thing seems clear: it is a time of readjustment. Old habit patterns as well as feelings and attitudes about the roles of parent and spouse give way to new ones. Father and mother face the loss of their parental roles, and they face each other differently. With the children gone, she is no longer Mom (in some ways), and he is no longer Dad (in some ways). Their bond reverts back to what it was before the children arrived.

APRON STRINGS—NO TANGLES

For years, researchers have been trying to determine what the transition is like for mothers.[13] After analyzing interviews of 160 middle-aged women, Lillian Rubin found that for all of the women, the departure of the children spelled R-E-L-I-E-F, even for those who were most involved as housewives.[14] The rewards were not hard to imagine: less complex life-style, more relaxation, and new opportunities to pursue goals long ago put on the shelf.

11. Henry Still, *Surviving the Male Mid-Life Crisis*, pp. 43–57 as cited by Golan, p. 137.
12. Philip Yancey, *Open Windows*, p. 73.
13. Golan, p. 132.
14. Lillian Rubin, *Woman of a Certain Age: The Mid-life Search for Self*, pp. 13–30.

Other research, however, suggests that for some women the nest is indeed empty. Some mothers apparently tie their selves into their children's lives. When the kids go, depression moves in.[15]

Naturally, there are some negative aspects for all women, especially those who have devoted most of their time to the family.[16] The event may be coupled with the present or impending menopause. With the parenting task reduced or gone, the mother will have to establish some sense of worth beyond that role.

Problems are not only caused by the child's leaving, but the "where" and "how" as well. According to Rubin, mothers who are most upset are those

- who are disappointed in their children
- whose relationships with the children are unsatisfactory
- whose disapproval of the child's life-style makes their interaction with the children difficult and tenuous[17]

If the children are a disappointment, the mother often blames herself and accepts blame placed on her by others. The whole matter may be complicated by resentment if she gave up her career dream to invest herself in the children's lives.

FATHER'S LOSS

Recent studies indicate that fathers may have more difficulty adjusting to the departure of children than mothers. My wife and I were surprised by our friends' response when we asked them how things were going now that the last child had moved out. Joy flowed from the woman's face as she told us how great it was. But both of them quickly acknowledged that Dad was having the toughest time. Men often keenly feel the loss when children leave. Contrary to popular belief, Rubin said that her interviews showed fathers more often than mothers wanted to halt the march of time and keep the children home longer.[18] The father's reaction may have less to do with his involvement in the day to day activities of the children's lives than with his feeling that life is going by all too fast.

Golan analyzes the intricacies of father-child relationships leading up to the child's departure from home. A qualitative change in the man's relationship with his children occurs during the child's adolescence. The teenager is growing distant. The father does not feel as close to his child as he did, creating a sense of loss. Groping for some explanation, he may reflect upon his own adolescence: *Perhaps I can't communicate with my teens because my Dad and I were too distant.* That, along with other matters, pressures him to "interiorize," pushing him into constant, sometimes tormenting, self-analysis.[19]

15. Sophie Lowenstein, "Toward Choice and Differentiation in the Mid-life Crisis of Women," mimeographed, as cited by Golan, p. 132.
16. Douglas C. Kimmel, *Adulthood and Aging,* p. 60.
17. Rubin, pp. 13–30.
18. Ibid.
19. Golan, p. 137.

My own struggle comes to mind. The closeness I felt with my two sons during their childhood faded during their teens. Confused and guilt-ridden, I sorted through all sorts of explanations, from blaming myself for lack of communication skills to assuring myself all fathers go through the same thing. Eventually, I was sure the answer lay in how my father and I related during my youth. He and I never shared feelings; thus, my sons and I could not share ours. Long talks were never part of my life with Dad; therefore, long talks were not part of my life with my sons. Somehow, I thought that I could not play the parent adolescent game because my dad had not played it very well with me. I did not know how, I thought.

At the time, I sensed a compelling need to relate to my father, then in his late seventies. Judging the talk between us to be largely superficial, I felt I hardly knew him. During visits, I asked questions about his background, eagerly struggling to know him in more depth. Once, by his hospital bed, when doctors thought he would die, I sensed an urgency to communicate what hung over me like a heavy weight. For just a few moments we talked about sensitive matters, and in response to my questions we shared our feelings as never before. I floated down the hospital corridor. I had been close to my father.

At the time, I wondered why those few moments meant so much to me. Now I believe I know. My almost obsessive concern for my relationship with my father was largely a concern for my relationship with my sons. In my subconscious, the two were intertwined. I had two unresolved conflicts, the past one connected to the present one. Somehow, if I could feel close to my father, my sons could feel close to me someday.

For many fathers, apparently, those conflicts are unresolved when the time comes for the adolescent to leave home. Possibly, in the father's mind, the departure serves to widen the gap between himself and his child. Yet most fathers do not have that severe a problem and are not distressed by a child's departure.[20]

HUSBAND AND WIFE TOGETHER

If the nest is not emptying on the anticipated schedule, it may be an anxious place. Like birds, the mother and father are wrapped up in whether or not the fledgling can fly. In middle-class families, the parents usually anticipate the child leaving for college at age eighteen, which creates a sort of halfstep in the letting-go process. Studies show that children who leave home at that age have a better relationship with parents than those who continue to live there. Because college may not be part of the plan in some families, older teens living at home become a problem. Children are not expected to leave home until married. The time for departure is indefinite, and preparation for the eventual separation is hard. Millions of parents with adult children at home are upset by the question "Will he ever leave?" Not all of those adults have serious troubles, or want to push the kids out, but there can be considerable stress and struggle. Elizabeth Harkins's study ended with this conclusion: the empty nest is not a particularly

20. Ibid., p. 138,

stressful period in most women's lives. The major threat to well-being is when a couple has a child who ought to be independent but is not.[21]

It seems, then, that the empty nest is not so difficult as supposed. For all women, changes are demanded. For some, the major struggle is letting go of the child. That not only means allowing the young adult to go his own way but freeing oneself from a sense of responsibility for what he does. With her control, she must also give up anxiety, allowing the fledgling young adult to make his own decisions and bear his own pain. Parents sometimes wallow in guilt and stew in frustration because they are too deeply tied to their adult child's behavior. In those situations, the children eat sour grapes, and the parents' teeth are set on edge. Such parents need to know that parents are influential but not omnipotent. "Train up a child in the way he should go and, when he is old, he will not depart from it" (Prov. 22:6, KJV) shows the power of family influences. Other Scriptures combine to balance that with the realization that adult children may go their own way, despite home training. The Proverb gives no guarantee. In the Old Testament, the rebellious young adult was to be stoned, showing that he, not his parents, took the onus for his behavior. Other forces, external and internal, determine what a person will be. Adult children must bear the burden of their own choices; parents should be set free.

The church's role is a prominent one since many of the parent's ideals of parenting may have been formed there. At that juncture of life, parents' needs will be spiritual and psychological. As church leaders, a quick response might be to enlist newly freed parents in church ministry. Bible studies, teas, social work, and evangelistic visitation are helpful opportunities for them. But it is important to see that their situation demands more than frantic activity. They also need lots of understanding. Many will need support groups and contact with other parents to help them work through the anxiety, guilt, and disappointment that can go with launching children from home. Practically, they will be constructing a new life-style.

What is most crucial about the new empty nest life-style is the relationship of the two "birds" that are left alone there. For the most part, research indicates that at that time, the nest is a cozy place to be. Both men and women report they look forward to it as a time of greater closeness between them. And they are right; in most cases, the intimacy increases. There is less tension, simply because they are no longer each playing two roles on a day by day basis (father-husband; mother-wife). Sexual relationships improve, sometimes dramatically.

Stories about mid-life separations and extramarital affairs should not be taken as the norm. The great majority of couples report greater companionship in all aspects during that period of life. Only a minority of mid-lifers' marital relationships are jeopardized by the emptying of the nest. Their marital welfare is determined primarily by how they have related all along and by how much they have neglected their relationships for the sake of the children. If, from the start, family satisfaction primarily came from the children, not from the husband-wife bond, they obviously

21. Elizabeth Harkins, "Effects of Empty Nest Transition on Self-Report of Psychological and Physical Well-Being," *Journal of Marriage and Family* 40, no. 3 (August 1978):547-56.

have little left when the kids are gone. Ralph Johnson's study gives scientific credibility to what is suspected: husbands who had affairs scored lower on marital adjustment tests and indicated they received less satisfaction in their marriages than those who did not.[22] The same was not true for women. Wives who took lovers did not report the same dissatisfaction. Sex, of course, is not the only problem area for empty nesters. Any conflict that was laid aside for the sake of giving attention to the children can resurface, causing fierce tension.

Contentions of one sort or another eventually lead many couples to separate or divorce although counseling is quite successful for many. The church is in a strategic position to offer hope to those couples, showing them that the option to divorce need not be continuing in a miserable relationship. Learning, change, and growth can take place—and often does.

The church can head off a lot of unhappiness through preventive measures. The time to begin preparing for the empty nest is when the couple is building it. Premarital counseling and marriage enrichment programs will help young adults build a relationship that will not quit when the children leave home and they find themselves alone again.

22. Ralph E. Johnson, "Marital Patterns During the Middle Years" (Ph.D. diss., University of Minnesota, 1968), as cited by Joan Aldous, *Family Careers,* p. 191.

16

Living After Death:
Grief and Widowhood

GOOD GRIEF[1]

Trying to comfort himself and his team after their worst loss, Chicago White Sox manager Tony LaRussa said, "Losing build's character; winning just is." Somehow everyone knows that LaRussa is right, but when something important has been lost, the last thing wanted is to hear "It's good for you." "Wouldn't it be better for me to still have what I lost?" could be hurled back.

The person dealing with grief is like the little girl whose mother was trying to comfort her as she took the candle from the room, leaving the small daughter in darkness. "God will be with you," the mother said. "Mother," the fearful girl pleaded, "could you take God and leave the candle?" A person in grief might be thinking: *Take character and give me back my wife.* Loss is terrible. Grieving is painful. Grief smears our thinking with sorrow and sometimes anger.

Beneath the sorrow, however, is the awareness that character is important and that grieving is a fertile soil in which character may grow. The loss may leave scars, but better Christians can emerge. "Tribulation brings about perseverance; and perseverance, proven character; and proven character, hope" (Rom. 5:3–4).

Maturity demands that everyone learn how to handle grief, simply because all face loss. Losses come in many varieties. Death is only one means of deprivation. A geographic move finds people mourning a whole community and a host of friends left behind. Adults of all ages lose jobs, billfolds, friends, and loved ones. Loss is almost synonymous with old age, when one loss after another occurs.

In the young adult section, the grief suffered by persons enduring what may be the worst loss of all, the death of one's child, was examined. Grief was also touched on in

---

1. This section is based on the larger treatment in my booklet *Grief*.

the section on divorce. Later, bereavement in the older widow and widower experience will be looked at. The treatment of grief, however, will be most thorough here in this middle adult section. Though grieving becomes a more likely passage as one grows older, it is the middle period when a first serious loss is most likely to occur.

Handling smaller losses up to the time of more critical ones trains one for grieving. Little losses can greatly disturb. Living down a lost twenty dollar bill can be difficult for some people. It may take days to forget about it. Thoughts about where it was last seen or put keep seizing the control center of the mind like terrorists demanding that attention be paid to them. Waking hours are colored with sadness, while the mind keeps saying, *It was only twenty dollars.*

GRIEF IS NORMAL

Since grief is normal, it is not an enemy to be attacked with Scripture verses and sweet sounding phrases. Grief is not something to escape. It is a tunnel to go through, not fly over. God's Word and presence enable those experiencing grief to make it to the only exit—the other end of the tunnel. Along with God's help, the best thing to help a person through grief is knowing about the shadows, turns, corners, and cracks inside the tunnel.

Even positive changes can produce grief, because every change is a loss. Though a person goes to a better job, he may still feel a sense of loss related to the old one. Taking a trip or vacation is a good example of how a pleasant, long anticipated change can have its mixture of mourning and joy. When climbing into the car or when the plane surges into the sky, a tinge of sadness or fear, despite intense anticipation, may be felt. Anxiety puts its trembling arms around us, aroused by the loss of what is being left behind. Grief, of course, is not always severe. It helps, though, to know what is happening even when the reaction is slight.

Today, quite a bit is known about the grieving process. Nonetheless, grief is not an easy subject to study, because death is not an easy thing to face. Experts say that death is more of a taboo subject in the American culture than sex. The fear of death holds all mankind in slavery (Heb. 2:15).

Since there are so many compelling reasons for learning about grief, anxiety must not be permitted to prevent the study of it. To be effective counselors, something must be known about grief's mysteries. The damage of unknowing sympathizers is as old as the work of Eliphaz, Bildad, and Zophar, who were so clumsy in their attempt to comfort Job.

GRIEF IS COMPLEX

Simply put, grief is the reaction to loss. It is not only sadness; it may include many emotions, including mental anguish and searching. Grief is different from bereavement in that bereavement is more a summary of the events of a certain time period. Mourning may not be synonymous with grief, though the two words are used in that way. Mourning may have more to do with the cultural pattern for handling a loss, particularly the death of a close one, such as certain social practices.

This discussion will deal with the emotional, mental, and practical parts of the grief process, somewhat interweaving them together.

Triggered by loss. Loss is what causes grief as well as explains it. Even in a death, it is the loss that is central to the grieving. In death, grieving is somewhat double: one grieves over his own loss as well as the dead one's losses. When my close friend died recently, I mourned his absence but also was saddened by what he had been denied: seeing his daughter graduate, for example, or being with us at Christmas time. My comfort comes in part from knowing he is with the Lord, since—for Christians—to die is gain (Phil. 1:21). But I still continue to feel sadness over his death and absence, along with many other feelings and thoughts. Grief being a loss reaction explains why Christians are not completely comforted at a time of death by the confidence that their loved one is safe and happy in God's presence. Their sadness is for themselves as well as for their loved one. To tell a widow she should not mourn because her husband is in a better place is to miss a crucial point. It is like telling a lonely wife not to feel bad because her absent husband is basking in the sunlight and relaxing on the golf course during his two-week business trip to Florida. She may be happy for him, but that can hardly be expected to take away the pain of her loss.

Inner conflict. Some experts talk about the conflict that goes on inside a person—a conflict between reality and desires. In reality, something is lost, but in the griever's heart, he wants that lost thing or person to exist. It is normal to want the valuable relationship to continue while the loss itself makes it evident that the relationship has already been severed. What is desired does battle with what must be faced. That conflict is part of grief.

Detachment—reattachment. In the grief process, a person must detach from the past relationship with the lost thing or person and then attach himself to a new relationship. For example, a man who has lost his wife must give up all he had with her while she was living: the warmth of her body, the companionship, the emotional support she offered. He must then establish a new relationship with her. He must be able to think of her and relate to her differently, cherishing the memories and being able to talk of her without undue sadness and conflict. The bereaved must also re-establish other relationships and patterns of life. Disengaging from the former ways of behaving, he must reinvest in a new and productive direction. For example, when a person loses a job he must move in both directions: severing the attachment to the past one and entering a new one. The conflict comes because of the emotional contact with the past. When strong, it will interfere with the adjustment to the present and future.

Searching. Under almost any circumstances, a person will search for something when it is lost. If a person did not care about the loss of food or other valuable items, he would not be able to survive. Have you ever misplaced your car keys or wallet right before attending a meeting? If you have, then you know how difficult it is to forget about the loss while you wait for the meeting to end. Your mind, like an uncontrolled computer, keeps retracing your steps, trying to locate the lost item. Collin Parkes has argued that the "urge to search" characterizes all grief as well. Particularly present in the early grief stages, "typical searching behavior includes anxiety, restlessness, preoccupation with the lost person, . . . focus of attention toward those parts of the environment in which the lost person is likely to be, and even 'calling for the lost person.' "[2]

Emotional puzzle. The emotional complexity of grief makes some phychologists think it is a unique human reaction. That is, they believe it is different from sadness and anger and so deserves a separate category. Others believe it is merely a combination of many emotions. Grieving does include a whole range of responses. It is more than sadness and can include anger. If the lost item was taken by force (as in a robbery or murder), bitterness combines with sorrow. Therefore, it cannot simply be said that the difficulty one has with grief will be proportionate to the degree of love a person had for the lost. Grief difficulty is not merely related to the intensity of love, it is also associated with the complexity of the loss situation. For example, a wife who has greatly loved her husband of fifty years may not have a severe bereavement at his death. Her thankfulness for a lifetime of happiness may balance her sorrow. On the other hand, a person may have more trouble grieving at times when the relationship with the departed person was not close. Take, for example, the reaction of a father to the death of his rebellious teenage son. Recalling years of tension prior to the son's death may produce a terrible mixture of bitterness, resentment, disappointment, and anger. Now that his son is gone, there is no chance for reconciliation. Loss, in that case, is not merely the loss of what the father had but what he might have had. He lost the future. Along with regret for the past, he may deeply resent not having a chance to restore his relationship with his son.

Grief is complex because it includes adjustment on two levels: the mental and the emotional. Life must be reconstructed, and questions raised by a loss must be grappled with. At the same time, all of the complex, emotional responses must be managed, even while the emotional and rational are intersecting and interfering with each other. Anger prompts bitter thoughts about God. Thoughts about missed opportunities push the griever to the brink of depression.

TO GRIEVE IS GODLY

Sex, age, religious belief, and personality structure all play a part in how a person reacts to loss. Though grief will be different for each individual, there is something similar about it for everyone. Scriptures teach that grief is proper for the Christian. Godliness does not exclude grief. For example, after Stephen was killed, "godly men buried Stephen and mourned deeply for him" (Acts 8:2, NIV). Today, mourning may be judged a weakness. In ancient times, people were not ashamed to display grief. The great generals Cyrus and Alexander are known for their public weeping at times of crisis. The apostle Paul acknowledged that he was capable of severe mourning. Speaking of God's healing of his friend, he wrote: "God had mercy on him, and not on

2. Collin Parkes, *Bereavement* (New York: International, 1972), p. 40, cited by R. Scott Sullender, "Three Theoretical Approaches to Grief," *The Journal of Pastoral Care* 23, no. 4 (December 1979): 243–51.

him only but also on me, lest I should have sorrow upon sorrow" (Phil. 2:27). "Sorrow upon sorrow" is an expression based on a Hebrew idiom that portrays intense mourning. When Paul said that Christians are to "sorrow not, even as others who have no hope" (1 Thess. 4:13, KJV), he was referring to the manner of sorrowing, not the fact. A Christian's grieving may be somewhat different, but it will still be present.

Accepting the idea that grieving is an acceptable response to loss will help people be better prepared for it. The one who believes he should not sorrow or "break down" may have the worst time. His grieving will be compounded by guilt if he responds in a way he thinks a Christian should not, even though that response is acceptable and normal.

GRIEF REACTIONS

LOSS REACTIONS

Preoccupation with the deceased is one of the first reactions to loss. Some attempt is made to bring back the loved one by fixing him in the mind. The griever relives past moments, perhaps talking continually about them with friends and relatives. Like taking treasures out of a jewelry box, a person lifts one moment after another from the mind's storehouse, holding them up, examining them, making certain they are intact, safe and secure.

Another means of "bringing back" is through trying to shape a clear mental picture of the one lost. Sometimes grievers are surprised by the difficulty of doing this. One can sense C. S. Lewis's panic and perplexity as he writes about his departed wife: "I have no photograph of her that is any good. I cannot even see her face distinctly in my imagination."[3] It seems it is more difficult to reconstruct the face than it is to recreate the sound of a voice or a feeling of what it was like to be near the departed one.

Sometimes the griever identifies with the lost person as if to continue that person's life. He may gaze at a sunset as if looking on behalf of the loved one. A widow will do things for her child, mentally attributing the deed to the deceased parent. *This hug is from Daddy,* she thinks, for example. Widows or widowers in the initial grief stages may so closely identify with their dead spouse that they begin to think like them. Sometimes the griever will actually try to take the lost one's place. A widow of a senator may run for office, trying to "keep her husband alive."

Things may be substituted for the deceased person. A griever may fix on a room, a piece of clothing, or article that brings a sense of the dead one's presence. The passion for hanging on may even cause hallucinations, some of which are merely altered perceptions. A person spotted in a crowd looks like the loved one, and the mourner is overcome by a moment of joy. Sounds in the next room may sound like the departed's voice. Apparently, people can miss someone so much that their feeling-saturated minds try to produce the sight and sound of the departed. People may need to be told

3. C. S. Lewis, *A Grief Observed,* p. 16.

that such things are common, while clearly stating that the Bible gives no evidence the living can communicate with the dead.

EMOTIONAL REACTIONS.

Like stirring a stagnant pond, loss brings all kinds of emotions to the surface. Some, like fear, may be surprising. "No one ever told me that grief feels so like fear. I am not afraid, but the sensation is like being afraid. The same fluttering in the stomach, the same restlessness, the yawning. I keep on swallowing."[4] Grief does actually produce fear: fear of the future, of being able to cope, of death. Sudden loss makes a person feel vulnerable. "If this could happen, what next?" is asked.

Perhaps fear takes the form of a general anxiety. Everyone, at some time, does battle with the dread of the future. After Job's tragedies, that godly man said,

> What I feared has come upon me;
> What I dreaded has happened to me.
> (Job 3:25, NIV)

Special to grief may be the fear of being abandoned, an anxiety that may be traced back to infancy. David Switzer makes a strong case for seeing grief as anxiety. Death triggers a basic personal anxiety about one's own existence.[5]

Deeper expressions of the fear of death occur. The griever struggles to regain some sense of the meaning of life. He ponders what it might be like to not exist. Fear digs up doubts about eternal life. Responsibilities threaten. The pressure of caring for others continues all the while the bereaved is wrestling with questions about the worth and significance of life.[6] Emotions are the driving force behind those questions. The reader of Job sees an outpouring of questions mixed with a cascading stream of emotion.

> Why is life given to a man
> whose way is hidden? . . .
> (Job 3:23, NIV)
> Where can wisdom be found?
> (Job 28:12, NIV)

are questions asked by a man who says he is "terrified" (23:16, NIV), in "thick darkness" (23:17, NIV), with "no rest, but only turmoil" (3:26, NIV), and whose "groans pour out like water" (3:24, NIV).

In dealings with oneself and others in grief, it is crucial to see that there is an emotional link to the rational. Questions prompted by grief may be legitimate quests for insight, but they should not all be taken seriously. Resolved emotions, not

4. Ibid., p. 7.
5. David Switzer, *The Dynamics of Grief*, pp. 102-9.
6. Ibid., pp. 169-70.

answered questions, will most often be the final answer to loss. The book of Job teaches that some questions remain unanswered.

In grief, Lewis can be excused for pondering God as some sort of monster who loves to torture people. Later, he explains that his mental pictures were painted by emotional brush strokes. "Why do I make room in my mind for such filth and nonsense?" he asks. "Do I hope that if feeling disguises itself as thought I shall feel less? Aren't all these notes the senseless writhings of a man who won't accept the fact that there is nothing we can do with suffering except to suffer it?"[7]

Be careful not to rebuke others or oneself for raising hard questions or saying hopeless things. Job accused God of being unjust and cruel, yet Job did not sin. *God's terrors are marshaled against me,* he wrongly thought (Job 6:4, NIV). The emotional context of statements should always be considered. Often, the griever is only using words to let out the foul vapors of an oppressed soul. An appropriate response may be to merely say, "I can understand how you could think that," or rest a hand on a trembling arm and just listen.

Anger, like fear, is a common grief response that must be kept in hand. It can break out in any direction—at the doctors, at circumstances, at God. To show how irrational it can be, it is often hurled at the one who has died or is dying. One woman recalls her irate thoughts as her husband lay dying in her arms after fourteen years of marriage, "You . . . you're not going to be there for me when I die."[8] Hebrews 12:15 warns against allowing bitterness to control responses to crises.

Anger is best handled by bringing it into honest light. "In your anger do not sin," (Eph. 4:26, NIV). Anger needs to be admitted to be controlled. Those who minister to the bereaved learn to accept their caustic words, bitter thoughts, and furious outbursts.

Guilt too, may clothe the mourner. "There is no grave beside which a flood of guilt feelings does not assault the mind," says Paul Tournier. Scores of things can create guilt. Some are real; most are imaginary. Guilt sometimes flows where there is no tie in reality to the crisis. A surviving spouse might accuse: "If only we would have gone to the hospital sooner," or, "If only we would have gotten different doctors." Others around know there has been no fault, but the griever sometimes carries a burden he does not deserve. Grievers need assurance from others. Since their own thinking is distorted, they need words from those whose thoughts are untempered by emotion. A more objective viewpoint can still be offered even while accepting the griever's thoughts and trying to understand them. "You know you got the best doctors you could," might be offered. They need clear statements of fact and reality.

Depression and sorrow are the primary grief reactions. As Job mourns, he showers his comforters with bleak, black statements:

> Why is light given to those in misery,
> and life to the bitter of soul,

---

7. Lewis, p. 29.
8. David Gelman et al., "A Great Emptiness," *Newsweek,* 7 November 1983, p. 120.

> to those who long for death that does not come,
> who search for it more than for hidden treasure.
> (Job 3:20-21, NIV)
> Sighing comes to me instead of food;
> my groans pour out like water.
> (Job 3:24, NIV)

He has all the symptoms of depression: sadness (3:20); desire for death (3:21); helplessness (3:25); sleep disturbance (7:4); a sense of worthlessness about life (9:21); pessimism about life (14:1); and physical distress (17:7). One griever described her feelings as a journey "down, down into the depths of depths in hollow, dark desolation."[9] The good news with the bad is that with time, depression will go away. Living with it is the way to get through it. Like early morning fog, depression will slowly fade as the griever moves through the stages of grief.

SOCIAL AND SPIRITUAL REACTIONS

Besides the emotional reactions, a person dealing with grief will deal differently with others than he normally would. Sometimes, a person will withdraw, desiring to be alone. Although friends and relatives will want to comply with their wishes, it may be best not to leave them entirely alone in the initial stages. Someone should be quietly with them or in a nearby room. The griever will often want company. "There is a sort of invisible blanket between the world and me. I find it hard to take in what anyone says. . . . Yet I want the others to be about me. I dread the moments when the house is empty. If only they would talk to one another and not to me."[10]

Reactions in the spiritual area may startle the griever. A Christian who has imagined himself to be spiritually tough even though he has had little prior experience with loss to test him, may be dismayed when he goes to pieces, or may be plagued by doubts when he has no sense of God's presence. Even those who have been close to God tell of how their feelings drive a wedge between them and their Lord. "Meanwhile, where is God? When you are happy, . . . if you . . . turn to Him . . . you will be—or so it feels—welcomed with open arms. But go to Him when your need is desperate, . . . what do you find? A door slammed in your face."[11]

Sometimes a person loses confidence in his own faith, thinking *My faith was never real.* The prior trials may seem so tiny; the previous exercise of faith like playing a game. Perhaps the griever is correct, but the size of past faith is irrelevant. What counts is present trust. Scripture tells us to have faith in God, not in our faith.

---

9. Stephanie Ambrose May, from her diary *In God's Hands,* as cited by B. Clayton Bell and Peggy Bell, "A Look at Grief," *Leadership* 1 (Fall 1980):44.
10. Lewis, p. 7.
11. Ibid., p. 9.

MENTAL REACTIONS

The mind will have its own response to grief. Losing raises many rational issues. First, the loss will have to be explained or rationalized. If one has no religious resources, he may become philosophical. *I'm just unlucky,* a person may explain to himself, or fatefully reason, *Losses are part of life.* People will grope for answers to spiritual questions never thought of before their loss brought the questions to their attention. Christians close by can play a big part in answering questions—voiced and unvoiced. Grievers need biblical insight, but they disdain being force-fed spiritual milk and meat.

Misfortune gives birth to puzzling questions. "Why is there suffering?" is the most complex. No honest Christian claims to have a simple answer for it. Suffering, pain and God are co-existent realities. Scripture says that He is a good God, One who loves and suffers with mankind. Space does not allow a discussion of the way theologians put those realities together. Joseph Bayly, a man who has seen his three young children die, says, "I cannot explain it, but my wife and I have never been more convinced of His love for us and our children than when we have turned from a fresh grave. . . . Reason gropes in the dark for answers, while faith waits for God."[12] The Scriptures promise eventual solace and peace to those who mourn. God is "the Father of mercies and God of all comfort, who comforts us in all our affliction" (2 Cor. 1:3-4). Tranquility in the mind and soul may not come instantly to those who suffer loss. Grief has a course to run.

GRIEF STAGES

Those who have studied grief have charted its stages.[13] Research is not complete enough to be certain that the following are the precise steps. Individuals will have varying experiences. Exploring these stages may help remove some of the mystery, confusion, and guilt feelings grieving people have. Knowing these stages will not remove the grief's pain but may help make the journey less difficult.

STAGE ONE: SHOCK

This first stage may last for hours or even days. "Shock" is both the emotional and the physical reaction to the crisis. The griever's emotions may simply make it impossible for him to believe what is happening.

In serious losses, the denial can be stubborn. Eventually, the griever must face the loss. Those nearby should help him do those things that make it evident: telephoning

---

12. Joseph Bayly, *The View from a Hearse,* p. 105.
13. Erich Lindeman, professor of psychiatry, was among the first to research the grief process. He published his results in an article entitled "Symptomatology and Management of Acute Grief" in the *American Journal of Psychiatry* 101:141-48, September 1944. Following Lindeman, Granger Westberg described ten stages of grief in his practical book, *Good Grief,* Philadelphia: Fortress Press, 1961. A Harvard study of grief was published under the title *The First Year of Bereavement,* New York: John Wiley and Sons, 1974. Elisabeth Kübler-Ross's studies also contributed to the knowledge of grief's stages. See *On Death and Dying,* New York: Macmillan, 1969.

relatives to share the news, viewing the body in the case of a death and when appropriate. The griever should not be protected from those "hard things," since that will prolong the denial stage. Allow the person in shock to take the lead in the conversation and listen without blame to statements of bitterness or anger. Encourage "grief work" immediately. Explain it is proper to cry, to express thoughts. If they are confused or distressed, confirm that that is normal, but allow him to do for himself whatever he can. That will help him come to terms with what has happened as well as with his shocked state.

STAGE TWO: CONTROL

This controlled stage ends, in the cases of death, when the funeral is over and the loved ones have departed. The bereaved is still influenced by grief and will need others to guide. Passivity, lack of reaction, feelings of emptiness, difficulty in making decisions, panic, fear, and anxiety may be present. Sometimes a person will feel a lack of connection to himself or have other strange perspectives and feelings.

It is best to allow those feelings to flow and not prevent them. The best way to deal with them is for the griever to continue life's activities. He must eventually go to work, though he may feel emotionally detached from what he is doing. Though his thoughts may be elsewhere, he should be with other people. At this time, the griever may complain of attacks of weeping and wonder if he is abnormal. Other things may happen to make the person question his sanity. Quiet assurance can be given along with companionship. The best human pain reliever for the agony of separation is a supporting, empathetic friend.

STAGE THREE: REGRESSION

The regressive stage, in the case of death, lasts about three months. A person may become more active handling the loss. But, coping is more selfish and may, at times, seem to be moving backwards to stage two. At this time, the griever is spending a lot of energy on keeping himself in control. Holding back tears and trying to concentrate on the task at hand saps his strength. He may become apathetic and helpless. "Tension" is a good way to describe his emotions, thoughts, and even physical condition. At this stage a person may simplify complex matters: "If we had not gone on vacation this would not have happened" is a sample of his reasoning. This is the time for being preoccupied with the deceased.

A person's own self-respect might diminish at this point. Public weeping, still not under control, may make him feel ashamed. The mind will be dealing with spiritual questions and with other issues. Religious behavior may become simplified, as answers are sought: "If I give a large portion of money to the church, I'll feel better," a person might say. Communion with God may be difficult. Guilt, anxiety, and depression still linger. Anger may flare up again and again.

This is a stage for handling the myriad of possible grief reactions.

During this stage, a good grief companion will:

- *Listen.* Allow the person to direct the conversation, and hear him out, even if what he says may not sound very reasonable.
- *Be alert* to questions. When the griever asks, he is reaching out for help. Not always willing to agree with you, the griever still needs to hear other points of view.
- *Ask questions.* Gently challenge what the griever says. You are a link to reality. Help the griever to see how feelings distort thinking. Ask him to talk, but do not force.
- *Be patient.* Rebuke for feelings and thoughts is not what the griever needs. If the griever is out of touch with reality it is not unkind to face him with the facts. Saying, "Your husband is dead; you must realize this," is not cruel if a woman is continuing to deny what has happened and thwarting the grieving process.
- *Make suggestions.* Depressed people sometimes need someone to prod them a bit. Urge the person to get out of the house more, to get at things that must be done.
- *Be kind and approving.* Communicate your acceptance through loving touch and word.

STAGE FOUR: ADAPTATION

Adaptation is the term used for this final step. A number of things occur:

- *Liberation.* The person feels free of the image of self as mourner. Sometimes, happiness seems to suddenly surge. Perhaps the emotional composure comes more slowly, but eventually the negative emotions are offset by the joy of being alive.
- *New perspective.* The lost one or thing is now seen in a new light. There is still an attachment, but it is now a different kind. The absence is accepted. Before, memories, furniture, places, and people associated with the loved one brought painful awareness of the loss. Now, the one who has grieved can comfortably be with those people and things. That is possible because the person has detached from the lost one and become reattached in a new way.
- *A reality focus.* Coming through the previous stages makes it possible to have a true focus on reality once again. The distorted, simplistic thinking of earlier grieving gives way to rational reasons and biblical truth. He can now again live without a complete rational explanation for all issues.

If the prior stages are handled properly, the griever will arrive at stage four. If "grief work" has not been done, he may end up with physical ailments or even delayed grief reactions. Unresolved anger, bitterness, or guilt may prevent normal relationships, thinking and living. Sometimes, for example, the loss of a child will damage the couple's relationship because one or both of them did not go through grief successfully.

In addition to the kind of support the companion gives in grief stage three, the person on stage four may need someone to watch for symptoms of trouble with the grief journey. Inhibited grief is one thing to look for. If, during the months following the loss, little emotion has been shown or discussed, the person may not have allowed grief to progress. Certain problems may occur as a result: alcoholism, continued loss of sex drive, physical illness, social problems, and the like. The person may need counseling to see the link between his current problems and his loss.

Delayed grief may cause an individual to have a sudden emotional outbreak over a loss that occurred years earlier. That may happen because during the grief period the person bravely controlled emotions to be a "good testimony" or not to "disturb the children." Grief may be delayed for other reasons. Something else may interfere with grieving, like an illness or another death. Once a woman was driven from one of my classes by an uncontrollable weeping spell that overcame her while viewing a film on babies. Later, we sought an explanation. We concluded that her extreme sadness and lengthy crying spell were delayed grief reactions. Several years before, her husband had died only a few weeks after she lost her newborn baby. She remembered that she had spent little time mourning the loss of her child because of her grief for her husband.

Elongated grief is another sign grieving has not gone well. Just how long the grief process should last is anybody's guess. The initial phase of shock can last from a few hours or days to a week or gradually change into a second phase of denial and acute grief, which reaches a peak of intensity between the second and fifth weeks of bereavement. It usually takes six to twelve weeks for intense grief to diminish. Normalcy might not occur before a year is up.[14] The kind of loss, the circumstances, and the personality of the individual along with many other factors make it impossible to say what is normal. A person headed for trouble might be identified by watching the progress through the stages. If, for example, a wife is still denying the death of her husband in spite of the funeral and all other evidence, she may need some special counseling. Or, sometimes a person stays on stage three, unable to successfully detach and reattach to the lost person. A Chicago man, for example, has never adjusted to the death of his young son. Years later, his son's room is as it always was. He has substituted the objects in the room for his departed son, never fully getting a new perspective of his child as one who is now gone. It may be unfair to judge people for what seems a peculiar way of handling a loss. The major standard is that they come to live a normal life and, of course, that they continue in their Christian walk.

ANTICIPATORY GRIEF

Recently, it has become evident that a person can start through the grief stages before a loss has occurred. It happens with the terminally ill. Anticipatory grief can even show up prior to a person's leaving on a trip such as in families in which one

14. Bertha Simos, "A Time to Grieve: Loss as a Universal Human Experience," as cited by Golan, p. 177.

member travels for business reasons or a tour of duty. They may become depressed and irritable with each other and slowly back away from the relationship that will soon be severed.

The terminally ill person experiences that kind of grief. The hope of eternal life and eventual reunion with loved ones does not keep them from the sting of eventual separation. Persons experiencing grief before loss may feel guilty. A husband of a terminally ill wife may chastise himself for a growing feeling of detachment from her. He cannot understand why he is pondering practical things like selling the home after she is gone.

Anticipatory grief can spawn loneliness if it is not understood. The dying person might begin to shut others out because he is trying to reduce the pain of leaving them. Those who remain behind may begin to turn off feelings for the departing one, isolating them. Everyone involved should try to stay emotionally close and resist the tendency to withdraw. Anticipatory grief should not be permitted to rob people of affection and companionship at such a critical time.

GRIEF: A HEALING PROCESS

Grief is a process of healing that needs to be helped along. People can assist, but they cannot heal themselves or others. B. Clayton Bell and Peggy Bell put it graphically. "A competent physician knows how to clean a wound, apply antiseptic, suture when necessary, bandage, *and then wait for the healing process.* A doctor is not a healer. He aids the healing process. The same is true of the wounds of grief. God is the healer and fellow Christians . . . can mediate His comfort. Yet they must also know how to keep their hands off to allow God to do His own healing."[15]

When everything is said and done about grief, the final word is this: it is God who comforts. Under His control and presence, grief must be allowed to run its course. Stephanie May endured a terrible tragedy. In one instant, a plane crash took her husband, two children, and a son-in-law. Here is the final entry in her diary.

> I cannot replace or compare my loss. It is my loss. I am not strong, I am not brave. I am a Christian with a burden to carry and a message to share. I have been severely tested, but my faith has survived, and I have been strengthened in my love and devotion to the Lord. Oh, God, my life is Yours—comfort me in Your arms and direct me in my life. I walked in hell, but now I walk with God in peace . . . His love surrounds us.[16]

GOING IT ALONE: WIDOWHOOD

"The first thing you think about is how she isn't there. And suddenly you feel death all around you." That feeling is the worst part of losing a spouse, according to Ron Landsman, a thirty-four-year-old Washington attorney.[17] The pain and sorrow of

15. Bell, "A Look at Grief," p. 50.
16. May as cited by Bell and Bell, pp. 49–50.
17. Gelman et al., p. 120.

widows and widowers is mixed with practical day-to-day struggles. Just as in divorce, the separated party faces a combination of emotional and pragmatic issues.

Becoming a widow or widower as a young or middle adult is more difficult than when older. Part of the problem is the lack of encouragement available from others. Whereas society and churches have a fairly strong support network for older widows it does not have the same for younger ones even though social support seems to be the most important factor for adjusting to the loss of a spouse. One middle-aged woman pointed out her need: "A listener's the only medicine a widow really needs. And let me tell you from bitter experience there aren't any. I'd call up people who were very close to me and try to tell them what I was feeling. I didn't get half a sentence out before they were breaking in with, 'Tillie, you're being morbid. You'll never get over it by dwelling on it. You can't live in the past. Think of the future.' "[18]

Studies show that sources of compassion are few. In a poll conducted in the Minneapolis-St. Paul area by the University of Minnesota's Center for Death Education and Research, the majority of widows reported receiving scant support from family, friends, doctors, or psychologists. What is most disappointing is that only 15 percent of those widowed said they had received church assistance.[19] Too often the church's advice is to accept the loss as God's will.

FIFTH WHEEL BLUES

Besides working through their grief, younger widows, like those divorced, have a host of practical matters to deal with. The surviving spouse may have to learn about financial matters, cope with household chores, and possibly with the care of children. At first she will try to make up for the lost parent by being both mother and father to the children. Spouses must learn that cannot be done and instead just try to be the best mother or father they can be.

A METAMORPHOSIS

Transition in widowhood is a metamorphosis of kinds. A person is suddenly forced to go from being a married person to a single. The roles are quite different.

The resocialization process requires three things: new friends, dating, and participation in social activities with other widows.[20] Younger widows and widowers may have as difficult a time finding those as they do finding someone to help them with their bereavement. Old friends may no longer be there. The widowed person is the "fifth wheel" at social gatherings. Jealousy and fear make some couples see the new widow or widower as a threat to their marriage.

Dating becomes a problem for those who feel remarriage is an answer to their loneliness. Just learning the skills and etiquette of dating is a major problem. Not only have they forgotten how to act in such a situation, they are not sure how to act as an

18. Alfred Allan Lewis with Barrie Berns, *Three Out of Four Wives*, pp. 31–32.
19. Gelman et al., p. 123.
20. Douglas C. Kimmel, *Adulthood and Aging*, p. 238.

older and formerly married person. Additionally, the emotional reactions of guilt, sorrow, and pain related to their former partner may surface while trying to build a relationship with someone else, making dating difficult to manage.

Strong physical and psychological sexual feelings compound the new status. Behind sex interest is the need to be intimate and close, to be cuddled and loved. The temptation to use sex as a form of comfort is powerful. The sexually aggressive person may even use comfort as an excuse to have an affair. Widows and divorcees often tell of awkward situations when the husbands of their friends proposition them sexually.[21]

Specialists have found that contact with other widowed persons is crucial. In fact, the widowed themselves sense this so much that they are behind the formulation of numerous groups throughout the country to facilitate that contact.

Remarriage is one answer to the practical and emotional problems of widowhood. Remarriage is more likely for younger widowed persons. Men remarry faster than women. On an average, remarriage occurs 1.7 years after the death of a spouse for men and 3.5 years after the death of a spouse for women.[22]

In New Testament times, the apostle Paul counseled younger widows to remarry (1 Tim. 5:14). But, it is clear that that counsel was not for all then, nor is it suitable for all now. Many will build meaningful lives as singles. Whatever choice the bereaved makes, the loss of a spouse can be an occasion of growth and a means of finding a new nearness to the Lord. He may emerge with greater self-confidence and esteem as well as trust in God.

21. Robert Weiss, *Marital Separation*, pp. 287-88.
22. David F. Hultsch and Francine Deutsch, *Adult Development and Aging*, p. 331.

17

Getting It from Both Ends: Delinquent Teenagers and Dependent Parents

TEENS IN TROUBLE

"He couldn't have hit us with his billy club any harder than he did with those words: 'We've got your son here in our jail. He's charged as a juvenile for carrying a concealed weapon.'" Those words tumbled from the trembling lips of a high school teacher, a respected member of his local church. He had just talked by phone to a policeman from another state. "We felt as if the bottoms of our hearts dropped out and all the feelings fell through," the father said. "We couldn't even cry."[1]

Margie Lewis tells another story.

> Wilma fled to the bedroom, leaving the aftermath of supper on the kitchen table. Alvin followed her. Silently they undressed. And when they climbed into bed, the nightstand clock flashed 8:05. For a time they lay side by side, as if bound and gagged by their emotions. Minutes passed before Wilma could manage an anguished sigh, "Why, Alvin, why?" Her emotions finally broke through and her body began to heave with sobs.

Minutes before, at the supper table, Wilma and Alvin's teenage son had said: "I don't really know how to tell you this, but I'm gay."[2]

Maybe before their children were teens, fear awakened parents such as those, its somber voice warning "That little child asleep in the next room will grow up a homosexual or a criminal." Most likely, though, they were not so distressed. Having a

---

1. Margie Lewis, *The Hurting Parent,* p. 22.
2. Ibid., p. 101.

teen in terrible trouble is part of other parents' horror stories, people think. But, the teenage rocky road sometimes leads to bad trouble for parent and teen.

TWO TYPES OF TROUBLE

In trouble does not refer to the normal developmental woes and stresses. It refers to two types of teens. First, there are those who willfully break the law. Classified as delinquent, they are involved in such things as drug use, theft, vandalism, frequent reckless driving, or driving while under the influence of drugs. Second are those, not socially delinquent, whose behavior is so deviant from the parents' (and sometimes from society's) that they are thought to be abnormal in their developmental pattern. Homosexuals and alcoholics are among those. Also, there are those who get caught up in unacceptable cults like the Children of God and the Unification Church (Moonies), where youths are coerced and taken advantage of.[3]

No research, to my knowledge, has established just how many troubled teens are in evangelical homes. It is known, though, that if one or both parents attend Sunday school and church, the teen is more likely to attend also. And those who regularly attend Sunday school are less likely to be troubled teens. Since teens eventually follow their parents' value system, troubled teens are less likely to come from moral homes.

Other statistics suggest that evangelicals might have their share of troubled teens. One factor most clearly related to delinquency is the strictness and conservative nature of the home.[4] Delinquents regularly complain that their parents give them too little freedom, treat them "like babies," and deny them privileges their peers are given. It cannot be absolutely determined that evangelicals tend to be more strict than their non-evangelical neighbors, but it can be supposed that conservative religious homes might harbor that kind of parent.

Counselors know that there are many hurting parents in churches whose teens are alcoholics, homosexuals, or delinquents. Through tearful, anxious eyes they will be looking to the Body of Christ for help.

CAUSES

Some causes of delinquency have been established. If a young (twelve- to fourteen-year-old) adolescent's relationship with the opposite sexed parent is poor, there is likely to be trouble. For high school teens, the scene of the cause shifts from the home to the school. Teens who have trouble adjusting and succeeding there will more likely become delinquent.

Incidences of delinquency can be traced to the absence of the father in the home. If the father is absent for at least one year during the child's life, there is greater likelihood of antisocial behavior. The absence does not always result from a broken

---

3. Martin Gold and Richard J. Petronio, "Delinquent Behavior in Adolescence," in *Handbook of Adolescent Psychology,* ed. Joseph Adelson, pp. 495–99.
4. Ibid., pp. 522–23.

home since many fathers in the study were taken away by military service.[5] Lack of success in grade school is another factor according to F. I. Nye and J. F. Short's study. Youngsters who complained of too much schoolwork or who had little motivation to study, ended up with more delinquents among them during their teens.[6] "Their findings suggest that adjustment in grade school has a significant effect on adolescent adjustment."[7] Other data soundly confirms that school is crucial to a young person managing his teen years.

The school can help the teen to know himself. Juvenile delinquency is usually linked to a search for autonomous identity. Normally, teens get a sense of self from their roles at school, home, church, or community. Acceptance and affirmation are the soils in which the unique self grows. If the identity does not flourish in the family, school or church, the youth will turn to a delinquent group to nourish the self. Joining the gang is in itself an autonomous act, setting the teen apart from his family. The delinquent group is distinctive as a rebellious group. That gives it its identity. It fosters and condones delinquent acts. It bestows honor upon those who steal hubcaps or throw rocks through school windows.

Research findings and information like that given above should not needlessly alarm parents. The research that exists indicates that every teen should be looked at individually. Not all kids who have a difficult time in grade school end up in trouble, for example. One generalization, however, is comforting to those who have troubled teens: delinquent teens seldom grow up to be delinquent adults.[8] Unless a teen's behavior is extremely serious from a criminal standpoint and is quite frequent, there is no indication he will end up a criminal. Even those who use drugs heavily or have less formal education or commit more crimes have the same chance of being responsible adults as those who do not.[9] It seems clear that drug use does not produce delinquent youth. Although delinquents do use drugs, those who use drugs do not statistically become more delinquent than other teens.[10]

Knowing those generalities might help some parents. Parents can try to solve early problems that might relate to later delinquency. They can muster all the help possible for a child struggling in grade school, for example. Parents can also watch for their child's cries for help. Laura J. Singer counsels:

> If a youngster is constantly yelling, screaming and flailing against his parents, if a depressed, sullen and withdrawn child retreats in his room and shuts the door on conversation; if there is extreme chaos or ominous silence in the household; if there are signs of self-destructive behavior or evidence that the child doesn't want to be at all honest

5. Ibid., p. 513.
6. F. I. Nye and J. F. Short, Jr., "Scaling Delinquent Behavior," *American Sociological Review* 22 (1957):326–31, as cited in Gold and Petronio, p. 513.
7. Gold and Petronio, p. 513.
8. Ibid., p. 515.
9. Ibid.
10. Ibid., p. 514.

with his parents; if there is no way of making real contact with the child; these are absolute danger signals and it's time to see outside help.[11]

All or none of the above may happen in any normal household, with any normal child. Too often and too pronounced may be too much. It is better to check it out than to worry about it.

HELPING THE HURTING

Those who help parents of troubled teens will find the parents' emotions to be in turmoil. When their child is linked to drugs, alcoholism, theft, or homosexuality, they feel terrible pain. Guilt, shame, embarrassment, and feelings of failure will play havoc with them. Often, when parents search for a cause for a teen's trouble, they think more emotionally than logically. Feelings compel them to ask, "Why?" and to search for someone or something to blame. No matter how smart, they can never be absolutely sure what created a certain problem. The best treatment for parents' emotional reactions is rational action. That may help the parents' marriage, too, since too much brooding can hurt the relationship—particularly if they start leveling blame at one another.

The first thing for such parents to do is to seek counseling along *with* their teen. Reading, also, can play a part. Two outstanding evangelical books for them are *When Parents Cry,* by Joy B. Gage, and *The Hurting Parent,* by Margie M. Lewis.

The most effective counseling strategy is contracting, in which teens and their parents enter into a formal contract. For example, if the issue is the time the teen should come home at night, the pact looks like this: for prompt homecoming for a given number of nights the teen is rewarded by use of the family car. If school is the problem, then a grade average is rewarded with certain privileges. The privelege given is for responsibility shown, and is not to be considered a bribe. A study has shown that contracting succeeds more than all other methods. Only 16 percent of the teens so treated had subsequent appearances in court compared to half of those not so treated.[12]

Parents should be directed to other authorities and social agencies in addition to family counselors for the specialized help they need. A lawyer to help fight the child's legal battles is not sufficient if the problem is to be solved in the long run. Short-term hospital treatment centers for drug and alcohol abusers are proving effective. Educational programs are also available for those who need less intensive treatment.

In order for the delinquent to break away from his peer group, he will need to find some encouragement elsewhere. School, family, and church loom large in his eventual rehabilitation. In other words, delinquency is in part a social problem; therefore, the

11. Laura J. Singer, *Stages,* p. 145.
12. Gold and Petronio, p. 521. Research is by N. C. Klein, J. F. Alexander, B. V. Parsons, "Impact of Family Systems Intervention on Recidivism and Sibling Delinquency: A Model of Primary Prevention and Program Evaluation," *Journal of Consulting and Clinical Psychology* 45 (1977):460–74.

cure is somewhat social. That is not meant to whitewash the problem; sin, too, is there. Pointing to the social causes of delinquency shows that delinquency is a many-sided problem that may call for a multifaceted treatment.

In addition to the family relationship problems confronting the parents of troubled teens, loneliness stalks such couples. Problems like homosexuality, delinquency, and alcoholism bear social stigmas that isolate people connected to them. Plenty of smug, self-righteous, pseudo-pious people will show up to hurl scalding water on parents' tender hearts. Parents with teens in trouble will need a support group where they can find acceptance, understanding, and encouragement. A special group consisting of parents like themselves would be most helpful, although they may also benefit from the ordinary small groups in the church.

There is plenty of evidence that the church *can* help families with special problems. The prescription for teens in trouble and their families calls for the warm, continuous touch of loving, accepting, affirming adults. That is one prescription the church ought to be in a position to fill.

IS THERE LIFE AFTER TEEN TROUBLE?

A final reminder: life goes on. Too often, parents think they would not be able to enjoy life if their offspring do not turn out right. People who teach about family life sometimes unwittingly teach that. I heard a nationally-known Christian family expert do as much in a television interview. He meant no harm, I'm sure, because he was driving home his point that Christian parenting is a serious responsibility. To make it stick, he said, "If your kids don't turn out right, then what's left in life?" "Life is left," I wish I could have said to all his listeners. No crisis or problem permits any Christian to wallow in sorrow, guilt, anger, or self-pity, glumly waiting for death to take him out of misery. The lives of the parents should not become part of the wreckage a teen in trouble brings down around him.

THE OTHER GENERATION GAP

"I can't believe this is happening now," Carol pressed her fingertips against her forehead. "Phil and I have just straightened out our problems and now he wants his mother to come live with us. It's either that or put her in a home, which he can't face. But if I have her with me, I'll be miserable. And if I refuse, I'll be guilty the rest of my life. How can I win?"[13]

Carol's words exhibit about half of the turmoil and dilemma aging parents can create for middle adults. Just about the time mid-lifers are waving good-bye to their children, they may find themselves with a new set of dependents, their aging father and/or mother. Dealing with the problems of the elderly can cause middle adults to shake their heads and gasp the now familiar words "I wasn't prepared for this!" Stephen Cohen and Bruce Gans claim that this is the case for most. "More and more

13. Singer, p. 192.

middle-aged persons find themselves unprepared for the real and often destructive feelings of anxiety, confusion and guilt that they experience because of their parents' difficulties."[14]

To obtain a clear understanding of middle adult agitations relating to dependent parents, it is necessary to form a clearer picture of the life and times of those elderly. It is important to see that the relationship between aging parents and their grown children can become rather complex and problematic. Having to depend on their children for housing and care, as sometimes happens, requires giving up their own independence, at least to some degree. By then, they have probably lost a lot: job, health, friends, home, driver's license, to name a few. To lose more of their independence is difficult. If they seem a bit reluctant and thankless, it is not hard to understand.

A complication for the middle adult concerns what is happening to him internally. The older person threatens the middle adult as the teenager does. The teen is a constant reminder of youthfulness—where the middle adult has been. The older parent represents old age—where the middle adult is headed. The middle adult is psychologically very much in the middle.

Deciding how the aged dependent parent is cared for is becoming a complicated matter due to an increasing number of alternative living arrangements. It is fortunate that the aged need no longer be forced to choose between an institution and living with a grown child and his family. Whether or not a mid-life man, for example, decides to take a parent into his home will depend upon a lot of things, including the stability of his marriage and his willingness to invest time in caring for the parent. Strong emotions flood the decision to institutionalize the elderly. An unpopular thing to do, that act is often done with a lot of guilt feelings. A friend's careless word or doubtful look can sting the middle adult who needs affirmation.

Middle-agers may also have to tackle marital problems that revolve around the care of parents. Conflict is especially painful when a person is confronted by two opposing loyalties, as when parents want to live with a son and the wife is against it. Even if the parent moves in, the wife may disagree about how the parent should be treated. An elderly mother may take advantage of her son and manipulate him to favor her. Needless to say, middle-aged persons must give priority to their marriage and stick together when facing problems—especially those concerning time, finances, space at home, and privacy.

Whatever care is needed, the Christian middle adult should not sidestep his responsibility for aging parents. The commands to honor father and mother include the idea of caring for them in their old age. Paul underscored that when he urged adults to care for their widowed mothers. "If any one does not provide for his own, and especially for those of his household, he . . . is worse than an unbeliever" (1 Tim. 5:8).

In society, the responsibility for parents is not clearly defined. The federal government and other agencies step in even before children have an opportunity to assist. Children of aging parents become emotional over wondering, *How much do I owe my*

14. Stephen Cohen and Bruce Gans, *The Other Generation Gap*, pp. 3–12.

parents? Inside their graying heads, parents may be asking, *How much do my children owe me?* Those questions arouse feelings that are difficult to deal with when middle adults have limited financial resources and constant demands on their time from other quarters.[15] Feeling guilty on one side and resentful on the other does little good for any of them, especially when the parent's situation is becoming more stressful. They will have to make the best decisions they can in the circumstances.

THE BENEFIT BALANCE

Dealing with aging parents is not all problems. Many of them never have to become overly dependent upon their grown children. Even when living together, the benefits more than balance out the bother. Joy flows from the harmonious relationships of three generations being together. Having an aged parent around creates a link to the past for young children. The impact of a grandparent's example should not be underestimated. Besides all that, the family has a chance to care for another human being, one who is perhaps growing weaker and more helpless. What a family receives will probably surpass what they have given.

The bottom line in living with aging parents is the New Testament principle of love. Christlike compassion is needed to overlook the eccentricities of aging loved ones; kindness will overcome the troublesome inconveniences. Patience and long-suffering will give the middle-aged couple the ability to smooth their differences. And all of that will be girded by empathy toward the aging parents. Caring for them will demand a furious search for understanding. Carefully reading the third part of this book would be a good place for any aging parent's respectful child to begin.

How we care for our aged involves us all. A story I once heard makes that point. When the old man ate at the dining room table, he slobbered and made unpleasant sounds. His daughter-in-law was disturbed, wondering how the awful scene affected her young children who had to watch every evening. She and her husband decided the old parent should no longer eat with the family. His food was served to him in the kitchen in a large wooden trough. Some days later, the children were busy with a project. "What are you doing?" the mother asked. "We are making a wooden trough to feed you and Daddy when you are old," they said. Afterward, the old man was brought back to the table, loved, respected, and given the honored place at the head of the table.

15. Naomi Golan, *Passing Through Transitions*, p. 140.

PART 3

OLDER ADULTHOOD

18

Older or Better?
Attitudes Toward Aging

If I can make this—as I shall—it should prove that a person my age can do a great many hard things. How I loathe the expression *senior citizen.* These two words alone make older people outcasts, even lepers. On the other hand, back in California I had seen many older people who had given up. We must never let society thrust us aside, as it will try to do.

I may have a catastrophe, I thought, but fear is simply not in my nature. Death is only a phase of life, and life has many glories.[1]

Those are the words of William Willis, a sixty-nine-year-old American. They record his brave thoughts on July 5, 1963, as he set out from Peru to sail the Pacific Ocean, alone, on a raft. That courageous man symbolizes both the strength and struggle of older adulthood. A confidence fed by sixty-nine vivacious years made him want to do what no one had done to prove a "senior citizen" can do many hard things. Though he had the strength to master an ocean, he reeled from the beating given by a society that wanted to cast him aside. Useful, yet unwanted; that is the dilemma of those who grow old in the Western world.

SOCIAL INSECURITY

The problems of older adults are mostly social. They are the victims of modern values. As persons become older, they become less like what society most esteems: beauty, youth, strength, health, success, accomplishment. Getting older represents a kind of failure. Losing the superficial signs of success and beauty, the basis for the older person's personal dignity tends to be devalued. Unable to compete and get

1. William Willis, "One Man Against the Sea," in *Post True Stories of Daring and Adventure,* p. 71.

ahead economically, he is "relegated to the scrap-heap of old age."[2]

Secular culture has such a passion for youth that it goes to great lengths to deny aging and dying. Because wrinkles are treated with contempt, millions of dollars are spent on removing them surgically. Cosmetics "fix" the faces of the dead to make them look younger and healthier as they lie in their caskets. The ill and very old are often institutionalized—placed out of sight.

Experts in gerontology, the study of aging, are agitated by the results of those attitudes. "Old age in America is often a tragedy,"[3] because older persons are forced out of the mainstream of life to become part of an ignored and depreciated minority group. "We are so preoccupied with defending ourselves from the reality of death that we ignore the fact that human beings are alive until they are actually dead. At best, the living old are treated as if they were already half dead."[4] They may become victims of poverty, lacking adequate housing, nutrition, medical and psychological care. They are subjected to isolation and loneliness. Sociologists Robert Gray and David Moberg claim that the problems of old age and retirement are greater than and affect more people than any other social problem.[5]

The secular value system also affects the aging person's own attitudes. Older people tend to devalue other older people and in the process have a diminished personal self-esteem.

The Western culture's tendency to overvalue youthfulness has a toxic affect on everyone's life perspective. Enamored by youth, the prospects of illness, deformity, and death are frightening. Classes on thanatology, the study of death, are popular on college campuses, not because of baneful words about dying but because of bold statements about living. Life makes sense only if death is included. If wrinkled faces, deformed rheumatic hands, stooped shoulders, and all of the other features of aging are deplored, a large part of life is rejected. In a sense value is placed on only that segment of life in the middle. That drives society to ignore not only the aged but the aging part of themselves as well. No wonder Robert Butler gave such a pessimistic title to his book *Why Survive? Being Old in America.*

Nonetheless, Western societies are becoming wiser about the plight of the elderly. The sheer number of the elderly gives them increased public visibility. In the United States there are about three times as many persons past their sixty-fifth birthday as there are college students. Their numbers continue to grow since the median age of the population continues to climb upward. When the census was taken in 1970, the median age was under twenty-eight. But as the nation moves into its third century its people are getting older. The median age exceeded thirty in 1981, will reach thirty-five by the year 2000, and approach forty by 2030. Over the same span the number of people over sixty-five will more than double to 52 million—one out of every six Americans.[6]

2. Robert Gray and David Moberg, *The Church and the Older Person*, p. 16.
3. Robert Butler, *Why Survive? Being Old in America*, p. xi.
4. Ibid.
5. Gray and Moberg, p. 16.
6. Kenneth L. Woodward, "The Graying of America," *Newsweek*, 28 February 1977, p. 50.

Numbers do not provide the major reason for caring. Concern should be aroused because the contemporary attitude is so clearly contrary to the will of God. The biblical portrait of the elderly is colored by "honor" (1 Chron. 29:28) and "glory" (Prov. 16:31). They possess what should be valued highest: "wisdom and understanding" (Job 12:12). Older men and women are to receive special regard and widows are to be cared for (1 Tim. 5:1–3).

Some will argue that today's society is not so dishonorable in the treatment of the elderly. They point to the fact that older people are elected to public office and the media avoids labeling old persons as weak and senile. Reporters never tired of mentioning that Golda Meier worked twenty-hour days while in her mid-seventies or that William Douglas had keen and alert blue eyes at age seventy-five. Two experts, however, maintain that supports the mistaken concept that old age is a time of inactivity and mental laxity. "This sort of well-intended patronizing compliment betrays a widespread assumption that intelligence normally declines in advanced adulthood and old age, and that people like Meier and Douglas stand out as exceptions."[7] The idea that there is a general intellectual decline in old age is largely a myth.[8]

Others will point out that not that many older adults are institutionalized. Only 5 percent of all persons past the age of sixty-five in this country are in institutions like hospitals, retirement homes and convalescent facilities.[9] Yet, significantly, studies show that between 20 and 30 percent of the elderly in this country die in institutions.[10] Chances for institutionalization are two out of three for a person who lives to be over eighty-five. Institutionalization is not simply a 5 percent matter.

The poverty situation of the aged can also be looked at in several ways. Those who live below the poverty level constitute only 15.3 percent of the elderly. Thus, in reporting on the Harris poll on aging, one writer says, "While serious problems of not enough money, fear of crime, poor health, loneliness, inadequate medical care and getting where they want to go indeed exist among certain minorities of older people, they are by no means as pervasive as the public thinks." It is important not to confuse *having* a problem with *being* a problem. "Such generalizations about the elderly as an economically and socially deprived group can do the old a disservice."[11]

As a ratio, 15.3 percent may not sound too bad. But as a fact, it is tragic. Think for a moment that 15.3 percent represents millions of helpless, lonely, fearful people. That 15.3 percent is also higher than the percentage of the general population below the poverty level, thus revealing that economics is a problem for the aged.

7. Paul B. Bates and K. Warner Schaie, "The Myth of the Twilight Years," *Psychology Today*, March 1974, p. 35.

8. Ibid., p. 35.

9. Gray and Moberg, p. 152.

10. G. Lesnoff-Caravaglia, "The 5 Percent Fallacy," *International Journal of Aging and Human Development* 9 (1978–79):187–92.

11. Louis Harris, *The Myth and Reality of Aging in America*, as cited by Barbara Silverstone and Helen Kandel Hyman, *You and Your Aging Parent*, p. 66.

BECOMING A MYTH AT SIXTY-FIVE

Experts continue to point out that the root of older adult problems is society's lack of understanding. Myths and stereotypes flourish, partly because the fear of aging keeps people from squarely facing it. The view is also distorted by lumping together all people over sixty-five.

> What can be said about people between sixty-five and eighty is different from what can be said about those over eighty. In the thirty-to thirty-five-year age spread between sixty-five and ninety-five (and above), in addition to the enormous age differences the differences between individuals regardless of age are remarkable. I live in a retirement center [says John Bennett] and am impressed by the capacity for creative activity of many individuals in their late eighties, and sometimes into their nineties. Society's stereotypes of the elderly as people who are unhealthy, ingrown, inactive, out-of-date in their ideas, rigid, and vulnerable to "senility," often have the effect of self-fulfilling prophecies. When these stereotypes influence public policies or the policies within institutions for the elderly, they produce serious injustices.[12]

Before determining what to do for the elderly, the common stereotypes must be discarded. Not all are senile or intellectually deprived or poor, as has already been seen. Nor are all of them saintly. Morality is a problem for them as it is for others. Many of them live together instead of marrying, primarily because of the financial benefits of remaining single. Their behavior may become a problem to their middle-adult children, who worry about the example they set.

Not all of them live in the past, are cantankerous, or are disagreeable. A given group of elderly is as diverse in temperament as any other group of adults. Not all are afraid of or tired of sex. Studies of sexual behavior indicate that many married persons continue to have sexual relations into their eighties and nineties.[13] Not all of them are frustrated, disappointed, and depressed. A national survey disclosed that people over sixty-five felt much better off than is generally believed.[14] That poll, done by Louis Harris, showed that old people do not consider themselves as lonely as most people think they are. Serious loneliness was a problem for only 12 percent. It is interesting that 60 percent of those *under* sixty-five thought that that was a major problem for older adults.

Old age is an adventure. Florida Scott-Maxwell is among those who speak positively about it. People cheat themselves when they "squeeze out passion and excitement" and focus on dread of illness, infirmity, isolation and death.[15] "We who are old know that age is more than a disability. It is an intense and varied experience, almost beyond our capacity at times, but something to be carried high," she reminds us. "It is a long

12. John C. Bennett, "Ethical Aspects of Aging in America," in *Ministry with the Aging,* ed. William M. Clements, p. 137.
13. Gray and Moberg, p. 151.
14. Ibid., p. 54.
15. Florida Scott-Maxwell, *The Measure of My Days,* p. 110.

defeat, it is also victory, meaningful for the initiates of time, if not for those who have come less far."[16]

Old age is neither inherently miserable nor inherently sublime. Like every stage of life it has its problems, joys, fears, and potentials.[17] The Scriptures mention its dark side. "The evil days come and the years draw near when you will say, 'I have no delight in them' " (Eccles. 12:1). And the Psalmist concurs.

> As for the days of our life, they contain seventy years,
> Or if due to strength, eighty years,
> Yet their pride is but labor and sorrow.
>
> (Psalm 90:10)

For some, perhaps many, in modern society, old age is troublesome. The 12 percent who admitted they were critically lonely represent more than 3 million people. Even the simple pleasure of eating is taken away for many of them, since loneliness dissolves appetite. "The food was like ashes in my mouth," is an oft-reported statement.[18]

The normal transitions of older adulthood are without doubt most hazardous. Death of a spouse in earlier adult periods was unlikely; in older adulthood it is the norm, as is death itself. The challenges are weighty as the Bible confirms. Sorrow may be part of old age (Ps. 90:10). Evil may overtake those unprepared for it (Eccles. 12:1). Marks of old age include physical suffering, failing strength and feebleness (1 Kings 1:1; Ps. 71:9). There may be difficulties in walking about (Zech. 8:4; Heb. 11:21). Gray hairs and dimness of vision do not escape mention in Scripture (Gen. 27:1; 48:10; Job 15:10; Prov. 16:31).

Because of their circumstances, the old are of special concern to God.

AWARENESS UP, ANXIETY DOWN

The study of this stage is an alluring one. Much attention has been given to it, and the researchers have revealed some exciting insights into its joys and challenges. The church, unfortunately, seems to share society's prejudices against the aged. In two recent studies clergymen came out looking only a bit less like the rest of society in terms of attitude toward the elderly. They frequently evaluate the elderly as forgetful, traditional, slow, lonely, noncontemporary, worried, dependent, nonsexual. They do enjoy ministerial contacts with older people, but they prefer teaching youth and middle-age adults.[19] If it is a fair assumption that clergymen are the most influential persons in churches, then the average church record in dealing with the elderly may be somewhat blemished, pockmarked mostly with lack of empathy.

16. Ibid., p. 5.
17. Butler, p. 2.
18. Burt Kruger Smith, *Aging in America*, p. 45.
19. See David Moberg, "Needs Felt by the Clergy for Ministries to the Aging," *Gerontologist* 15 (1975):17–175; Charles Longino and Gay C. Kitson, "Parish Clergy and the Aged: Examining Stereotypes," *Journal of Gerontology* 31 (1976):34–345.

Raising the congregation's awareness level concerning senior adults is the church's first order of ministry for the aged. There is so much to be explored: the physiological, psychological, and spiritual dimensions; the relationship of the aged to the church's life and ministry; public policy and community resources related to older adults.

The effort will have to be substantial enough to achieve two crucial goals.[20] First, it must aim to make the study of aging less like reading one's own hospital charts. Discomfort over the subject of aging must be overcome, since ignoring aging is one of the root problems of growing older. Ignorance sustains the damaging myths and negative attitudes. A church ought to feature aging as a topic when most of the congregation are present. Church publications, the church library and other media can be employed to deal with the common uneasiness about the topic of growing old.

A second goal of the church's teaching must be to change people's feelings and attitudes toward the elderly. Empathy must be created by making people feel how older people feel. Films like *Portrait of Grandpa Doc* and *The Wild Goose* help them see life through aged eyes. Powerful awareness exercises could be used in smaller groups by placing restrictive devises of various sorts on people, for example. Conversing with plugs in their ears for a while ought to make people better understand an older person with a hearing loss. Wax paper can be taped to eyeglasses to simulate poor sight. Gloves will make people feel what it is like to lose a normal sense of touch. Those exercises can be fun, but most of all they do the job of creating badly needed empathy.

Older adults themselves may be the best resource for helping other people become acquainted with their joys and struggles. No teaching device can replace personal contact with the elderly. Ask them to share their testimonies. Urge them to publically share some of their difficulties. Put them on panels and have them speak in special forums. Include them in small groups where all generations are represented. Intergenerational contact may be the most important overall strategy the church has for fostering understanding between people of all ages. When personal contact is not possible, as when older adults are confined to home or to an institution, older adults can share via audio or video cassettes. As part of a pastoral prayer, one pastor played a recorded prayer of one confined older adult who in the past had been prominent in the life of the church. Interviews of older adults can be put on tape, along with a slide presentation.

Consider using resource people: gerontologists, nurses, hospice program personnel, recreational therapists, welfare workers. There is no lack of people or methods to make people aware of the aged.

The goal of all that teaching is not to make old people look or feel different from the rest of humanity. Actually, the objective is just the opposite. Older adults do not want to be singled out as odd. Moberg and Gray's research is quite conclusive on that point. The church should be like an extended family where older and younger are fully

---

20. The following four paragraphs contain information from Melvin A. Kimble, "Education for Ministry with the Aging," in *Ministry with the Aging*, ed. William M. Clements, pp. 212-19.

welcomed. When older adults are considered a part of the larger fellowship and not treated categorically as old people, "the morale of older members is greatly built up."[21] Up with old people!

21. Gray and Moberg, p. 139.

19

Enter Stage Last:
Becoming a Senior Citizen

I was going along, doing 'my own thing,' with each day filled with activities[, she said]. Then one day I received a letter from my insurance company and I checked with my desk calendar. [Then to herself she shouted:] . . . In three months, I'll be sixty-five! I'll be an old woman soon and I don't even feel it.[1]

That woman suddenly realized that life's next step was being old. It does not hit everyone at the same time or in the same way. Maps of the life span are not that accurate. There is no big, black arrow at the entrance to any of the adult stages saying, "You are here."

Nothing physical happens to tell a person he is now a senior citizen. Some people of seventy are more physically fit than many persons of forty or less. No sudden mental deterioration sets in. There is no age when all individuals begin to show signs of aging.[2] The gateway to older adulthood is a highly individual matter.

A birthday, perhaps the sixtieth, might trigger the transition for some. Round numbers seem to symbolize a new venture. "Few of us bother with becoming 23 or 47 . . . we are hooked on the decimal system and our anxieties are engendered by those zeros that materialize every ten years."[3]

Anticipation of imminent retirement—or retirement itself—may make some people think they have gone through a new doorway in life. Here again, variability is the norm. Vocationally, a football player is old at forty; a congressman not until age eighty-five.

1. Naomi Golan, *Passing Through Transitions*, p. 191.
2. Robert Gray and David Moberg, *The Church and the Older Person*, p. 18.
3. G. Neubeck, "Getting Older in My Family: A Personal Reflection," *The Family Coordinator* 27 (1978):445–47.

Physical illness or a sudden awareness of physical limitations may be a turning point. A surgeon said,

> You know, I got to thinking while I was doing that abdominal cancer this morning, Reverend. It was a long operation, one of those tedious, grubby ones. After about three hours, I got a crick in my shoulder. I looked around at all those young bucks assisting me and it suddenly hit me that any one of them could probably do that operation as well as I can or better and not get near as tired. I'm either going to have to go down to the 'Y' and get in shape or get out of this business.[4]

Apparently, three factors are behind one's beginning to see oneself as "old."

- *Subjective feelings.* The woman quoted earlier may have been repressing her thoughts of growing older by endless activity. The letter from her insurance company jolted her into noticing that she would be an old woman soon.
- *Objective realities.* In that case, both the approaching birthday and the changes in regard to insurance hit her. Other "marker events" are retirement and registering for social security or medicare.
- *Social expectations.* What a person perceives of as old is mostly determined by society. That woman did not feel old; rather she was internalizing society's standard that sixty-five means one has crossed the line. The sixty-nine year old who sailed the Pacific on a raft was protesting that social expectation. Neither objectively nor subjectively did he judge himself to be old. Old for him was a social label to which he was saying, "No, thank you."

Transition to old age is rather complex. Using Levinson's formula, the stage of late adulthood starts around age sixty-five. The five previous years would be transitional ones.

To more fully understand the transition period, the following discussion examines it in the three transition periods suggested by Golan: leaving middle adulthood, crossing the line, entering late adulthood.[5]

LEAVING THE MIDDLE

Aging actually begins in the thirties. Before a person is through the young adult period, he will feel the physical effects of getting older. Thus, in some sense, the process of preparing for old age begins long before the sixty-to-sixty-five time frame. Some believe there is a preparatory process that lasts a long time, probably beginning in the mid-thirties. Traumatic events like relative's or friend's serious illness or death might stir the person's thinking about mortality. He experiences an engagement-disengagement pattern. One undergoes the process of relating, becoming intimate,

4. Charles V. Gerkin, *Crisis Experience in Modern Life,* p. 52.
5. Golan, pp. 191-96.

and then tolerating loss and grief.[6] That pattern will be repeated often in old age. The mid-lifer must learn to deal with the emotions of depression, disappointment, and anger.

To leave this period, three tasks need to be mastered, according to Mary Parent.

- Completion of one's life goals
- Evaluation of one's failures and disappointments
- Preparation for decline[7]

COMPLETION OF LIFE'S GOALS

Experts tend to agree that persons in this culture search for some sense of completion in old age. Life's purposes need to be wrapped up. One or more things might happen to make a middle adult achieve that sense of completion. Launching the last child into the world may do it, especially for the woman whose life has been wrapped up in raising kids. Depending on what one has done for his parents, the death of the parents may signal the end of a set of goals and create a sense of fulfillment or failure. If a spouse dies, goals relating to the marriage are completed. A person may lose a job or deliberately change careers—another thing has come to an end. All of those completions are also losses; one's sense of identity is at stake.

EVALUATION OF LIFE PERFORMANCE

Even if a person has been evaluating his life all along the mid-life pathway, the completions of life goals will bring on a new surge of self-examination. The mid-life review is like a sailor's checking his course halfway across the Atlantic: He makes corrections and establishes new directions.

The older adult life review is the landed sailor's contemplation of the voyage. One of the most sorrowful positions for some persons to be in is when they say, "I am who I have been"[8] The older adult need not be hopelessly enslaved to the past. At this point, adults' spiritual needs are profound. Their hunger for forgiveness, grace and assurance of eternal life is tied not only to their impending death but to their past life.[9]

The emotional reactions to that life review can be painful. In severe form, they may include guilt, anxiety, depression and obsessive preoccupation with the past, and may even proceed to a state close to terror, resulting in suicide. Normally, reactions are less intense, consisting of increased reminiscence, mild nostalgia, and mild regret. Three groups appear to be susceptible to despair: those who have always placed great

---

6. Stanley H. Cath, "The Orchestration of Disengagement," *International Journal of Aging and Human Development* 6, no. 3 (1975):204, as cited in Golan, p. 193.
7. Mary Kay Parent, "The Losses of Middle Age and Related Developmental Tasks," pp. 147–50, as cited in Golan, pp. 192–93.
8. Henri Nouwen and Walter J. Gaffney, *Aging*, p. 40.
9. Cath, "Orchestration of Disengagement," p. 193.

emphasis on the future but have disliked the present; those who are afflicted by real guilt because they purposely injured others; and those who are highly self-centered, for whom death is the ultimate threat.[10]

PREPARATION FOR DECLINE

This third task needs work on the practical and emotional levels. Those approaching older adulthood often sell their large, family-oriented homes and rent homes closer to shopping and public transportation. Some look to warmer climates and make plans to enter retirement communities. At the emotional level, the individual is stirred by the look ahead, more aware that death is imminent. Parent says that that awareness lies somewhere between mental knowledge and a sort of emotional feeling of imminent threat.[11]

Not all developmentalists believe the threat of death casts a big shadow on older adults. Most, however, think it is the older adult's major emotional struggle. Erikson, in particular, believes so. He plants the mortality issue right in the center of older adult development. Not all elderly get caught up in a life review process. It is true that the elderly are more interested in the past than in their present and future. But sorting out and restructuring the past demands skills most people do not possess. The studies of Lieberman and Tobin suggest that life review may not be as prevalent among the elderly as has been supposed.[12]

CROSSING OVER

"Crossing the line" is a reaction to certain marker events that force someone to face the doorway to a new life phase.[12] "I retire tomorrow: I'm a senior citizen." Retirement is the most significant marker event, though there are others, as noted in the last chapter. The married woman who is not "retiring" will, of course, be impacted by her husband's retirement.

THE TOP FLOOR OR THE ATTIC?

Many persons seem eager and ready for this crossing although feelings are mixed for others. The big change is in going from being a contributor to society to being a dependent. Self-image must undergo a facelift: "I'm one of the old folks now." In the East, old age is welcome; the last stop is the top spot, a place of honor. In the West, the top floor is more like the attic, where discarded items are kept.

Older adults face that castaway image in the church as well as in society. "I sometimes feel that I am excess baggage over at the church and know of other older

10. R. N. Butler, "The Life Review: An Interpretation of Reminiscence in the Aged," *Psychiatry* 24 (1973):179–82.
11. Parent, pp. 147–50, as cited in Golan, p. 193.
12. Morton A. Lieberman and Sheldon S. Tobin, *The Experience of Old Age: Stress, Coping and Survival*, p. 308.
13. Golan, p. 195.

persons who feel the same," is one comment Gray and Moberg collected. "This problem of older members getting pushed out of their jobs in the church is one of the problems we have at our churches." "They don't seem to realize how much those jobs meant to them when they get old and can't do much of anything else," she continued. "My father was an elder since I was two. Just last year they put him out. It just about crushed my father."[13]

The anguish comes through another statement: "I am getting older and I have been a member of the church for a long, long time. There have been quite a lot of our older members leave the church on account of they are dissatisfied. . . . The two most important reasons for this trouble is that we get put out of office and because the pastor passes up the older ones and mingles with the younger."[14]

From those who study the aged, the message is clear: they want to be involved. They often feel discriminated against when excluded from offices and positions because of age. That raises one of the most disturbing questions of older adult ministry: should they be treated in special ways or not? Singling them out for special programs may be another way of making them feel different. A national survey showed that churches are most frequently the sponsoring groups for such activities.[15] "Moberg later found no difference in the adjustment of older persons in churches with special programs and without special programs."[16]

Do special programs make older adults feel like outsiders or, at best, peculiar insiders? Apparently, some experts think the answer is yes. However, the solution does not lie in dismantling all special older adult programming. What older adults want is to be integrated into the church's life. Single adults can teach the church something about feeling excluded. So central was that theme that J. Brittain Wood forged it into the title of his book *Single Adults Want to Be the Church, Too*. Single adults need separate programs, but they most of all need to feel included. Substitute the word "older" for "single" in the title and you have the older adult plea. The White House Conferences in 1961 and 1971 summoned churches to do that, finding that it would help persons make a happy and orderly transition to retirement and old age. They were quite specific in what they meant by involvement: "All of the following roles: that of worshiper, learner, teacher, counselor, leader or elder, volunteer aid, and member in congregational organizations." They cautioned: "When congregations over-emphasize some of these roles and underemphasize others, older persons are often placed at a disadvantage."[17]

13. Gray and Moberg, pp. 122, 124.
14. Ibid., p. 124.
15. Robert Decrow, *New Learning Opportunities for Older Americans: An Overview of National Effort*, as cited by Donald Miller, "Adult Religious Education and the Aging," in *Ministry with the Aging*, ed. William M. Clements, p. 246.
16. David O. Moberg, "The Integration of Older Members in the Church Congregation," in *Older People and Their Social World*, ed. Arnold M. Rose and Warren A. Peterson, pp. 125-42, as cited in Barbara Payne, "Religion and the Elderly in Today's World," in *Ministry with the Aging*, ed. William M. Clements, p. 168.
17. White House Conference, 1971 Policy Statement and Recommendations, as cited in Carol LeFevre and Perry LeFevre, eds., *Aging and the Human Spirit*, p. 217.

Special programs in some churches are more the symptom than the problem. Because older adults are pushed out of other areas, special provisions have to be made. If, however, older adults are mainstreamed in the whole life of the church, special programs will be no threat.

It must also be kept in mind that when special programs are planned, they should not so much be *for* the older adults as *with* them. As much as possible, older adults should lead their own ministries. The White House Conference of 1971 especially urged this: It is noted that "special attention should be given to allow older persons to share in the planning and implementation of all programs related to them."[18]

Ministry, of course, is not the only thing older adults want from the church. Foremost, they want spiritual food. "The church has meant everything to me and it helps me over everything," said one elderly woman. "It gave so much comfort to me, and I know that the church is the biggest part of our lives."[19] Confided another: "I am ancient and it seems impossible that I am this old. Going to church is the most important thing in my life."[20]

THE THREE BLOCK GAP

Older adults' church attendance confirms that interest. Earlier research data showed they attended church less than when younger, but present studies indicate that is untrue. Church attendance seems to be relatively constant throughout an individual's lifetime. Attendance might decline, but at a much older age (well into the nineties) than formerly assumed.[21]

The church facilities will tell older people how welcome they are. Since health and impairments will make it difficult for some of them to attend, church buildings can be an obstacle course: steps (some without handrails), slick floors, narrow restroom stalls (without handrails and off limits to wheelchairs), heavy doors. Lack of ramps, handrails and elevators, are subtly saying, "We make it hard for you to join us; we just aren't sensitive to you." Whenever a church pays the cost of remodeling to fit the elderly, the respect it shows is priceless. A gradual ramp is a way of loudly saying to them: "We want you."

Another psychological roadblock is in the form of a dollar mark. Attitudes toward finances may keep some away from church. If they cannot contribute, some older adults flatly say they will not continue to go to church. "You know I gave my first $24 to the church, but I would stay home if I couldn't pay up now," said one. "I would because they don't pay any attention to those who don't pay." A sixty-five-year-old widow told how she felt: "Money shouldn't matter in the church, but it does. I stayed home because I was offended because they preached on how stingy we were with God."[22] Money may be an embarrassment to those older adults who struggle financially.

18. Ibid., p. 220.
19. Gray and Moberg, p. 113.
20. Ibid., p. 101.
21. Payne, p. 157.
22. Moberg and Gray, pp. 126–27.

Lack of transportation also matters—at least for some. All research discloses that it is a major factor in failure to attend church or participate in social activities of any kind. Two studies found that for most older adults, the critical distance to church was only three blocks.[23] Those three blocks symbolize so much. To walk, even run, three city squares is nothing to a younger adult without handicap, yet to some older adults, three blocks are like three oceans.

23. Payne, p. 161.

20

Keeping It All Together:
Integrity vs. Despair

INTEGRITY

On his deathbed, my eighty-three-year-old father was sometimes coherent, sometimes not. When fully conscious, only hours before his death, he made provision for his regular offering to be taken to church the following Sunday. Pages could be written about the symbolism of that act for him and for others who have done similar things. Whatever meaning might be discovered, a certain dignity can be seen in that act. In life's final hours, he still believed he had something to "offer." My dad had found, in his own way, the "integrity" Erikson describes.

In short, integrity means a tendency to keep things together. As on the other rungs of life's ladder, a person has to make sense out of self and life. The adolescent has to "get it together" by forming some sense of who he is and then acting on that identity, testing and clarifying it. The older adult becomes increasingly hard pressed to keep some inward sense of togetherness during a time when things are coming apart. Erikson notes that that "coming apart" is actually part of the physical process of aging. The interplay between the connecting tissues, the blood vessels, and the muscle system actually begins to slacken. Psychologically, losses and troubles make it difficult for the older adult to see coherence in life events. Loss of work, family, community and other responsibilities gives a sense of his world falling apart. That disorientation, like shattered eyeglass lenses, distorts the person's general worldview. Constructing a sense of "order" is the task of integrity. Integrity includes "an acceptance of the fact that one's life is one's own responsibility," or accepting what he has made of his life as his own making.[1]

Integrity also includes a "love for the human ego." This is not selfishness but rather

---

1. Erik Erikson, *Childhood and Society,* pp. 268–69.

a respect for human life and in particular for one's own life. Because the person accepts his own life cycle as destined, he experiences "a new, a different love of one's parents." As the older adult accepts his life, he accepts in a new way the parents, who originated and shaped it. A new respect for parents (even those who have died) may emerge.

In his later writings, Erikson expanded the notion of integrity to include a kind of "comradeship with men and women of distant times and of different pursuits who have created orders and objects and sayings conveying human dignity and love."[2] With that statement, Erikson brought religion and philosophy into the concept of integrity. Integrity sees that though one's life on earth is nearly over, it makes sense and, in one way or another, it will continue. The generativity of the middle adult period, the urge to create, to be useful, will continue as the fruit of one's life.

Achieving integrity takes "wisdom," which has little to do with the amount of intelligence a person has. In this context wisdom is an attitude—a worldview, wherein persons are willing to give up what is no longer theirs to occupy. It is the ability to face death without despair. Religion is a resource for this, since integrity comes from wrestling with "ultimate concerns."[3] Wisdom never evolves on its own but is related to a tradition, Erikson claims.[4]

Without wisdom, the older person lives in despair, which Erikson insists is the lot of those who do not attain integrity. Hopelessness and the fear of death breed disgust, and disgust gives birth to chronic complaining and disdain for everything.[5] Mental and behavioral problems of old age, psychoanalysts say, may be the spasms and tremors of the inner battle for integrity.

Robert Peck lists three developmental tasks that are steps toward integrity:[6]

- Finding personal worth outside work and roles
- Finding greater enjoyment in mental and social activities than in physical activities
- Finding in unselfish service to others a means of self-perpetuation

The first job is to view personal worth in terms broader than those contained in work and roles. The self-esteem question begs for an answer: "Am I a worthwhile person only insofar as I can do a full-time job, or can I be worthwhile in other roles and because of the kind of person I am?" A man or woman gives up a job, a housewife her role in the home. Until a person loses those jobs and roles, he is not conscious of how much they have been a part of his self-image. Loss of dignity must be handled.

The older person must not make "usefulness" his only fuel for self-esteem. Eventually, old age will impose its limitations. The diet that feeds integrity will have to change as

2. Erik Erikson, *The Life Cycle Completed*, p. 65.
3. Ibid., p. 64.
4. Erik Erikson, *Identity, Youth and Crisis*, p. 140.
5. Jo Eugene Wright, Jr., *Erikson: Identity and Religion* (New York: Seabury, 1982), p. 99.
6. Robert Peck, "Psychological Development in the Second Half of Life," in *Middle Age and Aging*, ed. Bernice L. Neugarten, pp. 90–92.

a person's contribution lessens and dependency upon others increases. The core of the Christian faith speaks to this.

Christians are not to judge people solely by their contribution. Christians have a "celebration of *uselessness.* We are not sufficient to our own salvation; our lives—our relationship with God—are a gift. We have not generated ourselves; we cannot, finally, justify ourselves."[7] Man's value is based upon His forgiveness. God creates no junk, neither has sin destroyed man's worth. Sin cannot be purged by human efforts. Grace, not works, ultimately justifies man's existence.

People of all ages need that truth. In modern society, where people's worth is equal to their productivity, it is easy to fall into making works the basis for feeling good about oneself. The very old, who have much less to offer than before, will need to realize that. Everyone should be reminded to celebrate uselessness. Dignity remains because, in God's sight, dignity has never depended upon being productive. It stems from being created and redeemed. Jesus loves man; that is enough. The Christian can cope by finding meaningful roles and jobs in church and community. "The ability to find a sense of self-worth through a variety of activities seems to make the difference between maintaining a continued vital interest in living or losing it in despair."[8]

The second task relates to the body. Older adults will have to find more fulfillment from mental and social activities than from physical. Persons who are too concerned with their physical well-being will find physical decline a serious insult. Worry about health will dominate their waking hours. Integrity means enduring physical discomfort but still enjoying the things that do not require large amounts of physical exertion. People learn to transcend physical distress. Studies show that people who move into middle life without balancing their focus on physical activities (often working-class men) have trouble adjusting in old age. The Christian has an advantage here because Scripture places high value on mental and spiritual efforts and on personal relationships. Some middle and older adults will be surprised by the fact that Christian values have not had first place as they might have thought.

Peck's description of the third task is most helpful because it pierces the core of the Christian struggle. Adapting to the eventuality of death consists of an unselfish devotion to others. In Peck's words, a person "can live so generously and unselfishly that even the prospect of personal death becomes less important than the secure knowledge that one has built for a broader, longer future through one's children, through contributions to the culture, and through friendships as a way of self-perpetuation."[9] That attitude results in a deep, active effort to make life more secure and happy for those who go on after one dies.

The hope of eternal life gives Christians a basis for achieving the kind of integrity Erikson describes. The Christian must deal with death by coming to terms with this

7. Evelyn Eaton Whitehead and James D. Whitehead, "Retirement," in *Ministry with the Aging,* ed. William M. Clements, pp. 133–34.
8. Peck, p. 91.
9. Ibid., pp. 91–93.

life as well as the next. Old age does not signal an end of life for the Christian, but it is a passageway, complete with entrance and exit.

Peck has described a basic non-Christian approach to eternal life: self-perpetuation through others on earth. Although concern for that type of "legacy" is not wrong, the hope of eternal life is far more that that for the Christian. Peck's task is, nonetheless, a good one. Christians, too, should permit their thoughts of death to turn them outward to others.

Before leaving Erikson's theory of the integrity-despair struggle, mention should be made of the opposition to it. One theorist claims that relatively few individuals ever achieve a commitment to integrity in old age. A secular society lacks the tradition required to do so. "We are living in an era that cannot provide the elderly person with a feeling of continuity," V. Clayton argues.[10] Clayton might be right, considering the shallowness of secular society. As he says, present culture is rootless in nature and without a sense of tradition. Apart from religious faith, it might be difficult for an older person to have some feeling of contributing to an ongoing evolution of the race, which is the only meaning secular society has to confer.

Other critics also charge that few individuals achieve the higher stages of Erikson's life cycle, and, therefore, it does not provide a true, general description of adult development.[11] Perhaps they are correct; Erikson may be describing what *ought* to be rather than what *is*.

Erikson's theory should be taken for whatever light it can shed on one's own experience. We do not know definitively what the common mental and spiritual groanings of adult souls are on life's journey. What is known is that older adults tend to struggle with forging an integrity and dignity in the face of death.

THE CHURCH'S ROLE

What older adults most need from the church is what the church has most to offer: answers to basic life and death questions. Gray and Moberg concluded from their survey that there is a direct relationship between a person being a closely affiliated church member and that person's adjustment in old age. Though the church gave the elderly fellowship and opportunity for service, its primary contribution to them was spiritual. Church life helped them deal with anxiety, fear and guilt.[12] That fact is also confirmed by a survey of adults over fifty-five. When asked, the majority said religion was the topic of study they most preferred.[13]

Those findings are consistent with other studies that show that the older person believes he is more religious than he was earlier in life.[14] However, after surveying

10. V. Clayton, "Erikson's Theory of Human Development as It Applies to the Aged: Wisdom as Contradictive Cognition," *Human Development* 18 (1975):119–21.
11. David F. Hultsch and Francine Deutsch, *Adult Development and Aging*, p. 316.
12. Robert Gray and David Moberg, *The Church and the Older Person*, p. 79.
13. Joann Menkus and Belden Menkus, "Adult Sunday School Needs to Grow Up," *Christianity Today*, 25 April 1975, p. 7.
14. Gray and Moberg, p. 65.

both sides of the question, Barbara Payne judged that it is impossible to tell if religious questions will be more important to a person when he is an older adult.[15] In any case, it appears that praying increases. "From the results of the American Piety Study, R. Stark has concluded that personal devotional activities provide the primary outlet for the anxieties and deprivation of old age and that the increasing piety of the elderly is manifested through prayer. The widespread notion that people become increasingly pious as they age is true only if piety is carefully defined as private devotionalism and belief in an immortal soul."[16]

Theoretically, it is logical for older adults to be more concerned about religious matters. For one thing, the interest would be tied to their increased interiority, which research has shown to be true of them. Also their developmental tasks would press for some ultimate answers: facing death, accepting losses, maintaining meaning and keeping a sense of worth.[17]

Religious interest may make older adults more open to the gospel than is generally believed. Most churches report increases in participation of those over sixty far above the population increase in that age group.[18] Research shows that older persons are more exposed to religious radio, television, and literature than middle and younger adults.

More open to faith, older adults may not be so open to changing faiths, however. Gray and Moberg observed that the aged will usually turn back to childhood beliefs to resolve their agony over past failure and sin. That is often done simplistically. "I just take it for granted," offered one man, "what I've been taught all my life and what I understand is true and do not fear when my turn comes."[19] Thus, non-Christian older adults may not be so eager to turn to Christianity. However, those with some childhood background in evangelical faith, need evangelism and Bible teaching. Is it possible that the investment in child evangelism and nurture by parents and church may eventually pay dividends in the late decades of life? Perhaps the dropouts of youth groups and Sunday schools who have some leaning toward Christian faith may come back when their hair is gray and their needs are great.

Addressing that renewed spirituality, Donald E. Miller suggests that the church can move in at least three directions.[20]

1. *Education for awareness.* The feelings of fear and being threatened that keep people from learning about aging must be confronted. Educating for awareness includes learning to speak about the changes taking place, freedom to express the

15. Barbara Payne, "Religion and the Elderly in Today's World," in *Ministry with the Aging,* ed. William M. Clements, p. 163.
16. Ibid., p. 165. Payne references R. Stark, "Age and Faith: A Changing Outlook as an Old Process," *Sociological Analysis* 29 (1968):1–10.
17. Milton L. Barron, "The Role of Religion and Religious Institutions in Creating the Milieu of Old People," in *Organized Religion and the Old Person,* ed. D. L. Scudder, pp. 12–33.
18. Payne, p. 167.
19. Gray and Moberg, pp. 101–2.
20. Donald E. Miller, "Adult Religious Education and the Aging," in *Ministry with the Aging,* ed. William M. Clements, pp. 236–39. All direct quotes in the following discussion are found in the above cited material.

feelings they generate, and then learning to accept them. It requires the of what is so often found in the church, as in society; aging like death hovers in the background, ignored. It is joked about, worried about, but seldom given serious understanding or exploration for the enrichment that it can bring to life.

2. *Education for intentionality.* By this, Miller means "the owning, acceptance, and cognitive expression of the urges and impulses of our own personal existence." It means teaching older adults to maintain whatever control of their lives they can. "Aging is often a time of declining responsibilities, yet it is frequently a time of making very stressful decisions—moving one's residence or changing one's vocation. . . . Aging persons must be pressed to risk making their own decisions.

There have been outstanding examples of elderly people who have kept control and maintained direction for their lives. That is usually the result of their continuing to do what they have always done. An outstanding eighty-year-old Christian leader died recently. Friends discovered on her desk a list of goals she had set out to accomplish in the next ten years of her life. She was not quitting. Disease and other impairments may make it difficult for some elderly, but they need to be taught to continue, by God's grace, to take hold of life and not allow it to take hold of them. The question "How can I know the will of God?" will still be important to the elderly, who will need to be guided to apply God's Word to the issues and circumstances they face. They will need to be challenged to take risks, to act in obedience to His purposes and direction.

3. *Education for coherence.* If some integrity of personality is to be maintained, the elderly must make sense out of life. As in the other transitions, changes will force them to reassess and reinterpret their values, thoughts, beliefs. It is reasonable that for most of them, putting it all together will be more difficult than at any other period of life. They have seen more tragedy, have endured more losses, have experienced more failure. There is simply more life history to summarize and make sense of. Surely, the elderly should see things in God's Word that others would not.

Doctrines of heaven and hell will interest them, as well as other subjects dealing with prophecy. Discussions relating biblical truth to the aging process will need to address questions like: What is aging? What does the Bible say about old age? What does it say about older adults? Is aging the result of sin? What are Christian answers to ethical matters like euthanasia?

One of the most important things that can be done for older persons is to understand their spiritual struggles. Too often, older people are not accepted for who they are. They are expected to be pious, to be spiritual. Yet, like people of all ages, they have their faith problems. Gray and Moberg showed that they are plagued by uncertainty about the resurrection and nagging doubt about the nature of the future life. They may think that their fear of death is equivalent to a lack of faith in God and assurance of salvation. In other words, studies show that they do not come up to the ideals set for them by the church.[21] They need to be accepted as they are.

---

21. Gray and Moberg, pp. 139–40.

Thus, Miller points out that the Christian education program is not merely a matter of adding electives to give them practical help with retirement, illness or handling grief. It should not merely be bound up in coping strategies but in true spiritual growth and personal development.

The thought that older adulthood may be a time of unusual spiritual maturity should be kept alive. Perhaps older adults possess capacities for wisdom and holiness unachievable at previous stages. They do not merely know about life; they taste it deeply.[22] They know its bitterness and sweetness better than most. Surely, when old, one should have some feel for what is genuine and real—what it truly means to be alive.

22. Alfred McBride, "Adult Education: A Ministry to Life Cycles," *Religious Education* 72, no. 2 (March–April 1977):171.

21

The Downhill Side: Coping with Loss and Psychological Disorders

LOST HATS AND THINGS

There is a story about an old man who left a suicide note that read something like this: "I lost my hat today; after losing so much, that was one more loss than I could handle." If one word could envelope all the problems of old age, it would be the word "loss." Authorities attribute the high rate of depression and suicide among older adults to the pain from multiple bereavements.[1] Unlike other adults, the older adult has little hope of recouping losses. They also may occur so rapidly that he faces additional grief while the "grief work" of a previous loss is yet unfinished.

Losses, of course, are not only in the form of loved ones. Job, financial resources, status, health, and familiar surroundings are part of a long list. I felt great sorrow for my eighty-year-old father when we stood outside the open door of his garage looking at his two-year-old Ford Granada. Wistfully, he explained that he had been unable to renew his driver's license a few weeks before. Always an active man, he deeply felt the loss of his freedom to move about. I stood with my father beside his car as I have often stood in a hospital room with others beside the body of their loved one—tearfully sharing his grief with little to say.

The major loss is the loss of place. Being recognized as old in a youthful society, they lose status. Retirement takes away all that the workplace has meant. Those forced into retirement especially feel this. For some, it is a crisis.

Loss of place, as has already been noted, might occur in church. Older people studied by Gray and Moberg reported that they withdrew more from their church responsibilities; men were more likely than women to give up ministry and leadership

---

1. Francis J. Braceland, "Senescence—The Inside Story," *Psychiatric Annals* 11, no. 10 (October 1972):57.

positions. Some believed the younger people should take over. Others felt pushed out because their ideas were no longer accepted.

If, at retirement, they move or if their children move, they lose contact with close relatives. Apparently, though, the lack of contact with adult children is no major problem. Children do not seem to be a form of old-age happiness according to a study by the National Opinion Research Center. People over fifty who have had children are no happier than those who have never had them.[2] The researchers noted that other studies on older people show that friendships, particularly with people the same age, are often more satisfying to older people than are the relationships with children, grandchildren, and other relatives.

Older adults who outlive friends feel "left behind." Greatest grief comes from the spouse's death. Women usually outlive their husbands because they marry older men and have a longer life expectancy.[3] More than half of the women over sixty-five will have to attend their husband's funeral. The percentage gets higher for women after age seventy-five: two-thirds of them will be widows. If widowhood forces a woman to change residences, she faces additional losses: home, familiar surroundings, neighbors, friends, community.

Losses amount to isolation. Some experts maintain that such "disengagement" from others and from life is healthy for the elderly. Solitude provides them more opportunity for pursuit of the spiritual life. The loss of energy makes them more willing to live with aloneness. However, most discredit that theory and maintain that social losses greatly disturb the elderly. Disengagements are difficult to accept and adjust to. They must learn to accept grief and to work it through.

CAN MAN LIVE BY MEMORIES ALONE?

Some may think that memories will sooth the elderly. Making up for losses with good memories is probably more a young adult ideal than an older adult reality, however. Among others, two great writers remind us of the bitterness of remembering. "The memory of happiness makes misery woeful," said Thomas Fuller.[4] Oliver Goldsmith put it in verse in 1770 in "The Deserted Village:"

> Remembrance wakes with all her busy train,
> Swells at my breast, and turns the past to pain,[5]

Those close to older adults can help them most by prompting them to talk out their sorrow and properly mourn their losses. Our friendship can add something to their lives. Service and fellowship activities in the Body of Christ can be offered them. Quality relationships with others are closely tied to their emotional health.

2. Christopher T. Cory, "Parenthood's Dim Rewards," *Psychology Today,* May 1981, p. 14.
3. David Moberg and Robert Gray, *The Church and the Older Person,* p. 127.
4. Thomas Fuller, "Gnomologia," no. 4650 in *The Howe Book of Quotations,* ed. Burton Stevenson, 10th ed. (New York: Dodd, Mead, 1976), p. 129.
5. Oliver Goldsmith, "The Deserted Village," 1.81, in *The Norton Anthology of English Literature.*

KEEPING A MENTAL GRIP

Mental and emotional problems of the aged are related to their life struggles. Since depression is common to grief, it is easy to see why it is their most common psychiatric complaint.[6] A young adult, for instance, might be depressed with little apparent cause. The depressed older adult, on the other hand, may have plenty of reason to be because of the many losses he experiences. Life's stresses may be what create mental illness among the aged. Older persons do battle with anxiety, guilt, and depression. Those may spring from feelings about the past or just about being old. Most older adults bring a reservoir of rich experiences and coping strategies to bear, adequately handling those feelings, but some will succumb to more serious psychological ills. When they do, they may not get adequate treatment. Concerned persons state that older adults are shortchanged when it comes to psychological help. It has been proved that the elderly do not receive counseling and psychological treatment comparable to that received by younger adults. One major reason is that people do not separate the elderly person's mental disorders from his aging. Experts point out that the elderly are portrayed as apathetic, insecure, out of control, temperamental hypochondriacs.[7] Because of that, professionals, relatives, and friends may tend to think an aged person is beyond help. They accept abnormal behavior as normal. Older people are permitted to continue in their deep emotional and mental suffering simply because no one understands enough to get help for them. Just a little knowledge will help one respond better to a disturbed aging parent or friend.

SENILITY IS A WORN OUT TERM

The complexities of the mental condition of older adults should be recognized. All psychological disorders are not simply due to aging. There are some physical causes of mental impairment. Things can go wrong mentally if the brain cells are damaged or stop working properly. That creates a condition of organic brain syndrome. Functions that break down are: the ability to remain oriented to what is going on; short- and long-term memory; visual-motor coordination; and the ability to learn and retain how things are spatially arranged.[8] The older person suffering from that will have a terrible time recalling phone numbers, will get mixed up over whether the window is on one side of the bed or the other, will have trouble getting food from plate to mouth. It may become so serious that he cannot remember children's names or eat without help. That state of affairs is called *senile dementia* and may be the most dreaded part of growing old. An eighty-two-year-old man tells of the anguish that came from observing his wife's dementia. She has constant illusions and is disoriented. He says: "It's not the physical decline, I fear so much. It's becoming a mental vegetable inside a healthy

6. Margaret Gatz, Michael A. Smyer, and M. Powell Lawton, "The Mental Health System and the Older Adult," in *Aging in the 1980's*, ed. Leonard W. Poon, p. 11.
7. Sandra M. Levy et al., "Intervention with Older Adults and the Evaluation of Outcome," in *Aging in the 1980's*, ed. Leonard W. Poon, p. 41.
8. Naomi Golan, *Passing Through Transitions*, p. 217.

body. It's a shame that we can rehabilitate or treat so much of the physical ills, but when your mind goes, there's nothing you can do."[9]

Too often an older adult with some of those symptoms is diagnosed as having senile dementia. In reality, only 3 to 5 percent of the elderly actually suffer from dementia. Senile dementia has become a catchword for all kinds of treatable problems. Senility is not a common old age problem.

One third of those who are diagnosed as senile are that way because of things other than aging. Errors in medication, malnutrition, and metabolic imbalance may be the culprits. Those things can be changed and the brain's functions restored. Too often, especially in nursing homes, a temporary problem is considered a permanent malady.

Social conditions can also cause symptoms of mental illness. For example, old persons in nursing homes are often confused and disoriented. A relative or nurse may have to explain over and over again exactly where the bed is and why the bathroom is in one direction and not another. However, given a couple of facts, the situation can be easily explained. The elderly person is struggling with a new situation. Everyone has awakened in the middle of the night in a strange bed and has had to do some fast thinking to orient himself. Imagine what moving to a nursing home means for the older person. It is another loss. Points of reference have been taken away. They lack a reference group and often face isolation and boredom. Some researchers conclude there is a circular relationship between not being with people and losing the ability to think. People provide stimuli to the senses, which keeps the wires to the brain humming. When the stimuli are decreased, the brain does not get as many messages. Cells may begin to shut down, then atrophy. Loss of memory occurs, along with general thinking ability. That is enough to make a person confused and anxious about what is happening to his head. That fear drives the lonely elderly person into more depression, apathy, and withdrawal. They then hear, see, and touch less, and the brain cells have even less to get excited about. And on it goes, a cruel circle.

Some other facts about senility should be better known. There are three types. *Senile Brain Disease* is the gradual, progressive decline caused by atrophy, the kind just discussed. *Alzheimer's Disease* causes "presenile dementia," which refers to mental decreases much earlier than the average onset of senile brain disease. "Presenile dementia" occurs in the forties and fifties. *Cerebrovascular Disease* refers to the blockage of blood flow to the brain that kills off brain cells by cutting off their oxygen. Other symptoms like paralysis appear at the same time in what is normally referred to as a *stroke*. However, if there are repeated episodes of blockage, a condition that parallels senile brain disease might exist.[10]

Just as peculiar behaviors are not always caused by senility, they are not always caused by mental and emotional disorder either. For instance, symptoms like loss of appetite and sleep disturbance can be traced to physical illness rather than depression.[11]

9. Gatz, Smyer, and Lawton, p. 12.
10. Douglas C. Kimmel, *Adulthood and Aging*, p. 422.
11. Levy et al, p. 43.

It is sometimes very hard to discern whether a mood may be causing a physical problem or a physical illness may be creating a certain mood.

HANDLE WITH TLC

"Handle the elderly with care" should be the outcome of this discussion. Any diagnosis that says nothing can be done for an elderly friend should be greeted with extreme caution. They may just need a change in environment, counseling or physical care. Also, one should watch for physicians who use drugs too freely when treating the emotional and mental states of the elderly. Changes in their physical system make them susceptible to being harmed by drugs. For one thing, they are often more sensitive to side effects than are younger people. A confused state may be drug induced, rather than a sign of senility.[12] Being in an institution will increase the likelihood of such side effects. Apparently, many physicians have a tendency to freely prescribe drugs without enough concern for potential problems that may be caused. Pastors and relatives should urge doctors to cooperate with them in analyzing the aged person's situation before using chemicals to treat them. *The danger of overmedicating and undercaring is very real.*

The same warning relates to treating actual mental illness with drugs. Pharmaceuticals do help with some problems. Tricyclic drugs are effective in treating depression, for example, but, as with all drugs, the side effects can be harmful. The older person and those concerned for him should reach for help in other ways before reaching for the medicine cabinet.

In general, what is known about the mental problems of the elderly should make us treat them as we would any other, younger adult. A forty-year-old woman would not be labled senile because she is irritable after losing a spouse; being eighty years old should make no difference. Being irritable and withdrawn is normal in a person coping with loss. Even if the elderly person starts complaining like a hypochondriac, he may be temporarily under stress. Writers in the field of gerontology say that the elderly do not receive quality psychiatric treatment. Perhaps their mental suffering is seen as less important because they do not have long to live. Those in Christian ministry should resist that discrimination. Families can be supported in their efforts to get the best care possible for their elderly loved ones. In church counseling clinics, more emphasis can be placed on providing help to the elderly and their families.

THE TERRIBLE THREE

Depression. Depression is the number one psychological complaint of the elderly[13] as it is for the population in general.[14] Popular terms like "being down" and "being in the pits" show how preoccupied people are with "blue" moods. It is an awful state to be

---

12. Ibid., p. 50.
13. Eric Pfeiffer, "Psychopathology and Social Pathology," *Handbook of the Psychology of Aging,* p. 653, as cited by Golan, p. 215.
14. John Altrocchi, *Abnormal Behavior,* p. 56.

in. "It was horror and hell," said one survivor. "I was at the bottom of the deepest pit there ever was. I was worthless and unforgiveable. I was as good as—no, worse than—dead."[15] The features of depression tend to make life seem worthless. First, there are the inner feelings: a sense of helplessness, a feeling of worthlessness, a loss of self-esteem. Feelings of pessimism about the future couple with intense sadness. Certain behaviors go with those feelings: a loss of interest in the ordinary events of life, a tendency to withdraw from activities, a downcast expression and a slump in posture. The depressed may complain that simple daily tasks are like mountains to climb, that food tastes like sand, and that appetite is only a memory. Loss of sleep, sluggish flow of thought, poor concentration, and even physical symptoms like headaches, chest pains, muscular aches, and lack of sex drive can occur.[16] Constipation and weight loss may also be present.[17]

Because the causes of depression are not generally known, little is certain about what makes an elderly person depressed. Some suggest that the aged person's depression is different than the young adult's since it, in part, results from the loss of self-esteem that comes from aging. In younger adults it is tied to an anger that is turned in on oneself. In the aged, depression may simply be the fruit of remorse, resentment, and guilt.

Depression can give birth to tragic things. Alcohol problems affect 2 to 10 percent of the elderly, with higher rates for widowers and the chronically ill.[18] Suicide is one of depression's macabre offspring. Although older people represent only about 18.5 percent of the American population, they commit 23 percent of the suicides in this country. The higher incidence among white males suggests that losses of job and self-esteem may be a leading cause. Those among the white males most likely to take their lives are the widowed, ones who have lost a confidant or never had one, and those who have recently seen a physician. Most, by the way, give some clue of their intentions, but the physicians do not recognize it or else fail to act.[19]

Paranoia. Golan writes that, after depression, paranoid reactions are probably the next most common psychiatric disturbance in old age.[20] Persons suffering paranoia are suspicious of persons and events and often give faulty explanations for what is happening around them. A woman may misplace her purse and accuse her daughter of stealing it. If there is less mail than before, the elderly man may be certain the postman is stealing it. The paranoid person attacks and attacks.

Pfeiffer thinks most paranoid conduct is an attempt to fill in blanks in the person's

15. Ibid., p. 436.
16. Paul E. Huston, "Depression: Psychotherapy," *International Encyclopedia of Psychiatry, Psychoanalysis and Neurology,* 4:59, as cited by Lloyd M. Perry and Charles M. Sell, *Speaking to Life Problems,* p. 108.
17. Eric Pfeiffer, "Psychopathology and Social Pathology," in *Handbook of the Psychology of Aging,* ed. James E. Birren and K. Warner Schaie, p. 653.
18. Levy et al. p. 43.
19. M. Miller, "Geriatric Suicide: The Arizona Study," *Gerontologist* 18 (1978):488-95, as cited by Levy et al.
20. Golan, p. 215.

view of his situation.[21] Paranoia is more common in persons who are hard of hearing, partially blind, or lower in mental capacities. They have reasons for their suspicions. Questions are not answered. Unheard, unseen things are happening. They try to make sense out of those. For example, the person who accuses the mailman of a federal offense is simply trying to figure out why the letters are not coming as before. A person who claims others are trying to poison him may be grappling with why food does not taste the same as it used to. Understanding that may make it easier for the people who must care for those with suspicious reactions, but it will still be hard. The caretakers will have to cope with the fact that the nurse or housekeeper may quit after being accused of stealing. They may find it next to impossible to get prescribed medicine into the person who thinks someone is poisoning him. Pfeiffer states that as much as 60 percent of drugs given in pill form may never be taken. Paranoia may account for some of that.[22]

Hypochondria. Hypochondria, the third most prevalent psychological disorder, increases with advancing age. Concern for the body's functions and ills gets so intense that it interferes with the aged person's relationship to family and others. The hypochondriac, like a frightened turtle, turns inward, believing that the outside world is too hostile and unrewarding. More often a woman than a man, the person shares a long list of physical symptoms and complaints with everyone. Inwardly, the individual knows something is wrong but seeks medical attention, instead of counseling. That is no doubt due to the fact that he knows physical illness can be a proper excuse for not performing, whereas emotional troubles are not seen as acceptable. Such a person withstands the most persuasive attempts to convince him that the origin of his symptoms is psychological not physical.

Care must be taken to avoid concluding too soon that an aged person's complaints are not physically caused. Although it is true that depression can cause physical complaints, physical disorders can also cause depression. It is difficult for doctors to sort out the psychological and physical causes.[23]

Peculiar Patterns or Survival Strategies?

Older people, like younger ones, develop special behavior patterns that help them ward off anxiety, depression, or uncontrollable rage. They depend on those patterns for survival. Some are in the normal range, some are more exaggerated. Understanding the coping mechanisms will go a long way in helping to understand the person using them.[24]

---

21. Pfeiffer, p. 656, as cited by Golan, pp. 215–16.
22. Ibid.
23. L. Epstein, "Symposium on Age Differentiation in Depressive Illnesses: Depression in the Elderly," *Journal of Gerontology* 31 (1976):278–82, as cited by Levy et al., p. 43.
24. The following discussion is taken from Barbara Silverstone and Helen Hyman, *You and Your Aging Parent* (New York: Pantheon, 1976), pp. 88–92.

LIVING IN THE PAST

As death approaches, many older people spend much time reminiscing. Although painful, it can also be comforting. Sometimes people wrongly attribute that reaction to brain damage. On the contrary, it is a sign of health, not deterioration, and should be encouraged.

PREPARATORY MOURNINGS

This protective form of behavior includes a morbid interest in death, a fascination with obituaries, and a preoccupation with funerals—even those of strangers. This gloomy look at life is a means of coping with the anticipation of death.

DENIAL

The older person may notice all the signs of aging in others but not in himself. "Old Mr. Jones is really showing his age, isn't he?" the eighty-year-old man, bent with arthritis and hard of hearing, may shout to you. Denial, in moderation, is a useful tool for maintaining a sense of stability. If carried too far, it can be hazardous. The elderly may deny pain and physical symptoms until beyond help. A person may even continue to spend and deny the financial change of status. Denial is normal and proper until it interferes with reality to the degree that it prevents proper decisions and behavior.

A pastor recalled a conversation he had with an eighty-two-year-old woman, lying in a hospital bed in a cardiac ward. Her medical record indicated she was rapidly dying of heart failure. Her appearance, however, displayed her denial of her condition. Dressed in a frilly pink bed jacket, her nails freshly polished, hair carefully set, she spoke in a tiny but strangely seductive voice. She talked of her past independence, the business she formerly owned and managed, the automobile she drove until entering the hospital. Recognizing all of those as signs of denial, when he prayed, the pastor quoted Paul's Corinthian letter: "Though our outer man is decaying, yet our inner man is being renewed day by day" (2 Cor. 4:16). As he said goodbye and turned to leave, the woman shouted to him: "But my outer nature isn't wasting away!" Within forty-eight hours she was dead, having refused to face dying and death.[25]

MISTRUSTFUL BEHAVIOR

An older person can become cautious and suspicious of others. Perhaps he doubts others because he has begun to doubt himself and subsequently projects his own uneasy feelings to others. When the elderly have lost a certain amount of their independence, they suspect persons of wanting to cheat or neglect them. A certain amount of such mistrust is normal, but it can become a mental illness. Too much of it will surely test the mental balance of those who live with and/or care for them.

25. Charles V. Gerkin, *Crisis Experience in Modern Life*, pp. 84-85.

STUBBORNNESS AND AVOIDANCE OF CHANGE

This pattern of behavior is a defense against loss. The elderly may want to control the losses and cling tenaciously to what is left; change becomes a terrible threat. Those close may call them stubborn, saying things like "I can't budge him," or, "He won't listen." The aged one might fear travel and shun new activities—even refuse to meet new people. "Stubbornness is used as a magical solution to fight the forces which disrupt life."[26]

WORSHIP OF INDEPENDENCE

Independence, like resistance to change, is another protective garb. The elderly have had their share of change—of interference. Doing their own thing is one way they can protect what they own. They may ignore health care and safety, endure drably furnished rooms, and do seemingly foolish—but independent—things.

OVERDOING

Activity is a common defense against depression, anxiety, and other emotional pains. The problem is that it can jeopardize health and cause important matters to be neglected.

RITUALISTIC BEHAVIOR

Some elderly become slaves to routine. Everything must be "just so." There is a schedule and a pattern to coming in, going out, dressing, eating, and going to bed. They unconsciously think that will ward off evil and give assurance that tomorrow will be the same. It is another way of dealing with loss and change. It bolsters their command of the environment and compensates for their losses.

THE IMPORTANCE OF SUPPORT

THE COMPANIONSHIP CURE

Companionship may be the most effective prevention and treatment for mental and emotional problems. Although the impact of people networks, like the church and family, has not been systematically studied by psychologists, their role in sustaining others is obvious, and some data is emerging to prove their importance. G. Niederehe reported a connection between depressed persons and their lack of people contact.[27]

---

26. Barbara Silverstone and Helen K. Hyman, *You and Your Aging Parent*, p. 91.
27. G. Niederehe, "Psychosocial Network Correlates of Depression in Later Life," paper presented at the thirty-first annual meeting of the Gerontological Society, Dallas, November 1978, as cited by Delores Gallagher, Larry W. Thompson, and Sandra M. Levy, "Clinical Psychological Assessment of Older Adults," in *Aging in the 1980's,* ed. Leonard W. Poon, p. 31.

Frequency, type, and quality of contact are all important. In another study, research showed that having a person to talk to helps people maintain mental health when going through bereavement.[28] Christians need no scientific data to know the power of fellowship. The New Testament makes clear that God ministers through others. The value of comforting one another (1 Thess. 4:18; see also 2 Cor. 1:4) is known. Christians are told to be sympathetic (1 Pet. 3:8), and to encourage one another (Heb. 10:25). The love of God is felt and seen within His family (1 John 4:11-12). Being immersed in the warmth and acceptance of the community of God is to be soothed and bathed by His love, which is made visible there (1 John 4:11).

IN THEIR STEPS

Along with fellowship, older adults need empathy. It is not hard to figure them out. Like understanding others, it demands putting oneself in their shoes. Stop and imagine what it would be like to be depressed or afraid merely because of age. It is easy to see that what they are going through can strike them with anxiety, fear, perplexity, tearfulness, and feelings of helplessness. Emotional turmoil may show up in acute physical troubles—like tense muscles, trembling, rapid heartbeat, shortness of breath, and an upset stomach. Those who care for them need to stretch their ability to listen and empathize. Talk to them, accept them, and counsel them. Explore with them what they are thinking and feeling and then help them see how normal they are. When they are mentally distressed, make sure they get help. An emotionally disturbed older adult is already fighting hopelessness. Ignoring him or saying in so many words that "nothing can be done" adds to that battle. Like heavy sand, hopelessness is poured upon hopelessness, burying the person in sadness and fear. No wonder the last days are difficult for so many. Understanding family and friends can change that for some of them.

---

28. Gallagher, Thompson, and Levy, p. 31.

22

Taking Care of the Old Equipment: Physical Changes

FEAR OF AGING

The spector most people fear in old age may not be the grim, gray ghost with the scythe but the white-coated surgeon with a scalpel. Fear of death may actually take second place to anxiety over the illnesses and ailments of the body. *I dread being old if it means lying around helpless and painfully decrepit* a lot of people think. Such fears are justified, but they are greatly exaggerated. Aging does change the body for the worse. The old equipment will have some break downs, and there will be an increased chance of getting certain diseases. Physical problems vary a great deal among individuals, and persons react quite differently to them. Only a minority of aged persons suffer restrictions severe enough to keep them from normal life activities. For example, a study found only 5 percent of the people over sixty were confined to their homes due to physical disabilities. Even life after eighty-five is not all that confining. Seventy-five of every one hundred of those people do not live in nursing homes.[1]

THE MYSTERIES OF AGING

There is still much mystery surrounding the process of aging and related diseases. Note how the following technical definition includes both: Aging is "a decline in physiological competence that inevitably increases the incidence and intensifies the effects of accidents, disease, and other forms of environmental stress."[2] Disease and

---

1. U.S. National Center for Health Statistics, "Characteristics and Activities of Nursing Home Residents," in *Vital and Health Statistics,* series 13, no. 27, as cited by Douglas C. Kimmel, *Adulthood and Aging,* p. 339.
2. P. S. Timiras, *Developmental Physiology and Aging* (New York: Macmillan, 1972), p. 465, as cited in Kimmel, p. 328.

aging are actually separate, but they are related. Biological aging is actually a decline in physiological competence, called *senescence,* which makes a person more susceptible to disease and its effects.

Drawing a line between aging and disease is not simple since both often play a part in the aged's eventual death. Can it be said, for example, that a ninety-year-old man dies of old age when he succumbs to pneumonia while being treated in a hospital with a disease of the heart? Gerontologists are still working on identifying exactly what happens biologically to make a person grow old and exactly how much decline occurs apart from disease. Theories and hypotheses exist, but no certain answer. Aging may have something to do with change in the cells or declining efficiency of the body's systems. One researcher believes there may be many causes of aging, not just one.[3]

If scientists unravel the mystery of aging, they might be able to slow it down with some sort of "cure" or even prevent it's happening. If that ever happens, the social consequences and ethical questions would be awesome. If the life span is doubled, how do we handle the population problem? Should criminals who are serving life sentences be kept alive indefinitely? If such treatment costs a great deal of money, should the government finance it? Those questions can wait, since no plunge into the fountain of youth will soon be available for the rich or poor.

Right now, scientists do not understand aging. Think for a moment of the matter of untangling the tie between aging and disease. For example, old age results in some change in the walls of the arteries. But although such change might be called "natural," it is also possible it results from a circulatory disease. Thus, normal age changes may eventually be found to be *diseases.* In fact, one theory of aging holds that disease accumulates over time so that disease itself is the actual cause of aging.[4]

The best way to look at aging is to consider both disease and natural decline. The so-called normal aging changes in the body will be examined first, followed by a survey of the kinds of illnesses older people face.

SLOWING DOWN

Ear trumpets and other hearing aids have become typical old age equipment. Almost one-third of all persons over sixty-five and about three-fourths of those between seventy-five and seventy-nine have some hearing loss. Vision declines, too. Only a slight majority (57 percent) of those between sixty and sixty-nine have 20/20 vision in their best eye. The statistics and the sight grow dimmer with age: only 27 percent of those aged seventy to seventy-nine and 14 percent of those eighty and over retain perfect vision. Over one-third of those over eighty have vision so poor that reading and driving are limited for them. Cataracts, a disease in which the lens of the eye becomes so opaque that it keeps light from entering, increase with age.[5]

3. Nathan W. Shock, "Biological Theories of Aging," in *Handbook of the Psychology of Aging,* ed. James E. Birren and K. Warner Schaie, as cited by Kimmel, p. 334.
4. Kimmel, p. 334.
5. David F. Hultsch and Francine Deutsch, *Adult Development and Aging,* pp. 73, 77.

Loss of teeth is clearly a mark of old age. Only one-half of all persons between fifty-five and seventy-four have any natural teeth.[6] Tooth loss, however, may not be necessary. Some maintain that it is due to periodontal disease. Little is done to teach young and middle adults about preventing such loss, although the loss may be due to aging itself. Teeth turn up in young and middle adults' dreams, falling out or breaking. Apparently, they are an unconscious image of what it means to be old. "The dreams point to the fear of losing one's bite, of becoming feeble, of losing something irreplacable . . . of failure to take hold of life."[7]

The body's skeleton changes with age. The perception that older people seem to get a bit shorter is true. The discs between the spinal vertebrae may compress a little to cause this. Shortness may be exaggerated by stooping brought on by weakening muscles. Advancing age changes the chemical composition of the bones, making them break more easily. The risk of damaging them by accident is especially high for women. Diseases of the joints such as arthritis increase greatly and might be caused by some aspects of aging.

As the advertisements constantly state, the skin is affected. Paleness, change in texture, dryness, and spots appear.[8]

Fat can build up while muscles get smaller unless the older person cuts back on food and conscientiously exercises. Because of a lower level of activity, the older person needs less food although quality and balance are essential. Proper nutrition is crucial.

Even sleep is not the same. Getting older means being more easily awakened at night and spending more time lying awake. The aged even lose a type of sleep enjoyed earlier: the deepest level of sleep. Older people may spend more time in bed to compensate for that loss. Psalms that speak of the night may become priceless to them:

> His song will be with me in the night
> (Psalm 42:8)
> When I remember Thee on my bed,
> I meditate on Thee in the night watches
> (Psalm 63:6)

Nighttime can become prayer time.

The digestive system is least affected by ordinary aging.[9] Constipation does not increase, as some seem to think. Taste buds will be fewer, making eating a bit different and less enjoyable. Decrease in the ability to smell may add to that. Eating good food regularly may become a problem, underscoring the need for help in having a proper diet.

6. National Council on Aging, *Fact Book on Aging: A Profile of American Older Population* (Washington: National Council of Aging, 1978), as cited by Kimmel, p. 336.
7. Kimmel, p. 347; Ann Belford Ulanov, "Aging: On the Way to One's End," in *Ministry with the Aging*, ed. William M. Clements, p. 112.
8. Kimmel, p. 347.
9. D. B. Bromley, *The Psychology of Human Aging*, as cited in Kimmel, p. 348.

The cause of all such physical changes could be attributed to illness as well as to aging. Actually, there does seem to be some hard evidence that few changes are caused by years alone. One true aging change seems to be the slowing in the central nervous system. Reaction time increases, thus accounting for the fact that older equals slower. In the threat of an accident, for example, a person who is beyond the mid-twenties will have slower responses as his years increase. Other factors are at work also, such as how much training a person has had to respond in a certain way. Yet, when all things are equal, there is a gradual slowing in reaction time. The change of pace may be linked to the difference in electric brain activity. It is clear that the recording of brain waves shows a different pattern with age.

The reaction time increase also makes older adults more accident prone. Nothing in developmental literature suggests that a person up to sixty-five (or even older) has trouble doing his job. But in later years, the older person may respond less quickly in an emergency situation. One bit of evidence for this is that fact that drivers over sixty-five are in more auto accidents than middle-aged drivers. (However, younger drivers have the highest accident rate of all).[10] There is some controversy over what causes the higher accident rate. But it seems fair to caution older adults not to take needless risks.

The central nervous system slowdown may be the most important physical change to remember. It shows up in the older person's intellectual life. An older person takes longer to learn even though he has as much capacity to learn as ever. When teaching older adults it is necessary to allow them to go at a slower pace.

Some other unwelcome, highly visible alterations include graying hair, baldness, and a gravelly voice. Any of those changes, or a combination of them, will make a person feel older. Since being older in our culture is not desirable, the fight for self-esteem is on. But until there is a very marked decrease in response in the very old, an older person should not feel handicapped or limited or be treated as such. What the older person lacks in speed, he makes up for in skill and experience. The elderly actually do not come out any less efficient. Younger adults, who lack the skills and wisdom of the older, may have to work at their physical peak to achieve the same results. Remember, too, that capacities decline quite gradually. Decline is not inevitable and universally the same for all. Not all the systems are affected equally; hearing loss and dimness of vision do not always go together, for example. Some of the changes are modifiable. Hormone therapy and physical exercise make a difference. The point is this: biological functioning affects behavior only at certain points, and not very seriously for most. That is the good news. The bad news is that if aging does not get you, illness probably will.

ILLNESSES YOU MAY HAVE TO LIVE WITH

Sickness, in general, seems to impact older persons more than aging, although old age should not be equated with disease. Many older people are quite healthy. It is not

10. Kimmel, p. 352.

known whether the skill level and appearance of sick old people results from their advanced age, from their illness, or from the interaction of both.[11]

Certain kinds of diseases attack older people. Old persons have more chronic diseases, long-term illness, or frequently recurring ones such as arthritis, rheumatism, heart conditions, and high blood pressure. Some chronic diseases like hay fever and peptic ulcers do not occur any more frequently in the aged than in the general population, however. Older adults also have fewer acute (severe but temporary) diseases. Among chronic diseases, heart and blood vessel problems are the most prevalent.[12]

Eighty-six out of every one hundred Americans age sixty-five or over are afflicted with one or more chronic diseases. Though not all are permanently disabled by their chronic disease, 20 percent of those sixty-five or older are subject to being restricted in their activities. Compare that to 1 percent under forty-five and 5 percent of those between forty-five and sixty-four.[13] The four major chronic diseases are arthritis, heart disease, hypertension, and diabetes. Eighty percent of older Americans have arthritis although heart and blood vessel problems are the most prevalent in the long run.[14]

Aging alone does not seem to cause illness. Some of the things that go with aging make a contribution: stress, for example. Tension over the death of a spouse or a change in residence can affect health. Persons who are impatient, unable to relax without guilt, always feeling a sense of urgency about time, or afraid to stop hurrying are more likely to have heart problems[15] than easy-going individuals. Lack of exercise may be another problem. It is clear that a vigorous life and physical exercise promote good health for any aged person.

Perhaps the church should say more about physical and mental health care. One of the major problems associated with poor health should be a major concern of the church: loneliness. People who are sick or think they are sick are more lonely and alienated than those who think they are well. Feelings of poor health bring with them feelings of loneliness.[16]

No matter how Jesus' words "I was sick, and you visited Me" (Matt. 25:36) is interpreted, they do show His desire that Christians be sensitive to the needs of the ill. The sick old person is often doubly shunned, since people in our culture avoid contact with both the aged and the ill. Visitation programs to nursing homes and other senior citizen facilities should be encouraged in people and by church programs. Older people themselves can be mobilized to help the sick in their infirmity and loneliness.

11. Ibid, p. 335.
12. Hultsch and Deutsch, p. 85.
13. Herman J. Loether, *Problems of Aging*, p. 30, as cited by David Moberg and Robert Gray, *The Church and the Older Person*, p. 29.
14. Hultsch and Deutsch, p. 85.
15. Ibid., p. 84.
16. Ethel Shans et al, "The Psychology of Health," in *Middle Age and Aging*, ed. Bernice L. Neugarten, p. 217.

COPING WITH SEXUAL CHANGES

Sex is gone forever with the coming of middle and old age according to many people. Half of college students, when asked, said they believed their parents had sexual intercourse only once a month or less. And one quarter of them thought their parents had given sex up altogether, or if they had any, it was less than once a year.[17] There is a widely held misconception that sex is for the young. It just does not fit with the elderly's image. Surveys of the elderly, however, should put that myth to rest. Capacity for sexual relations continues into the eighties for healthy persons, report sex experts William H. Masters and Virginia E. Johnson.[18] "Most people can and should expect to have sex long after they no longer wish to ride bicycles."[19]

The acid of truth should dissolve the damaging fables of old age sexuality. For example, "sex in old age is unnatural," or, "it might put too great a strain on the heart." Reality sets no time clock in the human body that turns off sexual feelings and needs. Nothing about growing old suggests that it should. Research suggests that sex is an enriching activity. "Old age is for many people an opportunity to explore new and creative forms of sexual expression, and to become free from the performance forms of sexuality that early marriages seem to require."[20]

In marriage enrichment sessions, I am frequently asked about the rightness of certain sexual practices between married partners. Often, the elderly are the ones asking. Sometimes one of them will tell me how close he feels to his partner as a result of some variation they have brought to their sex life. There is no right or wrong in what a couple chooses to do in private, as long as it is neither forced on one or harmful to either of them.

Besides being a form of pleasure, sex is a powerful expression of companionship. Older persons need the joy and intimacy a warm sexual relationship brings to marriage. With the procreation function of sex gone, the other aspects will become more important. Sex for the aged may take on new meaning, or at least be somewhat distinct from earlier years, and can still be very important.

Preparing for satisfying sexual relationships in old age is much like preparing for other areas of life; it begins in young adulthood. What satisfaction the older person gets from sex will be determined primarily by what satisfaction he or she experienced earlier. Two researchers found that if sex was a problem earlier in life, the individual will be happy for an excuse to avoid it.[21] In the case of "empty nest couples," with children gone the sexual relationship often improves, feeding on its new-found privacy and freedom.

17. Ollie Pocs et al., "Is There Sex After 40?" *Psychology Today,* 11 June 1977, pp. 54–56 and 87.
18. William H. Masters and Virginia E. Johnson, *Human Sexual Response,* pp. 238–47, 26–70.
19. Alex Comfort, "Sexuality in Old Age," *Journal of American Geriatrics Society* 22, no. 1 (1974):440–42.
20. Allen J. Moore, "The Family Relations of Older Presons," in *Ministry with the Aging,* ed. William M. Clements, p. 187.
21. Eric Pfeiffer and Glenn Davis, "Determinants of Sexual Behavior in Middle and Old Age," in *Normal Aging,* ed. Erdman Palmore, as cited by Kimmel, p. 222.

How late in life sex actually continues (and with what frequency) depends upon how often the person actually practices it. Kimmel says, "The greatest risk to male sexuality in the later years is abstinence.[22] The same is true for a woman, though a woman's sexual capacity seems to be less affected by age than a man's.

CHANGES, NOT HINDRANCES

Potentially, aging can bring with it some health complications into the bedroom. They are not serious, however, and can be easily overcome. Indeed, perhaps health is not as important to enjoying the sex relationship as one's attitude toward health. The way a person looks at the soundness of his body may make a difference. For example, there is no connection between sexual activity and heart attacks, though it is commonly believed that there is. Couples should get information from their doctors in regard to their special cases. People with illness may be unnecessarily denying themselves or their partners needed companionship. Health seems to be less important to women than men.[23]

Couples should be alert to possible sexual troubles for the aging man. The possibility of impotence increases sharply after age fifty. Not knowing what to do is more serious than the problem, which may be psychological rather than physical. Too often couples do not talk about such things. They may be embarrassed to seek help. Since attitudes toward sex are closely related to one's spiritual views, church leaders have some responsibility for teaching middle and older adults about the matter. A good sex manual may help the older couple. A trip or two to a physician or counselor might spare them years of frustration and distress.

Sexual functioning may change for older adults but, for the most part, such changes do not hinder them. Both the man and the woman may desire the sex relationship less often as they grow older. But quality in their love life can make up for less quantity. The focus of the sexual relationship becomes more relational and less physical. Each is comforted and affirmed by the physical and emotional fusion. In old age, they know that it is not good to be alone. Perhaps a man and a woman need each other then more than ever.

22. Kimmel, p. 220.
23. Ibid., p. 222.

23

Retirement: Retiring, Not Retreating

LAST OR TOP RUNG OF THE LADDER?

According to studies done a few decades ago retirement is a crisis. Current data, however, shows that is not true. People react in individual ways toward retirement. Circumstances, especially financial, make the difference. "Retiring as a widowed Chicano domestic worker in poor health is quite different from retiring as a corporate executive with a well-financed pension and stock options."[1] Values also play a part. How valuable has the job been to the person? What satisfaction and meaning has it given? Psychological factors affect a person's attitude toward retirement. If someone has been dreading growing old, retirement may be a terrible threat, since it is another rung in the ladder toward old age.

Retirement will be a challenge for most people. According to gerontologists, it is the most crucial life change for the older adult.[2] Retirement is complex because it is both an ending and a beginning. It ends years of dedication to a job and represents new opportunities for using time and energy. It concerns both the individual and the family. Most of all, it is a symbol of a passage into a new era of life. Because it involves so much, people are quite varied in how they decide to retire, prepare for it and adjust to it.

PREPARING FOR RETIREMENT

Though persons usually begin preparing for retirement long before the age of sixty, some still fail to prepare at all. When Abraham Monk questioned both administrative and professional men between the ages of fifty and fifty-nine, he found them reluctant

---

1. Evelyn Eaton Whitehead and James D. Whitehead, "Retirement," in *Ministry with the Aging*, ed. William M. Clements, p. 124.
2. Naomi Golan, *Passing Through Transitions*, p. 197.

to talk about retirement, let alone get ready for it. Neither group of men had a consistent pattern for discussing their plans of making financial preparations. Even reading about retirement was not important to them. When asked why they avoided preparing for retirement, they tended to respond with rationalizations: they might not live long enough to retire, or they expected to keep active all their lives.[3]

That confirms the suspicion that some people are reluctant to face retiring because they see it as something negative. However, broader research shows that most men do look forward to and plan for it.[4]

AN ENDING AND A BEGINNING

Church leaders can help by prodding the reluctant to make retirement plans and by providing retirement education with a spiritual thrust to it. It will be necessary to help people see the time of retirement as both an ending and a beginning. Being ready for it and adjusting to it requires dealing with the past as well as the future. A person might deal with one phase and not the other. Take the person who longs to retire from a boring or difficult job. He may see retirement only as relief from the negative. Because of this, the person may not be ready to cope with retirement losses. He may have given little thought to how some aspects of the job will be missed, such as the companionship of fellow workers or the sense of accomplishment at the end of the day. Such a person may also be so wrapped up in escaping from the job that few plans have been made for what happens afterward. He is like the child who sees summer only as a time when there is no school. Retirement must be seen as a period with something to do, not merely as a period with something to not do.

THE RELUCTANT AND THE READY

Men with higher economic and social status give more thought to retirement plans than those of lesser means. As might be suspected, adequate financial resources make for a more positive attitude. The prospect of maintaining one's standard of living is most important. In addition, if a person has good health and a robust interest in leisure time activities he will more eagerly look forward to retirement. Higher education also plays a part. The higher the education for a man, the less he wants to retire, although women with higher education are positive about leaving their jobs.[5] Women with higher incomes want to continue to work longer than women with lower incomes. Those who retire early may not be as positive about it as might be thought. More often than not, they are retiring because they have to. Adjustment for them may be especially difficult. Ministers and counselors need to be watching for those for whom retirement will be difficult and urge them to face it boldly.

3. Abraham Monk, "Factors in the Preparation for Retirement by Middle-Aged Adults," *Gerontologist* 11, no. 5 (Winter 1971):348–51, as cited by Golan, p. 198.
4. B. McPherson and N. Guppy, "Pre-retirement Life-style and the Degree of Planning for Retirement," *Journal of Gerontology* 34 (1979):254–63 as cited by David F. Hultsch and Francine Deutsch, *Adult Development and Aging,* pp. 319–20.
5. Hultsch and Deutsch, p. 320.

TWO PARTS OF GETTING READY

Psychological preparations. Dealing with loss will be first on the agenda. Sometimes a person will not be fully aware of all that will be missed: tools, desk, fellow workers, familiar sights, even coffee breaks. To the degree he forsees the coming loss, the person will begin anticipatory grief, mourning before the losses take place. Depression, sleep disturbance and loss of appetite may occur. A person might become more irritable and distant to fellow workers. Jealousy and bitterness may create a critical stance. The Christian should be careful to avoid resentment, anger, and other negative reactions. He should seek to be responsible and gracious during the final years and months in the work place.

Besides coping with loss, the prospect of retirement might kindle the *life review*, which characterizes the older person.[6] This, of course, is more true of men and career women. Women, in general, begin their life review when the last child leaves home.[7] Since, this is the time of the end of one's vocation, it will demand some sort of evaluation of what has been done with one's life. The Christian perspective can be a priceless asset. The Christian knows that life's purposes are not bound up in making automobiles, selling encyclopedias or doctoring the sick. To evaluate oneself, a Christian must evaluate his many roles as servant of Christ: parent, Sunday school teacher, citizen, friend, brother in Christ, and so on.

Practical planning. Lots of questions need answers. If a person does not think ahead, retirement can be quite confusing. Questions to be dealt with include: How will I have to adjust, if at all, to living on my income? How will I use my time? Should I have a busy or leisurely schedule? How can I use my time to serve the Lord? Do I want to live near the children and spend time with the grandchildren? Should I do some volunteer service? Should I keep my present house or move to a smaller one? Do I want to move to a place with a different climate?

Couples, it is to be hoped, share those questions together.

Many couples do a sort of rehearsal. To test their desire to live in a smaller house, they close off a number of rooms to see what more cramped quarters would be like. They may rent or purchase a motor home and take a trip to see if they would enjoy that.[8]

The actual retirement is a major event. The church should go out of its way to celebrate with the retiree and stress the crucial things it symbolizes: personal fulfillment, a record of faithful financial provision for one's family, contribution to society, and new opportunities for service. Remember that it will not be a happy occasion for many, especially those who retire involuntarily. One study showed that 48 percent of retirees did not want to leave their jobs.[9]

Overall, though, the effects of retirement are good. Retiring does not affect a

6. See chapter 20 for a further discussion of the life review.
7. Golan, p. 201.
8. Evelyn Eaton Whitehead and James D. Whitehead, *Christian Life Patterns*, pp. 125–26.
9. Douglas C. Kimmel, Karl F. Price, and James W. Walker, "Retirement Choice and Retirement Satisfaction," *Journal of Gerontology* 33, no. 4 (1978):575–85.

person's overall morals or cause poor health. There is no evidence that retirement has any effect on when a person dies. However, retirement can be very stressful, particularly if some other difficulty occurs about the same time, such as the death of a spouse or a serious illness or injury. The negative impact then is quite dramatic.[10]

ADJUSTING TO RETIREMENT

The adjustment tasks for the retiree are quite clear. He must shift the central point of reference for life from the job sphere to the family and world of retirees.

That shift touches some crucial areas. Financial adjustments may be called for. Those who have the most difficulty handling retirement are those with reduced income—about 40 percent of retirees.[11] In today's consumer-oriented culture, a person's buying power adds to his sense of worth. An elderly man may feel guilty, believing that he is not providing a good retirement life for his wife. He may criticize himself and his past choices and "failures." A wife might harbor resentment over the level of income. Those who are accustomed to giving to charities and to the Lord's work may feel bad that they cannot continue to do so as before.

Lower income may not only spawn psychological struggles but practical problems as well. The church will need to be alert to the fact that many in the community who are in need are elderly and direct social ministries toward them.

Besides assistance from the church, the elderly should be receiving help from their grown children. According to the New Testament, children are to be responsible for their parents' needs. In 1 Timothy 5:3-8, the apostle Paul makes clear that the first responsibility for the care of widows belongs to the children. The church should help only when no children do so.

Developing relationships with others will be another task of the retiree. A job loss means losing a whole network of contacts with people. The retiree will have to make up for that, at least in part. Retired women seem to feel that loss the most.[12] Research leaves no doubt that social contacts at church make retirement easier.

MEANWHILE, BACK HOME

Living with one's spouse will be a major area of adjustment for the married retiree. A wife has plenty of apprehension about having her husband around the house all day. Adapting to that demands some changes in attitude as well as practical effort.

Lowenthal suggests that adjustment to retirement means shifting from being instrumental to being emotional and expressive. The working person values himself for what he produces. In retirement, that view has to change. He must not only

10. Golan, p. 204; Delores Gallagher, Larry W. Thompson, and Sandra M. Levy, "Clinical Psychological Assessment of Older Adults," in *Aging in the 1980's,* ed. Leonard W. Poon, p. 29.

11. Robert C. Atchley, "Adjustment to Loss of Job at Retirement," *International Journal of Aging and Human Development* 6, no. 1 (1975):17-27.

12. J. H. Fox, "Effects of Retirement and Former Work Life on Women's Adaptation in Old Age," *Journal of Gerontology* 32 (1977): 196-202, as cited by Hultsch and Deutsch, p. 324.

develop the relational aspects of life but see how affection can be expressed through helping out. A retired man, therefore, will learn to express his care for his wife through running errands and doing housework with her. White-collar men adjust to that way of giving support in a relationship better than blue-collar men do. Working-class husbands think "woman's work" is demeaning and that sharing in it devalues them.[13]

Eventually couples adjust to each other, especially where there has been a history of marital happiness. For them the increase in time will mean more marital satisfaction. Those who have had a history of conflict will be in for some trouble at retirement.[14]

Getting used to a new schedule will tax their patience. Before, they spent weekends and evenings together. Now the longer hours together every day will require some reorganization of their time.[15] Problems include more than simple complaints: "He wants to watch television while I want to vaccum the living room." "He wants to tell me how to run the house."[16] More serious problems may fester underneath the issues. Anger and bitterness can result whenever one spouse presses for a closer relationship than they have had in the past.

Whatever the conflicts a husband and wife have, Paul Tournier speaks glowingly of the possibilities of their life together in the latter years: "Growing old together, husband and wife can come to know a love which is in a way prefiguration of heaven, for it is less tumultuous than the love of youth, being less directed towards selfish pleasure-seeking, and because a slow advance in mutual comprehension permits more authentic communication."[17]

THE MAJOR OCCUPATION OF THE RETIRED

Coping with loss of involvement is the major occupation of the retired person and is central to the older person's state of affairs. Some cope with loss of involvement by continuing a high level of activities; others tend to disengage from life. Both ways of adjusting are satisfactory, as long as a distinction is made between disengaging from some activities and withdrawing from life. It should not be assumed that frantic activity is the only way to fill up life.[18] Older adults who choose the less busy way of life must not be made to feel guilty if they turn down some opportunities for service.

Retired adults are quite distinct in their choice of post-retirement activities. According to one study, those who reported that work was a major source of satisfaction for them often sought other employment. Seventy-three percent of those so in-

---

13. L. E. Troll, "The Family of Later Life: A Decade Review," *Journal of Marriage and the Family* 33 (1971):263-90. Note: This study was done over a decade ago. It is possible that the blue collar attitude is different today.

14. H. Z. Lopata, "The Life Cycle of the Social Role of Housewife," *Sociological and Social Research* 51 (1966):5-22 as cited by Hultsch and Deutsch, p. 323.

15. Golan, p. 207.

16. Ibid., p. 298.

17. Paul Tournier, *Learn to Grow Old*, p. 94.

18. Suzanne Richard, Florine Livson, and Paul G. Peterson, "Adjustment to Retirement," in *Middle Age and Aging*, ed. Bernice L. Neugarten, pp. 178-80.

clined obtained other jobs after retirement. Those people were healthier, more educated, and held positions of higher status than those who did not return to some sort of work.[19]

Those who do not return to financially gainful work often find work-substitute activities such as volunteer service, hobbies, traveling, and recreation. Retired people usually expand their leisure activities gradually and in moderation.[20] The most mentioned activity done during the week is that of watching television. On weekends they entertain or visit friends. Only a small proportion engages in crafts, hobbies, or artistic activities. Gardening and walking are the only outside activities reported. Vacation and travel are limited to comparatively few who can afford the expense. Education programs, self-development courses, seminars, and classes are becoming more popular. Most significant, L. G. Peppers found that there is a strong relationship between life satisfaction and the number of activities the older person reported.[21]

Apparently, most older adults try to deal with their sense of uselessness and inactivity by continuing to keep busy. The church can assist in that by keeping them involved in Christian service.

A CALLING IS NOT JUST A VOCATION

All adults need to have a proper sense of *calling*. A calling or *vocation* is a summons to service in all realms of life. This culture tends to narrow the definition of vocation. Supposedly a person possesses no basis for self-respect if he is unable to work or has no children to care for. Those are distortions of the Christian understanding of life's vocation. Every person is to have a calling at any moment, from birth till death. A child's vocation, for example, is to attend school, submit to parents, and mature in Christ. The calling alters as life progresses. A person's calling must be found and exercised at every stage of existence.[22]

The older person will discover that vocation in old age is in part a relational calling. Even a severely ill elderly person, unable to care for the most basic personal needs, will find some sense of usefulness as a person to whom others can relate.

During all of life, vocation must be found in God's calling, not in work alone. Such a broader outlook will help retired people with the adjustments they face. A person whose life is oriented primarily around work will have the most traumatic time with retirement.[23]

19. G. F. Strib and C. J. Schneiderm, *Retirement in American Society: Impact and Process,* cited by Hultsch and Deutsch, p. 322.
20. Golan, p. 205.
21. L. G. Peppers, "Patterns of Leisure and Adjustment to Retirement," *Gerontologist* 16, no. 5 (1976):441–46, as cited by Golan, p. 206.
22. Seward Hiltner, "A Theology of Aging," in *Aging and the Human Spirit,* ed. Carol LeFevre and Perry LeFevre, p. 52.
23. M. F. Lowenthal, "Some Potentialities of a Life Cycle Approach to the Study of Retirement," in *Retirement,* ed. F. M. Car, as cited by Hultsch and Deutsch, p. 322.

INVOLVEMENT

One of the most important things the church can do to help persons cope with retirement is to permit and promote their involvement in the church's ministry. A sense of well-being comes from making a contribution. The elderly will need to develop some sense of vocation in later years that will replace the feeling they had during their "productive" years. "This new sense of vocation would not be based on financial remuneration, but rather on such values as feeling needed, bringing joy and pleasure to another, exploring and expressing unknown and unused skills and abilities, developing a talent that had been buried, or as one older person said, paying back some of the rent for the ground he had been using."[24] In other words, as Elbert Cole so eloquently puts it, the retired person must shift from making a "contribution to the gross national product . . . to [making] a contribution to the gross national 'human situation' by caring for and helping another human being."[25]

The White House Conference of 1971 emphatically recommended that older adults guide ministries for older adults, stating that "special attention should be given to allowing older persons to share in the planning and implementation of all programs related to them."[26] The reasons for doing this are as demanding as they are clear. First, there is no reason why older adults should not direct and staff such programs. Complaints are often heard that older adults are not being visited or served. Yet it is quite clear that older adults themselves have not spearheaded those ministries. The closest thing to an explanation is this: upon reaching retirement age older adults are often made to feel they have little to offer, or else they begin to expect a life of leisure. Somehow they think they have neither the power nor responsibility for having a meaningful ministry. For some reason, there is a feeling "that older adults are not able to lead themselves and therefore need younger leadership. . . . "[27] Cole maintains that that belief is not true. Younger leaders should assist in providing for ministries but only with a view toward helping them obtain their own goals. Older adults have ability, drive, and leadership skills. The church must increase its own awareness of "gray power" and help older adults to become aware of it as well.

Getting older adults into ministry is not just a nice way to keep them busy. With the number of adults over sixty in this society constantly increasing, it is going to be very difficult for adults of other ages to minister to them. Without older adults raising the funds and doing the work, there is no hope of providing all the services they will need.[28]

Ministries can take many forms: evangelistic, visitation, Bible studies in homes and nursing homes, special senior citizens clubs, and social, recreational and educational

24. Elbert C. Cole, "Lay Ministries with Older Adults," in *Ministry with the Aging,* ed. William M. Clements, pp. 252-53.
25. Ibid., p. 252.
26. U.S. White House Conference, 1971, "Section on Spiritual Well-Being," as cited in Carol LeFevre and Perry LeFevre, eds., *Aging and the Human Spirit,* p. 220.
27. Cole, p. 255.
28. Ibid., pp. 254-55.

programs. Many ministries can be done in cooperation with other churches or be part of a community based effort.

A model for such a ministry is call Shepherd's Center. Located in Kansas City, it

> focuses on people, not on programs or activities. [It rests on a] "people base" (a population base of older people living in a specific geographical area), and involves a covenant relation between center leaders and people assuring that every effort will be made to assist the people in achieving those goals needed or desired in their later years. In turn, the people provide the program leadership and participate in whatever way possible in maintaining a supportive network capable of helping themselves survive while finding some meaning and purpose in life. . . .

> The goal from the beginning was to utilize older people in providing those services required by other older people to remain in their own homes and to continue independent living. . . .

> Early plans to build a retirement home were scrapped when the team realized that . . . 95 percent [did not need it. Two questions were uppermost]: how can I get help when I need it in order to remain independent as long as possible; and what can I do in the later years to find meaning and purpose for my life?[29]

At first, they began with a single service, Meals on Wheels, initially conducted by retired men of one church. Later, a Shoppers Service was begun to help those who did not need hot meals delivered but who found shopping very difficult.[30]

> The Handyman program was created to assist older homeowners in making minor repairs to their homes. . . .

> The Night Team . . . is [a reassuring] but seldom used service. After-hours telephone calls are monitored by a professional answering service, which . . . refers emergencies to a select list of persons who are prepared to respond immediately. . . .

> The Care XX Program refers to keeping in touch with low-income older people who qualify for some of the services provided through Title XX of the Social Security program. The . . . staff refers those who need and qualify . . . to the authorized public agency. . . .

> The Friendly Visitors program utilizes the services of volunteers . . . who make regular visits to isolated and homebound individuals. . . . [31]

The Companion Aides are those who help elderly persons in their homes and are chosen for their ability to care. That services does not include maid or nursing services but rather those things "that children might do for their parents."[32]

29. Ibid., pp. 255–56.
30. Ibid., p. 256.
31. Ibid., pp. 259–60.
32. Ibid., p. 260.

The Security and Protection coordinator holds sessions on maintaining personal security in the home and on the street. . . .

The newest home service is the Shepherd's Center Hospice Team, specially trained to give assistance to the terminally ill. . . . [33]

"The Shepherd's Center has grown from a single service to nineteen major services, and to about 350 volunteers helping over 4,000 people."[34] A local church may independently seek to establish its own ministries, but, because of limited church resources and the great needs in most communities, it is advisable that a local church urge its elderly to participate in community agencies and united church programs, rather than start competing groups. They can make their Christian presence known within those programs and use contacts as opportunities for evangelism.

In a guidebook for the local congregation, Mark Bergmann and Elmer Otte offer some steps for a local church to begin a ministry with the aging.[35]

1. Gather a group of persons committed to establishing a ministry by the elderly. Invite adults of all ages to meet to initiate some ministry. From the start emphasize that it is not to be a ministry of *doing for* but rather of *doing with.*
2. Offer a method of determining some of the needs of the older person. Start with some discussion of questions like: Who are the elderly? What can the older person do? How can the older person be enabled to perform? Then, gather some facts about the elderly in your congregation and community. The Shepherd's program began with the finding that the two major concerns of the elderly were loneliness and lack of purpose. Find out what agencies are already serving the elderly. Each state has a State Commission on Aging that can be contacted. There are also state Area Agencies on Aging that have professionals who can be helpful. Many counties have a County Commission on Aging that handles discount programs, nutrition programs, and others. Communities have Senior Citizens Centers, Golden Age Homes, and other such organizations. Check around and begin to tie in with existing programs and staffs.
3. Discover what help is needed in the existing agencies and watch for services and people who are overlooked. Perhaps a questionnaire distributed among the congregation can help to locate persons and needs. List the needs and ask which should have the highest priority. Try to determine where God is leading. At that point, it may be time to form an organized group with a chairman. Projects and programs can be considered.

Bergmann and Otte suggest the following: special church services to deal with the concerns of the elderly; annual inter-generational events; prayer partners chosen by

33. Ibid.
34. Ibid., p. 256.
35. Mark Bergmann and Elmer Otte, *Engaging the Aging in Ministry,* pp. 19–31.

drawing names; surrogate children and grandchildren; trips and tours to such places as the zoo, flower gardens and historic centers; promotion of gardens among senior citizens; a telephone reassurance program; providing transportation for elderly; and provision of craft programs. Other potential programs include: a senior center, visitation and tape ministries, nutrition services, crime watch security, legal services, and referral resources.[36]

Older people report that some time after retirement, they sense something is missing. "For a time there might well be a glorious holiday, but then sooner or later there is that haunting question: is there more to life than this?"[37] If someone answers no to that, it may cause that person to hit a bottom from which he never recovers. Meaningful ministry can be a way up and out.

36. Additional information is available from the National Council on Aging, 1828 L Street, NW, Washington, D.C. 20046.
37. Cole, p. 252.

24

Grandparenting: A Grand Opportunity

IS IT GRAND?

Some people use the back of their cars to declare: "Happiness is being a grandparent." In general, the bumper sticker is true. For most, grandparenting is grand. Two-thirds of grandparents questioned said they were satisfied with the role.[1] One-third of them said it was disappointing or difficult for them and created stress. About 30 percent of the grandmothers and grandfathers surveyed said they felt remote from their grandchild and that the role of grandparent had relatively little effect on their lives.[2] Exactly what difficulties do they have? What kind of conflicts do grandparents have with their grown children over the grandchildren? What is expected of grandparents? How does grandparenting affect the grandparents marital relationship? What contribution do grandparents make to their grandchildren? How much grandparent power is there?

Writing in 1980, Lillian E. Troll said that there are almost no scientific answers to those questions, noting that fewer than a dozen studies of grandparenting had been done at that time.[3] Particularly for the middle class, grandparenting is a role-less role, since rights and duties are not clearly spelled out for them. That uncertain nature of grandparenting apparently causes some problems. Expectations vary with social class and ethnic group. Grandparents are not sure what their job is, and they may not know when they are doing it properly. They may believe they are denied any major part in their grandchild's life. Some, on the other hand, may be pressed into doing a great deal for their grandchild, which creates a heavy burden for them, particularly when they face health or financial problems.

1. B. L. Neugarten and K. K. Weinstein, "The Changing American Grandparent," *Journal of Marriage and the Family* 26 (1964):199–204.
2. Ibid.
3. Lillian E. Troll, "Grandparenting," in *Aging in the 1980's*, ed. Leonard W. Poon, p. 475.

Recent research finds that the relationship of grandparent to grandchild is far more important than was originally thought although there is not enough research to know what is a normal pattern. Right now, it is best to conclude that there is no general pattern as much as there is diversity in grandparent-grandchild relationships.[4]

RENEWAL AND IMPACT

Becoming a grandparent is a time of renewal for some. "It's through my grandchildren that I feel young again," they say. Others feel good about the idea of biological continuity. "It's carrying on the family line that counts." Without doubt, many feel a sense of self-fulfillment. "I can do for my grandchildren things I could never do for my own kids.... Now I have the time to be with them."[5] If the older adult did not have a close relationship with his own children, he may find himself making up for it by relating to the grandchildren. Grandchildren offer older adults a second chance. If they did not enjoy their own children, they can enjoy their children's children.

Giving gifts and spending time with grandchildren can strengthen the tie between the older adult and his grown children. That being true may make the opposite true—sparse grandparent-grandchild contact may foster a feeling of separation between parents and grown children.

Some grandparents feel good about being a resource person to their grandchildren. They give financial support, advice, and encouragement. Sometimes the satisfaction grandparents get is vicarious. That is, they feel they are able to achieve something through their grandchildren that they and their children were not able to accomplish. Perhaps that accounts in part for the obvious pride grandparents show in their grandchild's achievements.

In a society that tends to shelve its elderly, the grandparent role may be quite important for them. One study showed that the grandparent-grandchild relationship is especially meaningful to older grandmothers. "My grandchildren make me feel young," or, "They make me less elderly," they often say. Younger grandmothers are apparently busier with other concerns and do not depend upon the relationship so much. They tend to view their job as one of setting a good example, encouraging grandchildren to work hard and be honest. Older grandmothers, however, place emphasis on the personal relationship, centering on the joys and pleasures of being a grandmother.[6]

Though the significance of being a grandparent varies, studies show that it is important. Young parents should be made aware of this. Research shows that they play a large part in building the grandchild-grandparent tie. J. F. Robertson found that the relationship will be established to the extent that parents encourage and facilitate

4. Ibid., p. 480.
5. Neugarten and Weinstein as cited by Douglas C. Kimmel, *Adulthood and Aging*, p. 215.
6. J. F. Robertson, "Interaction in Three Generation Families, Parents as Mediators. Toward a Theoretical Perspective," *International Journal of Aging and Human Development* 6 (1975):106-9.

it.[7] There is a tendency for grown children to require grandparents to "earn" the rights and privileges of being grandparents.[8] Christian parents should be urged to resist that. They should be sensitive to their parents' needs and do what they can to cultivate their parents' contact with the grandchildren.

The classic study of Neugarten and Weinstein done in 1964 uncovered five different styles of grandparenting. They are:

- *Formal*—maintaining clearly demarcated lines between parent and grandparent, with an occasional gift or minor service (22 percent grandmothers, 23 percent grandfathers)
- *Fun-seeker*—a leisure orientation characterized by grandparental self-indulgence and mutuality of pleasure (20 percent grandmothers, 17 percent grandfathers)
- *Surrogate parent*—almost always the grandmother (10 percent grandmothers, 9 percent grandfathers), who substitutes for the children's mother if she is employed or otherwise unable to care for the children
- *Reservoir of family wisdom*—more the grandfather (1 percent grandmothers, 4 percent grandfathers); a sort of power role
- *Distant figure*—emerging "from the shadows" ritually and fleetingly (13 percent grandmothers, 20 percent grandfathers)[9]

A study done of grandparent-grandchild dyads in 1978 showed clearly that grandparents not only try to influence their grandchildren but that they usually succeed. Over 80 percent of the grandparents and even more of the grandchildren said there are attempts on both their parts to influence each other. The influence covers many areas of life: style of life, values, outlook, work, education, and interpersonal relationships.[10] Children eight to nine and eleven to twelve mention that they see value in the grandparent's character. They say things like, "He's a good man."[11]

That influence seems to be exerted beyond the time when the grandchildren are young. Evidence exists to prove that young adults value their relationship with their grandparents.[12] Robertson used a questionnaire to assess attitudes toward grandparents. She found that young adult grandchildren have very favorable attitudes toward grandparents. For example, 92 percent agree that children would miss much if there are not grandparents when they are growing up; 90 percent agree that grandparents are not too oldfashioned or out of touch to be able to help their grandchildren,

7. Ibid.
8. L. E. Troll, "The Family in Later Life: A Decade Review," *Journal of Marriage and the Family* 33 (1971):263-90.
9. Neugarten and Weinstein as cited by Troll, "Grandparenting," pp. 478-79.
10. G. Hatestad, "Patterns of Communication and Influence Between Grandparents and Grandchildren in a Changing Society," paper presented at the World Congress of Sociology, Sweden, 1978, as cited by Troll, "Grandparenting," p. 481.
11. B. Kahana and E. Kahana, "Grandparenting from the Perspective of Developing Grandchild," *Developmental Psychology* 3 (1907):98-105, as cited by David F. Hultsch and Francine Deutsch, *Adult Development and Aging*, p. 329.
12. Troll, "Grandparenting," p. 477.

and 79 percent indicate that teenagers do not think their grandparents are a bore.[13]

I saw this confirmed in a small way among our adult Christian sharing group. We were asked to tell who was the first example of a dedicated Christian we remembered meeting. Most of the fifteen adults in the group said it was a grandparent.

There is no absolute confirmation that a grandparent will impact grandchildren spiritually, but the research shows that the potential is there. Grandparents need to be reminded of that to give hope for results in ministry. It may also alert them to an opportunity they may think does not exist.

GRAND TROUBLES

Grandparenting, for some, is not just an occasion to fatten their billfold with pictures. Grandparenting can be burdensome. Quarrels over how the grandchildren are to be raised are not the most severe problems. Being forced to be surrogate parents is. Increased divorce and the movement of young mothers into the labor force is no doubt increasing the number of grandparents who care for grandchildren. Once especially true for lower class families, it is now true for the middle class. When child care is coupled with illness or poverty, it can be oppressive. Besides the effort child care takes, circumstances can make it emotionally painful. Especially troubled are those grandparents who take over the care of children because the child's parents are divorced or irresponsible. Their care of the grandchild is mixed with guilt and anger over their child's "failure" to care for his offspring. Grandparents like these will need the special support of relatives and friends in Christ. Such a person came to me following a meeting at which I spoke. "My wife and I are taking care of two teenage grandchildren," he told me. While I was speaking, I had noticed this over-seventy-year-old gray-haired man in the audience. I had pictured him as one of those happy empty-nesters, retired, and enjoying life among his elderly peers in the church. On the contrary, he was far from happy, and his nest was not tranquilly empty. Both teenagers under his care were disobedient and in trouble. His son, divorced twice, had left town, literally abandoning the children to his parents for the past eight years.

His wife, he said, was too permissive, and he was too ill to help discipline the youngsters or help with housework. A heart attack a month ago had put him into the hospital. Upon release the doctor told him to go home and rest. His wife constantly harassed him for not doing anything around the house. Life was hard. He was confused. He had no idea how he could manage the future. Nonetheless, he accepted his hardship as something he deserved. Until he had become a Christian a few years before, he had lived a terrible example to his children, who, he believed, had turned out badly because of it. Reaping what he had sowed, he told me he would somehow have to continue.

That man's plight is exceptional. It nonetheless points out that in teaching and other ministries it is important to be aware that some older adults carry the heavy

---

13. J. F. Robertson, "Significance of Grandparents: Perceptions of Young Adult Grandchildren," *Gerontologist* 16 (1976):137–40 as cited by Hultsch and Deutsch, p. 329.

burden of raising grandchildren. They may need direct help as well as counseling and teaching.

Grandparents with other kinds of problems may be present in the church. Some will have troubled relationships with their children over how the grandchildren are being brought up, even though grandparents in general tend to leave the parenting to the parents while they have fun with the grandchildren. Elderly who live with their grown children are especially prone to having conflict over childrearing issues. Those grandparents need to learn to let go of their grown children and not assume parental responsibility for them.

Laura J. Singer warns couples of some possible irritations. A man or woman for whom being a grandparent means being old may resent being referred to as grandpa or grandma. For example, one woman said, "My husband made some wisecrack about my being a grandmother and I was furious."[14] A person may resent the way his spouse behaves with the grandchild. A grandfather may feel free to cuddle and play with the youngster in carefree, childish ways. His wife may say, "I never knew you had it in you!" If she is feeling pushed out or less cared for by her mate, she may discredit his new way of being and say, "Can't you see you're making a fool of yourself when you play like that and get down to an infant's level?"

Grandparents may also tend to see each other as diminished. A man may think, *My wife was such a strong woman. Look at her now, trying to please her daughter; letting herself be bossed so she can be with our grandchild.*[15] The lessening of power over one's children is natural. Couples should discuss it and not allow it to make them feel devalued in each other's eyes.

Another problem might develop over an excessive preoccupation with the grandchildren as an attempt to refill the empty nest. In order to avoid closeness and hide problems in the marriage, a spouse may use the grandchildren as he did the children to keep a distance from the partner. When that happens, all the family relationships become strained. Resentment builds up in the neglected spouse. Left out, he fights mixed feelings of love for and jealousy over the grandchildren. The grown children become upset over the grandparent's excessive absorption in the grandchildren. "For everyone's well-being, the grandparents must not use their children and grandchildren to meet their own needs." Singer claims it is usually the grandmother who becomes overinvolved—especially if she cares for the child while the mother works. In such cases, a woman has to make her primary relationship the one with her husband if her marriage is going to be healthy.[16]

Grandparents may also have conflict between them when one responds to pressures to babysit or to spend more time with the grandchildren, and the other thinks the grown children are using them. Especially when the children have been quite dependent all along, they sometimes expect grandparents to be in touch with every little thing that happens in the grandchildren's lives, and resent their parents' lack of

14. Laura J. Singer, *Stages: The Crises That Shape Your Marriage,* p. 223.
15. Ibid.
16. Ibid.

involvement. A grandparent may be made to feel guilty even if he is giving attention to the grandchild.

Special situations occasion special difficulties. Grandparenting can be quite complicated when there has been divorce and remarriage. Three or four sets of grandparents can be party to a blended family, making keeping in touch with grandchildren quite a problem.

Despite those difficult cases, the adjustments related to grandparenting seem to be few and easy. Anyone who has been caught in the beaming glow of a grandparent reaching for the most recent snapshots of the grandchildren realizes that the rewards usually outweigh the responsibilities.

25

Deceased or Deserted: Death and Divorce in Old Age

DEATH OF A SPOUSE

"I want to go first" is a quip older people sometimes toss at one another. Apparently most mean it. Dying is better than surviving. Anticipating either one's own or one's partner's death is a normal, though anxiety ridden, part of old age. Widowhood is apparently a bleak prospect for either a man or a woman. Because of their longer average life and the tendency for them to marry older men, it is a more likely prospect for the female, resulting in widowed women outnumbering widowed men five to one. Some suggest that widowhood is worse in anticipation than it is in actuality, and that it is less traumatic in older adulthood than younger.[1]

Of course, no one can predict if and how she will become a widow, but there are some averages to consider. For some, it will be sudden and unexpected, through an accident or sudden heart failure. Half of all persons who live to be fifty die of heart disease and its complications. Many others will have clear warning in the form of a terminal illness. Helena Z. Lopata, in an important research project, found that many widows cared for husbands at home for one year during their last illness. They had time to mentally rehearse for widowhood.[2] Actually, in later adulthood, a number of chronic illnesses and conditions might be present in both husband and wife, making death imminent for either of them. That the other died first may become a factor in the following bereavement since the ill survivor may feel cheated or abandoned.

The passage to widowhood may be one of the most dramatic challenges of the life span. Since the death of a spouse and widowhood has already been discussed in the

---

1. Naomi Golan, *Passing Through Transitions*, p. 231.
2. Helena Z. Lopata, *Widowhood in an American City*, p. 48.

middle adulthood chapters, the following will touch on only those features that are especially typical of widowhood in older adulthood.

DYING "WITH" A PARTNER

Older adults are most likely to have some warning that they are going to lose their spouses. Sometimes, the partner will be quite ill long before either spouse actually faces what is happening. The terminally ill person and the partner may not come to grips with the hard reality until symptoms become quite ominous or a sudden collapse takes the sick person into a hospital.[3]

By that time, as a couple, they will have faced numerous losses such as social roles, activities, and some degree of health. In past installments, they have given up by degrees those things that were theirs together. Now they may encourage one another, talking about their impending losses and eventual separation. Studies show that elderly Christians do not greatly fear death and they share the hope of reunion.

Both the dying elderly and his spouse may go through the stages uncovered by Kübler-Ross: disbelief, anger, and resentment. People who support them will do so by listening, accepting, and offering assurances that the anger will pass.

Anticipatory grief. Expecting the ultimate separation, both the dying person and the survivors may go through the bereavement process before the actual death. All signs of grief may present themselves: anger, resentment, sadness, depression, remembering past events, withdrawal from the relationship. It is helpful if both the dying and the surviving are counseled to understand that and act properly in regard to it. Two extremes are to be avoided. First, the parties involved should be careful not to withdraw from one another leaving both the dying and the loved ones lonely, confused, and even forsaken. After decades of closeness, the elderly surviving spouse may feel a great deal of hurt when the terminally ill spouse moves away. Assurances that such is normal and the dying one is not himself will comfort. The other extreme in improperly handling anticipatory grief is to press too hard for maintaining closeness right up to the end. Persons should remain completely available to each other, but they should also permit one another to let go if necessary.

Sometimes the loved ones will feel guilty about beginning to work on the thoughts and feelings related to the dying one's death. A woman may feel bad about beginning to work on her grief or of thinking about whether she should sell the house after her husband is gone, even though it is proper and wise for her to do so. The one who will be left should be encouraged to answer the practical questions that arise: "Where will I live now? How can I face being alone in the house?" Friends and close relatives should give assurance that it is all right to think of those things even while the spouse is dying.

To tell or not. Whether or not to tell the terminally ill aged person that death is near is another predicament for the spouse. Physicians often do not know what to do and sometimes not only refuse to tell a patient but prohibit other staff members from

3. Golan, p. 231.

doing so.[4] That question is best dealt with on an individual basis. Much depends on how the ill person is coping with his situation. If he is a person who likes to face problems head on, he will probably want to know and ask a lot of questions. On the other hand, many elderly cope with dying by denying and avoiding it. Such a person may not even ask about his condition and seem to project the message that he does not really want to be told. Most patients are able to tell they are dying by such things as their own bodily changes, the comments and behavior of the hospital staff, and remarks by family and friends.[5]

There are good reasons for telling the terminally ill person about his condition. Scripture encourages truthfulness. Telling the dying person also creates an opportunity to say good-byes and care for other final matters, including the spiritual.

Hospice: The new way to die. "Where shall my loved one die?" is a question that the surviving spouse must answer. No more is it taken for granted that the terminally ill person needs to be in an intensive care unit or even in a hospital. The cry for death with dignity is being heard, which in turn is encouraging the rapid spread of the hospice movement. The concept of hospice originated in England and is dedicated to keeping the patient pain-free, comfortable, and fully alert during the final phases of the dying process. A mixture called "Brompton's Cocktail," consisting of ditmorphine (heroin) or morphine, cocaine, gin, sugar syrup, and chlorpromazine syrup is given in small doses around the clock before severe pain begins. It reduces the patient's fear of pain and enables him to maintain a clear mind.[6]

Care, too, is given to the family's needs. Visiting hours are not restricted. Often, comfortable chairs and couches are provided. Family members are allowed to participate in the care of the patient. Personnel in the hospice are trained to help the relatives and friends by giving information on what is occurring, suggesting things they can do, how they can respond and how they can cope with their emotions. Even after the death, the personnel continue their support, permitting the family to stay as long as they would like, answering questions, providing anything they can to help. After leaving the hospice, family members are encouraged to contact hospice personnel during their time of bereavement.

It seems as if this movement will become entrenched in the United States. The government's recent decision that Medicare may pay for hospice care will surely establish hospices further.

Perhaps the hospice program will help the aged couple deal better with one of the aspects of being terminally ill: the loneliness it brings to the dying. People may stay away because it is too painful for them to see a person in that physical condition or because they do not know what to say. Cancer victims often are made to feel like they have a contagious disease. The church can do a great deal to help in those matters by training adults to understand the terminally ill and how to act around them. Pastors

---

4. Ibid.
5. Ibid.
6. David F. Hultsch and Francine Deutsch, *Adult Development and Aging*, p. 361.

and church members can also stand behind the hospice program and encourage families to use it.

THE ETHICS OF DYING

Couples will face the controversial, ethical questions about euthanasia whenever a terminal illness "condemns a person to a future of long unconscious existence or unrelieved pain. Few subjects related to death are more discussed in both medical ethics and ethics informing legal policy,"[7] says John C. Bennett.

There are two types of euthanasia, active and passive. *Active euthanasia* refers to deliberate actions (e.g. injecting air bubbles) to end an individual's life when in a state of terminal illness. Withholding or withdrawing treatment that is sustaining life and thereby permitting a person to die is termed *passive euthanasia.*[8]

In a number of states, it is legally accepted that a patient has a right to refuse treatment. When no such law exists physicians make their decisions based on what is called "the living will." The patient signs "a directive to physicians to withhold life-supports under appropriate circumstances"[9] should they arise. So far, that does not have legal force, but some doctors do lean upon it. It is obvious today that some physicians often make decisions on their own quite apart from the legal situation. In general, evangelicals may have little argument with the practice of withholding medical support for sustaining life at appropriate times. Since those means are within the power of man to give, they are also within his will to take away or refuse. The questions revolving around who makes the decision and under what circumstances are not so easily answered. Bennett maintains there is broad moral support for "indirect euthanasia."[10]

Active euthanasia is another matter. "Not only has traditional Christian teaching been adamant against it, but so have the legal and the medical traditions. Bennett reminds us that "because mercy killing is deliberate and premeditated, in the U.S. it is legally classified as first-degree murder."[11] Though this is the legal situation, the current ethical discussion is very brisk. In fact, a 1974 poll disclosed that 53 percent of Americans said yes to actively ending a patient's life if requested by the patient or the family. That was up from 36 percent in 1950.[12]

Two realities complicate the question. The first has to do with a practice very close to euthanasia: intentionally "giving drugs to people in great pain, even though the drugs are known to shorten life. Such a policy should be regarded as a step toward positive euthanasia, although the shortening of life is a secondary effect, not the intention," argues Bennett.[13] Since, however, the resulting death is not intended, there seems to be moral support for the practice. The other complication is created

7. John C. Bennett, "Ethical Aspects of Aging in America," in *Ministry with the Aging,* ed. William M. Clements, p. 146.
8. Hultsch and Deutsch, p. 362.
9. Bennett, p. 147–48.
10. Ibid., p. 148.
11. Ibid.
12. Hultsch and Deutsch, p. 363.
13. Bennett, p. 148.

whenever the ill person takes his own life. Is "terminal suicide"[14] always immoral?

Both Catholic and Protestant theologians are presently tending to move in the direction of the moral acceptance of positive euthanasia. Catholic theologian Paul Ramsey "now admit[s] that in extreme cases of hopeless suffering, or when a person is permanently in a comatose condition, direct euthanasia may be permitted.[15] Bennett cautiously endorses the possibility, basing his reasoning on an ethic of love.

> I believe that the traditional positions in Christian morality and in Western law have been too much separated from concrete human experience, imposing abstract and absolute laws. One of the tendencies in the current development of ethical thinking is to pay greater attention to living and changing experience, to the exceptional situations which produce exceptional hardship and suffering. There is now less tendency to sacrifice individual persons to an abstraction. I believe that this humanizing of ethics is a better expression of love and compassion than is the absolutism of the ethical and legal tradition, and it is, therefore, more in harmony with the ethic of love itself, which is at the heart of the Judeo-Christian tradition and the humane secular ethic that has been influenced by it.[16]

Three major objections are leveled at any practice of euthanasia.[17] First of all, there is the matter of the sanctity of human life. This has been a foundational value in Western society. Modern medicine has, in fact, been based upon it. Therefore, whatever decision is to be made about prolonging or ending life must take that into account. Of course, present medical practices have created the question of when life actually ends.

Second, those who argue against euthanasia regard the practice as taking into one's own hands what belongs only to God. Evangelicals, especially, concur with the concept that "letting nature take its course" is the only acceptable way, since that is the realm controlled by God. Those who argue for euthanasia take the stand that God, too, may be present in the medical profession and in the actions of those who care. The whole matter is sometimes complicated by the fact that medical science may have already contributed to the person's present condition (as through a transplant that allows the person to go on living, but in a coma). Just what is natural? Just where *is* God in all of that?

The third objection is perhaps the most formidable. It is possible that positive euthanasia may lead to similar practices on a broader scale. That opens the door to the possibility that old people may be eliminated by persons or societies because they are considered useless. Bennett "recognize[s] the "dangers of this possibility. When it is discussed, the practices of the Nazis are always used as an illustration. . . . Ethical thinking and law should guard against these dangers."[18]

Evangelical theologians will need to continue to wrestle with the questions.

14. Ibid., p. 150.
15. Ibid., p. 149.
16. Bennett, p. 150-51.
17. These three objections are from Bennett, pp. 149-50.
18. Bennett, p. 150.

Meanwhile, Christians caught up in those situations will be forced to find an answer under the most grievous of circumstances.

THE WIDOW'S PLIGHT

A study by Lopata of over 300 widows revealed that grief for four out of five of them lasts longer than one year. Twenty percent believe a person never gets over it.[19] If the death occurs in the seventies or later, couples seem to be more resigned to it. Sometimes it is considered a relief from suffering and the heavy problems related to care.

Loneliness is the critical issue for the widowed. Widowers have more trouble living alone than widows. A man's depression is usually more severe than a woman's.[20] Groups of other widows in the church and community seem to rally around the new widow. The same is not true for the men. Both men and women find meaningful contact with children and grandchildren. The most satisfactory companionship comes through remarriage. Older adults are remarrying with increased frequency. Men remarry more than women and the likelihood of a woman remarrying declines as she gets older.[21] Remarriages are typically successful.

Not all widows adjust to their situation in the same way. Lopata found three different styles.

1. The self-initiating woman is quite flexible, willing to change and build new social relationships, constructing a new life.
2. The widow who lives in an ethnic community, as part of its life, is compared by Lopata to being in the traditional village life-style of the past. The widow does not experience much change since she has many social relationships.
3. The social isolates have never been too highly involved with others. Friends died or moved away.[22]

The financial costs of dying are high whenever the death is a lingering one. Funds may be exhausted, bills and loans accumulated, making financial woes a somber prospect of widowhood. When older widowers or widows have other problems such as poverty and ill health, they are especially vulnerable to life's stresses and in need of the church's ministry. The Bible does say with great significance: "This is pure and undefiled religion in the sight of our God and Father, to visit orphans and widows in their distress, and to keep oneself unstained by the world" (James 1:27).

19. Lopata as cited by Kimmel, *Adulthood and Aging,* p. 238.
20. Marjorie Fiske Lowenthal, "Social Isolation and Mental Illness in Old Age," *American Sociological Review* 29, no. 1: 54–70, as cited by Kimmel, p. 420.
21. U.S. Bureau of the Census, 1977.
22. Lopata, pp. 263–66, as cited by Kimmel, p. 238.

DIVORCE IN OLD AGE

Being divorced in old age is probably far worse than being widowed. In the United States each year 10,000 persons over sixty-five divorce. In addition to those, many persons enter older adulthood already divorced and still unmarried. By the year 2000 there will be over 1 million divorced older people—likely a conservative estimate.[23]

There is reason to believe divorce is more traumatic for the older than the younger adult. Although there is no research on what actually happens to the elderly, there are studies of divorced people in general. Those inquiries indicate that divorced singles often lose contact with friends once shared by the married couple. Older adults, in general, face the loss of friends. Since a divorced person carries a certain stigma, he may lose a whole social network upon separation from a spouse.[24] Some evidence suggests that women may suffer more censure from society than men. Since elderly women are less likely to remarry than men, they will compose the greater number of divorced elderly.

Lost friendships may be just part of the diminishing social support. Relationships with children and grandchildren may be in jeopardy, as well. The likelihood of reduced quality contact is large because of the disruption of family ties that divorce generally brings with it.

Loss of friends is just one potentially serious vexation the divorced elderly face. Two gerontologists speculate that the divorced are also candidates for psychological and economic struggles. Though no research supports their suggestions, it is reasonable that that is true. Divorce, it may be imagined, is more likely to grind away on a person's feelings of self-worth if the person is older, since other life changes are already challenging the older person's self-esteem. The effect of multiple transitions (for example, retirement, geographic move, divorce) may generate self-blame and self-pity, making it considerably more difficult for a person to adjust.[25]

Divorced older people also face profound economic consequences as a result of marital breakup. Divorce usually reduces financial income. Legal battles related to alimony and the rights to a husband's pension can be painful for an older woman to face. A divorced man can also be hard pressed to pay costs to maintain two separate households.

Whatever the church's view about divorce, it cannot ignore the summons of a gracious God to minister to the suffering.

23. Michael R. DeShane and Keren Brown-Wilson, "Divorce in Late Life: A Call for Research," *Journal of Divorce* 5 (Summer 1981):83.
24. Ibid., p. 84.
25. Ibid.

26

Institutionalization: Next to Last Steps

THE "HOME" STRETCH

Two or three generations ago, Americans refused to go to the hospital, believing it was the place of no return. For the most part, that feeling is gone. Instead, there is a new final stop on life's journey: the nursing home. Its reputation alone may account for the idea that the passage to institutional care may be the most difficult of all for the elderly (or for anyone).

Death is not so much the issue as the *lack of living* the nursing home represents. Death is there, to be sure. A bed across the hall mysteriously becomes empty some morning. The residents know why. It may not be the fear of dying that is the worst part but that a person has gone there to die. There is little hope of getting better—there is no prospect of going back home. The problem is that waiting to die offers little reason to live. Nursing homes are the ultimate in people shelves, labeled for the useless, the helpless, the dependent. "Houses of Death," one knowledgeable researcher calls them.[1] They are a problem for the aged who go there, for the children who may have to place them there, and for the nation as a whole. Many facilities are described as "human junkyards" and "warehouses."[2]

Some try to minimize the problem by citing statistics to show that only 4 or 5 percent of the elderly are in such institutions. While that is true, other research shows that the chances for ending up in a care facility are much higher—as high as two out of three—if one lives beyond eighty-five years of age.

The care of the elderly is moving in two positive directions: institutional facilities are improving, and other alternatives are increasing. This discussion will look at the possible steps an aged person takes toward an institution, but first a picture of what institutions actually exist needs to be developed. It is important to avoid lumping

---

1. Robert N. Butler, *Why Survive? Being Old in America,* p. 260.
2. Cited by Butler, p. 260.

them all together because today there are varieties of care facilities.

Commercial nursing homes are distinct from homes for the aging. Commercial nursing homes are operated for profit by anyone[3] and constitute the greater percentage of institutional facilities. Homes for the aged are sponsored by religious, benevolent, and trust organizations and are nonprofit and voluntary. Some of the nonprofit facilities are run by federal, state, county, and municipal governments.[4] The nonprofit agencies tend to focus on residential and personal care for those who are fairly healthy and independent.

The great majority of elderly are in commercial nursing homes, generally described by one gerontologist as "a facility that has few or no nurses and can hardly qualify as a home."[5] Although he admits there are some fine commercial nursing homes, he claims most are terribly deficient. His description supports the worst suspicions:

> I continue to visit nursing homes regularly—sometimes disguising myself as though I were inquiring about a family member, sometimes visiting openly as a physician. I have seen patients lying in their own urine and feces. Food is frequently left untouched on plates. Boredom among patients and weariness among staff are common.[6]

Many of those homes do not provide proper medical care; some states do not require they employ a directing physician. Doctors seldom conduct regular rounds.[7] Patients rely upon family doctors or private physicians assigned by the welfare agency.

The above description makes a search for other alternatives attractive. Older people have a negative view of nursing homes that is largely justified.[8] Those who go to them usually have no choice. As many as 60 to 80 percent are poor. Half of them have no living relatives or direct relationship with even a distant relative. The majority have more than one physical ailment. Only a third live beyond one year.[9]

One researcher found no evidence to support the idea that families refuse to care for older relatives[10] or grossly neglect them by shunting them off to such places. Alternatives other than nursing homes are generally sought, and when a home is chosen, it is usually done carefully and as a last resort. The possible paths that lead elderly people to institutional care are many and varied, but a broad outline of the steps some will take can still be sketched.

3. Butler, p. 261.
4. Ibid.
5. Ibid., p. 263.
6. Ibid.
7. Ibid., p. 264.
8. Robert C. Atchly, *Aging: Continuity and Change*, p. 242.
9. Butler, p. 267.
10. Ethel Shanas, "Social Myth as Hypothesis: The Case of the Family Relations of Old People," *The Gerontologist* 19, no. 1 (1979): 2-9, as cited by Naomi Golan, *Passing Through Transitions*, p. 225.

STEP ONE: RELOCATION

Several factors may seem to make it advisable that an elderly person move. Concerned children may encourage a widowed parent to consider a smaller house, or to move closer to friends in order to avoid loneliness. When the elderly person comes to the place where he needs help with shopping and household tasks, it may seem wise to have him move closer to relatives who can assist him.

Moving to another location can be very upsetting. The fact that so many elderly choose to live in their old neighborhoods in spite of the fact that deteriorating conditions have made living there dangerous for them, shows they sometimes have a lot of emotional investment in their homes. "For them it is not simply one more change of mailing address. Instead, moving is experienced as a major loss, one more in an ever expanding list of losses. They have to leave behind the familiarity, security and sense of belonging that the old neighborhood gave them. They lose direct touch with the private memories so intimately bound up with the sights and sounds of their neighbors, shops, and parks."[11] Adult children who pressure them to leave and come live with them may not be doing what is best for the parents.

On the other hand, there is evidence that elderly people want to be close to their children. Ethel Shanas concluded from her investigation that three out of four people over sixty-five who have living children live within a half hour of them.[12] Before a move is too hastily made, all factors should be considered and alternatives explored to keep them where they are. Perhaps nearby friends can help with the shopping; a relative might go several times a month to help with heavy housecleaning.

If relocation seems best for all, there are at least three alternatives: moving to a residential institution, moving in with one of the children, or moving to an apartment near a close relative. It seems clear that most of the elderly do not want to live in their children's homes. Those who do so usually have no better alternative. Some might prefer their own apartment or home, whereas others seem to find a residential home run by a church or benevolent agency more to their liking. Several elderly people sharing an apartment can solve most of the practical problems of living alone.

Any arrangement should provide for privacy, freedom, and independence as long as possible. The problem with institutional care and some living arrangements is that adults are not given initiative or freedom to care for themselves. Making them more dependent than they should be is damaging to their self-respect and will to live. The golden rule for the elderly person is this: permit him to live independently as long as possible.

Both the aged and those who care for them recommend doing everything possible before persuading a reluctant elderly person to enter some sort of facility for the elderly, particularly if it is a commercial nursing home. If nutrition becomes a problem for them, the Meals on Wheels program can meet that need. Nursing care

11. Stephen Z. Cohen and Bruce Michael Gans, *The Other Generation Gap: The Middle-Aged and their Aging Parents*, pp. 203–4.
12. Golan, p. 225.

can be brought to their residence. Relatives or certain agencies can help them with house repairs. Church visitors can keep them company. Communities and churches have organized telephone programs to see they are called at least once a day. Day-care centers offer health care, recreation, and social programs without requiring the elderly to move in. Welfare, Medicare, and Social Security Senior Center offices can give information about what resources are available in the community.

STEP TWO: DECIDING TO INSTITUTIONALIZE

Despite all of those services, certain conditions may make an institution seem to be the only answer for the elderly person's care. Mental or physical illness may make it impossible for them to stay with children or live alone.

Judging when that point is reached is not easy. There is always the danger of overexaggerating the elderly person's disabilities, making around-the-clock care seem needed when it is not. Loss of memory is one condition that is overplayed. Because older people are expected to lose their memory they sometimes appear to do so when in fact they have not. A young adult can say, for example, that he forgot to let the dog out during the day. But, if an older person excuses the mess on the kitchen floor with "I forgot," people begin to suspect that the memory is failing. An elderly person who may go for a walk and fail to find his way back home is not necessarily permanently incompetent. Emotional stress can block memory. Sometimes counseling can help overcome the problem.

A serious illness, particularly one that takes the elderly to the hospital, often occasions their being admitted to a nursing home. When the doctors warn that the patient will need good care when leaving the hospital, the family panics. They cannot conceive of the person's continuing to live in his own apartment or even with them. Physicians do not always help the situation as they may be quick to recommend a nursing home. Because they are usually most concerned about the body and because they know the medical benefits of institutional care, they may not consider the whole person.

STEP THREE: GOING TO A HOME

Modern facilities may make an institution look attractive, but appearance does not change its institutional nature. Middle adults placing their elderly parents in an institution sometimes cannot see why they resist being in a place that is as luxurious as a grand hotel and stylish as a country club. If they would stop and think about it for a moment, they would realize that they would probably not want to live in a hotel or country club either. Hotels and resorts are good for vacations, but over the long haul they just do not match up to the homeyness of home.

Children should also recognize that commercial nursing homes may not be staffed by altruistic people who are devoting their life to the care of the elderly. Generally they are staffed by unskilled workers, employed at low wages. They may do little more than feed and clothe patients. If children complain, the staff may take it out on the elderly resident.

However, once the decision is made to institutionalize the elderly person some things can be done to make it easier for him. The best situation is the one that is most like where the person lived before. The fewer changes that have to make the better.[13] For that reason, some homes allow the elderly to move in some of their furniture along with their pictures and other personal items. Some smaller institutions have more homelike facilities.

Personality plays a major role in adjustment. The aggressive person will adapt more successfully. Being irritating and demanding, they tend to keep their independence and privacy by forcing the surroundings to bend to them. Those who are more introspective and hopeful will also adjust well.

Just as parents prepare a small child for going to school, relatives can help elderly persons get ready for entering a nursing home. They will need to grieve. Listening to them at that time may be important as they reminisce about old times. After the decision is made the elderly person may experience a sense of helplessness, lowered self-esteem, depression, and/or withdrawal. Naomi Golan suggests that the elderly visit old neighbors when possible.[14]

The elderly person's family may be enduring some emotional pain along with some guilt. Apparently, many grown children consider placing their parents in an institution to be an act of abandonment, even when it is a sensible step. Church leaders and friends in Christ should provide support. If nothing is said by those around, the silence may be taken as disapproval and swell their guilt feelings.

For a long time researchers have stated that being admitted to a nursing home hastens a person's death. Yet, there are not solid conclusions about this.[15] Counseling and continued support by others can make a difference in how well and how long they live. It is natural to feel a certain degree of stigma or loss of status when entering even the best of group residences. Relatives should watch for signs of fear, anxiety, confusion and immobility, hostility, and even intense rage—all signs of stress.

STEP FOUR: ADJUSTING

The transition does not stop when the older person has moved into the institution. Settling down in the new setting requires some time.[16] The move to an institution demands a great deal of change. Institutional life is just not like homelife, as anyone recently home from a hospital will testify. Bathroom facilities must sometimes be shared. Schedules are kept. Meals must be eaten at the same time each day. One is constantly adapting to strangers due to staff turnover. Some persons will view it as a challenge, get involved in activities, attempt to overcome their physical problems, and even reach out and minister to others.

Family members should not be too distressed if some elderly resort to other types of adjustment behavior. A frequent one is that of denial: "I don't see what I'm doing here

13. David F. Hultsch and Francine Deutsch, *Adult Development and Aging*, p. 343.
14. Beverly A. Yayney and Darrell Stover, "Relocation of the Elderly," pp. 166–67. Golan, p. 227.
15. Hultsch and Deutsch, p. 343.
16. Yayney and Stover. p. 167.

with these old people."[17] Caroline S. Ford cites examples to show that denial is not always bad. It enables some people to cope with a situation for a time. It may even show an undaunted strength that should command respect. She tells of a woman who entered a convalescent facility for the aged, following hospitalization for coronary heart disease. She continued to think of the home as a hotel and referred to the staff members as maids and waitresses. Each night she requested to be wheeled to the entrance of the home, confident that her son or daughter would come to take her home. That they did not do so did not bother her. She endured great pain and through it all remained reasonably sociable and relatively free from obvious stress.[18]

Another form of adaptation is "regression into dependency." In certain situations an individual may regress to an infantile level, making many excessive demands for help in daily living although there is no organic basis for the incapacities he claims to have. He may ask to be fed or bathed or ask for assistance in walking. That is basically an unsatisfactory defense. It does not permit a person to cope properly with reality. Counseling might help.[19]

Some aged persons take refuge from an apparently unbearable situation by running away. Sometimes it is carefully planned and executed. Often, it is an impulsive and restless wandering without any specific objective or wish to escape from the residence.

Withdrawal is a common ploy. Retreating from others, the person appears listless and passive and is emotionally neutral or detached. Perhaps, he will withdraw through excessive sleeping or resting in bed. Persons who withdraw should be helped according to their individual personalities and situations. If the person is terminally ill and near death, it may be a positive way of detaching oneself in preparation for death.

In other cases, the withdrawal does not seem to be healthy. If a lively, active person withdraws after entering a home, it might be tolerated without strong resistance for a while, but eventually, relatives and friends should talk with the person about his stress. At that point one must be careful not to be overly critical of the way a very elderly person chooses to live his final days.

Manipulation is another adaptive mechanism. Any available tool or circumstance is used to help him gain his ends. He may cry, threaten, sulk, or pout. His "sinking spells," feelings of faintness, agitated telephone calls to family or frantic calls to nurses are his means of attempting to control or change the rules of a facility or the behavior of the staff. He may do that to increase his status or prop up his feelings of self-esteem and, of course, gain some mastery over his affairs. Though not the best way of coping, manipulation is fairly healthy because the person is at least in touch with reality.

The presence of any of those mechanisms is not a sign of mental breakdown or senility. A mentally ill label should not be attached to someone who does something that is quite logical, or at least understandable in a difficult situation. All of those mechanisms should be seen for their positive as well as negative outcomes. A person

17. This and the next six paragraphs are a summary of Caroline S. Ford, "Ego-Adaptive Mechanisms of Older People," *Social Casework* 46, no. 1 (January 1965):16–21 as cited by William C. Sze, ed., Human Life Cycle, pp. 599–608.
18. Ibid.
19. Ibid., pp. 604–5.

who turns to manipulation—repeated phone calls to be taken out of the home, for example—should be seen for his strengths. Considering him to be stubborn, and informing him of that, would be a blow to a person who perhaps all of his life had contributed much to those around him by being a superbly independent person. The challenge is to understand his needs and reactions and seek to learn from them.

ATTITUDES ABOUT AGING

Many who live a very long life live their last years with dignity. Their self-respect, good cheer and unselfishness, blends with strong faith in a mixture that uplifts those around them. Circumstances, however, scratch and claw at many older adults to tear away self-respect. "I see the sick and the despised, the defeated and the bitter, the rejected and the lonely," says one concerned observer. "I see them clustered together and alone. I see them deprived and forgotten, masters yesterday, outcasts today. What we owe them is reverence, but all they ask for is consideration, attention, not to be discarded, forgotten."[20]

The problem of aging in this country is twofold: the attitude of society to the old and the attitude of the old toward being old. How can the old be saved from despondency and despair? How can *old* be made beautiful and be made to regain the authenticity that belongs to old age?[21]

How the aged are treated may be one of the most important social questions of modern times. Heschel maintains "the test of a people is how it behaves toward the old." "It is easy to love children," he claims. "Even tyrants and dictators make a point of being fond of children. But the affection and care for the old, the incurable, the helpless are the true gold mines of a people."[22]

Perhaps our attitude toward the aged is rooted in our attitude toward aging. Beauty shops and plastic surgery to keep people young are symbols of how severely we resist change. There is no true awareness of the blessings of growing old. When a closer relationship between maturing and aging is seen, a greater respect for others who are old, as well as for oneself's growing old, will develop. True, some of life's passages are traumatic, but it is a dismal view of living that equates change with decay. Christians pressing toward the mark of the high calling of God should hope and pray that all their transitions will be transformations.

---

20. Abraham J. Heschel, "The Older Person and the Family in the Perspective of Jewish Tradition," in *Aging and the Human Spirit,* ed. Carol LeFevre and Perry LeFevre, p. 35.
21. Ibid., p. 37.
22. Ibid.

Afterword

A young friend of mine was in a heated argument with an older woman. Like knights with poised lances, they charged at each other from opposite sides of the divorce issue. He fought for more empathy and better treatment, especially for those who had been left badly wounded by a marriage break up. She took a harder stand, suggesting the church would lose its stand on divorce if it accepted those people too readily.

When he pleaded for sympathy by portraying the plight of divorced people who had been ignored by the church, she impatiently countered: "You don't want a church; you want a support group." Silence followed. The young man smiled. Others in the room exchanged looks of amazement. The red flush on the woman's face signaled she was also startled by her statement.

This story points to the major theme of this book. We are fellow travelers who need each other. In part, this is why Christ bound us together in His church. *Transition* is designed to help us understand each other. It does not ask us to compromise our standards, but it urges us to make an effort to walk with each other through life's passages and urge each other on. A book like *Transitions* offers empathy but it cannot bestow compassion. That is Christ's to give. His apostle said our churches should be "harmonious, sympathetic, brotherly, kindhearted, and humble in spirit" (1 Pet. 3:8). That sounds a great deal like a support group. Why not be a part of one?

Bibliography

Aldous, Joan. *Family Careers.* New York: John Wiley & Sons, 1978.

Altrocchi, John. *Abnormal Behavior.* New York: Harcourt, 1980.

Atchley, Robert C. *Aging: Continuity and Change.* Belmont, Calif. Wadsworth, 1983.

———. "Adjustment to Loss of Job at Retirement." *International Journal of Aging and Human Development* 6, no. 1 (1975):17-27.

Barron, Milton L. "The Role of Religion and Religious Institutions in Creating the Milieu of Old People." In *Organized Religion and the Old Person,* edited by D. L. Scudder. Gainesville: University of Florida Press, 1958.

Barshinger, Clark Eugene. "Living the Single Life: On Singleness, Intimacy and Maturity." Paper presented to the Wheaton Bible Church Career Group Retreat, January 1976.

Bates, Paul B. and Schaie, K. Warner. "The Myth of the Twilight Years." *Psychology Today* (March 1974): 35-40.

Bayly, Joseph. *The View from a Hearse.* Elgin, IL: David C. Cook Publishing, 1973.

Beck, Melinda. "A Kennedy's Bout with Heroin." *Newsweek,* 26 September 1983.

Bell, B. Clayton, and Bell, Peggy. "A Look at Grief." *Leadership 1.* Fall 1980.

Bennett, John C. "Ethical Aspects of Aging in America." In *Ministry with the Aging,* edited by William M. Clements. San Francisco: Harper & Row, 1981.

Bergmann, Mark, and Otte, Elmer. *Engaging the Aging in Ministry.* St. Louis: Concordia, 1981.

Berman, William H. and Turk, Dennis C. "Adaptation to Divorce: Problems and Coping Strategies." *Journal of Marriage and Family* 43, no. 1 (February 1981):179-89.

Bloom, Bernard L.; White, Stephen, W.; and Asher, Shirley J. "Marital Disruption as a Stressful Life Event." In *Divorce and Separation,* edited by George Levinger and Oliver C. Moles. New York: Basic Books, 1979.

Bocknek, Gene. *The Young Adult.* Monterey, Calif.: Brooks/Cole Publishing, 1980.

Bolles, Richard Nelson. *What Color Is Your Parachute? A Practical Manual for Job-Hunters and Career Changers.* Berkeley: Ten Speed Press, 1972.

Braceland, Francis J. "Senescence—The Inside Story." *Psychiatric Annals* 11, no. 10 (October 1972):57.

Brewi, Janice, and Brennan, Anne. *Mid-Life: Psychological and Spiritual Perspectives.* New York: Crossroad, 1982.

Brier, Judith, and Rubenstein, Dan. "Sex for the Elderly? Why Not?" In *The Age of Aging: A Reader in Social Gerontology.* Edited by Abraham Monk. Buffalo: Prometheus, 1979.

Brooks, Linda. "Supermoms Shift Gears: Re-Entry Women." *Counseling Psychologist* 6, no. 2 (1976):33–37.

Butler, R. N. "The Life Review: An Interpretation of Reminiscence in the Aged." *Psychiatry* 24 (1973):179–82.

Butler, Robert. *Why Survive? Being Old in America.* New York: Harper & Row, 1975.

Chartier, Jan. "The Mid-Life Load: A Challenge for Creative Ministry." *Baptist Leader* 43, no. 1 (June 1981):25–29.

Cheleen, Cathy. "The Real Dream-Child Comes at Last." Belmont, Mass: Resolve, n.d.

Chiriboga, David A. and Cutler, Loraine. "Stress Responses Among Divorcing Men and Women." *Journal of Divorce* 1, no. 2 (1977):95–106.

Clayton, V. "Erikson's Theory of Human Development as It Applies to the Aged: Wisdom as Contradictive Cognition." *Human Development* 18 (1975):119–21.

Clinebell, Howard and Clinebell, Charlotte. *The Intimate Marriage.* New York: Harper & Row, 1970.

Cohen, Stephen and Gans, Bruce. *The Other Generation Gap: The Middle-Aged and Their Aging Parents.* Chicago: Follette, 1978.

Cole, Elbert C. "Lay Ministry with Older Adults." In *Ministry with the Aging,* edited by William M. Clements. San Francisco: Harper & Row, 1981.

Coleman, John. "Friendship and the Peer Group in Adolescence." In *Handbook of Adolescent Psychology,* edited by Joseph Adelson. New York: Wiley, 1980.

Comfort, Alex. "Sexuality in Old Age." *Journal of American Geriatrics Society* 22, no. 1 (1974):440–42.

Conger, John Janeway. *Adolescence and Youth.* 2d ed. New York: Harper & Row, 1977.

Cory, Christopher T. "Parenthood's Dim Rewards," *Psychology Today,* May 1981.

CRM Books editorial staff. *Developmental Psychology Today.* Delmar, Calif.: CRM, 1971.

Dasteel, Joan C. "Stress Reactions to Marital Dissolution as Experienced by Adults Attending Courses on Divorce." *Journal of Divorce* 5, no. 3 (Spring 1982).

Davidson, Spencer, "Proliferating POSSLQ." *Psychology Today,* November 1983.

DeShane, Michael R. and Brown-Wilson, Keren. "Divorce in Late Life: A Call for Research." *Journal of Divorce* 5 (Summer 1981):83.

Douvan, E. and Adelson, J. *The Adolescent Experience.* New York: Wiley, 1966.

Duska, Ronald and Whelan, Mariellen. *Moral Development: A Guide to Piaget and Kohlberg.* New York: Paulist Press, 1975.

Dykstra, Craig. *Vision and Character.* New York: Paulist Press, 1981.

Elkind, David. "Growing Up Faster." *Psychology Today.* February 1979.

Erikson, Erik. *Childhood and Society.* New York: Norton, 1959.

———. *Identity and the Life Cycle.* New York: Norton, 1980.

———. *Identity, Youth and Crisis.* New York: Norton, 1968.

———. *The Life Cycle Completed.* New York: Norton, 1982.

———. *Youth: Change and Challenge.* New York: Basic Books, 1963.

Farrell, Michael P. and Rosenberg, Stanley D. *Men at Midlife.* Boston: Auburn House, 1981.

Felker, Donald. *Building Positive Self-Concepts.* Minneapolis: Burgess Publishing Co., 1974.

Fowler, James. "Stages of Faith and Adults' Life Cycles." In *Faith Development in the Adult Life Cycle,* edited by Kenneth Stokes. New York: W. H. Sadlier, 1980.

_____. *Stages of Faith.* San Francisco: Harper & Row, 1981.

Fowler, Jim, and Keen, Sam. *Life Maps: Conversations on the Journey of Faith,* edited by Jerome Berryman. Waco: Word Books, 1978.

Fox, J. H. "Effects of Retirement and Former Work Life on Women's Adaptation in Old Age." *Journal of Gerontology* 32 (1977):196-202.

Frost, Robert. *Collected Poems of Robert Frost.* New York: Halcyon House, 1930.

Gage, Joy B. *When Parents Cry.* Denver: Accent Books, 1980.

Galinsky, Ellen. *Between Generations.* New York: Time Books, 1981.

Gallagher, Delores; Thompson, Larry W.; and Levy, Sandra M. "Clinical Psychological Assessment of Older Adults." In *Aging in the 1980's,* edited by Leonard W. Poon. Washington, D.C.: American Psychological Association, 1980.

Gallatin, Judith. "Political Thinking in Adolescence." In *Handbook of Adolescent Psychology,* edited by Joseph Adelson. New York: Wiley, 1980.

Galvin, Kathleen M., and Brommel, Bernard J. *Family Communication: Cohesion and Change.* Glenview, IL: Scott, Foresman, 1982.

Garrett, Cyril D. "Middle-Age Shadows and Adolescent Personas." *Baptist Leader* 43, no. 3 (June 1981): 2-4.

Gatz, Margaret; Smyer, Michael A.; and Lawton, M. Powell. "The Mental Health System and the Older Adult." In *Aging in the 1980's,* edited by Leonard W. Poon. Washington, D.C.: American Psychological Association, 1980.

Gelman, David; Gary, Sandra; Greenberg, Nikki Finke; Michael, Renee; and Bruno, Mary. "A Great Emptiness." *Newsweek,* 7 November 1983.

Gerkin, Charles V. *Crisis Experience in Modern Life.* Nashville: Abingdon, 1979.

Gillespie, Vergie. Review of *Mid-Life: A Time to Discover, A Time to Decide,* by Richard P. Olson. *Baptist Leader,* June 1981.

Golan, Naomi. *Passing Through Transitions.* New York: The Free Press, 1981.

Gold, Martin, and Petronio, Richard J. "Delinquent Behavior in Adolescence." In *Handbook of Adolescent Psychology,* edited by Joseph Adelson. New York: Wiley, 1980.

Goldsmith, Oliver. "The Deserted Village." *The Norton Anthology of English Literature.* New York: Norton, 1974.

Gould, Robert. *Transformations. Growth and Change in Adult Life.* New York: Simon & Schuster, 1978.

Greeley, Andrew. *Love and Play.* Chicago: Thomas More Press, 1975.

Griffiths, Richard. *Courtship.* Bramcote, Nottinghamshire: Grove Books, 1978.

Gubrium, J. F. "Being Single in Old Age." *International Journal of Aging and Human Development* (1975):19-41.

Gurnsey, Dennis B. *A New Design for Family Ministry.* Elgin, Ill.: David C. Cook Publishing, 1982.

Halem, Lynne Carol. *Separated and Divorce Women.* Westport, Conn.: Greenwood Press, 1982.

Hall, Douglas T. *Careers in Organization.* Pacific Palisades, Calif.: Good Year, 1976.

Hanchett, Mark, and Hanchett, Anne. "On Having a Family." *The Stony Brook School Bulletin* (February 1980):1.

Harkins, Elizabeth. "Effects of Empty Nest Transition on Self-Report of Psychological and Physical Well-Being." *Journal of Marriage and Family* 40, no. 3 (August 1978):547-56.

Harvard University. *The First Year of Bereavement.* New York: John Wiley & Sons, 1974.

Hayes, Maggie; Stinnet, Nick; and Defrain, John. "Learning About Marriage from the Divorced." *Journal of Divorce* 4, no. 1 (Fall 1981):23-29.

Heschel, Abraham J. "The Older Person and the Family in the Perspective of Jewish Tradition"; "Religion and Aging in Contemporary Theology." In *Aging and the Human Spirit,* edited by Carol LeFevre and Perry LeFevre. Chicago: Exploration Press, 1981.

————. *Who Is Man?* Stanford, Calif.: Stanford University Press, 1965.

Hiltner, Seward. "A Theology of Aging." In *Aging and the Human Spirit,* edited by Carol LeFevre and Perry LeFevre. Chicago: Exploration Press, 1981.

Holland, John L. *Making Vocational Choices: A Theory of Careers.* Englewood Cliffs, N.J.: Prentice-Hall, 1973.

Hultsch, David F., and Deutsch, Francine. *Adult Development and Aging.* New York: McGraw-Hill, 1981.

Johnson, David. *Reaching Out.* Englewood Cliffs, N.J.: Prentice-Hall, 1972.

Jones, J. David. "Singles in America." *Solo Magazine,* March/April 1982.

Jung, C. G. *Modern Man in Search of a Soul.* Translated by W. S. Dell and Gary F. Baynes. New York: Harcourt, Brace and World, 1933.

Jung, Carl G. "The Stages of Life." In *The Portable Jung,* edited by J. Campbell. New York: Viking Press, 1971.

Kaluger, George, and Kaluger, Meriem Fair. *Human Development: The Life Span.* St. Louis: C. V. Mosby Co., 1974.

Kay, Emanuel. "The World of Work: Its Promises, Conflicts, and Reality," in *The Middle Years.* New York: American Medical Association, 1974.

Kimble, Melvin A. "Education for Ministry with the Aging." In *Ministry with the Aging,* edited by William M. Clements. San Francisco: Harper & Row, 1981.

Kimmel, Douglas C. *Adulthood and Aging.* 2d ed. New York: John Wiley and Sons, 1980.

————. Price, Karl F.; and Walker, James W. "Retirement Choice and Retirement Satisfaction." *Journal of Gerontology* 33, no. 4 (1978):575-85.

Kirk, H. David. *Shared Fate.* New York: Macmillan, 1964.

Klein, N. C.; Alexander, J. F.; and Parsons, B. V. "Impact of Family Systems Intervention on Recidivism and Sibling Delinquency: A Model of Primary Prevention and Program Evaluation." *Journal of Consulting and Clinical Psychology* 45 (1977):460-74.

Knox, Alan B. "Issues of Mid-Life." In *Programming for Adults Facing Mid-Life Change,* edited by Alan B. Knox. San Francisco: Jossey-Bass, 1979.

Kohlberg, Lawrence. "Education, Moral Development, and Faith." *Journal of Moral Education.* 4 (1974):13-14.

————. "Stages of Moral Development as a Basis for Moral Education." In *Moral Development, Moral Education and Kohlberg,* edited by Brenda Munsey. Birmingham, AL: Religious Education Press, 1980.

Kübler-Ross, Elisabeth. *On Death and Dying.* New York: Macmillan, 1969.

Landgraf, John R. "Career Development in Mid-Life." *Baptist Leader* 43 (June 1981):16-19.

Landgraf, John K. *Creative Singlehood and Pastoral Care.* Philadelphia: Fortress Press, 1982.

Lasch, Christopher. "The New Narcissism." *The New York Review of Books.* September 30, 1976.

Lederer, William J. and Jackson, Don D. *The Mirages of Marriage.* New York: Norton, 1968.

LeFeber, Larry A. *Building a Young Adult Ministry.* Valley Forge: Judson Press, 1980.

LeFevre, Carol, and LeFevre, Perry, eds. *Aging and the Human Spirit.* Chicago: Exploration Press, 1981.

Lesnoff-Caravaglia, G. "The 5 Percent Fallacy." *International Journal of Aging and Human Development* 9 (1978-79):187-92.

Levinger, George. "A Social Psychological Perspective on Marital Dissolution." In *Divorce and Separation,* edited by George Levinger and Oliver C. Moles. New York: Basic Books, 1979.

Levinson, Daniel J. *Seasons of a Man's Life.* New York: Alfred A. Knopf, 1978.

Levy, Sandra M.; Derogatis, Leonard R.; Gallagher, Delores; and Gatz, Margaret. "Intervention with Older Adults and the Evaluation of Outcome." In *Aging in the 1980's,* edited by Leonard W. Poon. Washington, D.C.: American Psychological Association, 1980.

Lewis, Alfred Allan, with Berns, Barrie. *Three Out of Four Wives.* New York: Macmillan, 1975.

Lewis, C. S. *A Grief Observed.* London: Faber & Faber, 1961.

Lewis, Margie. *The Hurting Parent.* Grand Rapids: Zondervan, 1980.

Lewis, Robert A.; Freneau, Phillip J.; and Roberts, Craig L. "Fathers and the Postparental Transition." *Family Coordinator* 28, no. 4 (October 1979):514–20.

Lieberman, Morton A. and Sheldon S. Tobin. *The Experience of Old Age: Stress, Coping and Survival.* New York: Basic Books, 1983.

Lindeman, Erich. "Symptomatology and Management of Acute Grief." *American Journal of Psychiatry* 101(September 1944):141–48.

Loder, James. *The Transforming Moment.* New York: Harper & Row, 1981.

Loevinger, Jane. *Ego Development.* San Francisco: Jossey-Bass, 1976.

Lowenthal, Marjorie Fiske; Thurnker, Majda; Chiriboga, David; and Assoc. *Four Stages of Life.* San Francisco: Jossey-Bass, 1977.

Marshall, W. A. "The Body." In *The Seven Ages of Man,* edited by Robert R. Sears and S. Shirley Feldman. Los Altos, Calif.: William Kaufmann, 1973.

Masters, William H., and Johnson, Virginia E. *Human Sexual Response.* Boston: Little, Brown, 1966.

May, Stephanie Ambrose. A privately published diary. Dallas: Highland Park Presbyterian Church, 3821 University Blvd., n.d.

McBride, Alfred. "Adult Education: A Ministry to Life Cycles." *Religious Education* 2 (March–April 1977):171.

McBride, Angela Barron. *The Growth and Development of Mothers.* New York: Harper & Row, 1974.

McGoldrick, Monica, and Carter, Elizabeth A., eds. *The Family Life Cycle: A Framework for Family Therapy.* New York: Gardner Press, 1980.

Menkus, Joann, and Menkus, Belden. "Adult Sunday School Needs to Grow Up." *Christianity Today,* 25 April 1975.

Menning, Barbara E. *Infertility: A Guide for the Childless Couple.* Englewood Cliffs, N.J.: Prentice-Hall, 1977.

Merriam, Sharan. "Professional Literature on Middle Age." In *Programming for Adult Facing Mid-Life Change.* Edited by Alan Knox. San Francisco: Jossey-Bass, 1979.

Miller, Donald E. "Adult Religious Education and the Aging." In *Ministry with the Aging,* edited by William M. Clements. San Francisco: Harper & Row, 1981.

Miller, M. "Geriatric Suicide: The Arizona Study." *Gerontologist* 18 (1978):488–95.

Miller, Sherod; Nunnally, Elam E.; and Wackman, Daniel B. *Alive and Aware.* Minneapolis: Interpersonal Communications Programs, 1976.

Moberg, David, and Gray, Robert. *The Church and the Older Person.* Grand Rapids: Eerdmans, 1977.

Moore, Allen J. "The Family Relations of Older Persons." In *Ministry with the Aging,* edited by William M. Clements. San Francisco: Harper & Row, 1981.

Moran, Gabriel. *Religious Education Development.* Minneapolis: Winston Press, 1983.

National Council on Aging. *Fact Book on Aging: A Profile of American Older Population.* Washington, D.C.: National Council on Aging, 1978.

Neubeck, G. "Getting Older in My Family: A Personal Reflection." *The Family Coordinator* 27 (1978):445-47.

Neugarten, B. L., and Weinstein, K. K. "The Changing American Grandparent." *Journal of Marriage and the Family* 26 (1964):199-204.

————. "The Awareness of Middle Age." In *Middle Age and Aging,* edited by Bernice L. Neugarten. Chicago: University of Chicago Press, 1968.

————. et al. *Personality in Middle and Late Life: Empirical Studies.* New York: Prentice-Hall, 1964.

Newman, Barbara M., and Newman, Philip R. *Development Through Life: A Psychosocial Approach.* Homewood, Ill.: Dorsey Press, 1975.

Nouwen, Henry, and Gaffney, Walter J. *Aging.* Garden City, New York: Doubleday, 1974.

Offer, Daniel. *The Psychological World of the Teenager.* New York: Basic Books, 1969.

Olson, Richard P. "The Mid-Life Dropout." *Baptist Leader* 43, no. 3 (June 1981):32-36.

Packer, J. I. "Infallible Scripture and the Role of Hermeneutics." In *Scripture and Truth,* edited by D. A. Carson and John D. Woodbridge. Grand Rapids: Zondervan, 1983.

Palmore, E. et al. "Stress and Adaptation in Later Life." *Journal of Gerontology* 34 (1979):841-51.

Parent, Mary Kay. "The Losses of Middle Age and Related Developmental Tasks." In *Social Work with the Dying Parent and the Family.* Edited by Elizabeth Prichard and Jean Collard. New York: Columbia U., 1977.

Parks, Sharon. "Faith Development and Imagination in the Context of Higher Education." Th.D. dissertation, Harvard Divinity School, 1980.

Payne, Barbara. "Religion and the Elderly in Today's World." In *Ministry with the Aging,* edited by William M. Clements. San Francisco: Harper & Row, 1981.

Peck, Robert. "Psychological Development in the Second Half of Life." In *Middle Age and Aging,* edited by Bernice L. Neugarten. Chicago: University of Chicago Press, 1968.

Perry, Lloyd M., and Sell, Charles M. *Speaking to Life's Problems,* Chicago: Moody Press, 1983.

Perry, Jr., William, G. *Forms of Intellectual and Ethical Development in the College Years.* New York: Holt, Rinehart and Winston, 1979.

Pfeiffer, Eric. "Psychopathology and Social Pathology." In *Handbook of the Psychology of Aging,* edited by James E. Birren and K. Warner Schaie. New York: Van Nostrand Rienhold, 1977.

Pocs, Ollie; Godow, Annette; Tolone, William L.; and Walsh, Robert H. "Is There Sex After 40?" *Psychology Today,* 11 June 1977, pp. 54-56.

Powell, John. *Why Am I Afraid to Tell You Who I Am?* Niles, Ill.: Argus Communications, 1969.

Pressau, Jack Renard. *I'm Saved, You're Saved . . . Maybe.* Atlanta: John Knox Press, 1977.

Rapoport, Rhonda and Rapoport, Robert. "New Light on the Honeymoon." *Human Relations* 17 (1964):33-56.

Rappaport L. *Personality Development.* Glenview, Ill.: Scott, Foresman, 1972.

Raush, H. L.; Barry, W. A.; Hertel, R. K.; and Swain, M. A. *Communication Conflict and Marriage.* San Francisco: Jossey-Bass, 1974.

Reister, Bary W., Gordon, Alan L. and Strieby, Serena B. "The Boston Single Life Study: Implications for the Helping Professions." *Journal of College Student Personnel* 22, no. 5: pp. 422-27.

Richard, Suzanne; Livson, Florine; and Peterson, Paul G. "Adjustment to Retirement." In *Middle Age and Aging,* edited by Bernice L. Neugarten. Chicago: University of Chicago Press, 1968.

Robertson, J. F. "Interaction in Three Generation Families, Parents as Mediators. Toward a

Theoretical Perspective." *International Journal of Aging and Human Development* 6 (1975):106–9.

Rubin, Lillian. *Woman of a Certain Age: The Midlife Search for Self.* New York: Harper & Row, 1979.

————. *Worlds of Pain: Life in the Working Class Family.* New York: Basic Books, 1976.

Ryder, Robert C.; Kafka, John S; and Olson, David H. "Separating and Joining Influences in Courtship and Early Marriage." *American Journal of Psychiatry* 41, no. 3 (April 1971).

Scott-Maxwell, Florida. *The Measure of My Days.* New York: Knopf, 1968.

Seely, Edward. "Behaviors of Peer Leaders, Adult Teachers, Mothers and Fathers as Perceived by Young People Fourteen through Eighteen." Ph.D. Dissertation, Michigan State University, 1980.

Sell, Charles M. *Achieving the Impossible: Intimate Marriage.* Portland, Oreg.: Multnomah, 1982.

————. *Family Ministry: The Enrichment of Family Life Through the Church.* Grand Rapids: Zondervan, 1981.

————. *Grief.* Portland, Oreg.: Multnomah, 1984.

Shans, Ethal, et al. "The Psychology of Health." In *Middle Age and Aging,* edited by Bernice L. Neugarten. Chicago: University of Chicago Press, 1968.

Shapiro, Constance Hoenk. "The Impact of Infertility on the Marital Relationship." *Social Casework: The Journal of Contemporary Social Work* 63, no. 7 (September 1982): 387–93.

Sheehy, Gail. *Passages.* New York: Bantam, 1977.

Silverstone, Barbara, and Hyman, Helen Kandel. *You and Your Aging Parent.* New York: Pantheon, 1976.

Simenauer, Jacqueline, and Carrol, David. *Singles, The New Americans.* New York: Simon & Schuster, 1982.

Singer, Laura J. *Stages: The Crises That Shape Your Marriage.* New York: Grosset & Dunlap, 1980.

Smith, Burt Kruger. *Aging in America.* Boston: Beacon Press, 1973.

Spence, Donald, and Lonner, Thomas. "The Empty Nest: A Transition with Motherhood." *Family Coordinator* 20, no. 4 (October 1971):369–75.

Spense, Barbara. "The Death of a Marriage." *His,* February 1980.

Spreitzer, Elmer, and Riley, Lawrence E. "Factors Associated with Singlehood." *Journal of Marriage and the Family* 36, no. 3:533–42.

Stein, Peter. "Singlehood: An Alternative to Marriage." *The Family Coordinator* (October 1975):489–502.

Sullender, R. Scott. "Three Theoretical Approaches to Grief." *The Journal of Pastoral Care* 23, no. 4 (December 1979):243.

Switzer, David. *The Dynamics of Grief.* Nashville: Abingdon, 1970.

Symonds, P. *From Adolescent to Adult.* New York: Columbia, 1961.

Sze, William C., ed. *Human Life Cycle.* New York: Jason Aronson, 1975.

Thomas, Chris. "An Approach to the Problems of Single Adults from a Positive Perspective." Paper, Trinity Evangelical Divinity School, 1979.

Tillich, Paul. *Systematic Theology.* Chicago: University of Chicago Press, 1957.

Tournier, Paul. *A Place for You.* New York: Harper & Row, 1968.

————. *Learn to Grow Old.* Translated by Edwin Hudson. New York: Harper & Row, 1972.

————. *To Understand Each Other.* Translated by John S. Gilmour. Atlanta: John Knox Press, 1967.

Troll, Lillian E. "Grandparenting." In *Aging in the 1980's,* edited by Leonard W. Poon. Washington, D.C.: American Psychological Association, 1980.

_____. "The Family of Later Life: A Decade Review." *Journal of Marriage and the Family* 33 (1971):263-90.

_____. Miller, Sheila; and Atchley, Robert. *Families in Later Life.* Belmont, Calif.: Wadsworth Publishing, 1979.

"U. of C. Prof Wins Nobel Prize," *Chicago Tribune,* 20 October 1983, sec. 1, p. 4.

U. S. Public Health Service. *Working with Older People: A Guide to Practice.* vol. II, publication no. 1459.

Ulanov, Ann Belford. "Aging: On the Way to One's End." In *Ministry with the Aging,* edited by William M. Clements. San Francisco: Harper & Row, 1981.

Vaillant, George E. *Adaptation to Life.* Boston: Little, Brown, 1977.

Van de Kemp, Hendrika, and Schreck, G. Peter. "The Church's Ministry to Singles: A Family Model." *Journal of Religion and Health* 20, no. 2 (Summer 1981):148-55.

Wallerstein, Judith, and Kelly, Joan Berlin. *Surviving the Breakup.* New York: Basic Books, 1980.

Weaver, Peter. *Strategies for the Second Half of Life.* New York: Franklin Watts, 1980.

Weiss, Robert. *Marital Separation.* New York: Basic Books, 1975.

Westberg, Granger. *Good Grief.* Philadelphia: Fortress Press, 1961.

Whitehead, Evelyn Eaton, and Whitehead, James D. *Christian Life Patterns.* New York: Image Books, 1982.

_____. "Retirement." In *Ministry with the Aging,* edited by William M. Clements. San Francisco: Harper & Row, 1981.

Willis, William. "One Man Against the Sea." In *Post True Stories of Daring and Adventure.* New York: World Publishing, 1967.

Willis, R. Wayne. "Some Concerns of Bereaved Parents." *Journal of Religion and Health* 20, no. 2 (Summer 1981):133-140.

Wood, J. Brittain. *Single Adults Want to Be the Church, Too.* Nashville: Broadman Press, 1977.

Woodward, Kenneth L. "The Graying of America." *Newsweek,* 28 February 1977.

_____. with Brinkley-Rogers, Paul. "All of Life's a Stage." *Newsweek.* 6 June 1977, p. 83.

Wright, H. Norman, and Inmon, Marvin N. *Preparing for Parenthood.* Ventura, Calif.: Regal, Books, 1980.

Wright, Norman. *Premarital Counseling.* Chicago: Moody Press, 1976.

Yancey, Philip. *Open Windows.* Westchester, Ill: Crossway Books, 1982.

Yayney, Beverly A. and Darrell Stover. "Relocation of the Elderly." In *The Age of Aging: A Reader in Social Gerontology.* Edited by Abraham Monk. New York: Prometheus, 1979.

Young, Richard G. "Values Differentiation as Stage Transition: An Expansion of Kohlbergian Moral Stages." *Journal of Psychology and Theology* 9 no. 2 (Summer 1981):164-74.

GENERAL INDEX

Abortion, 51
Activism
    older adults, 7
    vocation, 16
    young adult, 15
    young adults, 6
Adolescence
    disciplining, 157-59,
    parents letting go of, 161-62
    and parents, 152-161
Adoption, 103-5
    agencies, 1-3
Aging
    attitudes toward, 195-99
    definition, 230
Aging,
    and disease, 230
Altruism
    young adult, 4
    young adults, 12
Alzheimer's disease, 222
Authenticity
    and church, 143-45,
    in midlife, 120
Authority
    biblical, 95
    internalizing, 96
    of parents, 158

Baby
    adjusting to, 52
Bible
    and courtship, 41, 42,
    description of aged, 199
    evangelical view of, 94-95
    and intimacy, 32
    and radical idealism, 14
    view of human nature, xix
    view of old age, xx

young adult, 24
young adults ministry, 17
young adults, 14

Campus Crusade, 83
Career
    changing in midlife, 152
    in midlife, 143
    personal identity, 23
    and women in midlife, 151,
    young adults, 12
Change
    contemporary times, x
    and crisis, xiv,
    fear of, xv
    unexpected, xiv
Characteristics
    young adults, 9
Children
    deciding to have, 49-50,
    first child, 49-50
    leaving home, 166-69
    nurture of, xx
    of divorced, 68-68
Christian maturity
    pattern, xx
Christian ministry
    young adults, 12
Church
    authenticity in, 144-43
    classes for parents, 54
    contemporary issues, 18
    contemporary worship, 18
    and dating, 43
    established adulthood, 23
    as family, 228
    and intimacy, 37, 38
    involvement of elderly, 243-44
    and middle adults, 120

279